Media Ethics

Issues and Cases

Ninth Edition

Philip Patterson
Oklahoma Christian University

Lee Wilkins
Wayne State University
University of Missouri

Chad Painter
University of Dayton

ROWMAN & LITTLEFIELD
Lanham • Boulder • New York • London

Executive Editor: Elizabeth Swayze
Assistant Editor: Megan Manzano
Senior Marketing Manager: Kim Lyons

Credits and acknowledgments for material borrowed from other sources, and reproduced with permission, appear on the appropriate page within the text.

Published by Rowman & Littlefield
An imprint of The Rowman & Littlefield Publishing Group, Inc.
4501 Forbes Boulevard, Suite 200, Lanham, Maryland 20706
www.rowman.com

Unit A, Whitacre Mews, 26-34 Stannary Street, London SE11 4AB, United Kingdom

British Library Cataloguing in Publication Information Available

Library of Congress Cataloging-in-Publication Data Available

ISBN 978-1-5381-1258-8 (pbk.: alk. paper)
ISBN 978-1-5381-1259-5 (ebook)

∞™ The paper used in this publication meets the minimum requirements of American National Standard for Information Sciences—Permanence of Paper for Printed Library Materials, ANSI/NISO Z39.48-1992.

Printed in the United States of America

For Linda, David, and Laurel

Brief Contents

Contents

Foreword

Clifford G. Christians
Research Professor of Communication,
University of Illinois–Urbana

The playful wit and sharp mind of Socrates attracted disciples from all across ancient Greece. They came to learn and debate in what could be translated as "his thinkery." By shifting the disputes among Athenians over earth, air, fire, and water to human virtue, Socrates gave Western philosophy and ethics a new intellectual center (Cassier 1944).

But sometimes his relentless arguments would go nowhere. On one occasion, he sparred with the philosopher Hippias about the difference between truth and falsehood. Hippias was worn into submission but retorted at the end, "I cannot agree with you, Socrates." And then the master concluded: "Nor I with myself, Hippias. . . . I go astray, up and down, and never hold the same opinion." Socrates admitted to being so clever that he had befuddled himself. No wonder he was a favorite target of the comic poets. I. F. Stone likens this wizardry to "whales of the intellect flailing about in deep seas" (Stone 1988).

With his young friend Meno, Socrates argued whether virtue is teachable. Meno was eager to learn more, after "holding forth often on the subject in front of large audiences." But he complained, "You are exercising magic and witchcraft upon me and positively laying me under your spell until I am just a mass of helplessness. . . . You are exactly like the flat stingray that one meets in the sea. Whenever anyone comes into contact with it, it numbs him, and that is the sort of thing you seem to be doing to me now. My mind and my lips are literally numb."

Philosophy is not a semantic game, though sometimes its idiosyncrasies feed that response into the popular mind. *Media Ethics: Issues and Cases* does not debunk philosophy as the excess of sovereign reason. The authors of this book will not encourage those who ridicule philosophy as cunning

rhetoric. The issue at stake here is actually a somewhat different problem—
the Cartesian model of philosophizing.

The founder of modern philosophy, René Descartes, preferred to work
in solitude. Paris was whirling in the early 17th century, but for two years
even Descartes's friends could not find him as he squirreled himself away
studying mathematics. One can even guess the motto above his desk: "Happy
is he who lives in seclusion." Imagine the conditions under which he wrote
"Meditations II." The Thirty Years' War in Europe brought social chaos
everywhere. The Spanish were ravaging the French provinces and even
threatening Paris, but Descartes was shut away in an apartment in Holland.
Tranquility for philosophical speculation mattered so much to him that upon
hearing Galileo had been condemned by the Church, he retracted parallel
arguments of his own on natural science. Pure philosophy as an abstract
enterprise needed a cool atmosphere isolated from everyday events.

Descartes's magnificent formulations have always had their detractors, of
course. David Hume did not think of philosophy in those terms, believing as
he did that sentiment is the foundation of morality. For Søren Kierkegaard,
an abstract system of ethics is only paper currency with nothing to back it up.
Karl Marx insisted that we change the world and not merely explain it. But
no one drew the modern philosophical map more decisively than Descartes,
and his mode of rigid inquiry has generally defined the field's parameters.

This book adopts the historical perspective suggested by Stephen Toulmin:

> The philosophy whose legitimacy the critics challenge is always the seven-
> teenth century tradition founded primarily upon René Descartes. . . . [The]
> arguments are directed to one particular style of philosophizing—a theory-
> centered style which poses philosophical problems, and frames solutions to
> them, in timeless and universal terms. From 1650, this particular style was
> taken as defining the very agenda of philosophy (1988, 338).

The 17th-century philosophers set aside the particular, the timely, the local,
and the oral. And that development left untouched nearly half of the philosophical agenda. Indeed, it is those neglected topics—what I here call "practical philosophy"—that are showing fresh signs of life today, at the very time
when the more familiar "theory-centered" half of the subject is languishing
(Toulmin 1988, 338).

This book collaborates in demolishing the barrier of three centuries
between pure and applied philosophy; it joins in reentering practical concerns
as the legitimate domain of philosophy itself. For Toulmin, the primary
focus of ethics has moved from the study to the bedside to criminal courts,
engineering labs, the newsroom, factories, and ethnic street corners. Moral
philosophers are not being asked to hand over their duties to technical experts

in today's institutions but rather to fashion their agendas within the conditions of contemporary struggle.

All humans have a theoretical capacity. Critical thinking, the reflective dimension, is our common property. And this book nurtures that reflection in communication classrooms and by extension into centers of media practice. If the mind is like a muscle, this volume provides a regimen of exercises for strengthening its powers of systematic reflection and moral discernment. It does not permit those aimless arguments that result in quandary ethics. Instead, it operates in the finest traditions of practical philosophy, anchoring the debates in real-life conundrums but pushing the discussion toward substantive issues and integrating appropriate theory into the decision-making process. It seeks to empower students to do ethics themselves, under the old adage that teaching someone to fish lasts a lifetime, and providing fish only saves the day.

Media Ethics: Issues and Cases arrives on the scene at a strategic time in higher education. Since the late 19th century, ethical questions have been taken from the curriculum as a whole and from the philosophy department. Recovering practical philosophy has involved a revolution during the last decade in which courses in professional ethics have reappeared throughout the curriculum. This book advocates the pervasive method and carries the discussions even further, beyond freestanding courses into communication classrooms across the board.

In this sense, the book represents a constructive response to the current debates over the mission of higher education. Professional ethics has long been saddled with the dilemma that the university was given responsibility for professional training precisely at the point in its history that it turned away from values to scientific naturalism. Today one sees it as a vast horizontal plain given to technical excellence but barren in enabling students to articulate a philosophy of life. As the late James Carey concluded,

> Higher education has not been performing well of late and, like most American institutions, is suffering from a confusion of purpose, an excess of ambition that borders on hubris, and an appetite for money that is truly alarming (1989, 48).

The broadside critiques leveled in Thorstein Veblen's *The Higher Learning in America* (1918) and Upton Sinclair's *The Goose Step* (1922) are now too blatantly obvious to ignore. But *Media Ethics: Issues and Cases* does not merely demand a better general education or a recommitment to values; it strengthens the communications curriculum by equipping thoughtful students with a more enlightened moral awareness. Since Confucius, we have understood that lighting a candle is better than cursing the darkness, or, in Mother Teresa's version, we feed the world one mouth at a time.

Preface

More than three decades ago, two of us began the quest of delivering a media ethics textbook grounded in the theory of moral philosophy and using case studies for students to be able to apply the theory learned. In our planning, the book would begin and end with theory—moral philosophy and moral development, respectively—and the chapters in between would be topical and cross all mediums. So instead of chapter titles such as "journalism" or "public relations" you see titles such as "loyalty" and "privacy."

Despite the passage of decades, our foundational assumption remains that the media and democracy need one another to survive. If there is a single animating idea in this book, it is that whether your focus is entertainment, news, or strategic communication, whether your role is that of a professional or a parent, your "job" is made easier in a functioning democracy. And democracy functions best with a free and independent mass media that spurs change, reifies culture, and provides opportunity to read and think and explore and create. We believe that thinking about and understanding ethics makes you better at whatever profession you choose—and whatever your role when you get home from work. This book remains optimistic about the very tough times in which we find ourselves.

Let's begin with what's been left out and conclude with what you'll find in the text. First, you'll find no media bashing in this book. There's enough of that already, and besides, it's too easy to do. This book is not designed to indict the media; it's designed to train its future practitioners. If we dwell on ethical lapses from the past, it is only to learn from them what we can do to prevent similar occurrences in the future. Second, you'll find no conclusions in this book—neither at the end of the book nor after each case. No one has yet written the conclusive chapter to the ethical dilemmas of the media, and we don't suspect that we will be the first.

All along, the cases were to be the "stars" of the book—mostly real life (as opposed to hypothetical), usually recent and largely guest-written, especially when we could find someone who lived in close proximity to the market where the case study happened. We would end each case with pedagogical questions. These began, at the lowest level, with the actual details of the case and were called "micro issues." The questions then went out in ever-widening concentric circles to larger issues and deeper questions and eventually ended at debating some of the largest issues in society such as justice, race, fairness, truth-telling, media's role in a democracy, and many others. We called these "macro issues." The questions were not answered in the textbook. It was left to the student and the professor to arrive at an answer that could be justified given the ethical underpinnings of the text.

This simple idea became popular and subsequent editions added to the depth of the chapters and the recency of the cases. As the field changed and student majors within the field changed, so did the book. Some additions, including an "international" chapter and a "new media" chapter, came and went, and the material was absorbed in other places in the book. Writing about "public relations" became "strategic communications" with all the nuances that entailed. Social media rocked our industry and changed our economic model, and the book followed with the obvious ethical issues that citizen journalism brought with it. At every stage, it remained a true media ethics textbook and not simply a journalism ethics book. Both the current chapters and current cases bear that out.

This ninth edition brings with it many changes, the major ones being a new publisher, a new co-author, and a new chapter on social justice. More than half of all cases also are new. But a large amount of the text remains the same and a significant minority of the cases also remain in the textbook. These decisions mirror the state of the field of media ethics: some of the problems media professionals face today are new; others are as old as our professions.

Each of us bears a significant debt of gratitude to families, to teachers and mentors, to colleagues, and to our new and delightful publisher. We acknowledge their contributions to our intellectual and moral development in making this textbook possible, and we accept the flaws of this book as our own.

1

An Introduction to Ethical Decision-Making

By the end of this chapter, you should be able to

- recognize the need for professional ethics in journalism
- work through a model of ethical decision-making
- identify and use the five philosophical principles applicable to mass communication situations

MAKING ETHICAL DECISIONS

No matter your professional niche in mass communication, the past few years have been nothing short of an assault on the business model that supports your organization and pays your salary, on the role you play in a democratic society, on whether your job might be better—and certainly more cheaply—done by a robot or an algorithm.

Consider the following ethical decisions that made the news:

- the *New York Times* choosing to call President Donald J. Trump a liar in its news columns as well as on the editorial pages. National Public Radio made a different decision, refusing to use the word in its news coverage;
- Facebook users who, in the last two weeks of the US presidential election, chose to share "news stories" originating with Russian bots more frequently than they shared news stories from legitimate news organizations. Meanwhile, Facebook founder Mark Zuckerberg continued to assert that Facebook is not a media organization;

1

- the Gannett Corporation and Gatehouse Media closed down copy desks at individual newspapers in favor of a regional copy hub system, thereby ensuring that local news would no longer be edited in individual media markets;
- H&R Block purchasing "native advertising" that included a photo of a woman "taking a break" after filling out her name and address on her income tax forms. Native advertising is now found ubiquitously online and in legacy publications such as the *New York Times* and the *Atlantic*. Comedian John Oliver has skewered the practice in multiple segments, noting, "It's not trickery. It's sharing storytelling tools. And that's not bullshit. It's repurposed bovine waste";
- television journalists and other cable personalities charging their employers, specifically Fox News management, with systemic sexual harassment;
- films such as *Get Out*—with its blend of horror and science fiction—that included some subtle and some in-your-face messages about race— earning critical and box office success. The year before *Get Out* was released, the Academy Awards were the focus of furious criticism for a lack of diversity in nominations, the Oscar-so-white movement;
- and last, but in many ways the most central, President Donald J. Trump, less than six months into his administration, labeling "the media" as the enemy of the people, a characterization that was greeted with anger and alarm by some and embraced by others.

In a campaign video released in August 2017, the day after the far-right rally in Charlottesville, Virginia, killed one and injured many others, African-American journalist April Ryan stated that she and other journalists had been singled out as an "enemy of the White House." The video, titled "Let President Trump do his job" included small images of a dozen journalists while the voiceover described "the media attacking our president" and referred to "the president's enemies" who "don't want him to succeed." Ryan, a veteran White House correspondent for the American Urban Radio Networks and a political analyst for CNN, responded with a tweet castigating the campaign's "racial hate."

Each of these instances represent an ethical choice, decisions that most often begin with individuals but are then reinforced by the profit-making organizations for which they work or by the social organizations in which people willingly participate. Almost all of them include the element of melding roles—am I acting as a news reporter or as a consumer, as a private citizen or as a professional, as an audience member who understands that comedians can sometimes speak a certain sort of truth, or as an objective reporter for whom words that imply or state an opinion are forbidden. As young professionals, you are told to "promote your own brand" while simultaneously promoting your client, your news organization, or your profession. It's a staggering array of requirements and obligations, made more difficult by the very public nature—and the potential public response—that your decisions will inevitably provoke. A simple Google search of each of the foregoing ethical choices will open up a world of conflicting opinions.

The Dilemma of Dilemmas

The summaries above are dilemmas—they present an ethical problem with no single (or simple) "right" answer. Resolving dilemmas is the business of ethics. It's not an easy process, but ethical dilemmas can be anticipated and prepared for, and there is a wealth of ethical theory—some of it centuries old—to back up your final decision. In this chapter and throughout this book, you will be equipped with both the theories and the tools to help solve the dilemmas that arise in working for the mass media.

In the end, you will have tools, not answers. Answers must come from within you, but your answers should be informed by what others have written and experienced. Otherwise, you will always be forced to solve each ethical problem without the benefit of anyone else's insight. Gaining these tools also will help you to prevent each dilemma from spiraling into "quandary ethics"—the feeling that no best choice is available and that everyone's choice is equally valid (see Deni Elliott's essay following this chapter).

Will codes of ethics help? Virtually all the media associations have one, but they have limitations. For instance, the ethics code for the Society of Professional Journalists could be read to allow for revealing or withholding information, two actions that are polar opposites. That doesn't make the code useless; it simply points out a shortfall in depending on codes.

While we don't dismiss codes, we believe you will find more universally applicable help in the writings of philosophers, ancient and modern, introduced in this chapter.

This book, or any ethics text, should teach more than a set of rules. It should give you the skills, analytical models, vocabulary, and insights of others who have faced these choices, to make and justify your ethical decisions.

Some writers claim that ethics can't be taught. It's situational, some claim. Because every message is unique, there is no real way to learn ethics other than by daily life. Ethics, it is argued, is something you have, not something you do. But while it's true that reading about ethics is no guarantee you will perform your job ethically, thinking about ethics is a skill anyone can acquire.

While each area of mass communication has its unique ethical issues, thinking about ethics is the same, whether you make your living writing advertising copy or obituaries. Thinking about ethics won't necessarily make tough choices easier, but, with practice, your ethical decision-making can become more consistent. A consistently ethical approach to your work as a reporter, designer, or copywriter in whatever field of mass communication you enter can improve that work as well.

Ethics and Morals

Contemporary professional ethics revolves around these questions:

- What duties do I have, and to whom do I owe them?
- What values are reflected by the duties I've assumed?

Ethics takes us out of the world of "This is the way I do it" or "This is the way it's always been done" into the realm of "This is what I should do" or "This is the action that can be rationally justified." Ethics in this sense is "ought talk." The questions arising from duty and values can be answered a number of ways as long as they are consistent with each other. For example, a journalist and a public relations professional may see the truth of a story differently because they see their duties differently and because there are different values at work in their professions, but each can be acting ethically if they are operating under the imperatives of "oughtness" for their profession.

It is important here to distinguish between *ethics,* a rational process founded on certain agreed-on principles, and *morals,* which are in the realm of religion. The Ten Commandments are a moral system in the Judeo-Christian tradition, and Jewish scholars have expanded this study of the laws throughout the Bible's Old Testament into the Talmud, a 1,000-page religious volume. The Buddhist Eightfold Path provides a similar moral framework.

But moral systems are not synonymous with ethics. *Ethics begins when elements within a moral system conflict.* Ethics is less about the conflict between right and wrong than it is about the conflict between equally com-pelling (or equally unattractive) alternatives and the choices that must be made between them. Ethics is just as often about the choices between good and better or poor and worse than about right and wrong, which tends to be the domain of morals.

When elements within a moral system conflict, ethical principles can help you make tough choices. We'll review several ethical principles briefly after describing how one philosopher, Sissela Bok, says working professionals can learn to make good ethical decisions.

A Word about Ethics

The concept of ethics comes from the Greeks, who divided the philosophical world into separate disciplines. *Aesthetics* was the study of the beautiful and how a person could analyze beauty without relying only on subjective evaluations. *Epistemology* was the study of knowing, debates about what constitutes learning and what is knowable. *Ethics* was the study of what is good, both for the individual and for society. Interestingly, the root of the word means "custom" or "habit," giving ethics an underlying root of behavior that is long established and beneficial to the ongoing of society. The Greeks were also concerned with the individual virtues of fortitude, justice, temperance, and wisdom, as well as with societal virtues such as freedom.

Two thousand years later, ethics has come to mean learning to make rational decisions among an array of choices, all of which may be morally justifiable, but some more so than others. Rationality is the key word here, for the Greeks believed, and modern philosophers affirm, that people should be able to explain their ethical decisions to others and that acting ethically could be shown to be a rational decision to make. That ability to explain ethical choices is an important one for media professionals whose choices are so public. When confronted with an angry public, "It seemed like the right thing to do at the time" is a personally embarrassing *and* ethically unsatisfactory explanation.

BOK'S MODEL

Bok's ethical decision-making framework was introduced in her book *Lying: Moral Choice in Public and Private Life.* Bok's model is based on two premises: that we must have empathy for the people involved in ethical decisions and that maintaining social trust is a fundamental goal. With this in mind, Bok says any ethical question should be analyzed in three steps.

First, consult your own conscience about the "rightness" of an action. *How do you feel about the action?*

Second, seek expert advice for alternatives to the act creating the ethical problem. Experts, by the way, can be those either living or dead—a producer or editor you trust or a philosopher you admire. *Is there another professionally acceptable way to achieve the same goal that will not raise ethical issues?*

Third, if possible, conduct a public discussion with the parties involved in the dispute. These include those who are directly involved such as a reporter or their source, and those indirectly involved such as a reader or a media outlet owner. If they cannot be gathered—and that will most often be the case—you can conduct the conversation hypothetically in your head, playing out the roles. The goal of this conversation is to discover *How will others respond to the proposed act?*

Let's see how Bok's model works in the following scenario. In the section after the case, follow the three steps Bok recommends and decide if you would run the story.

How Much News Is Fit to Print?

In your community, the major charity is the United Way. The annual fund-raising drive will begin in less than two weeks. However, at a late-night meeting of the board with no media present, the executive director resigns. Though the agency is not covered by the Open Meetings Act, you are able to learn most of what went on from a source on the board.

According to her, the executive director had taken pay from the agency by submitting a falsified time sheet while he was actually away at the funeral of a college roommate. The United Way board investigated the absence and asked for his resignation, citing the lying about the absence as the reason, though most agreed that they would have given him paid leave had he asked.

The United Way wants to issue a short statement, praising the work of the executive director while regretfully accepting his resignation. The executive director also will issue a short statement citing other opportunities as his reason for leaving. You are assigned the story by an editor who does not know about the additional information you have obtained but wants you to "see if there's any more to it [the resignation] than they're telling."

You call your source on the board and she asks you, as a friend, to withhold the damaging information because it will hinder the United Way's annual fund-raising effort and jeopardize services to needy people in the community because faith in the United Way will be destroyed. You confront the executive director. He says he already has a job interview with another non-profit and if you run the story you will ruin his chances of a future career.

What do you do?

THE ANALYSIS

Bok's first step requires you to *consult your conscience*. When you do, you realize you have a problem. Your responsibility is to tell the truth, and that means providing readers with all the facts you discover. You also have a larger responsibility not to harm your community, and printing the complete story might well cause short-term harm. Clearly, your conscience is of two minds about the issue.

You move to the second step: *alternatives*. Do you simply run the resignation release, figuring that the person can do no further harm and therefore should be left alone? Do you run the whole story but buttress it with board members' quotes that such an action couldn't happen again, figuring that you have restored public trust in the agency? Do you do nothing until after the fundraising drive and risk the loss of trust from readers if the story circulates around town as a rumor? Again, there are alternatives, but each has some cost.

In the third step of Bok's model, you will attempt to *hold a public ethical dialogue* with all of the parties involved. Most likely you won't get all the parties into the newsroom on deadline. Instead you can conduct an imaginary discussion among the parties involved. Such a discussion might go like this:

EXECUTIVE DIRECTOR: "I think my resignation is sufficient penalty for any mistake I might have made, and your article will jeopardize my ability to find another job. It's really hurting my wife and kids, and they've done nothing wrong."

REPORTER: "But shouldn't you have thought about that *before* you decided to falsify the time sheet? This is a good story, and I think the public should know what the people who are handling their donations are like."

READER 1: "Wait a minute. I am the public, and I'm tired of all of this bad news your paper focuses on. This man has done nothing but good in the community, and I can't see where any money that belonged to the poor went into his pocket. Why can't we see some good news for a change?"

READER 2: "I disagree. I buy the paper precisely because it does this kind of reporting. Stories like this that keep the government, the charities and everyone else on their toes."

PUBLISHER: "You mean like a watchdog function."

READER 2: "Exactly. And if it bothers you, don't read it."

PUBLISHER: "I don't really like to hurt people with the power we have, but if we don't print stories like this, and the community later finds out that we withheld news, our credibility is ruined, and we're out of business." [To source] "Did you request that the information be off the record?"

SOURCE: "No. But I never thought you'd use it in your story."

REPORTER: "I'm a reporter. I report what I hear for a living. What did you think I would do with it? Stories like these allow me to support my family."

EXECUTIVE DIRECTOR: "So it's your career or mine, is that what you're saying? Look, no charges have been filed here, but if your story runs, I look like a criminal. Is that fair?"

PUBLISHER: "And if it doesn't run, we don't keep our promise to the community. Is that fair?"

NEEDY MOTHER: "Fair? You want to talk fair? Do you suffer if the donations go down? No, I do. This is just another story to you. It's the difference in me and my family getting by."

The conversation could continue, and other points of view could be voiced. Your imaginary conversations could be more or less elaborate than the one above, but out of this discussion it should be possible to rationally support an ethical choice.

There are two cautions in using Bok's model for ethical decision-making. First, it is important to go through all three steps before making a final choice. Most of us make ethical choices prematurely, after we've consulted only our consciences, an error Bok says results in a lot of flabby moral thinking. Second, while you will not be endowed with any clairvoyant powers to anticipate your ethical problems, the ethical dialogue outlined in the third step is best when conducted in advance of the event, not in the heat of writing a story.

For instance, an advertising copywriter might conduct such a discussion about whether advertising copy can ethically withhold disclaimers about potential harm from a product. A reporter might conduct such a discussion well in advance of the time he is actually asked to withhold an embarrassing name or fact from a story. Since it is likely that such dilemmas will arise in your chosen profession (the illustration above is based on what happened to one of the authors the first day on the job), your answer will be more readily available and more logical if you hold such discussions either with trusted colleagues in a casual atmosphere or by yourself, well in advance of the problem. The cases in this book are selected partially for their ability to predict your on-the-job dilemmas and start the ethical discussion now.

GUIDELINES FOR MAKING ETHICAL DECISIONS

Since the days of ancient Greece, philosophers have tried to draft a series of rules or guidelines governing how to make ethical choices. In ethical dilemmas such as the one above, you will need principles to help you determine what to do amid conflicting voices. While a number of principles work well, we will review five.

Aristotle's Golden Mean

Aristotle believed that happiness—which some scholars translate as "flourishing"—was the ultimate human good. By flourishing, Aristotle sought to elevate any activity through the setting of high standards, what he called exercising "practical reasoning."

Aristotle believed that practical reason was exercised by individuals who understood what the Greeks called the "virtues" and demonstrated them in their lives and calling. Such a person was the *phrenemos,* or person of practical wisdom, who demonstrated ethical excellence in his or her daily activity. For Aristotle, the highest virtue was citizenship, and its highest practitioner the statesman, a politician who exercised so much practical wisdom in his daily activity that he elevated the craft of politics to art. In contemporary terms, we might think of a *phrenemos* as a person who excels at any of a variety of activities—cellist Yo-Yo Ma, the late poet Maya Angelou, filmmakers George Lucas and Steven Spielberg. They are people who flourish in their professional performance, extending our own vision of what is possible.

This notion of flourishing led Aristotle to assert that people acting virtuously are the moral basis of his ethical system, not those who simply follow rules. His ethical system is now called *virtue ethics*. Virtue ethics flows from both the nature of the act itself and the moral character of the person who acts. In the Aristotelian sense, the way to behave ethically is that (1) you must know (through the exercise of practical reasoning) what you are doing; (2) you must select the act for its own sake—in order to flourish; and (3) the act itself must spring from a firm and unchanging character.

Figure 1.1. *Calvin and Hobbes* © 1989 Watterson. Reprinted with permission of Andrews McMeel Syndication. All rights reserved.

It is not stretching Aristotle's framework to assert that one way to learn ethics is to select heroes and to try to model your individual acts and ultimately your professional character on what you believe they would do. An Aristotelian might well consult this hero as an expert when making an ethical choice. Asking what my hero would do in a particular situation is a valid form of ethical analysis. The trick, however, is to select your heroes carefully and continue to think for yourself rather than merely copy behavior you have seen previously.

What then is a virtue? *Virtue lies at the mean between two extremes of excess and deficiency*, a reduction of Aristotle's philosophy often called the "Golden Mean" as shown in table 1.1. Courage, for example, is a mean between foolhardiness on one hand and cowardice on the other. But to determine that mean for yourself, you have to exercise practical wisdom, act according to high standards, and act in accordance with firm and continuing character traits.

In reality, therefore, the middle ground of a virtue is not a single point on a line that is the same for every individual. It is instead a range of behaviors that varies individually, while avoiding the undesirable extremes. Candor is a good example of a virtue that is most certainly contextual—what is too blunt in one instance is kind in another. Consider two witnesses to a potential drowning: one onlooker is a poor swimmer but a fast runner, the other is a good swimmer but a slow runner. What is cowardice for one is foolhardy for the other. Each can exhibit courage, but in different ways.

Seeking the golden mean implies that individual acts are not disconnected from one another, but collectively form a whole that a person of good character should aspire to. A virtue theory of ethics is not outcome-oriented. Instead, it is agent-oriented, and right actions in a virtue theory of ethics are a result of an agent seeking virtue and accomplishing it. As Aristotle wrote in *Nicomachean Ethics*, "we learn an art or craft by doing the things that we shall have to do when we have learnt it: for instance, men become builders by building houses, harpers by playing on the harp. Similarly we become just by doing just acts, temperate by doing temperate acts, brave by doing brave acts."

Table 1.1.   Aristotle's Golden Mean

Unacceptable Behaviors (Deficiency)	*Acceptable Behaviors*	*Unacceptable Behaviors (Excess)*
Cowardice	Courage	Foolhardiness
Shamelessness	Modesty	Bashfulness
Stinginess	Generosity	Wastefulness

Far from being old-fashioned, Aristotle's concept of virtue ethics has been rediscovered by a variety of professions. As Kenneth Woodward (1994) states in a *Newsweek* essay entitled "What is Virtue?" a call for virtue is still relevant today:

> But before politicians embrace virtue as their latest election-year slogan, they would do well to tune into contemporary philosophy. Despite the call for virtue, we live in an age of moral relativism. According to the dominant school of moral philosophy, the skepticism engendered by the Enlightenment has reduced all ideas of right and wrong to matters of personal taste, emotional preference or cultural choice. . . . Against this moral relativism, advocates of the "ethics of virtue" argue that some personal choices are morally superior to others.

Kant's Categorical Imperative

Immanuel Kant is best known for his *categorical imperative*, which is most often stated in two ways. The first asserts that an individual should act as if the choices one makes for oneself could become universal law. The second states that you should act so that you treat each individual as an end and never as merely a means. Kant called these two rules "categorical" imperatives, meaning that their demands were universal and not subject to situational factors. Many readers will recognize the similarity between Kant's first manifestation of the categorical imperative and the Bible's golden rule: Do unto others as you would have others do unto you. The two are quite similar in their focus on duty.

Kant's ethical theory is based on the notion that it is in the act itself, rather than the person who acts, where moral force resides. This theory of ethics is unlike Aristotle's in that it moves the notion of what is ethical from the actor to the act itself. This does not mean that Kant did not believe in moral character, but rather that people could act morally from a sense of duty even if their character might incline them to act otherwise.

For Kant, an action was morally justified only if it was performed from duty—motive matters to Kant—and in Kant's moral universe there were two sorts of duties. The strict duties were generally negative: not to murder, not to break promises, not to lie. The meritorious duties were more positive: to aid others, to develop one's talents, to show gratitude. Kant spent very little time defining these notions, but philosophers have generally asserted that the strict duties are somewhat more morally mandatory than the meritorious duties.

Some have argued that consequences are not important in Kant's ethical reasoning. We prefer a somewhat less austere reading of Kant. While Kant's view is that the moral worth of an action does not depend on its consequences, those consequences are not irrelevant. For example, a surgeon may show moral virtue in attempting to save a patient through an experimental procedure, but the decision about whether to undertake that procedure requires taking into account the probability of a cure. This framing of Kantian principles allows us to learn from our mistakes.

The test of a moral act, according to Kant, is its universality—whether it can be applied to everyone. For instance, under Kant's categorical imperative, journalists can claim few special privileges, such as the right to lie or the right to invade privacy in order to get a story. Kant's view, if taken seriously, reminds you of what you give up—truth, privacy, and the like—when you make certain ethical decisions.

Utilitarianism

The original articulation of *utilitarianism* by Englishmen Jeremy Bentham and later John Stuart Mill in the 19th century introduced what was then a novel notion into ethics discussions: *the consequences of actions are important in deciding whether they are ethical.* In the utilitarian view, it may be considered ethical to harm one person for the benefit of the larger group. This approach, for example, is the ethical justification for investigative reporting, the results of which may harm individuals even as they are printed or broadcast in the hope of providing a greater societal good.

The appeal of utilitarianism is that it has proven to mesh well with Western thought, particularly on human rights. Harvard ethicist Arthur Dyck (1977, 55) writes of Mill:

> He took the view that the rightness or wrongness of any action is decided by its consequences. . . . His particular understanding of what is best on the whole was that which brings about the most happiness or the least suffering, i.e., the best balance of pleasure over pain for the greatest number.

The benefit of utilitarianism is that it provides a principle by which rightness and wrongness can be identified and judged, conflicts can be resolved, and exceptions can be decided. The utilitarian calculus also has made possible the "quantification of welfare" Dyck says, allowing governments to make decisions that create the most favorable balance of benefits over harms.

With its focus on the consequences of an action, utilitarianism completes a cycle begun with Aristotle (see table 1.2). Aristotle, in developing the golden mean, focused on the *actor.* Kant, in his categorical imperative, focused on the *action,* while Mill, in his utilitarian philosophy, focused on the *outcome.*

Utilitarianism has been condensed to the ethical philosophy of the "greatest good for the greatest number." While this pithy phrase is a very rough and

Table 1.2. The Shifting Focus of Ethics from Aristotle to Mill

Philosopher	Known For	Popularly Known As	Emphasized
Aristotle	Golden mean	Virtue lies between extremes.	The actor
Kant	Categorical imperative	Act so your choices could be universal law; treat humanity as an end, never as a means only.	The action
Mill	Utility principle	An act's rightness is determined by its contribution to a desirable end.	The outcome

ready characterization of utilitarian theory, it also has led to an overly mechanistic application of the principle: Just tally up the amount of good and subtract the amount of harm. If the remaining number is positive, the act is ethical. However, when properly applied, utilitarianism is not mechanical.

To do justice to utilitarian theory, it must be understood within a historical context. Mill wrote after the changes of the Enlightenment. The principle of democracy was fresh and untried, and the thought that the average person should be able to speak his mind to those in power was novel. Utilitarianism, as Mill conceived of it, was a profoundly social ethic; Mill was among the first to acknowledge that the good of an entire society had a place in ethical reasoning.

Mill was what philosophers call a *valuational hedonist*. He argued that pleasure—and the absence of pain—was the only intrinsic moral end. Mill further asserted that an act was right in the proportion in which it contributed to general happiness. Conversely, an act was wrong in the proportion in which it contributed to general unhappiness or pain. Utilitarianism can be subtle and complex in that the same act can make some happy but cause others pain. Mill insisted that both outcomes be valued simultaneously, a precarious activity but one that forces discussion of competing stakeholder claims.

In utilitarian theory, no one's happiness is any more valuable than anyone else's, and definitely not more valuable than everyone's—quantity and quality being equal. In democratic societies, this is a particularly important concept because it meshes well with certain social and political goals. In application, utilitarianism has a way of puncturing entrenched self-interest, but when badly applied, it can actually promote social selfishness.

Utilitarianism also suggests that moral questions are objective, empirical, and. even in some sense, scientific. Utilitarianism promotes a universal ethical standard that each rational person can determine. However, utilitarianism is among the most criticized of philosophical principles because it is so difficult to accurately anticipate all the consequences of a particular act. Different philosophers also have disputed how one calculates the good, rendering any utilitarian calculus fundamentally error prone.

While utilitarianism is a powerful theory, too many rely exclusively on it. Taken to extremes, the act of calculating the good can lead to ethical gridlock, with each group of stakeholders having seemingly equally strong claims with little way to choose among them. Sloppily done, utilitarianism may bias the user toward short-term benefit, which is often contrary to the nature of ethical decisions.

Pluralistic Theory of Value

Philosopher William David Ross (1930) based his ethical theory on the belief that there is often more than one ethical value simultaneously "competing" for preeminence in our ethical decision-making, a tension set up in the title of his book *The Right and the Good*. Commenting on the tension, ethicist Christopher Meyers (2003, 84) says,

> As the book title suggests, Ross distinguished between the *right* and the *good*. The latter term refers to an objective, if indefinable, quality present in all acts. It is something seen, not done. Right, on the other hand, refers to actions. A right action is something undertaken by persons motivated by correct reasons and on careful reflection. Not all right actions, however, will be productive of the good.

In acknowledging the competition between the good and the right, Ross differs from Kant or Mill, who proposed only one ultimate value. To Ross, these competing ethical claims, which he calls duties, are equal, provided that the circumstances of the particular moral choice are equal. Further, these duties gain their moral weight not from their consequences but from the highly personal nature of duty.

Ross proposed these types of duties:

1. those duties of *fidelity,* based on my implicit or explicit promise;
2. those duties of *reparation,* arising from a previous wrongful act;
3. those duties of *gratitude* that rest on previous acts of others;
4. those duties of *justice* that arise from the necessity to ensure the equitable and meritorious distribution of pleasure or happiness;
5. those duties of *beneficence* that rest on the fact that there are others in the world whose lot we can better;
6. those duties of *self-improvement* that rest on the fact that we can improve our own condition; and
7. one negative duty: the duty of *not injuring others.*

We would recommend two additional duties that may be implied by Ross' list but are not specifically stated:

1. the duty to tell the truth, *veracity* (which may be implied by fidelity); and
2. the duty to *nurture,* to help others achieve some measure of self-worth and achievement.

Ross' typology of duties works well for professionals who often must balance competing roles. It also brings to ethical reasoning some affirmative notions of the primacy of community and relationships as a way to balance the largely rights-based traditions of much Western philosophical theory.

Like Kant, Ross divided his duties into two kinds. *Prima facie duties* are those duties that seem to be right because of the nature of the act itself. *Duty proper* (also called actual duties) are those duties that are paramount given specific circumstances. Arriving at your duty proper from among the prima facie duties requires that you consider what ethicists call the *morally relevant differences*. But Ross (1988, 24) warns that

> there is no reason to anticipate that every act that is our duty is so for one and the same reason. Why should two sets or circumstances, or one set of circumstances *not* possess different characteristics, any one of which makes a certain act our *prima facie* duty?

Let's take an example using one of Ross' prima facie duties: keeping promises. In your job as a reporter, you have made an appointment with the mayor to discuss a year-end feature on your community. On your way to City Hall, you drive by a serious auto accident and see a young child wandering, dazed, along the road. If you stop to help you will certainly be late for your appointment and may have to cancel altogether. You have broken a promise.

But is that act ethical?

Ross would probably say yes because the specific aspects of the situation had a bearing on the fulfillment of a prima facie duty. You exercised discernment. You knew that your commitment to the mayor was a relatively minor sort of promise. Your news organization will not be hurt by postponing the interview, and your act allowed you to fulfill the prima facie duties of beneficence, avoiding harm and nurturing. Had the interview been more important, or the wreck less severe, the morally relevant factors would have been different. Ross' pluralistic theory of values may be more difficult to apply than a system of absolute rules, but it reflects the way we make ethical choices.

Ross' concept of multiple duties "helps to explain why we feel uneasy about breaking a promise even when we are justified in doing so. Our uneasiness comes from the fact that we have broken a *prima facie* duty even as we fulfilled another" (Lebacqz 1985, 27).

Communitarianism

Classical ethical theory places its dominant intellectual emphasis on the individual and individual acts by emphasizing concepts such as character, choice, liberty, and duty. But contemporary realities point out the intellectual weakness in this approach. Consider the environment. On many environmental questions, it is possible for people to make appropriate individual decisions—today I drive my car—that taken together promote environmental degradation. My individual decision to drive my car (or to purchase a hybrid car) doesn't matter very much; when individual decisions accumulate, however, the impact is profound not only for a single generation but for subsequent ones as well.

Communitarianism, which has its roots in political theory, seeks to provide ethical guidance when confronting the sort of society-wide issues that mark current political and business activity. Communitarianism returns to Aristotle's concept of the "polis"—or community—and invests it with moral weight. People begin their lives, at least in a biological sense, as members of a two-person community. Communitarian philosophy extends this biological beginning to a philosophical worldview. "In communitarianism, persons have certain inescapable claims on one another that cannot be renounced except at the cost of their humanity" (Christians, Ferré, and Fackler 1993, 14). Communitarians assert that when issues are political and social, community interests trump individual interests but does not trample them.

Communitarianism focuses on the outcome of individual ethical decisions analyzed in light of their potential to impact society. And when applied to journalism, you have a product "committed to justice, covenant and empowerment. Authentic communities are marked by justice; in strong democracies, courageous talk is mobilized into action. . . . In normative communities, citizens are empowered for social transformation, not merely freed from external constraints" (Christians et al. 1993, 14).

Communitarianism asserts that social justice is the predominant moral value. Communitarians recognize the value of process but are just as concerned with outcomes. History is full of "good" processes that led to bad outcomes. For example, democratic elections led to the 1933 takeover of Germany by a minority party headed by Hitler. It was a democratically written and adopted Constitution that included the three-fifths clause where African-Americans were equal to three-fifths of a single Caucasian for purposes of population count. Under communitarianism, the ability of individual acts to create a more just society is an appropriate measure of their rightness, and outcomes are part of the calculus.

Communitarian thinking allows ethical discussion to include values such as altruism and benevolence on an equal footing with more traditional questions such as truth telling and loyalty. Indeed, Nobel Prize–winning work in game theory has empirically demonstrated that cooperation, one of the foundation stones of community, provides desirable results once thought to be possible only through competition (Axelrod 1984). Cooperation is particularly powerful when the "shadow of the future," an understanding that we will encounter the outcome of our decisions and their impact on others in readily foreseeable time, is taken into account.

Communitarianism suffers from a lack of a succinct summary of its general propositions. However, any notion of a communitarian community begins with the fact that its members would include, as part of their understanding of self, their membership in the community. "For them, community describes not just what they have as fellow citizens but also what they are, not as a relationship they choose (as in a voluntary association) but an attachment they discover, not merely an attribute but as a constituent of their identity" (Sandel 1982, 150). A communitarian community resembles family more than it resembles town.

Under communitarianism, journalism cannot separate itself from the political and economic system of which it is a part. Communitarian thinking makes it possible to ask whether current practice (for example, a traditional definition of news) provides a good mechanism for a community to discover itself, learn about itself, and ultimately transform itself.

Communitarian reasoning allows journalists to understand their institutional role and to evaluate their performance against shared societal values. For instance, the newsroom adage "if it bleeds it leads" might sell newspapers or attract viewers, but it also might give a false impression of community and its perils to the most vulnerable members. Communitarianism would not ban the coverage of crime but would demand context that would help viewers or readers decide if they need to take action.

Thinking as a communitarian not only mutes the competition among journalistic outlets, it also provides a new agenda for news. Rape stories would include mobilizing information about the local rape crisis center. Political stories would focus on issues, not the horserace or personal scandals, and the coverage would be ample enough for an informed citizenry to cast a knowledgeable ballot. Writers have linked communitarian philosophy with the civic journalism movement. But like the philosophy of communitarianism, the practice of civic journalism has not yet been embraced by the mainstream of society.

THE "SCIENCE" OF ETHICS

Life in the 21st century has changed how most people think about issues, such as what constitutes a fact and what does or does not influence moral certainty. But ethical theory, with its apparent uncertainties and contradictions,

appears to have taken a back seat to science. As people have become drawn
to ethics they seek "the answer" to an ethical dilemma in the same way they
seek "the answer" in science. Consequently, the vagaries of ethical choice as
contrasted with the seeming certainty of scientific knowledge casts an unfair
light on ethics.

We'd like to offer you a different conceptualization of "the facts" of both
science and ethics. Science, and the seeming certainty of scientific knowledge, has undergone vast changes in the past 100 years. Before Einstein, most
educated people believed that Sir Francis Bacon had accurately and eternally
described the basic actions and laws of the physical universe. But Bacon was
wrong. Scientific inquiry in the 20th century explored a variety of physical
phenomena, uncovered new relationships, new areas of knowledge, and new
areas of ignorance. The "certainty" of scientific truth has changed fundamentally in the past 100 years, and there is every reason to expect similar changes
in this century, especially in the areas of neuroscience, nanotechnology, and
artificial intelligence. Science and certainty are not synonymous despite our
tendency to blur the two.

Contrast these fundamental changes in the scientific worldview with the
developments of moral theory. Aristotle's writing, more than 2,000 years
old, still has much to recommend it to the modern era. The same can be
said of utilitarianism and of the Kantian approach—both after 100 years of
critical review. Certainly, new moral thinking has emerged—for example,
feminist theory, but such work tends to build on rather than radically alter
the moral theory that has gone before. Ethical philosophers still have fundamental debates, but these debates have generally tended to deepen previous
insights rather than to "prove" them incorrect. Further, thinking about global
ethics uncovers some striking areas of agreement. We are aware of no ethical system, for example, that argues that murder is an ethical behavior, or
that lying, cheating, and stealing are the sorts of activities that human beings
ought to engage in on a regular basis.

From this viewpoint, there is more continuity in thinking about ethics than
in scientific thought. When the average person contrasts ethics with science,
it is ethics that tends to be viewed as changeable, unsystematic, and idiosyn-
cratic. Science has rigor, proof, and some relationship to an external reality.
We would like to suggest that such characterizations arise from a short-term
view of the history of science and ethics. In our view, ethics as a field has at
least as much continuity of thought as developments in science. And while
it cannot often be quantified, it has the rigor, the systematic quality, and the
relationship to reality that moderns too often characterize as the exclusive
domain of scientific thinking.

SUGGESTED READINGS

Aristotle. *Nicomachean ethics*.

Bok, S. (1978). *Lying: Moral choice in public and private life*. New York: Random House.

Borden, S. L. (2009). *Journalism as practice*. Burlington, VT: Ashgate.

Christians, C., Ferré, J., & Fackler, M. (1993). *Good news: Social ethics and the press*. New York: Oxford University Press.

Gert, B.. (1988). *Morality: A new justification of the moral rules*. New York: Oxford University Press.

Mill, J. S. *On liberty*.

Pojman, L. (1998). *Ethical theory: Classical and contemporary readings*. Belmont, CA: Wadsworth.

Ross, W. D. (1930). *The right and the good*. Oxford: Clarendon Press.

ESSAY

CASES AND MORAL SYSTEMS

DENI ELLIOTT
University of South Florida–St. Petersburg

Case studies are wonderful vehicles for ethics discussions with strengths that include helping discussants

1. appreciate the complexity of ethical decision-making;
2. understand the context within which difficult decisions are made;
3. track the consequences of choosing one action over another; and
4. learn both how and when to reconcile and to tolerate divergent points of view.

However, when case studies are misused, these strengths become weaknesses. Case studies are vehicles for an ethics discussion, not its ultimate destination. The purpose of an ethics discussion is to teach discussants how to "do ethics"—that is, to teach processes so that discussants can practice and improve their own critical decision-making abilities to reach a reasoned response to the issue at hand.

When the discussion stops short of this point, it is often because the destination has been fogged in by one or more myths of media case discussions:

Myth 1: Every opinion is equally valid.

Not true. The best opinion (conclusion) is the one that is best supported by judicious analysis of fact and theory and one that best addresses the morally relevant factors of the case (Gert 1988). An action has morally relevant factors if it is likely to cause some individual to suffer an evil that any rational person would wish to avoid (such as death, disability, pain, or loss of freedom or pleasure), or if it is the kind of action that generally causes evil (such as deception, breaking promises, cheating, disobedience of law, or neglect of duty).

Myth 2: Since we can't agree on an answer, there is no right answer.

In an ethics case, it may be that there are a number of acceptable answers. But there also will be many wrong answers—many approaches that the group can agree would be unacceptable. When discussants begin to despair of ever reaching any agreement on a right answer or answers, it is time to reflect on all of the agreement that exists within the group concerning the actions that would be out of bounds.

Myth 3: It hardly matters if you come up with the "ethical thing to do" because people ultimately act out of their own self-interest anyway.

Any institution supported by society—manufacturing firms or media corporations, medical centers, and so on—provides some service that merits that support. No matter what the service, practitioners or companies acting only in the short-term interest (i.e., to make money) will not last long. Both free-market pragmatism and ethics dictate that it makes little sense to ignore the expectations of consumers and of the society at large.

The guidelines below can serve as a map for an ethics discussion. They are helpful to have when working through unfamiliar terrain toward individual end points. They also can help you avoid the myths above. While discussing the case, check to see if these questions are being addressed:

1. What are the morally relevant factors of the case?
   (a) Will the proposed action cause an evil—such as death, disability, pain, loss of freedom or opportunity, or loss of pleasure—that any rational person would wish to avoid?
   (b) Is the proposed action the sort of action—such as deception, breaking promises, cheating, disobedience of law, or disobedience of professional or role-defined duty—that generally causes evil?
2. If the proposed action is one described above, is a greater evil being prevented or punished by allowing it to go forward?
3. If so, is the actor in a unique position to prevent or punish such an evil, or is that a more appropriate role for some other person or profession?
4. If the actor followed through on the action, would he be allowing himself to be an exception to a rule that he thinks everyone else should follow? (If so, then the action is prudent, not moral.)
5. Finally, would a rational, uninvolved person appreciate the reason for causing harm? Are the journalists ready and able to state, explain, and defend the proposed action in a public forum, or would a more detached journalist be ready to write an expose?

CASE

CASE 1-A

HOW TO READ A CASE STUDY

PHILIP PATTERSON
Oklahoma Christian University

When you look at the photo, it stirs your emotions. It's the last moment of one girl's life (the younger survived). It's a technically good photo—perhaps a once-in-a-lifetime shot. But when you learn the "back story" of this photo, a world of issues emerges, and the real discussions begin. And that's the beauty of cases as a way of learning media ethics.

For this case, here is what you need to know. One July afternoon, *Boston Herald* photographer Stanley Forman answered a call about a fire in one of the city's older sections. When he arrived, he followed a hunch and ran down the alley to the back of the row of houses. There he saw a 2-year-old girl and her 19-year-old godmother, on the fifth-floor fire escape. A fire truck had raised its aerial ladder to help. Another firefighter was on the roof, tantalizingly close to pulling the girls to safety. Then came a loud noise, the fire escape gave way and the girls tumbled to the ground. Forman saw it all through his 135 mm lens and took four photos as the two were falling.

The case study has several possible angles. You can discuss the gritty reality of the content. You can factor in that within 24 hours, the city of Boston acted to improve the inspection of all fire escapes in the city and that groups across the nation used the photos to promote similar efforts. You can talk about the ingenuity and industry of Forman to go where the story was rather than remain in front where the rest of the media missed it. You can critique his refusal to photograph the girls after impact. You can debate why the Pulitzer Prize committee gave Forman its top prize for this photo and add in the fact that more than half of the various "Picture of the Year" awards over decades are of death or imminent death. You can argue whether the *Boston Herald* profited off of the death and injury of the girls and what Forman's role was once he witnessed the tragedy. And you can ponder what happens when this photo hits the internet, stripped of context.

You can talk about any or all of these issues or imagine others. That's the beauty of a case study—you can go where it takes you. From this one case, you can argue taste in content, media economics ("If it bleeds, it leads"), personal versus professional duty, etc.

Perhaps you will want to role play. Perhaps you will ask yourself what Kant or Mill would do if he were the editor or whether a communitarian would approve the means (the photo) because of the end (better fire escape safety). Perhaps you want to talk about the "breakfast test" for objectionable content in the morning paper, whether it passes the test or whether the test ought to exist. Or what values led the paper to run the photo and the committee to give it an award.

During the semester, you can do more than just work through the cases in this book—you can find your own. All around you are cases of meritorious media behavior and cases of questionable media behavior. And, quite frankly, there are cases where good people will disagree over which category the behavior falls into. Good cases make for good discussion, not only now but also when you graduate into the marketplace as well.

So dive in, discuss, and defend.

Figure 1.2. Stanley J. Forman, Pulitzer Prize 1977. Used with permission.

2

Information Ethics

A Profession Seeks the Truth

By the end of this chapter, you should be familiar with

- both the Enlightenment and pragmatic constructions of truth
- the development and several criticisms of objective news reporting as a professional ideal
- why truth in "getting" the news may be as important as truth in reporting it
- how to develop a personal list of ethical news values

Each traditional profession has laid claims to a central tenet of philosophy. Law is equated with justice, medicine with the duty to render aid. Journalism, too, has a lofty ideal: the communication of truth.

But the ideal of truth is problematic. We often consider truth a stable commodity: it doesn't change much for us on a day-to-day basis, nor does it vary greatly among members of a community. However, the concept of truth has changed throughout history. At one level or another, human beings since ancient times have acknowledged that how truth is defined may vary. Since Plato's analogy of life as experienced by individual human beings as "truthful" in the same way as shadows on the wall of a cave resemble the physical objects that cast those shadows more than 3,000 years ago, people have grappled with the amorphous nature of truth. Today, while we accept some cultural "lies"—the existence of Santa Claus—we condemn others—income tax evasion or fabricating an employment history. Most of the time, we know what the boundaries are, at least when we deal with one another face-to-face.

Compounding the modern problem of the shifting nature of truth is the changing media audience. When a profession accepts the responsibility of printing and broadcasting the truth, facts that are apparent in face-to-face interaction become subject to different interpretations among the geographically and culturally diverse readers and viewers. Ideas once readily accepted are open to debate. Telling the truth becomes not merely a matter of possessing good moral character but something that requires learning how to recognize truth and conveying it in the least distorted manner possible.

A CHANGING VIEW OF TRUTH

One pre-Socratic Greek tradition viewed truth—*alethea*—as encompassing what humans remember, singled out through memory from everything that is destined for *Lethe,* the river of forgetfulness (Bok 1978). Linking truth and remembrance is essential in an oral culture, one that requires that information be memorized and repeated so as not to be forgotten. Repeating the message, often in the form of songs or poetry, meant that ideas and knowledge were kept alive or true for subsequent generations. Homer's *Iliad* and *Odyssey* or much of the Bible's Old Testament served this function.

This oral notion of truth, as noted in table 2.1, was gradually discarded once words and ideas were written down. However, it has come to the fore with the advent of television and its computer cousins such as YouTube that allow viewers to hear the words of the president rather than wait for those words to be passed down to them. When we see something on television or our computer screen, we assume that it closely corresponds to reality. The maxim "seeing is believing" reminds us that truth has become entangled with pictures, an oral concept of truth that has been a dormant form of knowledge for hundreds of years until technology made "seeing" events live worldwide possible.

While the ancient Greeks tied truth to memory, Plato was the first to link truth to human rationality and intellect. In *Republic*, Plato equated truth

Table 2.1. A Philosophy of Truth Emerges

Source	Truth Equals
Ancient Greeks	What is memorable and is handed down
Plato	What abides in the world of perfect forms
Medieval	What the king, Church, or God says
Milton	What emerges from the "marketplace of ideas"
Enlightenment	What is verifiable, replicable, universal
Pragmatists	What is filtered through individual perception

with a world of pure form, a world to which human beings had only indirect access. In Plato's vision, there was an ideal notion of a chair—but that ideal chair did not exist in reality. What people thought of as a chair was as similar to the ideal chair as the shadows on the wall of the cave are to the objects illuminated by the fire. To Plato, truth was knowable only to the human intellect—it could not be touched or verified. We're living in the cave.

Plato's metaphor of the cave has had a profound influence on Western thought. Not only did Plato link truth to rationality, as opposed to human experience, but his work implies that truth is something that can be captured only through the intellect. Platonic truth is implicit within a thing itself; truth defined the "perfect form." Plato's concept of the truth separated the concept from the external world in which physical objects exist.

Subsequent centuries and thinkers adhered to Plato's view. Medieval theologians believed truth was revealed only by God or by the Church. The intellectual legacy of the Reformation centered on whether it is possible for the average person to ascertain truth without benefit of a priest or a king. About 200 years later, Milton suggested that competing notions of the truth should be allowed to coexist, with the ultimate truth eventually emerging (see table 2.1).

Milton's assertions foreshadowed the philosophy of the Enlightenment, from which modern journalism borrows its notion of truth. The Enlightenment cast truth in secular terms, divorced from the Church, and developed a "correspondence theory" of truth still held today. The correspondence theory asserts that truth should correspond to external facts or observations. The Enlightenment concept of truth was linked to what human beings could perceive with their senses harnessed through the intellect. Truth acquired substance. It was something that could be known and something that could be replicated.

This Enlightenment notion of truth is essential to the scientific method. Truth has become increasingly tied to what is written down, what can be empirically verified, what can be perceived by the human senses. Enlightenment truth does not vary among people or cultures. It is a truth uniquely suited to the written word, for it links what is written with what is factual, accurate, and important.

Truth and Objectivity

This Enlightenment view of truth is the basis for the journalistic ideal of objectivity. While objectivity has many definitions, minimally it is the requirement that journalists divorce fact from opinion. Objectivity is a way of knowing that connects human perception with facts and then knowledge. Objectivity is also a process of information collection (Ward 2004). Journalists view objectivity as refusing to allow individual bias to influence what they report or how they cover it. It is in journalism that all facts and people are regarded as equal and equally worthy of coverage. Culture, an individual sense of mission, and individual and organizational feelings and views do not belong in objective news accounts. An Enlightenment view of truth allowed objectivity to be considered an attainable ideal, and objectivity was often linked to the end result of reporting and editing: the individual news story or media outlet.

However, philosophy was not the only reason that objectivity became a professional standard in the early 1900s. The early American press garnered much of its financial support from political advertising and most of its readers through avowedly partisan political reporting. But America became more urban in the late 1800s, and publishers realized that to convince potential advertisers that their advertising would be seen by a large audience, they had to make certain their publications would be read. Partisan publications could not ensure that, for strong views offended potential readers. What publishers at the turn of the 20th century needed was a product that built on an Enlightenment principle that guaranteed that facts would be facts, no matter who was doing the reading. Opinion would be relegated to specific pages, and both facts and opinion could be wrapped around advertising (Schudson 1978). In this century, the niched political product has reemerged, first on cable television and then more robustly on the web. As advertising itself has become more targeted, financial support for political content that attracts some and repels others has not been a disadvantage.

The normative ideal of objectivity came along at an advantageous time for yet another reason. The mass press of the early 1900s was deeply and corruptly involved in yellow journalism. Fabricated stories were common; newspaper wars were close to the real thing. Objectivity was a good way to clean up journalism's act with a set of standards where seemingly none had existed before. It fit the cultural expectations of the Enlightenment that truth was knowable and ascertainable. And it made sure that readers of news columns would remain unoffended long enough to glance at the ads.

The Enlightenment view of truth also was compatible with democracy and its emphasis on rational government. People who could reason together could arrive at some shared "truth" of how they could govern themselves. Information was essential to government, for it allowed citizens to scrutinize government. As long as truth was ascertainable, government could function. Citizens and government needed information in order to continue their rational function. Information, and the notion that it corresponded in some essential way with the truth, carried enormous promise.

That changed when the 20th-century pragmatists—most notably Americans John Dewey, George Herbert Mead, Charles Sanders Pierce, and William James—challenged the Enlightenment view of truth. They held that the perception of truth depended on how it was investigated and on who was doing the investigating. Further, they rejected the notion that there was only one proper method of investigation—that is, the scientific method. Borrowing from Einstein, pragmatists argued that truth, like matter, was relative.

Specifically, the pragmatists proposed that knowledge and reality were not *fixed by* but instead were *the result of* an evolving stream of consciousness and learning. Reality itself varied based on the psychological, social, historical, or cultural context. Additionally, reality was defined as that which was probable, not as something intrinsic (the Platonic view) or something determined by only one method of observation (the Enlightenment view). Pragmatism found a comfortable home in 20th-century United States. Under pragmatism, truth lost much of its universality, but it was in remarkable agreement with the American value of democratic individualism. Soon pragmatism filtered through literature, science, and some professions, such as law.

Pragmatism provided a challenge to objectivity. No sooner had the journalistic community embraced objectivity than the culture adopted more pragmatic notions of truth. That clash fueled criticism of objectivity. Pragmatism challenged the journalistic product: the individual news story and the media ecosystem in which it emerged. However, if objectivity is defined as a method of information collection—a systematic approach to gathering "facts" from many points of view—then this philosophical development provides support for defining objectivity as a process rather than as a result.

Postmodern philosophy has taken these questions to their logical extension, suggesting that the concept of truth is devoid of meaning. Postmodernism asserts that context is literally everything, and that meaning cannot exist apart from context, which is directly opposed to fact-based journalism.

The last decade of the 20th century and all the years of the 21st century have added yet another level of complexity to the problem: the information explosion. Facts and truth come to us quickly from all over the globe. While objective reporting is still *one* standard, it is not the *only* standard. With the advent of websites that include not just words, but images, aggregated from many sources, yet a different notion of truth is resurfacing—what philosophers call the convergence or coherence theory of truth. Under this view, truth is discovered not through any single method of investigation but by determining which set of facts form a coherent mental picture of events and ideas investigated through a variety of methods. Convergence journalism—which uses sounds, images, and words to cover stories—is one professional response to the coherence theory of truth and the technological possibilities of the internet and the personal computer. Of course, convergence journalism requires an active audience, and an active audience brings its preexisting beliefs, values, and context to every message. All too often, it is possible to be overwhelmed by the information available to us rather than devoting the time and effort required to make sense of it. Reading the news sent to us by Facebook friends is less time-consuming and intellectually easier then seeking out a variety of information sources on our own.

In short, objectivity has been deeply undermined by both philosophical shift and technological innovation (Christians, Ferré, and Fackler 1993). Telling your readers and viewers the truth has become a complicated business as Sissela Bok points out:

> Telling the "truth" therefore is not solely a matter of moral character; it is also a matter of correct appreciation of real situations and of serious reflection upon them. . . . Telling the truth, therefore, is something which must be learnt. This will sound very shocking to anyone who thinks that it must all depend on moral character and that if this is blameless the rest is child's play. But the simple fact is that the ethics cannot be detached from reality, and consequently continual progress in learning to appreciate reality is a necessary ingredient in ethical action. (Bok 1978, 302–3)

WHO'S DOING THE TALKING ANYWAY?

The pragmatic's critique of objectivity has called attention to the question of who writes the news. Journalists—primarily male, Caucasian, well educated, and middle-to-upper class—are often asked to cover issues and questions that life experiences have not prepared them to cover. Stephen Hess (1981) noted that journalists (particularly the Eastern "elite" media), in terms of their socioeconomic status, look a great deal more like the famous or powerful people they cover than the people they are supposedly writing for. Work on the national press corps has shown similar results (Weaver, Beam, Brownlee, Voakes, and Wilhoit 2007). Journalists generally are better paid and better educated than the audience for their product.

Almost every professional journalistic organization has developed programs specifically to attract and retain women and minorities with only incremental and sporadic success. This lack of access to the engines of information has not been lost on a variety of groups—from religious fundamentalists, who have established their own media outlets, to racial minorities, who fail to find themselves either as owners or managers of media outlets, to political conservatives. They argue that the result is news about middle-class Caucasians, for middle-class Caucasians, and liberal in political orientation. How individual journalists and the corporations they work for should remedy the situation is unclear. But as demographics change us from a culture that is predominantly Caucasian to one that is not, the mass media will play a decreasing role unless journalists find a way to report news that is of interest to the new majority. In this century, worldwide newspaper readership and broadcast viewership continues to decline in favor of the internet (including newspaper websites) and magazines that focus on celebrities rather than public affairs (Thorson, Duffy, and Schumann 2007). Traditional journalists faced an audience in open rebellion with no clear strategy to remain financially viable and provide the public with the information that civic engagement requires.

DEFINING AND CONSTRUCTING THE NEWS

More than 80 years ago, journalist Walter Lippmann (1922) said, "For the most part, we do not first see, and then define, we define first and then see." He added that we tend to pick out what our culture has already defined for us, and then perceive it in the form stereotyped for us by our culture.

In one classic study (Rainville and McCormick 1977), a blind New York journalism professor claimed he could predict the race of football players being described in the play-by-play by what was said about them. Caucasian athletes were described as intellectually gifted while African-American athletes were described as physically gifted. In a culture that values brains over brawn, African-American football players were the subject of repeated stereotypical insults—all couched as praise. And even though the study is now more than 70 years old, the tendency to revert to these stereotypes continues on sports broadcasts today in which athletes are called "smart" and others are called "athletic." In the former, the quality was obtained by hard work; in the latter, it was a gift of genetics. Women, the elderly, and the gay community have been the focus of studies with similar results. Their conclusion has been that while journalists maintain that they are objective, they (like their readers and viewers) bring something to the message that literally changes what they see and what they report (Lester 1996).

How journalists do their work—what scholars call news routines—also has an impact on what readers and viewers "see." "Objectivity can trip us up on the way to truth," says Brent Cunningham (2003). "Objectivity excuses lazy reporting. If you're on deadline and all you have is 'both sides of the story,' then that's often good enough." Cunningham points to a study of 414 Iraq war stories broadcast on ABC, CBS, and NBC leading up to the 2003 conflict. All but 34 originated from the White House, the Pentagon, or the State Department. The result: the "official truth" becomes the received truth, and only the bravest journalists dared depart from it. Timothy Crouse in his 1974 campaign memoir *The Boys on the Bus* reported the same phenomenon. John Oliver's achingly funny take on reporting climate change repeats the criticism that objectivity misused can result in lies of staggering consequence (Nuccitelli 2014).

News reflects certain cultural values and professional norms. In a classic study, sociologist Herbert Gans (1979) studied how stories became news at *Newsweek* and CBS and found that almost all news stories reflected these six cultural values: (1) ethnocentrism, (2) altruistic democracy, (3) responsible capitalism, (4) individualism, (5) an emphasis on the need for and mainte-nance of social order, and (6) leadership. These dominant values helped to shape which stories were printed and what they said, what communication scholars call "framing."

Gans called these values the "para-ideology" of the media. He added that "the news is not so much conservative or liberal as it is reformist." Researcher James Carey (quoted in Cunningham 2003) says that it is this para-ideology that results in charges of liberal bias against the media. "There is a bit of the reformer in anyone who enters journalism. And reformers are always going to make conservatives uncomfortable."

News stories about middle-class or upper-class people, those who tend to successfully adopt the culture's values, made the American news "budget," according to Gans. While Gans focused on journalism about the United States, other scholars have noted the same phenomenon, called *domesticating the foreign*, in international coverage (Gurevitch, Levy, and Roeh 1991). Journalists working for US media outlets tell stories about international events in cultural terms Americans can readily understand but that also sacri-fice accuracy. For example, routine coverage of elections in Britain or Israel is conveyed in horse-race metaphors even though both countries employ a parliamentary system where governing coalitions are common and who wins the horse race is not nearly so important.

E. J. Dionne (1996) claims that the press is in internal contradiction. It must be neutral yet investigative. It must be disengaged but have an impact. It must be fair minded but have an edge. The conflicts make objectivity virtually impossible to define and even harder to practice.

Figure 2.1.   1993, Washington Post Writers Group. Reprinted with permission.

PACKAGING THE STORY: NEWS AS MANUFACTURED PRODUCT

The goal of telling a "good story" also raises other ethical questions, specifically those that focus on packaging to highlight drama and human interest. These questions have intensified as all media channels—from newspapers to documentary film to entertainment programming—have focused on coherent storytelling and the need for a powerful story to capture audience interest. Current research suggests that narratives are memorable, but news narratives are not always neat and the facts from which they emerge can be both chaotic and contradictory.

This drive to package has led to a profession that values finding an "event" to report and to be there first. Few consumers realize it, but news is "manufactured" daily, just as surely as furniture, cars, or the meal at your favorite fast-food restaurant—and often the process can be messy. Journalists start the day with a blank computer screen and with press time or broadcast time looming. On deadline—often a deadline of minutes—they produce a print story, a video package, a tweet, or a multimedia report—or often all four. And adding to the built-in tension of deadlines is the challenge to be fair, complete, accurate, and, above all, interesting. Whole industries—particularly public relations or "strategic communications"—have emerged to help journalists package their daily stories on deadline.

The need to find an event has meant that journalists have missed some important stories because they were not events but rather historic developments with both a past and a future. For example, major social developments such as the women's movement (Mills 1989), the Black Lives Matter movement, the Occupy Wall Street movement, and the civil rights movement and the anti–Vietnam War movements of the 20th century were under-covered until their leaders created events for the media to report. Director Michael Moore said he began his career with the 1989 film *Roger and Me* about the devastation of General Motors layoffs in his hometown of Flint, Michigan, because he "didn't see on the silver screen or the television screen what happened to people like us" (Smith 1992).

The preoccupation with events affects coverage of science, too, which is most frequently reported as a series of discoveries and "firsts" rather than as a process (Nelkin 1987). "New hope" and "no nope" drive most science reporting. We are treated to stories about cures often without the necessary context—political, economic, etc.—to interpret the latest research results. Other stories are missed or misreported when they lack the easy "peg" editors look for. The *Washington Post*'s Pulitzer Prize–winning stories on conditions at Walter Reed army hospital emerged only after dismayed veterans and their families contacted the newspaper multiple times (Priest and Hall 2007). When thousands of lives were lost in Bhopal, India, by a malfunctioning plant, coverage focused entirely on the picture-friendly event and not on the socioeconomic, scientific, and political causes that led to the disaster (Wilkins 1987). A deeper look at news coverage of the 1986 Chernobyl nuclear disaster, something Charles Perrow calls a "normal accident" in his book of the same title, found that coverage echoed the stereotype of American superiority and Russian inferiority rather an approach focusing on science and risk (Patterson 1989). Phenomena not linked to specific events—such as the growth of a permanent American under-class or the current opioid crisis—went unreported for years waiting for an appropriate news peg.

The phenomenon of "pack journalism" has been chronicled in several films, dating back to the classic *The Front Page* to the reboot of *The Manchurian Candidate* (2004). All emphasize journalistic excesses and an unwillingness to engage in independent thought that would disturb enlightened and pragmatic philosophers alike. They also expose a too-easily manipulated system, particularly as newsroom staffs have shrunk. This unwillingness to leave the "pack" with a breakout story has allowed some of the hottest political stories of the new century being reported first on the web where these institutional pressures are different. Seymour Hersh's original reporting of the My Lai massacre during the Vietnam War, which eventually appeared in the *New York Times,* was held up because no other reporter had a similar story. Some 30 years later, it wasn't until CBS broadcast images of prisoner abuse at the notorious Abu Ghraib prison in Iraq that Hersh's initial reporting of the scandal in *The Atlantic* received serious national attention.

Truth is more than just a collection of facts. Facts have a relationship to one another and to other facts, forming a larger whole. Yet, analytic coverage of American institutions, of science and technology, of politics, and of social movements is rare. What is more common—especially on cable news outlets—is to invite two or more parties with conflicting views, allot them too little time to discuss the issue at hand, and then sit back and let the resulting heated exchange take the place of reporting.

Stephen Hess (1981) has argued that journalists need to engage in reporting that looks more like social science than storytelling. Gans (1979) argues for news that is labeled as originating from a particular point of view. Other scholars argue for news that is analytical rather than anecdotal, proactive rather than reactive, and contextual rather than detached. On a practical level, working reporters and editors insist that individual journalists need to do a better job of understanding their own biases and compensating for them.

The accumulated evidence, both anecdotal and scholarly, today strikes at the core of objectivity (Craft 2017) and shows that, intellectually, we are living in a pragmatic era, but we seem to be unable professionally to develop a working alternative to the Enlightenment's view of truth. Because of this, mainstream media are increasingly seen as irrelevant, particularly to a younger audience for whom truth is more likely to be a segment on Stephen Colbert, who in 2012 won a Peabody Award for his coverage of the impact of SuperPacs on elections, than a report on the networks' nightly newscasts.

ON THE ETHICS OF DECEPTION: FAKE NEWS

Ethicist Sissela Bok in her book *Lying* (1978) notes that discerning the truth—and then telling it—is hard. Bok's book focuses intensely on human relationships. It would be fair to say that she did not anticipate the machine. In this decade, the confluence of a cultural shift about the nature of truth, the segmentation of an active audience on the one hand and the range of media outlets on the other, the emergence of Facebook as a purveyor of news through sharing, and the increasingly sophisticated technology associated with computers and widely available software has led to the emergence of yet another challenge to journalism: fake news.

So, let's begin with a definition. Bok defines lying in the following way: the lie must be stated, the liar must knowingly provide information that she/he is aware is incorrect or wrong, and the lie must be told in order to gain power over the person who is being lied to. For Bok and many other ethicists, lying as an act—like murder—starts out in the "moral deficit" column. The human default is "truth"; lying must be justified to be ethical, and satisfactory justification is rare.

We think the parallels between Bok's definition of lying and any definition of fake news are strong. First, fake news is "stated"—that is, publication on the internet, including the dark web, is the equivalent of saying something to a friend. Second, those who produce fake news—or set its production in motion through the use of bots or other technological tools—are aware that it is wrong or inaccurate. This sets fake news apart from a mistake (discussed later in this chapter) or a hoax, something that was common in journalism in the 19th century and was done primarily to garner attention and hence income. However, in the 19th century, both the perpetrator of the hoax and most members of the audience were "in" on the deception. No one was fooled, at least not for long. Fake news fooled lots of folks, and its impact persists as you read these words. Third, fake news is developed and distributed to gain power, in this context the economic power that comes from internet clicks linked to advertising content. The motive here is not better social relations or political activism; the goal is to gain power through wealth.

Take this example: A Macedonian teen and his mates who live in the rust belt town of Veles, once part of the former Yugoslavia, admitted to generating fake news content from multiple websites. The teen earned more than $60,000 in six months by producing fake news stories that were picked up through Facebook postings, drew thousands of readers, and earned the producers a penny-per-click that added up to a staggering income in comparison to others in that country. One teen, who was interviewed by NBC, bragged that his fake news stories had earned him more money than his parents earned in a year (Smith and Banic 2016). The teen was quoted as saying, "I didn't force anyone to give me money. People sell cigarettes, they sell alcohol. That's not illegal. Why is my business illegal?" These stories were difficult to spot; the only way a reader would know that the story's origin was a tip off to problematic content was a close look at the imitation URL on what was built to look like a legitimate news page from sources such as Fox News or the *Huffington Post*.

Much closer to the United States, a Maine resident operating under multiple pseudonyms but primarily on his website LastlineofDefense.org, published multiple stories that he said he intended as parody to "fool" political conservatives. Christopher Blair told Politifact, which had debunked more than 100 of his stories for months before the 2016 presidential election, that his goal was to "feed the Hoverounders their daily need for hate and their undying urge to blame everything in the known universe on Hillary Clinton and Barack Obama" (Gillin 2017). The problem is that it's unclear whether what Blair told that news organization and many others was the truth about the motive for his activities.

Journalists who unmask internet trolls—and thereby challenge their worldview—have themselves been threatened. Jared Yates Sexton, a *New York Times* contributor and assistant professor of creative writing at Georgia Southern University, shared with *HuffPost* several threatening messages directed at him since he unmasked an internet troll who created a video retweeted by President Donald J. Trump. In one, a Reddit user warns of a looming "journocaust"— presumably a holocaust for journalists. In another, a Twitter user says there's "a civil war coming" and that memes—specifically, the anti-Semitic one by the creator of the video that Trump shared—are "the least" of Sexton's problems.

"There's a fever pitch to this dialogue that is dangerous to everybody," Sexton told *HuffPost*. "And it's the people who are mentally ill, who are unhinged, who are unwell—they pick up on this stuff. And they are really, really moved to act by it" (D'Angelo 2017).

Bok's treatise on lying does not anticipate that those who tell the truth about lies will be physically threatened by those who lie. She assumes that, in civil society, the human need for truth in order to live an authentic life will triumph over the short-term need to ease difficult questions and difficult relationships by everything from fibbing to telling whoppers. But, as the above examples and many others suggest, getting "found out" about lying does not seem to deter the impulse, which can be fueled by a drive for wealth, notoriety, or both.

And, of course, by the time you read these words, this brand of fake news will seem "oh, so yesterday." Audio is even easier to fake than words and still images. Virtual puppeteering, as reported by NPR's Radio Lab, will allow you and anyone else with the right software and an inexpensive video camera to put your voice and thoughts in the mouth of someone who is perhaps more famous, say former president Barack Obama, in a way that is almost undetectable to the human eye and ear (Adler 2017). The NPR report left listeners with the startling, ethics-focused question: If we know that such technology can be used for both pro-social and malevolent purposes, what should society—including those who are inventing the technology—do to make certain that those with malevolent ends do not go unchecked?

And, why is fake news so pernicious? Because as human beings, we are attracted to things that seem outlandish and strange. In a study that examined how tweets were shared beginning in 2006 and continuing through 2013, social scientists found false tweets reached an audience of 1,500 or more six times faster than true ones, a pattern that emerged as more than 126,000 individual news items were shared 4.5 million times among more than 3 million people. As one of the researchers noted, "The crazy stupid . . . is the one that goes massively viral," (Lazer et al. 2018).

Fake news is a new frontier for journalists. There are too many fake news stories to spend the time and resources to debunk every one. Debunking itself may put journalists and their news organizations in harm's way. Technological solutions, for example, the development of real-time algorithms that would spot the fake and label it as such, are in development but not yet in the world. Facebook has started to tag some stories as "disputed," but that label comes only after stories have been posted and shared, and it is not as thorough as it needs to be, by Facebook's own admission. We will discuss the impact of "fake news" on democratic decision-making in chapter 6, but for our purposes in this chapter, one principle stands out. It has never been more important for professional journalists to tell the truth in their reporting and to make every effort to continue to do so. Minimally, trust in the profession and belief in its credibility are at stake.

ON THE ETHICS OF DECEPTION: THE JOURNALIST'S PERSPECTIVE

In a profession that values truth, is it ever ethical to lie? To editors? To readers? To sources, who may be liars themselves? Are there levels of lying? Is flattering someone to get an interview as serious a transgression as doctoring a quote or photograph? Is withholding information the same thing as lying? If you can only get one side of the story, do you go with it? Does it matter today if opinion mingles with news?

Crises of credibility have faced media outlets of all sizes including spectacular instances at both *USA Today* and the *New York Times* that resulted in front-page editorial apologies and multi-page retractions. In the case of the *Times*, it started when a 27-year-old reporter, Jayson Blair, fabricated all or part of more than 40 stories. After his resignation from the paper, the *Times* ran four full pages of corrections documenting every error discovered in Blair's reporting. The *Times'* correction made it clear that the *Times* had failed to correct the problem in earlier stages despite many opportunities to do so. In a subsequent analysis of the case, many at the *Times* and other places suggested that one reason Blair's actions had been unchecked for so long was because of his race. Blair was African-American, and he had been hired as part of the *Times'* diversity program. His mentors at the paper, Executive Editor Howell Raines and Managing Editor Gerald Boyd, who also was African-American, were among Blair's strongest supporters and both eventually resigned in the fallout. While the *Times* denied that race was the reason that Blair had been promoted, Blair himself did not.

Errors in Journalism: Inevitability and Arrogance

Confounding truth and deception in journalism is the problem of errors. Inadvertent mistakes in stories are common. One freelance fact checker (Hart 2003) wrote in the *Columbia Journalism Review (CJR)* that she had not experienced an error-free story in three years of fact checking for *CJR*, one of journalism's leading watchdog publications. Her calls to fellow fact checkers at other publications led her to believe that articles with errors are the rule, not the exception.

However, mistakes are different from fabrication and do not indicate a lack of dedication to the truth. Some, if not most, mistakes are matters of interpretation, but others are outright errors of fact. In her article "Delusions of Accuracy," Ariel Hart says that hearing journalists proudly claim to have had no errors or fewer errors than the *Times* found in Blair's writing is "scary, not the least because it encourages delusions of accuracy."

One problem seems to be audience members so disconnected from the media that they don't bother to correct journalists' mistakes or, worse, assume, as readers of the *Times* evidently did, that fabrication is *de rigueur* for journalists. "Journalists surely make mistakes often, but I think we don't—or can't—admit it to ourselves because the idea of a mistake is so stigmatized. . . . So mistakes need to be destigmatized or restigmatized and dealt with accordingly. They should be treated like language errors," Hart argues.

Figure 2.2. *Pearls Before Swine* © **Stephan Pastis/Distributed by United Feature Syndicate, Inc.**

However, Blair wasn't the only bad news for the *Times* during those weeks. Pulitzer Prize–winning reporter Rick Bragg also resigned from the paper after it became public that he, too, had published stories based largely on the reporting of stringers who did not receive a byline in the *Times*. Furthermore, some of his stories filed with non-New York datelines had been written on airplanes and in hotel rooms where Bragg was functioning more as a rewrite editor rather than doing actual on-the-scene reporting. Bragg said his practices were known at the *Times* and common in the industry. That comment aligns with one heard frequently in the Blair incident that sources did not complain to the *Times* about incorrect stories since they felt that fictionalizing stories was just the way things are done. This cynical appraisal of journalism threatens our credibility, which is the chief currency of the profession.

So, how do journalists feel about deception? A survey of members of Investigative Reporters and Editors (IRE) provides some insight into the profession's thinking (Lee 2005). Journalists think about deception on a continuum. At one end, there is almost universal rejection of lying to readers, viewers, and listeners. IRE members regard such lies as among the worst ethical professional breaches. At the other end, more than half of the IRE members surveyed said they approved of flattering a source to get an interview, even though that flattery could be considered deceptive and certainly was insincere.

In the same survey, lies of omission—such as withholding information from readers and viewers and also editors and bosses—were considered less of a problem than fabricating facts in a story or fabricating entire stories, which was almost universally condemned. IRE members were more willing to withhold information in instances when national security issues were involved. The journalists also said some lies were justified; they approved of lying if it would save a life or prevent injury to a source.

The journalists surveyed also noted that there were outside influences on these judgments. Broadcast journalists were more accepting of hidden cameras and altering video than were print journalists, although that difference might be changing as more print journalists get video experience via their newspaper's websites. And, those who worked in competitive markets were more willing to accept deception than were those who saw themselves in less competitive environments. The more experienced a journalist was, the less likely he or she was to accept any form of deception. Finally, the survey revealed what journalists worry about is the impact such reporting methods have on the believability of news accounts and on journalists' ability to cover subsequent stories if caught in an ethical lapse.

Is it ethical to lie to liars? Is withholding information the same thing as lying? If not, under what circumstances might it be appropriate? If it is, are there ethically based justifications for such an act? Sissela Bok (1978) argues that such an act raises two questions. Will the lie serve a larger social good, and does the act of lying mean that we as professionals are willing to be lied to in return?

Bok suggests that most of the time, when we lie we want "free rider" status—gaining the benefits of lying without incurring the risks of being lied to. In other words, some journalists may believe it's acceptable to lie to a crook to get a story, but they professionally resent being lied to by any source, regardless of motive.

Lying is a way to get and maintain power. Those in positions of power often believe they have the right to lie because they have a greater than ordinary understanding of what is at stake. Lying in a crisis (to prevent panic) and lying to enemies (to protect national security) are two examples. In both circumstances, journalists can be—either actively or without their knowledge—involved in the deception. Do journalists have a right to counter this lying with lies of their own, told under the guise of the public's need to know? Does a journalist have the responsibility to print the truth when printing it will cause one of the evils—panic or a threat to national security—that the lie was concocted to prevent?

Then there is the "omission versus commission" issue. In the first, the lie is that some part of the truth was conveniently left out; in the latter, the lie is an untruth told purposefully. Bok asserts that a genuinely white lie may be excusable on some grounds, but that all forms of lying must stand up to questions of fairness and mutuality. According to Kant's categorical imperative, the teller of the white lie must also be willing to be lied to. Even lying to liars can have its downside as Bok points out in her book *Lying* (1978, 140):

> In the end, the participants in deception they take to be mutually understood may end up with coarsened judgment and diminished credibility. But if, finally, the liar to whom one wishes to lie is also in a position to do one harm, then the balance may shift; not because he is a liar, but because of the threat he poses.

Reporting *via* the internet has given new urgency to the issue of lying by omission. In most instances, failing to identify yourself as a reporter when collecting information electronically from news groups, chat rooms, or other modes of public discussion is considered problematic. Journalists, when pressed, note that the US Supreme Court has ruled internet transmissions are public. The ethical issue emerges when most of those involved in the discussion are not aware of the legal standards and expect, instead, the more ethically based relations of face-to-face interactions. Ethical thought leaves journalists with difficult choices.

Reporting *on* the contents of the internet—and cable television—raises another series of challenges. How should journalists go about debunking internet rumors, which can sometimes be distinguished from fake news? Conventional wisdom for the legacy media holds that reprinting or rebroadcasting rumors only furthers them. News organizations in New Orleans covering Hurricane Katrina faced a series of difficult news decisions in the face of rumors sweeping the city. In some instances, they elected to print or broadcast rumors prevalent in the networked world that they could not substantiate. The same problems continue to plague journalists in stories as distinct as news of Michael Jackson's death, or terrorist attacks in Europe or India. Another equally serious challenge is how to treat information promulgated by well-known sources—information that is false. Calling someone a liar, at one level, seems the height of nonobjective journalism. However, when the facts suggest that a source is lying—even if that source is not held to the same standards of truth telling as journalists are—what becomes an acceptable professional mechanism to hold non-journalist sources to account?

ETHICAL NEWS VALUES

Most mass media courses present a list of qualities that define news. Most such lists include proximity, timeliness, conflict, consequence, prominence, rarity, change, concreteness, action, and personality. Additional elements may include notions of mystery, drama, adventure, celebration, self-improvement, and even ethics. While these lists are helpful to beginning journalists, they probably will not help you decide how to recount the news ethically.

We suggest you expand your journalistic definitions of news to include a list of ethical news values. These values are intended to reflect the philosophic tensions inherent in a profession with a commitment to truth. If news values were constructed from ethical reasoning, we believe the following elements would be emphasized by both journalists and the organizations for which they work.

Accuracy—using the correct facts and the right words and putting things in context. Journalists need to be as independent as they can when framing stories. They need to be aware of their own biases, including those they "inherit" as social class, gender, and ethnicity, as well as learned professional norms.

Confirmation—writing articles that are able to withstand scrutiny inside and outside the newsroom. Media ethicist Sandy Borden (2009) refers to this as the "discipline of confirmation," a concept that reflects how difficult it can be to capture even a portion of the truth in sometimes complex news situations.

Tenacity—knowing when a story is important enough to require additional effort, both personal and institutional. Tenacity drives journalists to provide all the depth they can regardless of the individual assignment. It has institutional implications, too, for the individual cannot function well in an environment where resources are too scarce or the corporate bottom line too dominant. In addition, news organizations need to trust journalists when they report independently rather than expect them to act as part of a pack.

Dignity—leaving the subject of a story as much self-respect as possible. Dignity values each person regardless of the particular story or the particular role the individual plays. Dignity allows the individual journalist to recognize that newsgathering is a cooperative enterprise where each plays a role, including editors, videographers, designers, and advertising sales staff.

Reciprocity—treating others as you wish to be treated. Too often, journalism is "writing for the lowest common denominator." Reciprocity demands respect for the reader. It also rejects the notion of journalism as benevolent paternalism—"We'll tell you what we think is good for you"—and recognizes that journalists and their viewers and readers are partners both in discovering what is important and in gleaning meaning from it.

Sufficiency—allocating adequate resources to important issues. On the individual level, sufficiency can mean thoroughness, for example, checking both people and documents for every scrap of fact before beginning to write. On an organizational level, it means allocating adequate resources to the newsgathering process. With virtually every media outlet suffering from declining readers or viewers, thanks mainly to the web, this is probably the central issue of the current media landscape.

Equity—seeking justice for all involved in controversial issues and treating all sources and subjects equally. Equity assumes a complicated world with a variety of points of view. Equity demands that all points of view be considered but does not demand that all sides be framed as equally compelling. Equity expands the journalistic norms of "telling both sides of the story" to "telling all sides of the story."

Community—valuing social cohesion. On the organization level, a sense of community means that media outlets and the corporations that own them need to consider themselves as citizens rather than mere "profit centers." On the individual level, it means evaluating stories with an eye first to social good.

Diversity—covering all segments of the audience fairly and adequately. There appears to be almost overwhelming evidence that news organizations do not "look like" the society they cover. While management can remedy part of this problem by changing hiring patterns, individual journalists can learn to "think diversity" regardless of their individual heritages.

In 2013, the Corporation for Public Broadcasting (CPB) decided to make an ethical news value—transparency—the cornerstone of its new standards and practices policy. We'll ask you to take a look at the impact of that ethical news value—and its implication for the other values we have listed—in a case study in this chapter. Regardless, no list of ethical news values should be considered conclusive. Collectively, they provide a framework within which informed ethical choices can be made.

SUGGESTED READINGS

Bok, S. (1978). *Lying: Moral choice in public and private life.* New York: Random House.

Gans, H. (1979). *Deciding what's news: A study of CBS Evening News, NBC Nightly News, Newsweek and Time.* New York: Vintage.

Jamieson, K. H. (1992). *Dirty politics.* New York: Oxford University Press.

Lippmann, W. (1922). *Public opinion.* New York: Free Press.

Plato. *Republic.*

Weaver, David H., Beam, R. A., Brownlee, B. J., Voakes, P. S., & Wilhoit, G. C. (2007). *The American journalist in the 21st century: U.S. news people at the dawn of a new millennium (LEA's Communication Series).* Mahwah, NJ: Lawrence Erlbaum Associates.

CASES

CASE 2-A

ANONYMOUS OR CONFIDENTIAL: UNNAMED SOURCES IN THE NEWS

LEE WILKINS
Wayne State University
University of Missouri

They are characterized in many different ways. Frequently, there are no names, just blurred references to job duties.

From the *New York Times* on Dec. 9, 2017, as it reported on President Donald J. Trump's daily routine:

> One adviser said that aides to the president needed to stay positive and look for silver linings wherever they could find them, and that the West Wing team at times resolved not to let the tweets dominate their day.
>
> Other times, they are slightly more anonymous.

From the *New Yorker*'s reporting about the Harvey Weinstein sexual abuse/harassment scandal by journalist Ronan Farrow:

> Two sources close to the police investigation said that they had no reason to doubt Gutierrez's account of the incident. One of them, a police source, said that the department had collected more than enough evidence to prosecute Weinstein. But the other source said that Gutierrez's statements about her past complicated the case for the office of the Manhattan District Attorney, Cyrus Vance Jr. After two weeks of investigation, the district attorney's office decided not to file charges.

There are those who have made journalistic history, such as Watergate's anonymous source, who was known in both the book and the film only as "Deep Throat." Journalists Bob Woodward and Carl Bernstein kept Deep Throat's identity a secret for more than 30 years until FBI agent Mark Felt, shortly before his death, announced that he had played this pivotal "follow the money" role in the investigation.

And, sometimes they even make it to the US Supreme Court as in *Cohen v. Cowles Media Co.*, 501 US 663 (1991), when the court ruled that journalists could not allow sources to remain confidential if such promises would violate normally applicable laws. Cohen v. Cowles changed the way newsrooms operated.

Anonymous sources may even change the course of history. Judith Miller, a former *New York Times* reporter who protected her anonymous sources in her reporting on the existence of weapons of mass destruction in Iraq in 2002 and 2003, was ultimately vilified in a profession that had once lionized her when it was revealed that the "anonymous sources" were, in fact, former president George W. Bush administration officials who had demanded anonymity in return for access. The weapons of mass destruction, of course, did not exist, and both Miller and the *Times* had to face the historic impact of erroneous reporting that supported the US decision to invade Iraq.

Anonymous sources are also used as political bludgeons. If a story is sourced anonymously, it's tantamount to "fake news." A reader voiced what many other were thinking in a February 2017 *New York Times* piece that reflected on its own sourcing practices, something that the newspaper has been criticized for since at least the early 1990s. The *Times'* article included the following: "Gene Gambale of Indio, Calif., is among the readers who wrote to complain in recent weeks. 'I have noticed a continuous and disturbing trend of relying upon unnamed sources,' Gambale said. 'I believe that is poor journalism and deprives the reader of any way to evaluate, on their own, the credibility of those sources or the accuracy of the statements they make.'"

Anonymous sources have become so much a part of what the public believes it knows about how journalists operate that every beginning reporter has faced this question, whether it comes from average citizens, or local elected, appointed, or nongovernmental officials: "I'd like to tell you this, but I don't want you to use my name."

How to handle such requests, and under what circumstances, has been a continual professional debate that dates back to the founding of the US republic when Benjamin Franklin used multiple "nom de plume" such as Silence Dogood and Richard Saunders, who published respectively in the *New England Courant* and as the author of the *Poor Richard's Almanac*. Ethical decision-making asks journalists to balance potential harm to sources—for example, ratting out a drug cartel in a news story is a life-threatening decision, the need for the public to know consequential information and to evaluate it, decisions that involve truth telling and transparency, and the ability for news organizations to defend their decisions in court—something that multiple news organizations have had to do since the Cohen decision and which is often threatened by the subjects of unflattering and often investigative pieces.

Micro Issues

1. How would you respond to a city councilperson who requests anonymity before speaking with you about an important local issue? Why?

2. Many journalists believe that the Cohen ruling is an example of "bad law" overriding important ethical principles. Evaluate this claim. What is the role of trust between a journalist and her supervising editors in such decisions? Between a journalist and the news organization's corporate owners?

Midrange Issues

1. How would you respond to the reader who wrote to the *New York Times* to question that paper's use of anonymous sources?
2. Is there a distinction between sources who are unknown to the general public but well known to the major players in specific stories and sources such as Deep Throat who are known only to journalists? Why?
3. The names of rape and sexual harassment victims are often allowed to remain anonymous. Evaluate this professional norm.

Macro Issues

1. Investigative journalist and *Washington Post* editor Bob Woodward has said that some institutions, such as the military and the courts, could not be covered were it not for anonymous sources. Assuming that Woodward is correct, what should journalists agree to in order to cover these important beats?
2. Judith Miller spent three months in jail rather than reveal the sources of her stories on weapons of mass destruction. Would you be willing to take such a stand? Do you think news organizations should support journalists who do make such decisions?

CASE 2-B

**DEATH AS CONTENT: SOCIAL RESPONSIBILITY
AND THE DOCUMENTARY FILMMAKER**

TANNER HAWKINS
Oklahoma Christian University

Eric Steele's documentary *The Bridge* tells the story of the Golden Gate Bridge—the leading location for suicide in the world—and the people who travel from around the nation to end their lives there. The documentary also features interviews with the families of the deceased and a lone jumper who survived.

Steele's crew spent 365 days recording the bridge and documented 23 of the 24 suicides that occurred in 2004. According to Steele, he and his crew were often the first callers to the bridge patrol office to report jumpers, but they never stopped recording during incidents with potential jumpers and those that followed through. To accurately portray the amount of suicides that take place annually at the bridge, Steele and his crew did not personally interfere with any of the jumpers.

In the United States, approximately 30,000 people kill themselves each year. The average age for the Golden Gate Bridge is in the 20s. Eleven men died building the structure. In an interview, Steele said he had once considered suicide. "It's that Humpty Dumpty moment when it's all going to fall apart," he said. "For me and many others, it didn't come. For the people in this film, it did" (Glionna 2006).

Soon after Steele's crew wrapped up filming, the *San Francisco Chronicle* reported that multiple government officials claimed that Steele lied about the intentions of his documentary. When applying for a permit to film in the Golden Gate National Recreation Area, Steele said he planned to film the "powerful and spectacular interaction between the monument and nature." He later emailed bridge officials to confess the true intentions of his documentary, knowing there was little they could do.

Many critics lambasted the documentary, claiming that featuring the bridge as a prominent suicide destination in such a somber manner would only increase the number of suicides. It was called "voyeuristic," "ghastly," and "immoral" in various reviews and called the equivalent of a "snuff film" by one San Francisco supervisor.

"This is like a newspaper carrying a front-page photo of someone blowing his head off; it's irresponsible, exploitive," said Mark Chaffee, president of Suicide Prevention Advocacy Network California.

Other detractors rebuked the film for failing to include interviews with any mental illness experts or psychologists. The review on the BBC website (Mattin 2007) noted that "despite the shocking, up-close look, we're no closer to a real understanding of the terrible urge to end it all."

The *New York Times* (Holden 2006) took a middle road, observing that *The Bridge* raises inevitable questions about the filmmaker's motives and methods and whether he could have tried harder to save lives. It raises age-old moral and aesthetic questions about the detachment from one's surroundings that gazing through the camera's lens tends to produce." The author goes on to say that such discussion was beyond the scope of a movie review.

However, just as many supporters came to the defense of the documentary, arguing that the film brought awareness to an important topic that is not discussed openly enough in society. Reviewer Jim Emerson (2006), writing for Roger Ebert's website, said of the film:

> *The Bridge* is neither a well-intentioned humanitarian project, nor a voyeuristic snuff film. It succeeds because it is honest about exhibiting undeniable elements of both. It's a profoundly affecting work of art that peers into an abyss that most of us are terrified to face.

Following the release of the film, the city of San Francisco voted to spend $2 million on a study to examine building a pedestrian suicide barrier, a move they had resisted in the past (Glionna 2006).

Micro Issues

1. Should the makers of the documentary have tried to intervene in any of the twenty-plus suicides they witnessed? Why or why not? Justify your answer.
2. If a news crew had been on the bridge at the time of a jumper, would their obligations be any different than a documentarian?
3. Because suicide is a crime, did the filmmakers have a duty to report the jumpers as they climbed to the top of the bridge?

Midrange Issues

1. Does the recording of the last moments of nearly two dozen lives violate the privacy of individuals suffering from severe mental illness? The privacy of their families? If so, is this violation justified?
2. Does Steele's dishonesty in obtaining a permit to film the bridge and the jumpers negate the integrity of his documentary? Discuss your answer in light of utilitarian theory.
3. Is there any merit to complaints that the documentary might encourage "copycats" among those struggling with suicidal thoughts? Justify your answer.
4. Do you agree with the comments by Chaffee that the film is equivalent to a newspaper printing a photo of someone blowing his head off? In what way is the comparison right or wrong in your opinion?

Macro Issues

1. Is there a difference between how a utilitarian such as Mill would view the decisions made by the documentarians and how it would

be viewed by a deontologist such as Kant? If so, discuss how they would differ?

2. Other documentarians have had to make decisions that allowed harm to come to their subjects or decisions to not render aid to their subjects in pursuit of a truthful outcome on film. What is the "greater good" in situations such as this? Is there a universal principle for all documentaries or should it be decided on a case-by-case basis?

3. Many believe that the decision by the city to finance a study to examine ways to prevent future suicides was motivated by the film. Does this change your opinion of the film in any way? If so, how?

CASE 2-C

NEWS AND THE TRANSPARENCY STANDARD

LEE WILKINS
Wayne State University
University of Missouri

By many measures, 2010 and 2011 were very bad years for the CPB and its radio arm, National Public Radio (NPR). CPB found itself under attack by members of the Tea Party and some other Republicans for what they viewed as a "liberal" media agenda. Congress threatened to cut CBP's $320 million funding, a move that would have placed the financial future of about 50 percent of public radio and public television stations (most of those in smaller markets) in fiscal jeopardy. At the same time, the great recession that began in 2008 also took a financial toll; audience fundraising activity—and corporate support—weakened.

Finances were not the only problem. These years included a series of significant controversies, beginning with the firing of NPR's Juan Williams for comments he made about Muslims that were broadcast on Fox News, where he also was a commentator. Ultimately, NPR's top news manager, Ellen Weiss, was forced to resign over the incident. Just weeks later, NPR's top executive, Vivian Schiller, who had come to public radio after working at the *New York Times*, was forced to resign after an audio tape of one of the organization's top fundraisers, Ron Schiller (no relation), surfaced on the internet. In that audio tape, Ron Schiller called some congressional Republicans and particularly members of the Tea Party racist, unchristian, and anti-intellectual. Schiller also said he believed that NPR and the CPB would, over the long run, be better off without congressional funding support. Both Vivian Schiller and Ron Schiller were forced out.

All this came in the midst of professional successes, including a listening audience for NPR of more than 27 million people—much above those watching television network and cable news—and reporting that won every professional prize.

CPB had last changed its editorial and organizational standards in 2005 but, beginning in 2009, launched a multi-year project to update those standards and to apply them to all aspects of CPB efforts—from program selection to fundraising to news. The intent was a single set of standards that would inform best practices throughout the corporation. Executives hoped these consistent standards would strengthen ties with audience members and funders, including Congress. Those new standards were adopted in June 2011 and may be accessed at: http://www.pbs.org/about/editorial-standards/. In many ways, these standards were similar to those that had informed the organization since its inception.

Those new standards included standards for the news organization that audiences know as NPR. The standards were based on a normative framework for NPR's journalism and included an acknowledgement of the following principles: fairness, accuracy, balance, responsiveness to the public (accountability), courage and controversy, substance over technique, experiment and innovation, and exploration of significant subjects, as well as subsections on what would be considered unprofessional conduct, unacceptable production methods, and NPR's use of social media, particularly as a source for news stories. Third on the normative list was the standard of objectivity, which those who developed the updated standards linked to transparency in this way:

> Beyond that, for a work to be considered objective, it should reach a certain level of transparency. In a broad sense, this spirit of transparency means the audience should be able to understand the basics of how the producers put the material together. For example, the audience generally should be able to know not only who the sources of information are, but also why they were chosen and what their potential biases might be. As another example, if producers face particularly difficult editorial decisions that they know will be controversial, they should consider explaining why choices were made so the public can understand. Producers should similarly consider explaining to the audience why certain questions could not be answered, including why, if confidential sources are relied on, the producers agreed to allow the source to remain anonymous. And the spirit of transparency suggests that if the producers have arrived at certain conclusions or a point of view, the audience should be able to see the evidence so it can understand how that point of view was arrived at. One

aspiration implicit in the idea of transparency is that an audience might appreciate and learn from content with which it also might disagree.

Opinion and commentary are different from news and analysis. When a program, segment, digital material or other content is devoted to opinion or commentary, the principle of transparency requires that it be clearly labeled as such. Any content segment that presents only like-minded views without offering contrasting viewpoints should be considered opinion and should identify who is responsible for the views being presented.

No content distributed by PBS should permit conscious manipulation of selected facts in order to propagandize.

Individual media outlets—both television and radio—may decide whether to adopt these voluntary standards.

Micro Issues

1. Are there certain sorts of agreements between journalists and their sources that would be jeopardized by the transparency standard?
2. Are there certain sorts of activities journalists do—for example, deciding which stories to cover—that might benefit from a "transparency" standard?
3. Does being transparent about process add unproductively to a journalists' workload?
4. Is transparency best considered a component part of objectivity?

Midrange Issues

1. Take a news story from any media source and evaluate how well it meets the CPB normative guidelines.
2. What values on the CPB list do you find internally consistent? Contradictory? Could you adopt these standards as part of your best practices?
3. Do you think labeling something news or opinion matters to most audience members? What about entertainment programming such as *The Daily Show*?

Macro Issues

1. Should the US taxpayer fund media organizations such as the CPB?
2. What definition of truth do you believe CPB is applying to news content—at least as reflected in its professional standards?

CASE 2-D

CAN I QUOTE ME ON THAT?

CHAD PAINTER
University of Dayton

During an Aug. 19, 2012, interview with St. Louis television station KTVI-TV, Missouri senate candidate Todd Akin said women cannot get pregnant from "legitimate rape" because their bodies have ways to block unwanted pregnancies. Republican presidential contender Mitt Romney quickly condemned the comments, calling them "insulting, inexcusable, and frankly, wrong" and saying that he found the comments "offensive" and "entirely without merit," according to an article in the *National Review*.

But did Romney actually say those words?

There is question because government and campaign officials regularly grant interviews to journalists only under the condition of quote approval, according to *New York Times* reporter Jeremy Peters. Quote approval, *Time* media critic James Poniewozik wrote, is when a journalist agrees to send his or her source quotes to be "redacted, stripped of colorful metaphors, colloquial language and anything even mildly provocative."

Peters wrote that Romney and his campaign advisers almost always require quote approval from any conversation, and that journalists quoting any of Romney's five sons use only quotations approved by his press office. Quote approval also is the accepted norm for President Barack Obama, his top strategists, and almost all of his midlevel aids in Chicago and Washington.

Several major news organizations—including the *New York Times*, *Washington Post*, *Reuters*, *Bloomberg*, *Vanity Fair*, and *National Journal*—have accepted the practice of quote approval in political stories, according to Peters. (There also is a long-standing, problematic tradition of quote approval for celebrity news and certain types of sports stories.) One reason for the acquiescence by reporters, Poniewozik wrote, is that a reporter who does not accept the condition could be scooped by another reporter who did. A second reason is that reporters often are desperate to pick the brains of a politician or his top strategists. Finally, each of the reporters Peters interviewed said that the meanings of quotes were not altered, and that changes were always small and seemingly unnecessary.

Many journalists perform accuracy checks with sources, ensuring that the quotes and information gained from a source are correct. Some publications require accuracy checks. However, quote approval is quite different from an accuracy check.

The quote approval requirement really is a struggle between reporters and politicians for power and control. News is a construction of reality (Gulati, Just, and Crigler 2004) dependent on the relationship of a news organization with other institutions, interests, or groups in a society (Baldasty 1992; Shoemaker and Reese 1996). News about political campaigns is an ongoing negotiation—or power struggle—between journalists, editors, and owners on one side, and candidates, campaign staffers, and party activists on the other (Gulati et al. 2004). The media need a steady, reliable flow of the raw material of news (Herman Chomsky 2002). Journalists become reliant on their sources because of this constant need for new information, and this reliance allows sources to dictate terms of coverage.

Politicians and their campaign staffs also could be asserting control, calling off the hounds of an attack-dog press. Sabato (2000) suggests that attack journalism during presidential campaigns causes candidates to become increasingly secretive because of their fear of reporters. The result is that politicians limit press access except under highly controlled situations (Sabato 2000). The ultimate highly controlled situation is for a politician to grant interviews only when he or she knows any quote can be deleted or changed.

Micro Issues

1. Citizens need information about candidates' and politicians' views on issues. However, what should journalists be willing to give up in order to obtain that information?
2. How reliable is information obtained after a politician or his or her advisers have massaged or altered quotes?
3. Are there certain sorts of stories, for example, stories about science or finance, where this practice might be more acceptable? Why or why not?

Midrange Issues

1. Quote approval is for newspaper journalists. Should there be such a thing as video approval? What would be the morally relevant distinctions?

2. Should reporters disclose to their readers when they have submitted a story for quote approval?
3. How is quote approval related to truth?

Macro Issues

1. Media based on social responsibility is premised on the idea that freedom of expression is a positive freedom (Nerone 1995). The moral right of freedom of expression is not unconditional (The Commission on Freedom of the Press 1947) but a right granted to do moral good (Nerone 1995). By agreeing to "quote approval," are reporters opening the debate as to whether they are serving the best interests of the public or serving the interests of politicians?
2. How does the notion of citizen journalism influence the concept of quote approval? Of candidates' willingness to speak "off the cuff" with citizens?

CASE 2-E

NPR, THE *NEW YORK TIMES*, AND WORKING CONDITIONS IN CHINA

LEE WILKINS
Wayne State University
University of Missouri

On Jan. 6, 2012, Ira Glass, host of American Public Media's "This American Life," devoted a 39-minute segment to a report on working conditions at manufacturing plants in China.

The show was based extensively on a single source, Mike Daisey, who recounted what he had seen and what he had been told through an interpreter on a visit to a Foxconn factory in China, a plant that makes parts for the popular iPhone and iPad. Daisey recounted stories about working conditions and stated some workers in the plant had been poisoned during the manufacturing process.

Less than a month later, the *New York Times* ran a series of investigative stories on working conditions at Chinese plants making Apple products.

"Mr. Daisey and the Apple Factory" quickly became the most popular "This American Life" podcast, with about 880,000 downloads. Daisey, a performance artist, became something of a celebrity and Apple critic, granting numerous interviews about his experiences. Faced with the publicity, Apple itself responded, announcing that it would for the first time allow third-party inspections of its Chinese manufacturing facilities.

NPR's "Marketplace" reporter Rob Schmitz also had spent a great deal of time in China and reported on working conditions there. He, too, heard the Mr. Daisey segment—and he told his bosses at NPR that there were facts included in it that did not ring true. He was given the go ahead to do independent reporting.

Less than three months later, Glass aired the following retraction:

> I have difficult news. We've learned that Mike Daisey's story about Apple in China—which we broadcast in January—contained significant fabrications. We're retracting the story because we can't vouch for its truth. This is not a story we commissioned. It was an excerpt of Mike Daisey's acclaimed one-man show "The Agony and the Ecstasy of Steve Jobs," in which he talks about visiting a factory in China that makes iPhones and other Apple products.
>
> The China correspondent for the public radio show "Marketplace" tracked down the interpreter that Daisey hired when he visited Shenzhen China. The interpreter disputed much of what Daisey has been saying on stage and on our show. On this week's episode of *This American Life*, we will devote the entire hour to detailing the errors in "Mr. Daisey Goes to the Apple Factory."
>
> Daisey lied to me and to *This American Life* producer Brian Reed during the fact checking we did on the story, before it was broadcast. That doesn't excuse the fact that we never should've put this on the air. In the end, this was our mistake.

Subsequent inspections at Foxconn plants did reveal numerous violations of agreements to working conditions there. Mr. Daisey, in subsequent interviews, has said that while the specifics of his allegations are fabrications, the overall indictment of Apple is "true."

Micro Issues

1. Justify Schmitz's decision to go to his editors, who work for the same organization that broadcasts "This American Life," asking to reinvestigate this story?
2. Download the original Mr. Daisey piece and the *New York Times* investigative report. Examine the sources for each. What principles regarding "knowing" and "telling" the truth emerge?
3. Was the retraction that Ira Glass provided ethically justifiable? Why?

Midrange Issues

1. Many reporters work in countries where they do not speak the native language(s). What are the risks to accurate reporting when the individual journalist does not understand the words that are being spoken? Should "helpers" such as translators receive some byline or on-air credit for their assistance with such coverage?
2. What journalistic norms made Mr. Daisey's accounts so believable? How do you see those norms expressed in other investigative reports?
3. The *New York Times* has never had to retract any of its reporting on this issue. Evaluate the distinctions between the *Times* report and the Mr. Daisey piece based on the ethical news values outlined in this chapter.

Macro Issues

1. How should journalists treat sources that lie to them, particularly after the lie has been discovered? Is what Ira Glass did in his retraction ethical?
2. Is Mr. Daisey right—even though his facts were wrong? Was the overall story "true"? What definition of truth do you use in responding to this question?

CASE 2-F

WHEN IS OBJECTIVE REPORTING IRRESPONSIBLE REPORTING?

THEODORE L. GLASSER
Stanford University

Amanda Laurens, a reporter for a local daily newspaper, covers the city mayor's office, where yesterday she attended a 4 p.m. press conference. The mayor, Ben Adams, read a statement accusing Evan Michaels, a city council member, of being a "paid liar" for the pesticide industry. "Councilman Michaels," the mayor said at the press conference, "has intentionally distorted the facts about the effects of certain pesticides on birds indigenous to the local area." "Mr. Michaels," the mayor continued, "is on the payroll of a local pesticide manufacturer," and his views on the effects of pesticides on bird life "are necessarily tainted."

The press conference ended at about 5:15 p.m., less than an hour before her 6 p.m. deadline. Laurens quickly contacted Councilman Michaels for a quote in response to the mayor's statement. Michaels, however, refused to comment, except to say that Mayor Adams's accusations were "utter nonsense" and "politically motivated." Laurens filed her story, which included both the mayor's accusation and the councilman's denial. Laurens's editor thought the story was fair and balanced and ran it the following morning on the front page.

The mayor was pleased with the coverage he received. He thought Laurens had acted professionally and responsibly by reporting his accusation along with Michaels's denial. Anything else, the mayor thought, would have violated the principles of objective journalism. The mayor had always believed that one of the most important responsibilities of the press was to provide an impartial forum for public controversies, and the exchange between him and the councilman was certainly a bonafide public controversy. Deciding who's right and who's wrong is not the responsibility of journalists, the mayor believed, but a responsibility best left to readers.

Councilman Michaels, in contrast, was outraged. He wrote a scathing letter to the editor, chiding the newspaper for mindless, irresponsible journalism. "The story may have been fair, balanced and accurate," he wrote, "but it was not truthful." He had never lied about the effects of pesticides on bird life, and he had "never been on the payroll of any pesticide manufacturer," he wrote. "A responsible reporter would do more than report the facts truthfully; she would also report the truth about the facts." In this case, Michaels said, the reporter should have held off on the story until she had time to independently investigate the mayor's accusation; and if the accusation had proved to be of no merit, as Michaels insisted, then there shouldn't have been a story. Or if there had to be a story, Michaels added, "it should be a story about the *mayor* lying."

By way of background: The effects of pesticides on bird life had been a local issue for nearly a year. Part of the community backs Mayor Adams's position on the harmful effects of certain pesticides and supports local legislation that would limit or ban their use. Others in the community support Councilman Michaels's position that the evidence on the effects of pesticides on bird life is at best ambiguous and that more scientific study is needed before anyone proposes legislation. They argue that pesticides are useful, particularly to local farmers who need to protect crops, and because the available evidence about their deleterious effects is inconclusive, they believe that the city council should not seek to further restrict or prohibit their use. The exchange between Mayor Adams and Councilman Michaels is the latest in a series of verbal bouts on the subject of pesticides and the city's role in their regulation.

Micro Issues

1. Did Laurens do the right thing by submitting her story without the benefit of an independent investigation into the mayor's accusations about Councilman Michaels?
2. Is the mayor correct in arguing that Laurens acted responsibly by providing fair and balanced coverage of both sides of a public controversy without trying to judge whose side is right and whose side is wrong?
3. Is the councilman correct in arguing that Laurens acted irresponsibly by concerning herself only with reporting the facts truthfully and ignoring the "truth about the facts"?

Midrange Issues

1. Is it sufficient when covering public controversies to simply report the facts accurately and fairly? Does it matter that fair and accurate reporting of facts might not do justice to the truth about the facts?
2. Does the practice of objective reporting distance reporters from the substance of their stories in ways contrary to the ideals of responsible journalism?
3. If reporters serve as the eyes and ears of their readers, how can they be expected to report more than what they've heard or seen?

Macro Issues

1. What distinguishes fact from truth? For which should journalists accept responsibility?
2. If journalists know that a fact is not true, do they have an obligation to share that knowledge with their readers? And if they do share that knowledge, how can they claim to be objective in their reporting?
3. Justify or reject the role of objectivity in an era where more media outlets are available than ever before.

CASE 2-G

IS IT NEWS YET?

MICHELLE PELTIER
University of Missouri

Every weekday afternoon, he screams, pouts, whines, stomps his feet, and throws things in rabid fits of frustration. It's Jim Cramer, the manic 54-year-old host of CNBC's "Mad Money" program. Cramer uses all the hyperkinetic bells, whistles, and special effects of a television game show to showcase the nonstop onslaught of his latest buy and sell recommendations for stocks.

"It occupies some sort of netherworld between sheer entertainment and useful financial advice," said *Washington Post* media writer Howard Kurtz, just a few months after the show began in 2005 (Farzad 2005).

"This show is about making money and educating you while we entertain you. There's no bones about that," Susan Krakower, the vice president of strategic development at CNBC, who cocreated the show with Cramer, told the *Hollywood Reporter* (Gough 2006).

Based on ratings, viewership rises along with the stock market's volatility, though it's difficult to know whether the people who tune in are more interested in entertainment or advice (Carr 2008). What is certain is that Cramer's over-the-top style appeals to viewers who might otherwise tune out the dense drone of financial news coverage. The information Cramer, a former hedge-fund manager, presents is both real and relevant. He reaches more younger viewers than traditional financial shows; in fact, Cramer tours US colleges on a regular basis.

However, during the financially disastrous year of 2008, the show's host made a number of high profile—and questionable—statements.

In March 2008, Cramer responded to a viewer who was tempted to sell his shares of struggling Bear Stearns stock.

"No, no, no! Bear Stearns is fine," Cramer said on air. "Don't move your money from Bear! That's just being silly."

When JPMorgan Chase took over the beleaguered investment bank less than a week later, the stock value plunged. Cramer justified his misplaced optimism, even suggesting that it was partly calculated, saying, "I guess I could have caused a run on the bank and said take your money out of Bear."

In September 2008, Cramer interviewed the CEO of Wachovia and called the bank's stock one of only a few potential "winners" in the $700 billion bailout (Sorkin 2008). Two weeks later, a chagrined and sullen

Cramer glowered an apology into the Steadicam, telling his viewers that he had "screwed up."

"I let you down 'cause I wasn't skeptical enough," he said. "I have to presume when it comes to banking right now, there is no objective truth, just negative, just terrible things."

Finally, in October, Cramer appeared on NBC's "Today Show" with a grim economic forecast. "Whatever money you may need for the next five years, please take it out of the stock market right now, this week," he advised viewers.

Amid accusations that such statements were akin to shouting "fire" in a crowded building, Cramer stood by his advice, emphasizing that he remained confident in the long-term investment potential of stocks (Carr 2008). "I am still committing for my retirement," he told Scott Collins of the *Los Angeles Times*. "I'm not backing away. Because, I have no intention of retiring in the next five years" (Collins 2008).

Legally, CNBC protects itself and its volatile show host with extensive disclaimers warning of the financial risk in the advice offered on the program. In part, the warning states viewers "should not take any opinion expressed by Cramer as a specific inducement to make a particular investment or follow a particular strategy."

Micro Issues

1. How important is it that Cramer intends to entertain as well as inform in terms of the way he presents financial news?
2. Is the disclaimer that runs at the beginning of every show ethically defensible? How would you defend it?
3. How should a rational actor evaluate the claims of Cramer?
4. How is Cramer's show like and unlike what a public relations person for your local bank might do? Are there ethical distinctions between Cramer's approach and more traditional advertising or public relations?

Midrange Issues

1. What is the ethical role of CNBC in presenting a show such as "Mad Money"?
2. Compare Cramer's brand of financial news with Comedy Central's Jon Stewart and his brand of mock news. Which is more ethically justifiable? Why?
3. Should a local newspaper's business or financial reporter treat Cramer's recommendations as a news story?

4. Do you think audiences are particularly vulnerable when it comes to complex topics such as financial news? Does that vulnerability result in any distinct ethical obligations?

Macro Issues

1. Are there some subjects that are too serious to be made entertaining in this way?
2. Cramer is an avowed capitalist. Can he also be trusted to be an objective critic of the capitalistic system—particularly considering the financial disasters of 2008? Is that his role?
3. Evaluate the usefulness of Cramer's show to individual viewers. Is he advisor or entertainer?

CASE 2-H

WHAT'S YOURS IS MINE: THE ETHICS OF NEWS AGGREGATION

CHAD PAINTER
University of Dayton

In June 2008, The *Hartford Courant* cut 95 jobs from its news department, roughly half of its news staff, in two rounds of layoffs. But within a few months, with an online news hole to fill and a reduced staff, the paper started aggregating local news from surrounding dailies.

In a search of the publication's website for Aug. 29–30, 2009, *Journal Inquirer* reporter Christine McCluskey counted 112 stories that were written by the *Courant*'s Connecticut competitors *Bristol Press*, *New Britain Herald*, *Torrington Register-Citizen*, *Waterbury Republican American*, and her own paper (McCluskey 2009). The stories were often—but not always—attributed to the original source, a practice Michael E. Schroeder, publisher of the *Bristol Press* and *New Britain Herald* called, "at best plagiarism, at worst outright theft" (McCluskey, 2009).

Jeffrey S. Levine, the *Hartford Courant*'s director of content, explained his paper's position. "Aggregation is the process of synopsizing information from other news sources, most commonly by placing a portion of the information on your website and linking to the original story" (McCluskey 2009). He cited a mistake in his paper's editing process that "inappropriately dropped the attribution or proper credit and in some cases credited ourselves with a byline to a *Courant* reporter" as the basis for the plagiarism claims.

The Society of Professional Journalists code of conduct states "Never plagiarize" and the Associated Press code warns its writers: "don't plagiarize." Similarly, an ethics primer in online journalism from the University of Southern California's Annenberg School of Journalism states "Don't steal others' work. Such theft is plagiarism" (Niles 2009). Bill Kovach and Tom Rosenstiel call it a "deceptively simple but powerful idea in the discipline for pursuing truth: do your own work" (2007, 99).

However, aggregation is not a black-and-white issue. Is it acceptable to disseminate another news organization's work as long as that work is properly credited? Should the rules be the same for newspapers, broadcast outlets, and online journalism? What about content-sharing organizations such as the Associated Press?

One of the core principles of journalism is the discipline of verification (Kovach and Rosenstiel 2007, 79). Aggregation violates that principle because it might not discriminate between rumor, fact, and speculation (Kovach and Rosenstiel 2007), and because it doesn't allow for independent confirmation of facts. Falsehoods and rumor go unchecked even if the original source issues a retraction if the aggregators fail to correct or pull the offending story.

However, aggregation isn't a new concept in the news business.

Time magazine was a notorious aggregator. First published March 3, 1923, Henry Luce's flagship magazine aimed to summarize the news quickly, but few of its busy readers would have guessed that *Time* was digested entirely from the dozens of newspapers it subscribed to, "gaining its greatest free lunch from the opulent tables of the *New York Times* and *New York World*" (Swanberg 1972, 58).

Radio, at least in its infancy, relied heavily on newspapers for a steady supply of news reports. For their part, newspapers at first either cooperated with radio for increased exposure or completely ignored the new medium (Chester 1949). That changed with the rise of the CBS and NBC chain radio broadcasting networks and increased advertising competition from radio. On April 24, 1933, the members of the Associated Press "passed a resolution directing the AP Board of Directors to refuse to give AP news to any radio chain" (Chester 1949, 255). State and national press associations "busied themselves with resolutions attempting to restrict news broadcasting, mostly because it was incongruous for newspapers to furnish free news" to their competitors in radio (Hammargren 1936, 93). Eventually the courts weighed in, punishing the most egregious uses of newspaper content on the radio airwaves as an unfair practice.

Currently, the Associated Press is battling aggregating websites such as Google News over use of unauthorized content. The Associated Press announced plans in July 2009 to create "a news registry that will tag and track all AP content online to assure compliance with terms of use." The proposed tracking system "will register key identifying information about each piece of content that AP distributes as well as the terms of use of that content, and employ a built-in beacon to notify AP about how the content is used" (Strupp 2009).

The Associated Press itself is a cooperative that supplies around-the-clock news content to its 1,500 US daily newspaper members, as well as international subscribers and commercial customers. There is also a recent trend among formerly rival papers to form localized content-sharing arrangements (Ricchiardi 2009). The newspapers cite budgetary constraints and the cost of Associated Press content as the major reasons for the arrangements.

But Alan Mutter, a former editor in Chicago and San Francisco who currently writes the blog *Reflections of a Newsosaur* speaks for those who regret the loss of diversity when he says: "Where there are multiple reporters covering the same beat or same event, you're going to get multiple views and everybody is going to try harder to go to a higher level of reporting. It's a fact of human nature that competition inspires better work" (Ricchiardi 2009).

Micro Issues

1. Does proper attribution solve the ethical problem of aggregation? If not, do you have an alternative idea?
2. If news organizations voluntarily agree to offer their content to be aggregated under specific conditions, does that eliminate the ethical issues?

Midrange Issues

1. Evaluate the following statement: Credibility, one of the foundations of journalism, is predicated on "the notion that those who report the news are not obstructed from digging up and telling the truth" and that the journalists can tell "the news not only accurately but also persuasively" (Kovach and Rosenstiel 2007, 53). Can an aggregator be expected to be a watchdog over information that their media outlet did not create?

2. How are content aggregators such as the *Huffington Post* distinct, in an ethical sense, from long-standing cooperatives such as the Associated Press?

Macro Issues

1. Is aggregation an issue primarily of economics or ethics? If aggregators such as Google News paid for content, would that solve the problem?
2. Who "owns" the news? Does a media outlet have the right to require that a consumer pay for information that he or she needs to be a participant in a democratic society? Did the framers of the Bill of Rights give any clues in this area?

3

Strategic Communication

Does Client Advocate Mean Consumer Adversary?

By the end of this chapter, you should be able to

- know how new technologies raise old ethical questions
- understand balance and cognitive dissonance persuasion theories and their role in persuasion
- understand the amplified TARES test for evaluating the ethics of individual messages
- understand why the relationship between the media and public relations is both symbiotic and strained

REACH OUT AND TOUCH SOMEONE

Most of the readers of this book are in their early 20s, and are most often seeking *someone* in addition to the *something* of a college education. Many of you will conduct your search for friends and life partners online—and increasingly on sites such as eharmony. Visitors to that site and others like it pay a subscription fee, complete various sorts of profiles, and are linked with possible matches. The non-virtual world and that human thing called chemistry seem to take it from there.

Not much of an ethical issue involved—that is, until you learn how such websites really make their money. They do it not exclusively through the matching service they advertise but more predominantly by attaching cookies to subscribers' computers and then selling that information—willingly provided in the form of the profile—to marketers who seek a specific demographic, for example, people of a certain age, or a certain income, and with specific likes and dislikes. Those electronic lists the websites sell—a process you must agree to in order to use the matching service—then allow marketers to push specific sorts of messages at you electronically and at times of their choosing, employing what the industry now terms behavioral marketing.

Behavioral marketing, which also is sometimes called behavioral targeting, is used to increase the effectiveness of advertising by tapping into data created by users as they surf the web. When you buy a book on Amazon, you've created a data point that the site's algorithm uses to advertise other similar books. When you "like" a cat video on Facebook, you have sent a signal that you might be interested in ads for cat food or pet adoption. Users somewhat involuntarily create a wealth of data, from which websites and pages they visit to the links they click on and the terms they enter into Google or other search engines. This information then can be combined with a person's geography and demographic area, as well as personal information they voluntarily disclose on websites and social media. Publishers love this data; they can charge a premium for targeted ads because consumers are more likely to purchase products from such ads when compared to random advertising. While the marketers never know your specific identify—in other words your name—they know enough about you for selling purposes, right down to the fact that you like terrier dogs but not cats and that your favorite musician is Post Malone.

It's all part of the brave new world of strategic communication, or the seamless connections between what professionals used to refer to as advertising and public relations.

And strategic communication, just like news, is facing a new economic reality: a business model that is no longer successful. What used to be the case, that entertainment or news content on either television or in a print medium was designed to deliver an audience to advertisers, is now increasingly problematic because people are finding ways to dodge persuasive messages as never before. Whether it's TiVo and skipping through commercials or getting news "for free" on the web, strategic communication professionals are being forced to find novel ways to get their messages to "eyeballs"—or people acting in their roles as consumers. Strategic communication professionals are also faced with the reality of an active audience—an audience that not only buys products or services but also expects to be able to evaluate those services and products on sites such as Yelp, which allows consumers to post their unfiltered opinions about local businesses, including restaurants, shops, and other sorts of local services. Local businesses particularly thrive with positive mentions and are punished by negative reviews. Several small business owners have filed lawsuits, complaining that Yelp has a financial interest in the listings, so consumer reviews posted on the site

were manipulated depending on which companies advertise on the site—
claims that Yelp executives deny, stating that both negative and positive
feedback provide authenticity and value. In April 2009, Yelp began allowing
local businesses to respond to comments on the site. These audience-based
measures of products and services have added new dimensions to efforts
to "control the message" that has been part of both advertising and public
relations for decades.

These novel approaches can raise serious individual ethical issues—issues
that once seemed more the realm of the journalist. Students who once said,
"I went into advertising because I don't feel comfortable forcing people to
talk to me, and I don't have to think about invading people's privacy" are
now facing decisions about whether and how to use computer-based technologies to do precisely these things—only this time to promote sales of various
products and lifestyles.

These facts of new media life also do not blunt some of the deepest continuing criticisms of persuasion, that the nature of the persuasive message
itself—short, highly visual, and intentionally vague—is overly reliant on
stereotypes, spins the truth, glorifies consumerism at the expense of community, and as an institution warps non-persuasive content in significant ways.
The ease of bypassing persuasive messages also challenges one of the most
significant justifications for advertising: that without the funding it provides,
broad-ranging political discourse would not be possible in developed democracies such as the Unite States. These new economic realities have heightened
the need for clear ethical thinking for those entering the persuasive end of the
business.

TECHNOLOGY: A ROOM OF REQUIREMENT
OR A SYSTEM OF VALUES?

The ubiquitous nature of social media and other forms of nearly instantaneous news and advertising consumption raises another issue: fake ads. The
problem came to a head following the revelation that Russian companies
with ties to the Kremlin purchased divisive, inflammatory, and false ads on
Facebook and Twitter in an attempt to tip the presidential election to Donald
Trump, as well as sow social discord throughout the United States. These ads,
which were seen by upwards of half of US adults, featured hot takes on gun
control, race and anti-racist groups, women's rights, immigration, and political rallies including the "Not My President" and "Down with Hillary!" rallies
that didn't exist. The information in these ads was false—including made-up
protest groups and events, as well as discredited information. However, some

ads were featured prominently on fact-checking sites such as PolitiFact and Snopes, sites that aim to dispel such falsehoods. Google, Facebook, and Twitter all are under scrutiny, including Congressional hearings, for how their automated ad systems were used by Russians to spread this false information.

Facebook's ad problems didn't stop there, however. Anyone can create an ad on Facebook; the tool is prominently displayed on its homepage, and it's easy and relatively cheap to use. It's also easy to discriminate: A ProPublica investigation in September 2017 revealed that advertisers can direct their pitches to specific groups—including to people who expressed interest in topics such as "Jew hater," "How to burn jews," and "History of 'why jews ruin the world.'" In November 2017, ProPublica revealed the results of a second investigation where its reporters bought rental housing ads on Facebook but asked that certain categories of users—including African-Americans, people interested in wheelchair ramps, and Spanish speakers—be excluded, a clear violation of the Fair Housing Act. ProPublica again found problems with Facebook ads in December 2017; this time, employers could target ads to job seekers under 40, allowing advertisers to skirt employment law. The problem comes from automation. Unlike legacy media companies, Facebook uses an algorithm instead of sales representatives. So, instead of a Facebook employee selecting audiences offered to advertisers, ad categories are created automatically based on what users share on Facebook and their other online activity.

Many of these issues arise because technology makes certain activities possible. Such activities, which most often require the enormous data processing capacities of the computer, also present professionals with two different ways of thinking about technology itself.

The first approach equates technology with efficiency. Those who subscribe to this school of thought assert that technology itself raises no ethical issues, but rather the ethical issues arise in how the technology is put to use. The second approach asserts that any technology is embedded with values. Think of the technology you are using right now: the written word and the printing press. What does writing value? A specific definition of truth, as reviewed in chapter 2 of this book. A specific standard of evidence, for example, written documents and sources for them are important. Some specific ways of organizing human community and of placing economic value on some activities are also emphasized by the written word. The act of writing and the technology of the printing press have made much of contemporary human community possible—but those communities privilege some values while minimizing others.

In this view, articulated by French theologian Jacques Ellul, technology is at core a system of values that must be understood before any decision to adopt a technology can be made. Failure to understand the values embedded in a technology can have many unintended consequences, some of them quite horrible.

Being a competent and ethical professional does not require you to resolve this deeply philosophical debate. But it does require you to acknowledge that it exists and to think clearly about whether, in the process of claiming efficiency, you have overlooked important questions of values.

THINKING ABOUT THE AUDIENCE: FROM PERSUASION THEORY TO PHILOSOPHICAL ANTHROPOLOGY

Psychologists first began to try to understand persuasion by working with a stimulus–response model. This early behaviorist approach led many to believe that the media could act as a "hypodermic needle" or a "magic bullet," sending a stimulus/message to an unresisting audience. These researchers, called "powerful effects theorists," found examples to support their theory in the success of propaganda during both world wars and the public panic after Orson Welles's *War of the Worlds* broadcast on Oct. 30, 1938 (though the extent of that panic has been overblown).

But, the stimulus–response model proved to be a poor predictor of much human behavior. Later, communication theorists focused on cognitive psychology. Rather than analyzing persuasion as a simple behavioral reaction to a sufficient stimulus, these scholars theorized that how people think and what they brought to the persuasive situation helped to explain persuasion. According to these theories, people strain toward cognitive balance. Simply put, we are most comfortable when all of our beliefs, actions, attitudes, and relationships are in harmony, a state theorists called "symmetry."

Such theories have become known as "balance theories" because they stress the tendency of people to strive for cognitive balance in their lives. A person achieves balance only when his or her attitudes, information, and actions are in harmony. Leon Festinger (1957) coined the term cognitive dissonance to describe the state where a message and an action give conflicting and uncomfortable signals. Think of it as knowing the hazards of smoking but choosing to smoke anyway, setting up a classic brain/action dissonance. The desire to eliminate that dissonance is a strong one, sometimes strong enough to influence purchasing behavior and voting habits—at least some of the time.

Advertisers use this theory. Knock a consumer off balance early in the commercial and promise restoration of that balance through the purchase of a product. For instance, the opening scene of a commercial might suggest that your dandruff is making you a social outcast, and the subsequent copy promises you social approval if you use the correct shampoo.

Figure 3.1. *Doonesbury* © 1988 G. B. Trudeau. Reprinted with permission of Andrews McMeel Syndication. All rights reserved.

Balance theories also explained why persuasive messages were sometimes quite effective while at other times inconsequential. No consequences to the problem, no lack of balance, and subsequently no sale. This individually focused approach also provided the ultimate practical justification for advertising, the ancient Roman phrase *caveat emptor,* "Let the buyer beware." The creators of the ads were willing to assume little responsibility for the impact of their work, and academic studies gave them partial cover: If you can't prove that something's been effective, then it's unreasonable to suggest you take some responsibility for it. Even the FTC allows "puffery in advertising but not deception"—but they never tell you where they plan to draw the line.

Anthropologists assert that human rationality exists on equal footing with daily experience, language, and symbols. Culture and our personal experience balance rationality (Wilkins and Christians 2001). If philosophical anthropology is correct, then ethical analysis of advertising founded in "Let the buyer beware" is morally unsustainable.

Instead, the ethical goal of advertising should be the empowerment of multiple stakeholders—from those who need to buy, those who need to sell, those who live in a community fueled by commerce and tax dollars, and finally those who depend on advertising-supported news to be participatory citizens in a democracy.

If the concept of human being as creator of culture and then a dynamic user of symbols becomes an ethical foundation for thinking about the audience, advertising practitioners should be expected to operate within the following framework:

- Clients and the public need information that gives them "a good reason to adopt a course of action" (Koehn 1998, 106). The reason needs to be non-arbitrary and capable of helping people support one action instead of others.
- Rather than offering only expert opinion, advertising should foster ongoing discussion so that people can explore when options are sound and when practical knowledge (common sense) is superior.
- Advertising, just like news, can help foster reflective community, including the community of consumers. Just like the Super Bowl results that are discussed at work the next day, often the creative ads that supported it are part of the social experience as well.
- Advertising needs to take seriously the role of culture in our lives. That means that advertising must authentically reflect the diverse voices that comprise our culture.
- Advertising will speak to the role of organizations in our lives. Questions of history and background can be conveyed in ads, but that must be done accurately and in context.

Given these general guidelines, let's explore a specific framework that puts ads to an ethical test.

THINKING ABOUT THE MESSAGE: A SYSTEMATIC TEST

The original TARES test is a checklist of questions the creators of every persuasive message should ask themselves to determine the ethical worthiness of the message (Baker and Martinson 2001). While the TARES test takes its inspiration from the "symbol formation" function of both advertising and news, public relations practitioners have added the significant element of advocacy to an ethical evaluation of public relations messages. Advocacy means "understanding and valuing the perception of publics inside and outside organizations" (Grunig, Toth, and Hon 2000). Advocacy also means communicating those perceptions to other publics, an effort that has become more complex because it involves relationships with multiple stakeholders "in a world of increasingly diverse and more active publics who are empowered by and connected through the Internet" (Fitzpatrick and Bronstein 2006, *x*).

Those who support the advocacy model argue that any misleading information put out by strategic communications professionals will be somehow "self-corrected" by the gatekeepers of the media or by the self-righting "marketplace of ideas." Those who reject the advocacy model do so on two grounds. First, they assert that advocacy too easily morphs into distortion and lies. Second, they argue that the long-term health of many enterprises, from business to government programs, is ill-served by "spin" and better served by honest, timely communication—even at the expense of short-term losses.

> Of course, public relations professionals do not enjoy the special status of the "Fourth Estate." Indeed, as representatives of *special* interests—as compared to the *public* interest—they and their clients and employers may have less protection from judicial forays into questions of ethics. Public relations professionals must consider both whether the special obligations associated with the freedom to communicate are being met and whether, in the absence of effective *self*-regulation, the government might step in to hold practitioners accountable for irresponsible behavior (Fitzpatrick and Bronstein 2006, 16) [italics in the original].

To help you think through the ethical issues that persuasion raises—particularly in the world of strategic communication where most professionals will be asked to meld traditional advertising and public relations, we have connected the approaches in both fields through a single, ethically based test of specific messages.

The first element of the test—**T**—stands for **truthfulness**. Are the claims, both verbal and visual, truthful? If the message communicates only part of the truth (and many ads do this), are the omissions deceptive? Conversely, a message would pass the test if it meets a genuine human need to provide truthful information, even if some facts are omitted. Does the technology used to convey the message obscure or help to reveal the truth about the claims? In addition, practitioners should be able to verify with clients the truthfulness of client claims, and they should provide information to their audiences that will allow them to verify the truthfulness of claims in messages aimed at the public (table 3.1).

The Cheerios television ads that emphasize eating Cheerios as part of a heart-healthy lifestyle could easily pass the first element of the TARES test. People do have to eat, and the ads provide needed information. The ads also omit some information—for example, the other components of a heart-healthy lifestyle or the fact that other breakfast cereals also meet these requirements. But the omitted information does not lead the mature consumer to make false assumptions and bad choices.

In addition, telling the truth in times of crisis, such as becoming an advocate rather than an adversary in the long-term healthcare of a particular client, tests the foremost professional principles for public relations practitioners. The history of the field would suggest that businesses and agencies whose

Table 3.1. The Amplified TARES Test of Ethical Persuasion

T	Are the ad claims **Truthful?**
A	Is the ad claim **Authentic?**
R	Does the ad treat the receiver with **Respect?**
E	Is there **Equity** between the sender and the receiver?
S	Is the ad **Socially** responsible?

actions demonstrate that public health and safety are more important than short-term profits—telling the truth even when it hurts—are quite likely to profit and survive in the long term.

Step two in the amplified TARES test—**A** for **authenticity**—is closely linked to step one. Authenticity suggests that it's important not only to do the right thing, but also "to do it with the right attitude" (Pojman 1998, 158). We link this notion to the concept of sincerity. First, is there a sincere need for this product within the range of products and services available? Second, are the reasons given to the consumer purchasing the product presented in such a way that they also would motivate the person who developed and wrote the message? Simply put: Would you buy your own reasoning about the uses and quality of the product advertised?

Authenticity, used in this way, is closely linked to disclosure, an important standard for public relations messages. The ethical end of disclosure is the generation of trust among and between various publics. "Ethical public relations professionals are forthright and honest and counsel clients and employers to adopt responsible communication policies built on principles of openness and transparency" (Fitzpatrick and Bronstein 2006, 13). Disclosure also demands providing information about who is paying for the message and who stands to profit from its success. Direct advertising of pharmaceuticals to consumers—once banned by law—often fail this part of the test.

Let's take a set of strategic communication messages about products designed to help elderly or infirm people live more independently. Although some of these products—for example, devices that turn on lights in response to a hand clap—may seem little more than high-tech toys, anyone with a grandparent in a wheelchair, a sibling crippled by an illness like rheumatoid arthritis, or even a young person suffering from the imposed immobility of a broken leg can readily understand the need for such devices.

Others, such as advertisements for extended care facilities or supplements to existing insurance plans, attempt to focus on the human desire of independent living. But in making this point, if the messages stereotype elderly people as frail, helpless, weak, or easily panicked, or if they knock otherwise healthy individuals off balance to sell a product based on fear, they do not authentically reflect the reality of life beyond age 65. The ad lacks authenticity based on an unrealistic stereotype of the early retiree. The TARES test would require rethinking the specific appeal in the ad to one that scares and stereotypes less and informs more. For creative people, such a switch is readily accomplished if they think about it. Just as important, a fresher approach might well sell more.

The **R** in the test stands for **respect**, in this case, respect for the person who will receive the persuasive message. However, as a shorthand way of thinking through this element of the test, it might be appropriate for advertising practitioners to ask themselves, "Am I willing to take full, open, and personal responsibility for the content of this ad?"

Take the recent anti-texting-while-driving public service campaign that began with an ad of an actual car crash filmed from inside the car and its devastating aftermath. Even though the ad itself, which originated with a European government and went viral through YouTube, was filmed as a documentary, the campaign was criticized for its "scare" tactics. However, while the campaign relied on fear as a primary emotional tactic, it also provided rational reasons to not text and drive. Even though it was created by a government agency, the ad and its emotional appeal provide evidence of respect for human life.

The **E** in the amplified TARES test stands for **equity**. We conceptualize equity as follows: Is the recipient of the message on the same level playing field as the ad's creator? Or, to correctly interpret the ad, must that person be abnormally well informed, unusually bright or quick-witted, and completely without prejudice? Equity is linked to **access** for public relations professionals, and it takes its ethical power from the role of free speech in a democratic society. Free people are the autonomous moral actors that philosophers have long insisted must be the foundation of ethical choice and access to information equalizes an individual's ability to participate in the marketplace of ideas.

Think about this corporate image ad for Mobil Oil—the one with the pristine scenery, glorious sunset, and an oil tanker. The ad claims that Mobil has the best interest of the environment at heart by building tankers with double hulls. While Mobil's claim—that it builds double-hulled tankers—is literally true, correctly interpreting the ad requires a recall of recent history. Mobil, and all other oil companies, were required by Congress to build double-hulled tankers after the single-hulled tanker, the *Exxon Valdez*, ran aground and spilled an enormous amount of oil in Alaska, an environmental disaster of the first magnitude. For the image ad to work, it counts on the average person not knowing—or not being able to connect—legal requirements with corporate behavior. The ad assumes (and actually depends on) an imbalance between the knowledge of the person who created the ad and the consumer. It flunks the concept of equity. Similarly, an airline company that brags about a point of customer service that has actually been codified by the congressionally mandated Passenger Bill of Rights is relying on customer ignorance or forgetfulness to score points for behavior required by law.

Finally, the **S** in the amplified TARES test: Is the ad **socially responsible**? This is perhaps the most difficult element of the test for the simple reason that advertising practitioners have duties to many groups, among them their clients, the agencies for which they work, consumers, people exposed to the ad whether they buy or not, and society at large.

Because this text emphasizes social ethics, we suggest interpreting this portion of the TARES test in the following fashion:

- If everyone financially able to purchase this product or service did so and used it, would society as a whole be improved, keeping in mind that recreation and self-improvement are worthy societal goals?
- If there are some groups in society that would benefit from using this product as advertised, are there others that could be significantly harmed by it? Are there ways to protect them?
- Does this ad increase or decrease the trust the average person has for persuasive messages?
- Does this ad take the notion of corporate responsibility, both to make money and to improve human life and welfare, seriously and truthfully?

For public relations practitioners, social responsibility also may be defined as **process**, whether public relations advocacy impedes or contributes to the robust functioning of the marketplace of ideas. An evenhanded process encourages both the journalists who use public relations–generated information for news stories and various audiences who must rely on those stories as part of their decision-making to use the information provided.

Using this concept of social responsibility should enable you to think ethically about television's decisions to air condom advertising. MTV, the network targeted at teenagers, chose to air such ads in 2000. More traditional network television outlets still do not. Which decision do you believe is more ethically justified? Why? Does the notion of social responsibility, and the process of democratic functioning, have any place in your analysis?

Or try this dilemma. With all the talk about global warming, there is one organism that thrives in a warmer subtropics environment—the mosquito that perpetuates dengue fever, a painful disease totally preventable by mosquito control. Does the "first world" have a right to advertise the comforts of energy consumption when a single degree's change in the world's climate allows more latitudes for the disease-bearing mosquito?

The amplified TARES test is a demanding one. But asking these questions, particularly during the process of creating an ad, can also be a spur to better, more creative execution and can be rewarded in the capitalistic marketplace. The TARES test may help advertising practitioners warn their corporate clients about the kind of advertising that could do them, as well as society at large, great long-term harm.

ADVERTISING'S SPECIAL PROBLEMS: VULNERABLE AUDIENCES

Advertising in a mass medium reaches large, heterogeneous audiences. Often, advertising intended for one group is seen by another. Sometimes the results are humorous, and maybe even a little embarrassing, as when ads for contraception or personal hygiene products make their way into prime-time programming.

However, in the case of Camel cigarettes' "Joe Camel" ads, this "confusion" of intended audience with actual recipients appeared quite deliberate. A few years ago, the Camel company agreed to withdraw the cartoon spokesperson "Joe Camel" from magazines and billboards after internal documents revealed the industry targeted underage smokers and sales figures bore out its success.

In other cases—for example, the beer industry—no such ban exists. Advertising intended for adults is often seen by those who cannot legally drink but do remember the catchy commercials and the presentation of drinking as something connected with fun and good times. These ads air in a society when most adult alcoholics report having had their first drink when they were underage.

Are there certain types of audiences that deserve special protection from advertising messages? US law says yes, particularly in the case of children. Legal restrictions on advertising targeted at children cover everything from Saturday-morning television programming to types of products and the characters that advertisers may employ. Children, unlike adults, are not assumed to be autonomous moral actors. They reason about advertising imperfectly, and in an attempt to protect them, American society has accepted some regulation of commercial speech.

However, the issue gets murkier when the target audience is formed of subgroups of adults—for example, ethnic consumers. Exactly when advertisers began to actively court ethnic consumers is uncertain. Dwight Brooks (1992) quotes a 1940 *BusinessWeek* article that reported that an organization was established in Los Angeles to help guide advertisers who wished to garner the patronage of African-American consumers. Amazingly, the businesses were cautioned against using such words as "boss," "boy," and "darkey" in their ads. Instead, the advertisers were urged to refer to African-American consumers as "Negroes" who want the same things as other shoppers.

America is on its way to being a nation with no ethnic majority, and the real attempt to court ethnic audiences began when those audiences acquired buying power. Hispanics are now the largest minority in the United States. The buying power of African-American consumers now tops more than $300 billion. The Asian American market also has increased substantially.

Yet, a relative handful of advertisements reflect this emerging demographic reality despite studies and surveys showing that consumers, especially millennials, are more likely to purchase products that include diverse families in advertisements. Companies such as Budweiser and 84 Lumber received good reviews following their 2017 Super Bowl ads that directly addressed immigration and diversity. However, commercials designed to appeal to this market segment sometimes employ troubling stereotypes or encounter other difficulties. For example, Dove apologized after publishing and then pulling an ad where a black woman, after using Dove body lotion, removes her top to reveal a white woman underneath. Dove was especially susceptible to criticism because it also produced a 2011 ad for its body wash depicting a before-and-after picture that charted the transition of a black woman into a white woman.

Magazines pointed at teenage girls seldom reflect the reality of teenage bodies. Studies have shown that women who are exposed to such advertising images find their own bodies less acceptable. The same goes for facial features. Scholars have noted that the ideal image of beauty, even in magazines targeted at African-Americans, is a Caucasian one of small noses, thin lips, and lighter skin tones. African-American women simply don't see themselves in these advertisements. Scholars in cultural studies argue that the impact of these repeated images is "cumulative." Ultimately, culture comes to accept without question what is nothing more than a gender or a racial stereotype, and the stereotype ultimately becomes a "truism."

Few scholars have suggested that adults who are minorities need special protection from advertising. What they have noted is that ads that abuse the trust between consumer and advertiser have consequences. In the short term, products may not sell or may find themselves the target of regulation. In the long term, cynicism and societal distrust increases. People sense they are being used, even if they can't explain precisely how. The buyer may resort to avoiding advertising itself rather than to using advertising to help make better decisions.

JOURNALISM AND PUBLIC RELATIONS:
THE QUINTESSENTIAL STRUGGLE

Public relations began as a profession in the late 19th century when newsmakers sought to find a way to get past journalism's gatekeepers to get their stories told from simple press releases to elaborate publicity stunts (such as the "torches of freedom" march for women smokers envisioned by Edward L. Bernays in the early years of the 20th century). For the client, public relations practitioners offered free access to the audience; for the newspapers, they offered "free" news to publishers.

Despite the occasional animosity between journalists and public relations practitioners, the relationship is truly symbiotic—they simply could not live without each other. No news organization is large enough to gather all the day's news without several public relations sources. Business pages are full of press releases on earnings, new product lines, and personnel changes, all supplied by writers not paid by the media. Travel, entertainment, and food sections of newspapers would be virtually nonexistent if not for press releases. On the other hand, media outlets provide the all-important audience for an institution wanting the publicity.

With this common need, why are the two professions sometimes at odds? Much of the problem stems from how each of the two professions defines news. To the public relations professional, the lack of breaking news is news-worthy. Plants that operate safely and are not laying off any employees, non-profit organizations that operate within budget and provide needed services, companies that pay a dividend for the 15th consecutive quarter are all signs that things are operating smoothly and make for a story that the public should hear. To the journalist, the opposite is true. Plants only make news when they endanger the public safety. Employees are at their most newsworthy when they bring a gun to work, not when they show up every day for 30 years.

One modern issue is native advertising, which is sponsor-funded content that matches the form and editorial and design function of news content. The issue really isn't new, though: David Ogilvy created the famous "Guinness Guide to Oysters" magazine advertorial in 1950. While there must be a clear disclosure such as the label "advertisement" or "sponsored content" to pro-tect consumers from being deceived, native ads are designed to trick readers or viewers into thinking that material presented was created by reporters or other journalists. Further muddying the water is that news organizations have started branded content studios, most notably the *New York Times*'s T Brand Studio, that create and sell native ads, as well as other advertising content. Examples of native ads are almost too numerous to list; consumers see them every day in sponsored posts on Facebook and Twitter, Google text ads in search listings, product placement such as characters eating Reese's Pieces in *E.T. the Extra-Terrestrial*, and in-feed ads such as the recommended content from "Around the Web" found at the end of almost every online news article.

The average news consumer rarely observes this constant struggle for control, yet he or she is affected by it. How should we evaluate a profession with the goal of persuading in a manner that does not look like traditional persuasion or the goal of preventing the dissemination of information that might harm the illusion that has been created? By undermining the concept of independent and authentic news messages accepted as credible by the public, are strategic communication practitioners undermining the central content vehicle for their messages? Doesn't persuasion need the contrast of news to succeed?

More recently, the focus of animosity has centered on the concept of "synergy," or the notion that consumers should receive multiple messages from distinct sources, thereby increasing sales or public perception of particular issues. At the ethical core of synergy is the concept of independence—for the journalists who report on the news and for the consumers of both news and persuasive messages who need to make independent decisions about them. The current economic pressures on both strategic communication and journalism have intensified this tug-of-war over independence.

PERSUASION AND RESPONSIBILITY

Louis Hodges (1986) says that the notion of professional responsibility can be summed up in a single question: To what am I prepared to respond ably? In other words, what have my education and my experience equipped me to do and to assume responsibility for? Ask a strategic communication practitioner, "To what are you ably equipped to respond?" and he or she might answer, "To respond to a crisis for a client" or "To generate favorable media attention for a client" or "To generate increased sales for my client." However, there are greater responsibilities.

Hodges further states that responsibilities come from three sources. First, there are those that are *assigned*, such as employee to employer. Second, there are those that are *contracted*, where each party agrees to assume responsibilities and fulfill them. Third, there are the *self-imposed* responsibilities, where the individual moral actor takes on responsibilities for reasons indigenous to each individual. It is our contention that public relations, practiced ethically, will not only fulfill the assigned or contracted responsibilities with the employer or the paying client but also take on the greater calling of self-imposed responsibilities. These self-imposed responsibilities could include such constructs as duty to the truth and fidelity to the public good. The more self-imposed responsibilities the strategic professional assumes, the more ethical the profession will become as practitioners see their personal good as being synonymous with the public good.

SUGGESTED READINGS

Fitzpatrick, K., & Bronstein, C. (eds.). (2006). *Ethics in public relations: Responsible advocacy.* Thousand Oaks, CA: Sage.

Hodges, L. (1986). Defining press responsibility: A functional approach. In D. Elliott (ed.), *Responsible journalism.* (pp. 13–31). Newbury Park, CA: Sage.

Baker, S., & Martinson, D. (2001). "The TARES test: Five principles of ethical persuasion." *Journal of Mass Media Ethics* 16(2 & 3).

Leiss, W., Kline, S., & Jhally, S. (1986). *Social communication in advertising: Person, products and images of well being.* New York: Methuen.

O'toole, J. (1985). *The trouble with advertising.* New York: Times Books.

Sandel, M. (2012). *What money can't buy: The moral limits of markets.* New York: Faffaf, Straus and Giroux.

Schudson, M. (1984). *Advertising: The uneasy persuasion.* New York: Basic Books.

CASES

<hr>

CASE 3-A

WEEDVERTISING

LEE WILKINS
Wayne State University
University of Missouri

In *Nichomachean Ethics*, Aristotle discusses the vice of gluttony, which included drinking too much. For the Greeks, gluttony was a violation of the ethical virtue of moderation—it was too much of a good thing. But, for the Greeks, and for multiple cultures throughout history, it was the excess, not the substance itself, that created potential problems.

Weed was initially used in the United States by African-Americans and was adopted by mainstream culture in the 1960s when it became the drug of choice for baby boomers (Weisman 2014). Because of its association with marginal and countercultures, as well as its intoxicating effects, possessing, growing, and selling marijuana was criminalized; in fact, for much of the second half of the 20th century, possessing even small amounts of weed was the criminal equivalent to possessing small amounts of heroin, at least in the United States. During this era in US history, it was the substance itself that was at issue.

People smoked dope anyway, and based on personal experience and perhaps some wishful thinking, the 1960s also gave voice to a small political movement that argued for its legalization, claiming it was no more harmful for most people than alcohol and almost certainly much less harmful than tobacco (which by this time had been linked to cancer) and less addictive than heroin. Marijuana laws also were selectively enforced: if you were a person of color and caught with a "baggie" or a "joint," you were far more likely to be criminally prosecuted than if you were a Caucasian caught in the same set of circumstances.

In later decades, the generation that had grown up with illegal—but popular—"Mary Jane"–obtained political power. Democratic Presidents Bill Clinton and Barack Obama both admitted to smoking weed, although Clinton claimed he "never inhaled." The underground market for the drug remained brisk, and marijuana became an economically viable cash crop (meaning no taxes were paid on the proceeds) in geographic areas as distinct as California, Oregon, and southern Missouri even though it continued to remain illegal at both the local and federal level. Scientists also systematically began to investigate the anecdotal claims about the drug. Marijuana was found to reduce the pain of cancer and other illnesses or long-term injuries, sometimes when other drugs would not. It did not appear to have the addictive qualities of some more traditional painkillers. Extracts of the plant (which did not produce a high for the average person) were prescribed for people with certain sorts of seizure disorders. In sum, scientific evidence coupled with personal experience prompted a culture change: Marijuana came to be viewed much more like alcohol, a legal product, or certain prescription drugs, a medically effective substance, than an underground street drug that put users in jail and providers with lengthy felony convictions.

As the way the culture viewed the drug changed, governments also changed their outlook: Alcohol and tobacco produce tax revenue, even though both continue to be regulated. Why not do the same with weed? The political movement to legalize marijuana that originated the 1960s began to see political success as first municipalities and then states began to legalize (but still control) marijuana, first for medical purposes and then for recreation, in much the same way that states and municipalities regulated alcohol consumption. As of January 2018, seven states and the District of Columbia have legalized marijuana for recreational use and another 22 states have legalized it for medicinal use, though it is illegal at the federal level. The political and cultural change had indeed been a long, strange trip.

With legalization at the local and state level, business sprang up. There were marijuana vacations, where the tour company would pick you up at the airport and take you to various vendors to sample everything from edibles to more traditional ways of consuming the drug. These tour companies would make sure that no one was "high" behind the wheel and also that people were guided through the various kinds and strengths of marijuana available. The experience was very much like a tour of the California wine country, only the intoxicant changed.

However, because the federal government continued to regard the drug as illegal, the clash of federal, state, and local law enforcement expectations resulted in transactions that were conducted only in cash. Businesses could not provide information to potential consumers about their existence or their services. In other words, marijuana-based businesses couldn't advertise.

However, given the history of the past 60 years, there is every reason to believe that the federal government will eventually begin to treat weed in the same way it regulates alcohol. Whether that change comes in the next year or the next decade, the prospect of advertising weed provides advertising practitioners with a rare opportunity to consider how that product can be effectively and ethically advertised to a growing group of consumers before such advertising becomes widespread.

Micro Issues

1. How is advertising weed like and unlike direct-to-consumer advertising of over-the-counter and prescription drugs?
2. How does the fact that marijuana is a "sin" product like alcohol or gambling influence your approach to developing ads?
3. How does thinking about vulnerable audiences influence your approach to weedvertising?
4. What sorts of images would be appropriate to employ in weedvertisements?

Midrange Issues

1. W. D. Ross provides a set of duties, reviewed in chapter 1. Could weedvertising be said to support any of Ross's duties?
2. Are there some uses of weed that should not be advertised? Compare your response on this question to how you would respond to similar questions about drugs, alcohol, or gambling.
3. Advertisers often employ testimonials in their ads. Would such a strategy be appropriate for weed?

Macro Issues

1. Should the advertising industry develop and enforce its own set of guidelines that regulate weedvertising? What might those guidelines be? How would these guidelines be like or unlike the current guidelines regulating advertising promulgated by the federal government for all products? For products such as alcohol?
2. How would developing a weedvertising campaign be like or unlike a campaign for selling seats on commercial ventures that promise to take passengers to outer space or the moon?

CASE 3-B

CLEANING UP THEIR ACT: THE CHIPOTLE FOOD SAFETY CRISIS

KAYLA MCLAUGHLIN AND KELLY VIBBER
University of Dayton

Between July and December 2015, more than 500 customers became sick after eating at a Chipotle Mexican Grill. Six different outbreaks of either *E. coli*, Norovirus, or *Salmonella* were reported in Chipotle restaurants from Seattle to Boston. While none of these outbreaks resulted in deaths, Chipotle still faced a vast public demand to address food safety concerns.

Chipotle also needed to restore its positive image, an image that had become the target of several unflattering social media memes. For example, customers tweeted using the hashtag #chipotleecoli and noted "paying extra for guac but not for the e.coli." For a company whose competitive advantage and brand image centered on locally and naturally sourced products, the issue of food safety was central.

Chipotle reported the majority of the outbreaks to the Center for Disease Control after the restaurants had been sanitized and the ingredients replaced, preventing the CDC from conducting any investigation.

Chipotle also failed to publicly address the outbreaks until after the fourth episode, publishing its first press release on Nov. 3, 2015. On Dec. 16, Chipotle purchased full-page advertisements in various outlets such as the *New York Times*, *Wall Street Journal*, and *USA Today*. The advertisement was an open letter from founder Steve Ells and focused on eight new food safety initiatives. In it, Ells wrote,

> Since I opened the first Chipotle more than 23 years ago, we have strived to elevate fast food, by using better ingredients which are raised responsibly, without synthetic hormones, antibiotics, added colors, flavors or sweeteners typically found in processed fast food. And I'm very proud of that. But in 2015, we failed to live up to our own food safety standards, and in so doing, we let our customers down. At that time, I made a promise to all of our customers that we would elevate our food safety program. (The full letter is available at www.chipotle.com/openletter.)

The outbreak incidents and the poor corporate response had financial and legal consequences. Bloomberg estimated that Chipotle lost nearly $73 million in sales after the outbreaks (Stock 2016). In January 2016, investors sued Chipotle for making "materially false and misleading statements" and not disclosing that "quality controls were not in compliance with applicable consumer and workplace safety regulations" (Wahba 2016). Also in January 2016, Chipotle received a subpoena requiring the company to release a "broad range of documents" related to the Simi Valley outbreak. Later in the month, Chipotle received a second subpoena for information regarding food safety measures from as far back as 2013 (Associated Press 2016). During this time, Chipotle also privately settled 96 cases with customers on a case-by-case basis (Jennings 2016).

Social media dramatically increased the awareness of the outbreaks as well as providing a platform for circulating false information without any filter.

Hoping to fuel a turnaround, Chipotle closed all of its restaurants on Feb. 8, 2016, for a four-hour food safety meeting to discuss new policies and answer outstanding questions. The new plan featured eight main actions the company would take to prevent future outbreaks and become a leader in food safety, including restaurant inspections at its more than 1,900 locations, farmer support and training, and ingredient traceability.

After Chipotle's dramatic closing, the company continued to promote new marketing initiatives aimed at gaining back customer trust and revenue. Between February and May 2016, Chipotle gave away nearly $70 million in free food (Taylor 2016). In July 2016, Chipotle executives announced they would be utilizing a loyalty program called "Chiptopia" as a way to bring back once-loyal customers.

Despite these multiple efforts to engage with and reestablish their customer base, financial indicators continued to lag. The company has experienced additional hurdles in 2017, including another Norovirus outbreak and video footage, which traveled quickly on Twitter, of mice in a Dallas Chipotle restaurant.

Micro Issues

1. Chipotle failed to publicly address food contamination until after the fourth outbreak. Analyze their response.
2. Evaluate the open letter from Chipotle founder Steve Ells.
3. What is the ethical responsibility of members of the public who have a bad experience with a local business to tell the truth or accurately report what happened?
4. What is the ethical responsibility of someone who reads such a post?

Midrange Issues

1. Chipotle has cultivated an image of providing locally and naturally sourced products, a contrast to many of their fast-food competitors. How did this image positively or negatively influence media coverage of the outbreaks?
2. Develop a strategic advertising campaign to help reestablish Chipotle's image following several unflattering social media memes. What ethical principles do you rely on to develop this approach?

Macro Issues

1. One reporter compared the Chipotle outbreaks to similar, yet more widespread, incidents at Jack in the Box restaurants in 1992. Chipotle suffered bigger sales losses, and the reporter attributed these decreases to social media and the power of news being widely available. Evaluate these claims.

CASE 3-C

KEEPING UP WITH THE KARDASHIANS' PRESCRIPTION DRUG CHOICES

TARA WALKER
University of Colorado Boulder

In 2015, Kim Kardashian-West posted a picture of herself on Instagram holding a bottle of pills with the caption, "OMG. Have you heard about this?"

The post touted the drug Diclegis and its benefits for morning sickness. Soon thereafter, Duchesnay, the drug manufacturer, received a warning letter from the Food and Drug Administration (FDA) saying that the post had been "false and misleading" because it failed to mention the drug's risks. Consequently, Kardashian-West posted a month later describing the potential side effects and the risks associated with Diclegis. She used the hashtag "#correctivead" with the post, and prefaced the list of side effects with the words "for US residents only" (see https://www. instagram.com/p/7B07j_uSww).

Kardashian-West's original post omitted any warnings, suggesting that Duchesnay deliberately sidestepped the regulations about direct-to-consumer drug advertising. According to Matt Brown, the CEO of Guidemark Health, Duchesnay "took a risk by having Kardashian-West promote the product without safety information." As a result, brand awareness increased substantially. "The concept of 'bad publicity is good publicity' was definitely embraced here," Brown said (McCaffrey 2015).

Kardashian-West's post is only one event in a long line of controversies associated with direct-to-consumer-advertising, or DTCA.

Proponents of DTCA claim that these ads provide an important source of health information, especially for hard-to-reach populations (Lee and Begley 2010). Additionally, advocates argue such advertising may help undiagnosed patients receive treatment and promote greater adherence to drug regimens (Calfee 2002; Hoek and Gendall 2002; Hoek 2008; Johar 2012). Critics argue such advertising contributes to high healthcare costs, weakens doctor-patient relationships, adds to an unnecessary demand for drugs, and oversimplifies complex health issues (Metzl 2002; Huh, Delorme, and Reid 2004; Grow, Park, and Han 2006; Payton and Thoits 2011).

Until the early 1980s, prescription drugs had been marketed almost exclusively to doctors. The justification was that consumers did not have the medical knowledge or experience to make decisions about prescriptions. However, cultural changes about patients' rights and the unquestioned authority of doctors in making medical decisions primed the political environment for the acceptance of advertising drugs directly to consumers. In 1985, the FDA loosened regulations (Donohue 2006). Approved advertising, however, had to include the same information that ads for physicians contained "a true statement of information in brief summary relating to side effects, contraindications and effectiveness" and a "fair balance" of both the drug's benefits and its risks (FDA/DHHS 1969). By default, these requirements made it difficult to advertise drugs on television because the safety information could not fit into a television spot.

In 1997, the FDA released a new set of guidelines specifically for broadcast DTCA. These new guidelines suggested that the "brief summary" could be avoided as long as the ad provided information on major side effects and contraindications and gave viewers a way to access the rest of the information. Ads could refer consumers to web pages, a corresponding print ad in a magazine, a toll-free number, and/or their pharmacists and physicians. These loosened restrictions resulted in drug companies dedicating more of their marketing budgets to television advertising, and less to print (Eaton 2004, 430).

DTCA for prescription drugs is legal only in the United States and New Zealand. Online, however, there are no national borders.

Micro Issues

1. Should pharmaceutical companies develop distinct standards for adverting drugs via social media?
2. Is the omission of a drug's potential risks deceptive?
3. To whom do celebrity endorsers such as Kim Kardashian-West owe loyalty? To the drug manufacturer? To readers or viewers?

Midrange Issues

1. DTCA is legal only in two countries but can be accessed almost anywhere online. What legal restrictions, if any, should be enacted for such advertising online?
2. Evaluate the claim "bad publicity is good publicity" in the context of direct-to-consumer ads.
3. Do drugs constitute a different category of advertised product, and hence require different sorts of standards/regulations, compared with other consumer goods? How are drugs like or unlike tobacco and beer, both products where advertising is more stringently regulated?

Macro Issues

1. How things are sold—the advertising appeal—is one of the enduring ethical issues in advertising. Evaluate the appeal in the original Instagram ad.
2. Does the use of a celebrity endorsement change the nature of direct-to-consumer drugs ads? Why?
3. Does the original ad pass the TARES test? Could any social media ad pass the TARES test?
4. Media organizations now make a great deal of money on the DTCA of drugs. Evaluate the impact of this revenue stream on potential decision-making about printing/broadcasting such ads.

CASE 3-D

BETWEEN A (KID) ROCK AND A HARD PLACE

MOLLY SHOR
Wayne State University

On Sept. 2, 2017, the *Detroit Free Press* published an opinion piece by editorial writer and Pulitzer Prize winning journalist Stephen Henderson. In his editorial, Henderson questions whether Kid Rock was an appropriate choice for the opening concert at Detroit's Little Caesars Arena, which was built with significant taxpayer support in a city with a large black population.

Henderson wrote: "This is a musician who got rich off crass cultural appropriation of black music, who used to wrap his brand in the Confederate flag—a symbol inextricably linked to racism, no matter what its defenders say—and who has repeatedly issued profane denouncements of the very idea of African Americans pushing back against American inequality."

Henderson called the opening of the arena with Kid Rock as public representative "tone deaf." He not only condemned Kid Rock as spokesperson for such a public opening, but also questioned the public and political sensitivity of the Illitch family. As owners of the new arena, and as operators of the Olympia Entertainment Division, the Illitch organization was responsible for booking the concert.

"Having Kid Rock open this arena is erecting a sturdy middle finger to Detroiters—nothing less," Henderson wrote. "And the Ilitches, who've done so much for this city and also taken so much from it, should be the last to embrace that kind of signaling."

In response to the *Detroit Free Press* editorial, Kid Rock's representatives pulled the press credentials for the paper, limiting the newspaper's access to report on the concert and the much-anticipated opening of the arena (Gross 2017). Journalists still would have access to the concert by buying a ticket and attending with the general public.

Numerous press outlets reported the retaliatory action. In many of the subsequent stories, Kirt Webster, Kid Rock's publicist, said the reason for denying access was that the *Detroit Free Press* "wrote a fucked-up story and allowed it to be published" (Herreria 2017). The publicist also contended that neither did the paper fact-check the article nor did Henderson report about Kid Rock's local charitable giving. Webster claimed that their response to the article was to show that they would not "reward bad behavior" (Greenwood 2017).

While the regional editor of the *Detroit Free Press* clarified that Henderson's column was an opinion piece, he also defended the paper's news coverage of the arena opening (Greenwood 2017).

Webster shuttered his public relations firm in November 2017 following sexual harassment claims, which Webster said were egregious and untrue. In December 2017, Henderson was terminated from the *Detroit Free Press* for misconduct.

Micro Issues

1. Was it reasonable or fair for Kid Rock's representatives to pull the *Detroit Free Press* credentials in response to commentary that they deemed less than favorable?
2. Kid Rock is a musician who uses his art as a platform for uninhibited public speech. Should he therefore be held to a higher standard regarding issues such as media access?
3. Should a hometown newspaper be held to a different standard than a national newspaper when covering local celebrities and civic events?

Midrange Issues

1. Compare this incident to Disney banning the *Los Angeles Times* from movie press screenings following the newspaper's investigation into Disney's Anaheim business dealings.
2. To whom does Kirt Webster owe loyalty? To whom does Kid Rock owe loyalty?
3. What do you see as the differences in getting excluded from a sporting event or public performance and a news event such as a press conference?

Macro Issues

1. What are the options for a newsroom that gets shut out of an event? Do you include that fact in your reporting of the event? Does it become a separate story?
2. Many news outlets have forums for opinion including editorial pages, on-air commentaries labeled as such, and so on, and one of the oldest tenets of journalism is the independence of this role from outside pressure, whether newsmakers or advertisers. If these clearly labeled opinions begin to affect the ability of reporters to get access to news, what do you do?

CASE 3-E

WAS THAT AN APPLE COMPUTER I SAW? PRODUCT PLACEMENT IN THE UNITED STATES AND ABROAD

PHILIP PATTERSON
Oklahoma Christian University

Michael Scott, the buffoon-like office manager in the Emmy Award–winning NBC comedy "The Office," shows up at casual Friday encouraging his shocked employees to check out his backside in his new Levi's jeans. In the wildly popular ABC drama/comedy "Desperate Housewives," Gabrielle (played by Eva Longoria) gets desperate enough for cash to model beside a Buick LaCrosse at a car show and for a mattress firm. In the now-cancelled "American Dreams," which portrayed American life in the 1960s, such American icons as Campbell's Soup and the Ford Mustang were woven into the show.

Hollywood calls it "brand integration." Its critics—some of them the very writers for shows using product placement—call it much worse. But by any name, the phenomenon is growing. During the 2004–2005 television season, more than 100,000 actual products appeared in American network television (up 28 percent in one year) according to Nielsen Media Research, generating $1.88 billion (up 46 percent in a year) according to PQ Media (Manly 2005). Advertising agencies have set up product placement divisions. Research organizations have cropped up to take on the task of measuring the effectiveness of product placement. And television shows in the United States seem to have an insatiable appetite for what they offer.

"The fact is, these brands are part of our lives, and brands exist in these television environments, so why not showcase them," said Ben Silverman, chief executive of the firm that produces "The Office" (Manly 2005, A14).

However, not everyone is pleased. In a 2005 meeting in New York during "Advertising Week," television writers protested outside a panel discussing the state of brand integration in television programming. Among their gripes, they want more of a say in how products will be placed and, inevitably, a share of the profits generated from writing a product into the script.

Most see the move as one of survival. Taking a cue from radio and its "soap operas," the original television shows were named for the sponsors

("The Colgate Comedy Hour" and "Texaco Star Theater"), and the audience had little option but to watch the ads. But while commercials undergirded the television industry for the first 50 years, the advent of the remote and, more recently, TiVo, have allowed consumers to avoid the very commercials that make the programming free.

"The advertising model of 10 years ago is not applicable today," according to Bruce Rosenblum, president of Warner Bros. Television Group. "At the end of the day, if we are unable to satisfy advertisers' appetites to deliver messages in new ways to the viewer, then we're destined to have a broken model" (Manly 2005, A14).

However, for government-sponsored television in Europe, the practice of product placement remains a sticky issue.

In a 2005 edition of "Spooks," a BBC drama, a logo for an Apple computer appeared in early airings of the show and then was removed in subsequent showings after British print media alleged that the Apple logo and others had slipped into BBC programming in exchange for cash and favors, which violates BBC rules. In Germany, firings occurred after public broadcaster ARD was found to have had shows full of illegal product placements for years (Pfanner 2005).

Not every European country has such a ban. In Austria, public broadcaster ORF airs more than 1,000 product placements a year on its shows and provides the ORF with about $24 million in funds to supplement its budget of approximately $1 billion. The ORF says that allowing the placements actually regulates what happens anyway. "If you don't regulate it, it exists anyway, in a gray zone," said Alexander Wrabetz, chief financial officer for ORF (Pfanner 2005, A15).

And even within the BBC, which has not announced any intent to change its ban on product placement, there are differing opinions. One BBC executive, speaking to the *International Herald Tribune* off the record, said, "Back in the '50s, everything was called Acme, or we stuck stickers over all the brand names. There isn't a TV company in the world that does that now. Viewers don't find it convincing" (Pfanner 2005, A15).

Ultimately, success in product placement still comes down to whether the placement fits the plot. "The needle we have to thread," according to Johnathan Prince, creator of "American Dreams" and now working on Madison Avenue, "is to have brand integration that is effective enough to have resonance, but . . . subtle enough so that it doesn't offend" (Manly 2005, A16).

Micro Issues

1. Would you personally prefer to go back to the days where made-up names such as "Acme" were placed on products to conceal the true brand names of the products?
2. Does the authenticity that real products such as name-brand computers bring to a television show outweigh the intrusiveness of inserting a product into the plot of a show?
3. Are products placed into television shows the "price" you pay for free television, just as watching 30-second commercials were the "price" your parents and grandparents paid?

Midrange Issues

1. News magazines such as *Newsweek* will often run multi-page special sections on issues such as "Women's Health," and all of the ads within the section will be for products promoting women's health. What do you see as the difference between this practice and product placement on television shows?
2. Do you see a difference in whether product placement should occur in scripted dramas and comedies as opposed to reality television?
3. How does product placement in television shows differ from naming sports stadiums or college bowl games after corporate sponsors, where presumably they will be mentioned on air for free during newscasts? Should newscasters avoid the corporate names of these places and events?
4. When a news show ends with rolling credits that attribute the wardrobe of the anchor to a certain store, is that product placement? Is that an intrusion on the objectivity of the news? Justify your answers.

Macro Issues

1. If consumers are "zapping" and "TiVo-ing" through commercials in free television, what will happen to the medium if product placement fails to deliver the needed revenue to keep the programming free? What will happen to the United States if free television is eliminated?
2. In trying to "thread the needle" between effectiveness and offensiveness, what are some of the guidelines you would write for product placement?

3. Is the argument made by Wrabetz in this case an ethical one?
   Compare the argument to the five standards of the TARES test found
   in this chapter and see how it measures up.

CASE 3-F

SPONSORSHIPS, SINS, AND PUBLIC RELATIONS: WHAT ARE THE BOUNDARIES?

LAUREN BACON BRENGARTH
University of Missouri

Sponsorships are a complicated yet essential tool for nonprofit organizations. Sponsorships from the for-profit world provide funds that are critical for nonprofit growth and operations, yet they come at a cost. Consider the example the for-profit University of Phoenix and a nonprofit organization that administers local Head Start services and provides free preschool to children living in poverty.

While interviewing the communication manager of the nonprofit, I asked him if he felt that social media enabled the organization to serve a news-producing function in the community. He affirmed that he not only believes that the organization is a news producer, but that the group's success in driving social media has led to new dollars coming to the organization. Some of those new dollars had raised troubling questions.

For example, contributions from the for-profit University of Phoenix included an exchange of promotional mentions and opportunities by the nonprofit preschool. For example, the preschool promoted the University of Phoenix as the lead sponsor of its annual fundraising breakfast through Facebook and Twitter posts. Additionally, at the breakfast, the nonprofit hosted a University of Phoenix "cyber café" where event attendees were encouraged to log on and tell others that they were at the event.

In previous years, the University of Phoenix local staff members volunteered at the preschool through events such as reading to the children, providing "literacy totes" filled with school supplies and books for the kids, and several other activities. The relationship between the two organizations prompted the preschool to nominate the University of Phoenix for a Head Start Corporate award for model corporate/community partnerships, which it won.

Meanwhile, the University of Phoenix has come under fire for its high tuition rates and tendency to cater to low-income students who often leave campus with a pile of debt, minimal job prospects, and no degree. Because of the substantial federal financial aid that students receive, graduation rates have received heightened government scrutiny (Gramm 2012).

Additional University of Phoenix criticisms highlight its reliance on part-time instructors and a pattern of pushing students through course curriculum in half the time of traditional postsecondary schools (Dillion 2007). In 2009, the institution paid a $78.5 million settlement when two whistleblowers filed a False Claim Act lawsuit against the university regarding its student recruitment practices. Officials counteracted widespread critiques by saying that the university structure caters to working students that many traditional schools ignore.

The University of Phoenix has experienced a sharp dip in enrollment because of widespread national criticism adding to a negative public image. In the third quarter of 2012, reports from the University of Phoenix reflect a 15 percent drop in average degreed enrollment and an 8 percent decline in new student starts. Net revenue for the Apollo group (the operator of the University of Phoenix) shows a 9.2 percent decline in the third quarter of fiscal year 2012; however, the company still brought in $3.3 billion in revenue.

Micro Issues

1. If working, lower-income students make up a large portion of the University of Phoenix student body, how does this partnership cause potential ethical conflicts?
2. Should nonprofits partner with for-profit organizations?
3. What are the appropriate conditions and parameters for a nonprofit to promote its sponsor(s)?
4. What do for-profit organizations hope to gain by partnering with nonprofits?
5. What are nonprofits willing to sacrifice in order to gain for-profit capital?

Midrange Issues

1. What differentiates sponsorships from advertising?
2. Many for-profit corporations encourage employees to volunteer their time and dollars to a variety of local and national organizations. What, if anything, should for-profit organizations expect for this effort?

Macro Issues

1. How do politics influence the appropriateness of sponsorship relationships and promotion (for example, the US Olympic Team received apparel from Ralph Lauren that was manufactured in China)?
2. How does social responsibility influence the appropriateness of sponsorship relationships (for example, Budweiser sponsoring football tailgates for a major university)?
3. What should nonprofits do to adequately research the history and practices of the for-profits that want to sponsor them?
4. Chapter 6 discusses the role of the corporate citizen as one element that can have a positive impact on the bottom line. Do you believe sponsorships such as the one described above contribute to the concept of the "good" corporate citizen? Do motives matter?

CASE 3-G

A CHARITY DROPS THE BALL

PHILIP PATTERSON
Oklahoma Christian University

Susan G. Komen for the Cure is a global organization dedicated to finding a cure for breast cancer, educating the public about the disease and aiding patients who have been diagnosed with cancer. The organization has raised nearly $2 billion in more than three decades of operation. Its signature event, the Susan G. Komen Race for the Cure, draws on a network of activists, survivors, and volunteers to create an event that is one of the largest in all US charities. Since 1982, the Komen organization has been a trusted brand in its chosen field of breast cancer research.

In February 2012, the leadership of Komen announced that it would end its long-standing relationship with Planned Parenthood, a women's health resource. Planned Parenthood delivers reproductive health care, sex education, and information to its clients worldwide. Their 800 centers in the United States serve nearly five million clients each year. According to their publicity information, one in five women in the United States has visited a Planned Parenthood health center at least once in her life. Nearly three-quarters of a million breast exams are provided by the organization each year. Three percent of the healthcare provided by Planned Parenthood are abortions or abortion referrals. This keeps them at odds with many religious groups and conservative causes as well.

Prior to the decision by Komen, it had been announced that Planned Parenthood was under congressional investigation to determine if they had used federal funding to finance abortions. In the midst of the inquiry, Susan G. Komen for the Cure announced that it would suspend its funding of Planned Parenthood—at the time a total of $680,000 annually.

Backlash to the decision was swift and came from many sources. Children's author Judy Blume was one who condemned the Komen organization, publicly saying, "Susan Komen (the namesake of the charity) would not give in to bullying or fear. Too bad the organization bearing her name did." Other criticism came from various sources around the country.

Days later, the Komen organization apologized for their actions and reinstated the funding to Planned Parenthood. Karen Handel, vice president for public affairs at Susan G. Komen for the Cure, resigned following the public apology. Handel had been an outspoken critic of Planned Parenthood, and most members of the media believed that her resignation was not voluntary and was instead connected to the bad publicity from the suspension of the funding to that group. However, in her resignation letter and in interviews afterwards, Handel said that while she had a role in the decision, both the Komen board and top executives were onboard with it.

Micro Issues

1. Does a charity such as Susan G. Komen for the Cure have a duty to reflect the views of its donors in its policies and its affiliations?
2. Should donors have a right to shape the way their funds are used after they have given them?
3. If the original decision to drop the funding had the support of the board of Komen, why did Handel have to resign?

Midrange Issues

1. The decision to break the affiliation with Planned Parenthood by Komen came in the midst of a congressional inquiry with largely Republican support. Was the subsequent decision of Komen to reinstate Planned Parenthood politically motivated?

2. If you are a spokesperson for a group, is it incumbent that you agree with all of its actions? Would you have resigned as Handel did? Why or why not? Does your opinion about abortion have anything to do with your decision?

Macro Issues

1. This controversy involved two of America's largest charities for women's health care. Much of the funding of these charities comes from large corporate donations. In light of that, what is your opinion of Komen's initial action against Planned Parenthood? What about its subsequent reversal?
2. Donations to organizations such as Komen are tax deductible. To what extent does that give the government a right to regulate them?

Loyalty

Choosing between Competing Allegiances

By the end of this chapter, you should

- understand why the articulation of loyalties is important in professional ethics
- know Royce's definition of loyalty and at least one of the major problems with that conceptualization
- understand how journalists' role in society provides them with an additional set of loyalties to consider
- be familiar with and able to use the Potter Box as a justification model for ethical decision-making

LOYALTY AS PART OF THE SOCIAL CONTRACT

Decisions involving loyalty occur routinely for media professionals. When editors and journalists decide which stories to cover and how to cover them, they are expressing a loyalty. When recording executives cancel the contract of a controversial artist to avoid a boycott, they have chosen a loyalty. Whether or not to cover a minor political candidate or an upcoming political movement is often rooted in loyalty. In fact, many ethical decisions come down to this question, "To whom (or what) will I be loyal?"

The original discussion of loyalty in Western culture was written by Plato in *The Trial and Death of Socrates* (see Russell 1967). In Plato's *Phaedo*, Socrates bases his defense against the charges brought against him on his loyalty to divinely inspired truth. When asked by his accusers if he will stop teaching philosophy, Socrates responds:

Men of Athens, I honor and love you: but I shall obey God rather than you, and while I have life and strength I shall never cease from the practice and teaching of philosophy, exhorting any one whom I meet. . . . For know that this is the command of God; and I believe that no greater good has ever happened in the State than my service to God.

While the word *loyalty* is not present in English translations of the *Phaedo*, the overall tone of the work is a tribute to loyalty, in this case a willingness to die for a cause.

Social contract theorist Thomas Hobbes was the first major Western philosopher to assert that God did not have to be the focus of loyalty. As a monarchist, Hobbes saw loyalty to the crown as the solution to the natural, selfish nature of humans. The solution, living inside of the "social contract" required loyalty to the crown. In his historic work, *The Leviathan*, Hobbes asserted that loyalty is a social act (Socrates saw it as political) and that the agreement allows people to form a "social contract" that is the basis of society. Unlike Socrates, Hobbes acknowledged that people could have more than one loyalty at a time and might, at certain times, be forced to choose among them—a notion most philosophers hold today.

Hobbes, unlike Socrates, also asserted that loyalty has limits. Loyalty to the ruler stops when continued loyalty would result in a subject's death—the loyalty to self-preservation being higher than loyalty to the ruler. The turmoil surrounding how the United States responds to terrorist acts and activities is a vivid example of how being loyal can inform decisions.

THE CONTRIBUTIONS OF JOSIAH ROYCE

American theologian Josiah Royce, who taught at Harvard in the early 1900s, believed that loyalty could become the single guiding ethical principle. In *The Philosophy of Loyalty* (1908), Royce wrote, "My theory is that the whole moral law is implicitly bound up in one precept: 'Be loyal.'" Royce defined loyalty as a social act: "The willing and practical and thoroughgoing devotion of a person to a cause." Royce would be critical, therefore, of the journalist who gets a story at all costs and whose only loyalty is to himself, or the public relations professional who lets loyalty to an employer cause her to bend the truth in tweets, posts, press releases, or annual reports. To Royce, loyalty is an act of choice. A loyal person, Royce asserted, does not have the leisure not to decide. For in the act of not deciding, that person has essentially cast his loyalty.

Loyalty also promotes self-realization. As a contemporary of Sigmund Freud, Royce spent much of his academic career fascinated with the new findings in psychology, writing a textbook in the field and, at one point, serving as the president of the American Psychological Association. Subsequently, he viewed loyalty in the light of psychology. As a person continued to exercise loyalty, Royce believed, he or she would develop habits of character that would result in systematic ethical action. Like other aspects of moral development (see the last chapter of this book), loyalty can be learned and honed, Royce believed.

Loyalty as a single ethical guide has problems. *First*, loyalty, incompletely conceived, can be bias or prejudice thinly cloaked. *Second*, few people maintain merely a single loyalty and if loyalty is to become a guiding ethical principle, we need to develop a way to help distinguish among competing loyalties. *Third*, in a mass society, the concept of face-to-face loyalty has lost much of its power. *Finally*, the most troubling question: whether it is ethical to be loyal to an unethical cause, for example, racism or gender discrimination.

However, Royce suggested a way to determine whether a specific cause was worthy of loyalty. A worthy cause should harmonize with the loyalties of others within the community. For Royce, community was all-important to his philosophy and inextricable from it. He wrote that "individuals without community are without substance, while communities without individuals are blind" (Royce 1908). This places the journalist in an important role in the community, and, for Royce, the loyalty of the journalist should be in harmony with the loyalty of the reader. The loyalty of the advertising agency should not conflict with the loyalty of either its client or the consumer. Our loyalty to free and unfettered political discussion as the basis of modern democracy and journalism meets Royce's test of loyalty but is also the core of the debate over campaign finance laws.

To Royce, the true problem of loyalty as an ethical principle was not the poor choice of loyalties but failure to adhere to proper loyalties: "The ills of mankind are largely the consequence of disloyalty rather than wrong-headed loyalty" (Royce 1908). Causes capable of sustaining loyalty, Royce noted, have a "super-individual" quality, apparent when people become part of a community. A spirit of democratic cooperation is needed for Royce's view of loyalty to result in ethical action. For instance, advertising agencies demonstrate an ethical loyalty when they view their role as providing needed information for intelligent consumer choice, but more often they opt for loyalty to the bottom line because they suspect that competing agencies do.

Royce's thought has been criticized on a number of grounds. First, some philosophers assert that Royce's concept of loyalty is simplistic and that the adoption of loyalty as a moral principle may lead to allegiance to troubling causes. For instance, the advertising copywriter who scripts distorted television spots about a political opponent in the belief that she must get her candidate elected is demonstrating a troubling allegiance to a politician over the democratic process. Similarly, a reporter who must get the story first, regardless of its completeness or accuracy, would be demonstrating a misplaced loyalty to beating the competition.

Second, others have noted that Royce provides no way to balance among conflicting loyalties. Media professionals such as journalists are faced daily with a barrage of potential loyalties—the truth, the audience, the sources, the bottom line, the profession—and choosing among them is among the most basic of ethical decisions. Other professions have similar dilemmas such as the documentarian who must be loyal to the truth in her art while at the same time being loyal to the producers who want large numbers of the ticket-buying public to see the final product.

Third, it is unclear how Royce's ethical thinking would balance majority notions against minority views. Strictly interpreted, Royce's notion of loyalty could inspire adherence to the status quo or strict majority rule. For instance, advertisements that stereotype groups of people despite evidence to the contrary help perpetuate incorrect images. The ads work because they appeal to the majority, but by stereotyping, they have crowded out more accurate impressions.

Yet despite these criticisms, Royce's thought has much to recommend it. First, Royce speaks to the development of ethical habits. Second, Royce reminds us that the basis of loyalty is social and loyalty requires we put others on an equal footing with ourselves. Most important is the overriding message of Royce's work: *when making ethical choices, it is important to consider what your loyalties are and how you arrived at those loyalties.*

JOURNALISM AS A PROFESSION

Loyalty is not a fixed point but a range within a continuum. In *Loyalty: An Essay on the Morality of Relationships*, George P. Fletcher (1993) identifies two types of loyalty. The first is minimal: "Do not betray me." The second is maximal: "Be one with me."

Between these two poles is a range of possibilities for allegiance and for corresponding media behavior. The location on the continuum for YouTube will differ from that of *The Nation* magazine. One of the problems modern news media face is that a large percentage of the US public subscribes to the notion that if the media are not maximally loyal—that is, one with government, with a particular political candidate, or with the military and so forth—then they are traitorous.

The media have been called disloyal by politicians, often for no greater sin than fulfilling the watchdog role. In *Unbelievable: My front row seat to the craziest campaign in American history*, MSNCB journalist and now anchor Katy Tur (2017) recalls the days she spent on the campaign trail covering candidate Donald Trump and his wild swings between criticizing her reporting—often publicly from the stage—and lavishing praises, and at one point, a kiss, on her depending on whether he was pleased with her recent reporting. In her recollection of the 500 days she spent with Trump, she writes of a candidate consumed with wanting loyalty out of reporters who were guilty only of trying to objectively perform their roles in covering his campaign. She remembers being booed at campaign rallies courtesy of comments by Trump and being called "little Katy Tur," "disgraceful," and "third rate" from the stage by Trump at various times, only to later be praised by the mercurial candidate.

Loyalty can be linked to role. A role is a capacity in which we act toward others. It provides others with information about how we will act in a structured situation. Some roles are occupationally defined—account executive, screenwriter, editor. Others are not: mother, spouse, daughter. We all play multiple roles, and they help us to define ourselves and to know what is expected of us and others.

When the role you assume is a professional one, you add the ethical responsibilities of that role. Philosophers claim that "to belong to a profession is traditionally to be held to certain standards of conduct that go beyond the norm for others" (Lebacqz 1985, 32), and journalism qualifies as one of those professions with a higher expected norm of conduct.

However, not all journalists agree in practice. Louis Hodges (1986) makes the distinction in this manner: when asked what she does for a living, one journalist says, "I am a journalist," while another says, "I work for the *Gazette*." Hodges claims the first speaker recognizes her responsibility as a professional while the latter merely acknowledges her loyalty to a paycheck. The first would be expected to be loyal to societal expectations of a journalist; the second may or may not.

Journalists and their employers have debated whether journalism should be considered a profession. Advocates of professionalism assert that professionalism among journalists will provide them with greater autonomy, prestige, and financial rewards. Critics see the process of professionalization as one that distances readers and viewers from the institutions that journalists often represent.

Despite these debates, we sense that journalists have two central responsibilities that are distinct in modern society. First, they have a greater responsibility to tell the truth than members of most professions. Second, journalists also seem to carry a greater obligation to foster political involvement than the average person.

Philosophers note that while ethical dilemmas are transitory, roles endure. Role expectations carry over from one situation to another. Loyalty to the profession means loyalty to the *ideals* of the profession. To Aristotle, loyalty to a profession also would mean maintaining high professional standards. The Aristotelian notion of virtue means being the best television producer or advertising executive you can be in the belief that you are being loyal to the profession and its ideals.

CONFLICTING LOYALTIES

As you can see, we are no longer talking about merely a single loyalty. We live in an age of layers of loyalties, creating added problems and complications.

Sorting through competing loyalties can be difficult, particularly when loyalties in one role appear to conflict with the loyalties of another. Much has been written about this issue, and we have adapted one such framework from William F. May (2001), who outlined these layers of loyalties for college professors, but they are adaptable to those who work in the media. He offers four types of loyalty.

1. Loyalties arising from shared humanity:
   - Demonstrate respect for each person as an individual.
   - Communicate honestly and truthfully with all persons.
   - Build a fair and compassionate environment that promotes the common good.
2. Loyalties arising from professional practice:
   - Fulfill the informational and entertainment mission of the media.
   - Understand your audience's needs.
   - Strive to enhance professional development of self and others.
   - Avoid the abuse of power and position.
   - Conduct professional activities in ways that uphold or surpass the ideals of virtue and competence.
3. Loyalties arising from employment:
   - Keep agreements and promises, operate within the framework of the law, and extend due process to all persons.
   - Do not squander your organization's resources or your public trust.
   - Promote compassionate and humane professional relationships.
   - Foster policies that build a community of ethnic, gender, and socio-economic diversity.
   - Promote the right of all to be heard.

4. Loyalties arising from the media's role in public life:
   - Serve as examples of open institutions where truth is required.
   - Foster open discussion and debate.
   - Interpret your professional actions to readers and viewers.
   - Serve as a voice for the voiceless.
   - Serve as a mirror of society.

The problem of conflicting loyalties is evident in the reality that most media professionals work for a corporation. They owe at least some loyalty to their corporate employers. However, such loyalty seldom involves a face-to-face relationship. Corporations demand employee loyalty but are much less willing to be loyal in return. The fear is that one's allegiance to the organization will advance the interest of the organization without any reciprocal loyalty to the employee. This is particularly true in the first years of this century when many news organizations, particularly newspapers, either went out of business, ceased their printing operations, or suffered severe economic cutbacks.

Most ethical decisions, however, are not about loyalties to corporations or loyalty to an abstract concept such as freedom of the press or the public's right to know. Most everyday loyalty decisions are about how you treat the subject of your interview or how you consider the consumer of your advertising. Such ethical decisions bring to the forefront the notion of *reciprocity*. Simply articulated, reciprocity requires that loyalty should not work against the interest of either party.

Even in a time of shifting loyalties, there are some loyalties that should only be reluctantly abandoned such as loyalty to humanity and loyalty to truth. *Virtually no situation in media ethics calls for inhumane treatment or withholding the truth.* You can probably articulate other loyalties you would rarely, if ever, abandon. Even if you can't foresee every possible conflict of loyalty in your media profession, knowing where your ultimate loyalties lie is a good start to avoiding conflicts.

THE POTTER BOX

Ethical decision-making models, such as the one in chapter 1 by Sissela Bok, help you make an ethical choice. In this chapter, you will learn a second decision-making model, one that incorporates loyalties into the reasoning process. The model was developed by Harvard theologian Ralph Potter and is called the Potter Box. Its initial use requires that you go through four steps to arrive at an ethical judgment. The case below will be used to help familiarize you with the model.

You are the editor of a newspaper of about 30,000 circulation in a western city of about 80,000. Your police reporter regularly reports on sexual assaults in the community.

While the newspaper has a policy of not revealing the names of rape victims, it routinely reports where assaults occur, the circumstances, and a description of the assailant, if available.

Tonight, the police reporter is preparing to write a story about a rape that occurred in the early-morning hours yesterday on the roof of the downtown bus station. Police report that the young woman who was raped went willingly to the roof of the bus station with her attacker. Although she is 25, she lives in a group home for the educable mentally handicapped in the city, one of seven women living there.

She could not describe her assailant, and police have no suspects.

Your reporter asks you for advice about how much detail, and what detail, he should include in the story.

The Potter Box has four steps that should be taken in order (see figure 4.1). They are (1) understanding the facts, (2) outlining the values inherent in the decision, (3) applying relevant philosophical principles, and (4) articulating a loyalty. You proceed through the four steps in a counterclockwise fashion, beginning with the factual situation and ending at loyalties. We will examine each step individually.

Step One: Understanding the facts of the case. In the scenario, the facts are straightforward. You have the information; your ethical choice rests with how much of it you are going to print.

Step Two: Outlining values. Values is a much-abused word in modern English. People can value everything from their loved ones to making fashion statements. In ethics, however, values takes on a more precise meaning. When you value something—an idea or a principle—it means you are willing to give up other things for it. If, as a journalist, you value truth above all things, then you must sometimes be willing to give up privacy in favor of it. In the case above, such a value system would mean that you would print every detail because you value truth and you would risk invading the privacy of a person who is in some important ways unable to defend herself. If, as a journalist,

Facts	Loyalties
Values	Principles

Figure 4.1. The Potter Box

you value both truth and privacy, then you may be willing to give up some truth, the printing of every detail, to attempt to preserve the victim's privacy.

Values often compete. An important element of using the Potter Box is to be honest about what you really do value. Both truth and privacy are lofty ideals. A less lofty ideal that most of us value is keeping our jobs. Journalists often value getting the story first or exclusively. A forthright articulation of all the values (and there will be more than one) in any particular ethical situation will help you see more clearly the choices that you face and the potential compromises you may have to make.

Step Three: Application of philosophical principles. Once you have decided what you value, you need to apply the philosophical principles outlined in the first chapter. For example, in the previous scenario, a utilitarian might argue that the greatest good is served by printing a story that alerts the community to the fact that some creep who rapes women who cannot defend themselves is still out there. Ross would argue that a journalist has duties both to the readers and to the victim and they must be weighed before making a decision.

Aristotle's Golden Mean might counsel a middle ground that balances printing every detail against printing no story at all. Kant would suggest that the maxim of protecting someone who cannot protect herself is a maxim that could be universalized, making a decision to omit some information justifiable. He would also argue to not use the woman as a means to your end—an exclusive story in this instance.

In this case, application of several ethical principles leads to the general conclusion that the newspaper should print some story, but not one that inadvertently reveals the victim's identity or that makes her out to be hopelessly naive in her trust of strangers.

However, you should be alert that while different ethical principles in this scenario lead to the same conclusion, many, if not most, ethical dilemmas may not produce such a happy result. The principles point to different and even mutually exclusive actions on your part, leaving you to decide your ultimate loyalty. But this is why the Potter Box demands that you apply more than one ethical principle, so that if (or when) they vary, you are able to explain why.

Step Four: Articulation of loyalties. The ultimate destination of the Potter Box is to arrive at a loyalty. Potter viewed loyalty as a social commitment and the results of using the Potter Box reflect that ethic. In the fourth step, you articulate your possible loyalties and decide whether they are in conflict. In the case above, you have a loyalty to the truth, to the community, to the victim, and to your job—just for starters.

But, your loyalties are not in severe conflict with one another unless you adopt an absolutist view of the truth the community needs to know. It is possible to counsel your reporter to write a story that tells the truth but omits some facts (for example, the woman's residence in a group home and her mental retardation), alerts the community to a danger (there's a creep out there who police haven't caught), protects the victim's privacy (you won't print her name or where she lives), and allows you to take pride in the job you've done (you've told the truth and not harmed anyone).

However, use of the Potter Box often highlights a conflict between loyalties. In these instances, we refer you to Royce's concept: What you choose to be loyal to should be capable of inspiring a similar loyalty in others who are both like and unlike you. Journalists are often accused of being "out of touch" with their viewers or readers, a fact for which we are highly criticized, and proper attention to loyalties can help to bridge this gap wherever it exists.

Our experience with the Potter Box has been that the vast majority of ethical decisions will allow you to sustain a variety of loyalties—they are sometimes not mutually exclusive as we saw above. However, those decisions that are most troubling are ones where a loyalty becomes so dominant that you are forced to abandon other loyalties that once seemed quite essential.

While you may initially find the stepwise process of the Potter Box somewhat cumbersome, as you learn to use it, you will become fluent in it. The following case study, "The Pimp, the Prostitute, and the Preacher," illustrates how you might use the Potter Box when making an ethical decision.

The Pimp, the Prostitute, and the Preacher

You are the court reporter for a daily newspaper in a city of about 150,000 in the Pacific Northwest. About a year ago, the local police force began to crack down on prostitutes working the downtown mall. However, the department sought to limit prostitution by arresting pimps rather than by arresting either the prostitutes or their customers. The first of those arrests has now come to trial, and your paper has assigned you to cover it.

In his opening statement, the local assistant district attorney tells the jury that in order to convict a person of pimping under state law, the state must prove first that money was exchanged for sexual favors, and second that the money was then given to a third party, the pimp, in return for protection, continued work, etc. During the first two days of the trial, he calls as witnesses four young women, ages 14 to 16, who admit they have worked as prostitutes in the city but are a great deal less clear on the disposal of their earnings. Your story after the first day of the trial summarizes the details without disclosing their names.

Near the end of the second day, the prosecutor calls as witnesses men caught paying one or more of the women to have sex with them. Among those who testify is a middle-aged man who in an almost inaudible response to a question lists his occupation as a minister at one of the more conservative Protestant churches in the city. He admits to having paid one of the young women for sex, and that day's portion of the trial ends soon after his testimony is complete.

About 45 minutes later, you are back in the office to write the story when the newsroom secretary asks you if you have a few minutes to speak with "Reverend Jones." You look up and realize you are facing the minister who testified earlier. In the open newsroom, he begs you, in tears and on his knees, not to print his name. He even holds out a copy of the story you wrote on page 1 of this morning's paper outlining why the names of the prostitutes had not been used. He asserts that, should a story with his name appear, his marriage will crumble, his children will no longer respect him, and he will lose his job.

After a few minutes, the paper's managing editor realizes what is happening and calls you, the minister, and the news editor into his office for a conference.

Using the Potter Box, determine how you would report this story. Your decision will reflect a set of loyalties as well as the values and principles you have chosen. Others may choose differently. A justification model such as Potter's or Bok's does not eliminate differences. What it will do, ideally, is ensure that your choices are grounded in sound ethical reasoning and justifiable on demand.

When you are finished, the final casting of loyalties will inevitably create another fact for the first quadrant of the box. For instance, in this case, if the decision is to run the name, anything that might subsequently happen to the minister as a result—firing, divorce, even possible suicide—is now a hypothetical "fact" for the first quadrant of the Potter Box and you go through again. If you decide not to run the minister's name and his parishioners discover his actions, the newspaper loses credibility. This is also a "fact" to be entered into the first quadrant of the Potter Box. Considering these additional although hypothetical "facts," you may want to go through the process again to see if your decision will remain the same. Regardless of your initial decision about the story, would the possibility of that subsequent "fact," obviously not known to the journalist at the time, make a difference in a later use of the Potter Box?

Now that you've made a decision about revealing the name of the minister based on the facts, we'd like to introduce additional facts. Read them and go through the Potter Box again, focusing less on the minister and more on larger issues that affect how the story is written and how it is run in the newspaper. This time, think about the notions of stereotyping, how minorities are portrayed in news reports, and what exactly we mean by "objectivity" and "truth."

As the trial continues, it becomes clear that there are other factors at work. In your largely Caucasian community, the only people arrested for pimping have been African-American. All the young women who work as prostitutes are Caucasian, as are the customers who testify. As far as prostitution goes, your Pacific Northwest version is relatively mild. There are no reports of drug use among the prostitutes and their customers, and none of the prostitutes has complained of physical violence. Further, the prosecuting attorney cannot make any of the young women admit under oath that they ever gave the pimps any money. The jury verdict in this case is not guilty.

Do the new facts change your loyalties? Do they change the way you look at the trial? If so, in what way?

We recommend that you try using both the Bok and Potter justification models at various times in your ethical decision-making. Becoming a competent practitioner of both methods will provide you with greater flexibility and explanatory power. We also recommend, regardless of the approach you use, that an unvarnished and critical discussion of loyalty become part of your ethical dialogue. We believe it will enable you to anticipate situations as well as react to them.

SUGGESTED READINGS

Fletcher, G. P. (1993). *Loyalty: An essay on the morality of relationships.* New York: Oxford University Press.

Fuss, P. (1965). *The moral philosophy of Josiah Royce.* Cambridge, MA: Harvard University Press.

Hanson, K. (1986). The demands of loyalty. *Idealistic Studies, 16*, 195–204.

Hobbes, T. (1958). *Leviathan.* New York: Bobbs-Merrill.

Oldenquist, A. (1982). Loyalties. *Journal of Philosophy, 79*, 73–93.

Powell, T. F. (1967). *Josiah Royce.* New York: Washington Square Press.

CASES

CASE 4-A

FAIR OR FOUL? REPORTER/PLAYER RELATIONSHIPS IN THE SPORTS BEAT

LAUREN A. WAUGH
Oklahoma State University

On New Year's Eve 2013, Red Sox third baseman Will Middlebrooks posted a photo of himself on Twitter with New England Sports Network (NESN) reporter Jenny Dell making "official" a romantic relationship that many both inside and outside the organization had already known about. Dell had been covering the Red Sox for two seasons and was becoming more popular with the Red Sox Nation. While they are married today, their relationship raised a months-long conversation about reporter/source relationships in one of the most storied franchises and largest markets in professional sports.

According to Yahoo! Sports (Oz 2014), a month after the tweet, NESN announced Dell would be reassigned to working two smaller roles that would lower the profile she had with the Red Sox. The network and Dell parted ways in May 2014, and Dell landed a job ten days later as an NFL reporter with CBS.

Dell had 100,000 Twitter followers while reporting for the Red Sox. The NESN Red Sox reporter position is a respected role among sports media, and the position tends to lead to more prestigious roles as witnessed by the fact that Dell's predecessor had left to be a reporter with the MLB Network. The job is one of the most popular media jobs in baseball due to the popularity of the team.

It had been reported that Dell was receiving offers for more prominent jobs (Finn 2014), such as a position with FOX Sports 1. The *Boston Globe* wrote, "There was frustration among management that she was entertaining offers and considering an attempt to get out of her contract" at the time her relationship with a player became public.

The fact that Dell was reassigned to smaller roles with NESN led followers to believe Dell was moved because of her relationship. Though NESN never confirmed the reassignment was about the relationship, Red Sox chairman Tom Werner acknowledged, "We came to the conclusion and Jenny came to the same conclusion, that it would be a distraction for her to be a reporter. We decided that in the end, it would be better to move on and not have it be a distraction" (Finn 2014).

Dell's job was not the same as a typical television news reporter. Dell's position with NESN was solely an in-house media role for the Red Sox and objectivity was not required. Her job was to report what was happening within the Boston team, and the job rarely required her to report on controversial topics or do any investigative reporting.

Some of the competitors to NESN thought that the relationship was a conflict of interest. Bleacherreport.com claimed that the relationship gave Dell an edge, and numerous Boston news outlets stated that Dell was reportedly reassigned to a different position in an effort to combat any conflict of interest concerns that might arise from a sideline reporter interviewing the same person she was dating.

The two did not interact professionally very often, if at all. Middlebrooks's rookie season was in 2012, Dell's first year with NESN. In 2012, Middlebrooks played well until he was injured in August. The following season, he only hit .192 and was optioned to the Red Sox Triple A team in June. Middlebrooks was not in Boston for much of the 2013 season. Dell was taken off the Red Sox beat before 2014 spring training and season.

Although the New Year's Eve post was the first public confirmation of the relationship by Middlebrooks or Dell, many people in the Boston area already assumed the two were together. Breitbart.com said their relationship "was never a well-kept secret" and the *Boston Globe* said the tweet confirmed what was one of "the worst-kept secrets in the city."

However, NESN waited until the couple made their relationship "Twitter official" before reassigning Dell.

Sports Illustrated reporter Richard Deitsch conducted a survey of female reporters to see if they believed it was okay to be in a relationship with an athlete on the team they are covering (Allen 2014). He found few female reporters who agreed with what Dell was doing. *Boston Globe* sports reporter (and former Red Sox beat writer) Amalie Benjamin said, "Never. Ever. And more, it hurts the credibility of every female reporter doing it the right way." *USA Today*'s Lindsay Jones said, "Never, never, never. Did I mention never?" And Deitsch's colleague at *Sports Illustrated*, Joan Niesen stated, "Under no circumstances. None whatsoever. No, no, no."

Micro Issues

1. Is there a real potential for a conflict of interest in this case, or is this largely about keeping up appearances on the part of NESN? Justify your answer.
2. Does your opinion change knowing Middlebrooks was not a major star of the Red Sox? That NESN is not an objective news source?
3. When the story broke that Dell was involved with a potential source, should she have been fired rather than transferred? Why or why not?

Midrange Issues

1. How does your opinion of this case change if the athlete was a female and the reporter was a male?
2. Does it make a difference that Dell was working at NESN, where the Red Sox are treated as a "home team?"
3. Does it matter that Dell is not a "hard news" reporter expected to be fair and objective, or expected to do investigative reporting?

Macro Issues

1. Is what Jenny Dell and others do at networks such as the NESN "real" journalism?
2. Critique the comments by the three females interviewed by Deitsch. Are they correct that this hurts all female reporters when one acts like Dell? Is this an overreaction given her job and his relative lack of success as a player?

CASE 4-B

TO WATCH OR TO REPORT: WHAT JOURNALISTS WERE THINKING IN THE MIDST OF DISASTER

LEE WILKINS
Wayne State University
University of Missouri

Millions saw it live. A CNN crew including Ed Lavandera, producer Jason Morris, and cameraman Joel De La Rosa filmed and then helped volunteer first-responder Austin Seth as he pulled 86-year old Elmore Jones, his 83-year-old wife JoAnne, and his daughter, Pam, from their Houston home in the aftermath of Hurricane Harvey.

Lavandera wasn't the only journalist to make this choice. "I'm a journalist, but I'm also a human being," said David Begnaud, who helped Houston residents out of a flooded house and into a rescue boat where he had been riding. The whole event was streamed live on CBSN digital.

The Weather Channel's Jim Cantore made the same decision. While on the air, he interviewed a man who was waiting for his daughter's family to be evacuated. Later, some residents who decided to leave the area told Cantore they had done so because of what he had said on television. His Weather Channel colleague was broadcast holding a crying baby, the youngest member of the family to be evacuated.

"I learned this 12 years ago to the date with Katrina's landfall," Cantore said in a *Washington Post* story. "When people are in trouble, you just do what you can to help. I could give a crap about TV at that point."

A woman struggling with a television set interrupted a live shot with Matt Finn, a Fox News reporter who was covering the hurricane from Port Arthur, Texas. Finn motioned the camera away from the woman and helped her when the shot ended. Finn also provided exhausted fire fighters with transportation—a detail that did not make it into his news coverage.

"I'm not making myself the story, and I'm not a hero," he said. "The people I'm looking at right now—the police officers and the firefighters—are the heroes."

Micro Issues

1. Kelly McBride, vice president of the Poynter Institute said that a reporter's job is to inform. "Any time you spend your energy on helping someone, that is energy and resources not spent on telling the story to the audience." Evaluate this statement in light of the journalists' actions and rationale outlined above.
2. How does your evaluation differ from the "shoot now, edit later" decision that sometimes explains how still photographers decide which images to capture?

Midrange Issues

1. Less than two weeks later, Hurricane Irma pounded the state of Florida. Coverage included multiple journalists broadcasting live in the teeth of the storm while simultaneously airing government instructions to evacuate. Evaluate these actions in light of the cases outlined above.

2. What philosophical theory supports your decision?
3. Should journalists broadcast (e.g., on personal Twitter feeds) photos or videos shot by citizens at the scene of a hurricane or other disaster despite the fact that those citizens have been encouraged to evacuate or take other measures to remain safe?

Macro Issues

1. How are the actions described above distinct from stating a personal opinion in a news story?
2. These decisions by news reporters occurred during a time when the media were being called the "enemy of the people" by President Donald J. Trump. Should footage of these actions be used to promote the profession as part of a public relations campaign?

CASE 4-C

PUBLIC/ON-AIR JOURNALIST VS. PRIVATE/ONLINE LIFE: CAN IT WORK?

MADISON HAGOOD
Oklahoma Christian University

On Oct. 9, 2017, viewers tuned in to the 6 p.m. SportsCenter offering on ESPN only to find that one of the hosts, Jemele Hill, had been suspended from the ESPN airwaves for two weeks for running afoul of the network's social media policy. Almost immediately, the question of whether public figures should be able to express their private political opinions on social media came under scrutiny in ESPN's handling of SportsCenter co-host Hill's series of tweets from her personal Twitter account.

Hill, who first got a chance to co-host ESPN's flagship program in February 2017, came under fire that September when she called President Trump a "white supremacist who has surrounded himself with other white supremacists" in a tweet that has since been deleted. Hill also claimed Trump was the "most ignorant, offensive president of [her] lifetime," a "bigot," and "unqualified and unfit to be president."

Despite issuing an apology for her tweets, which "painted ESPN in an unfair light," Hill found herself serving a two-week suspension after a second breach of ESPN social media conduct, when she encouraged "paying customers" to "boycott" Dallas Cowboys owner Jerry Jones' advertisers in light of the ongoing 2017 NFL controversy concerning player conduct during the national anthem.

Following the lead of ex-San Francisco 49ers quarterback Colin Kaepernick from the 2016 season, many NFL players had chosen to sit, kneel, or stay in the locker room during the playing of the anthem in the fall of 2017. Jones, however, had orchestrated his team's protest carefully—a well-televised knee before the anthem and respect during it. He had even participated in the pseudo-event himself. Later, Jones had been quoted as saying that any Cowboy who did not stand for the anthem would be benched. At that point, Hill took to social media.

"If they don't kneel, some will see them as sellouts," Hill said in a series of tweets on her personal account on Oct. 8, 2017. "By drawing a line in the sand, Jerry put his players under more scrutiny and threw them under the bus . . . If the rationale behind JJ's stance is keeping the fan base happy, make him see that he underestimated how all of his fan base feels."

ESPN, which has a partnership with the NFL through 2021, told ThinkProgress (Legum 2017) that the key factor in Hill's suspension was the reference to a boycott of Cowboys' sponsors, many of which also sponsor the network. In a statement, an ESPN spokesperson said that in the aftermath of Hill's suspension, "all employees were reminded of how individual tweets may reflect negatively on ESPN and that such actions would have consequences."

While on one hand, ESPN and other networks have encouraged their commentators and personalities such as Hill to "build their personal 'brand' through commentary." ESPN public editor Jim Brady told the *Washington Post* (Farhi 2017) that "media companies are simultaneously asking many of their personalities to be active and engaging on social media but not partisan or opinionated. It's a line that is, at best, blurry and, at worst, nonexistent."

Through two sets of guidelines for its employees, "Social Networking" and "Political and Social Issues," ESPN (2017) encourages its employees to "avoid personal attacks and inflammatory rhetoric . . . Think before your tweet. Understand that at all times you are representing ESPN, and Twitter (as with other social sites) offers the equivalent of a live microphone. Simple rule: If you wouldn't say it on the air or write it in a column, don't post it on any social network."

Employees of companies such as ESPN are held responsible, not only for the content they post on their personal accounts, but also for the audience their posts reach and the potential effects of an improper post.

ESPN's *Outside the Lines* anchor Bob Ley told *Sports Illustrated* (Deitsch 2017) following Hill's first breach in social media policy:

> The usual standard of saying only what you would with a microphone in your hand apparently no longer applies. These are emotional, political times. There are important responsibilities that come with the many perks, and chief among those these days is realizing your words carry the weight of your platform. You speak for more than yourself.

Hill left SportsCenter in January 2018. She now writes for the ESPN site *The Undefeated*, which blends sports, race, and culture.

Micro Issues

1. Was it right for Hill to be suspended by ESPN for tweets published on her personal account? Justify your answer.
2. As an employee, do you believe you represent your employers, even when you are "off the clock?"
3. Should one be forced to sign a social media policy to gain employment?

Midrange Issues

1. If Hill had not been previously warned about social media after her tweets about President Trump, do you believe her calling for a boycott of Jerry Jones would have been enough by itself for a suspension by the network? Justify your answer.
2. Hill is an African-American woman. Do you see any hints of either sexism or racism in this case, and, if so, where? Would a popular male anchor have been treated differently?
3. If Hill had a lesser role within ESPN, do you think her punishment would have been as severe?

Macro Issues

1. Is a sport event's integrity lost if there is no playing of the national anthem beforehand?
2. In the context of the Black Lives Matter movement and the protests in Charlottesville in 2017, do you believe minority television personalities' comments and views are met with more scrutiny than those of caucasian commentators?

CASE 4-D

WHEN YOU ARE THE STORY: SEXUAL HARASSMENT IN THE NEWSROOM

LEE WILKINS
Wayne State University
University of Missouri

By the time you read this case study, this list will be longer:

Roger Ailes, Fox News
Matt Lauer, NBC's Today Show
Mike Oreskes, NPR
Charlie Rose, CBS
David Sweeney, NPR
John Hockenberry, WNYC
Leonard Lopate and Jonathan Schwartz, WNYC
Harvey Weinstein, The Weinstein Company
John Lassater, Disney/Pixar
Glen Thrush, *New York Times*
Bill O'Reilly, Fox News
Garrison Keeler, The Prairie Home Companion

But, the names on *this* list epitomize a series of important questions. The first, how to report a story when your own organization, and specifically your own newsroom, is involved?

NBC chose to announce Matt Lauer's firing on the *Today Show* less than 12 hours after the initial complaint surfaced. *Today Show* host Savannah Guthrie fought back tears as she read the announcement, noting, "This is a sad morning at NBC News." The show's ratings jumped after the announcement. Lauer waited a little more than two days to respond, and then released a statement that read, "There are no words to express my sorrow and regret for the pain I have caused others by words and actions. To the people I have hurt, I am truly sorry. As I am writing this I realize the depth of the damage and disappointment I have left behind at home and at NBC."

Fox played it differently. Charges against Bill O'Reilly dated back to 2002, and his contract was continually renewed while some of the women involved received financial settlements totaling about $13 million. It was only after those settlements were reported in the *New York Times* that

O'Reilly was fired. Months later, the *Times* reported that O'Reilly had settled yet another claim for $32 million right before he signed another contract renewal with the network. O'Reilly characterized his firing as a "political and financial hit job." He added, "There were a lot of other business things in play at that time and still today that 21st century was involved with." (Some of those considerations are outlined in the case study Murdoch's Mess in chapter 7.)

NPR played it yet a third way. On Nov. 19, 2017, it aired an hour-long special, reported by women at NPR, in which the network's response to sexual harassment claims was part of the focus of the in-depth coverage. That coverage explored why sexual harassment had become a flash point at this time in history, explored how men felt about the issue, and defined sexual harassment in the workplace. NPR's reporting about the issue, even when it involved other news organizations, always included a mention that NPR itself is involved in the harassment scandal.

In December 2017, the #MeToo movement was named a person of the year by *Time* magazine.

Micro Issues

1. Is sexual harassment a legitimate news story?
2. Evaluate the distinct approaches of the news organizations outlined above, as well as others that you may be familiar with, in terms of transparency and privacy (discussed in chapters 2 and 5, respectively).
3. If you were to write a "best practices" guide to how news organizations should report on sexual harassment within the organization, what would you suggest? Why?
4. Compare the reporting about sexual harassment by the news organizations outlined above with that conducted by the *Boston Globe* and described in the Spotlight case in chapter 9.
5. How does the fact that other news organizations are reporting on sexual harassment charges in news organizations that compete with them influence your response?

Midrange Issues

1. In most jurisdictions, certain kinds of sexual harassment are also criminal conduct. In the United States and in criminal cases, people are considered innocent until proven guilty. Do charges of sexual harassment carry a different standard of proof and evidence? Why?

2. Sexual harassment is the most obvious and vicious form of
   misogyny in contemporary culture. How are changes in tolerance
   of acts of sexual harassment likely or unlikely to change underlying
   patterns of discrimination and marginalization of women, either
   in the workplace or as the focus of news and entertainment
   programming?

The second set of questions these responses to sexual harassment
raise are more philosophical in nature. In general, they center on the
role and effectiveness of punishment in human relationships, from the
political to the personal. Most people consider being fired over charges
of sexual harassment a form of punishment. In the current climate, Emily
Lindin, a columnist at *Teen Vogue*, summed up one view concisely on
Twitter: "I'm actually not at all concerned about innocent men losing
their jobs over false sexual assault/harassment allegations," she wrote.
"If some innocent men's reputations have to take a hit in the process of
undoing the patriarchy, that is a price I am absolutely willing to pay."
Lindin, who was criticized for the comment, noted that women had
been afraid for decades and disbelieved and discounted when they
attempted to report the issue. Lindin voiced the anger many women felt
and continue to feel about the issue.

Feminist philosopher Martha Nussbaum notes that in any society,
in situations of profound oppression and systematic injustice, trust is
nonexistent. "It is very easy for the oppressed to believe that trust is
impossible and that they can win their struggle only by dominating
in their turn." In her 2016 book *Anger and Forgiveness: Resentment,
Generosity, Justice*, Nussbaum examines the lives and work of Gandhi,
Martin Luther King, and Nelson Mandela as examples of revolutionary
justice. Nussbaum sees more potential in Mandela's approach, noting,
"A nation torn by horrible acts may find itself unable to move forward.
Angry feelings may have such a deep grip on people's minds that they
cannot be changed to forward-looking projects and feelings" (Nussbaum
2016,. 244). With Mandela, Nussbaum suggests that anger itself,
while understandable, is a philosophical error, one that replicates the
dominant/dominated relationship that produced it in the first place.
Instead, she recommends generosity and reciprocity. Nussbaum notes,
"If this book achieves anything, I hope it achieves that sort of square-
one reorientation, getting its readers to see clearly the irrationality and
stupidity of anger" (Nussbaum 2016, 249.) "Our institutions should
model our best selves, not our worst. . . . Furthermore, when there is
great injustice, we should not use that fact as an excuse for childish

and undisciplined behavior. Injustice should be greeted with protest and careful, courageous strategic action. But the end goal must remain always in view: As King said so simply, "A world where men and women can live together" (Nussbaum 2016, 249).

Macro Issues

1. Evaluate this statement: Sexual harassment is an expression of power that has been confounded with sex.
2. How might news organizations that have been plagued by sexual harassment and other forms of misogyny develop the "forward-looking projects and feelings" of which Nussbaum speaks?
3. Is Nussbaum's approach too idealistic for the current cultural climate? If your answer is yes, what alternative do you believe might be effective?

CASE 4-E

WHOSE FACEBOOK PAGE IS IT ANYWAY?

AMY SIMONS
University of Missouri

Barrett Tryon joined the *Colorado Springs Gazette* staff in April 2012. He was hired to help draw users to the newspaper website, providing updates on breaking news and enterprise stories.

Tryon was no stranger to the Colorado Springs market. He'd spent more than a decade working for KRDO-TV, an ABC affiliate. In 2011, he won an Emmy for "Best Newscast" in a medium-sized market. That same year, the station's website—of which Tryon was the managing editor—was given the award for best website by the Associated Press. On his station bio, he is described as "the face behind KRDO.com and KRDO's Facebook and Twitter pages." As the face of those pages, Tryon drew in more than 200 new followers to the station's sites each week.

If there was one thing Barrett Tryon was confident he knew, it was how to use social media responsibly.

That's why what happened to him at the *Gazette* surprised so many.

It started with a *Los Angeles Times* story published on June 12, 2012, announcing Freedom Communications Holdings Inc.'s sale of

Barrett Tryon shared a link.
5 hours ago

The new owner hopes to spin off the smaller papers in separate deals by the end of the summer to help finance the purchase of the Register, according to an editor at the paper who was not authorized to speak publicly. These are the Gazette in Colorado Springs, Colo.; the Appeal-Democrat in Marysville, Calif.; the Desert Dispatch in Barstow; the Porterville (Calif.) Record; the Daily Press in Victorville; and the Sun in Yuma, Ariz.

Orange County Register, six sister papers are sold to Boston group
www.latimes.com

The Orange County Register and six other daily newspapers have been sold to a Boston investment group in

Figure 4.2.   Barrett Tryon

the *Orange County Register* and six other newspapers to a Boston investment group. One of those papers: the *Gazette.*

Tryon posted a link to that story to his Facebook page, along with a pull quote highlighting his employer's direct involvement.

Three hours later, Tryon's boss, Carmen Boles, told him via email that the Facebook post was a violation of Freedom Communication's social media policy, stating the *Los Angeles Times* article "does not meet our standards of factual information." Soon after, in a second email, she included this passage:

> Freedom Communications, Inc.'s Associate Handbook/Confidentially and Proprietary Rights policy prohibits you from posting disparaging or defamatory . . . statements about the company or its business interests, but you should also avoid social media communications that might be misconstrued in a way that could damage the company's goodwill and business reputation, even indirectly.

Tryon maintained he was acting within his rights under the First Amendment, telling his boss in an email, "it's on my personal account, and from an LA Times article, I'm not removing it."

The email exchange continued for several hours, and Boles told Tryon that corporate human resources would be handling the matter. Tryon, standing his ground, told Bowles "it's only natural for someone to be interested in something that directly affects you. . . . I think there's a huge difference between saying 'eff off' versus pulling a quote. But, since I violated the policy, I'll deal with the consequences."

The human resources department scheduled a meeting with Tryon for June 14, 2012. That meeting never happened because, Tryon told the *Colorado Springs Independent*, he insisted on bringing an attorney. Instead, Freedom Communications put him on administrative leave without hearing his side of the story. Meanwhile, the paper's decision ignited debate over the ethics and legality of social media policies.

Almost all news organizations and professional associations have some kind of social media policy or guideline. Many, such as NPR, the *New York Times*, and the *Roanoke Times*, even make them public. Most read like a list of common sense reminders: identify yourself as a journalist and a representative of your newsroom, maintain standards of confirmation and attribution, maintain copyright by linking to content instead of reposting, assume anything you post is public, etc. Some, such as the Associated Press and ASNE, urge journalists not to break news on social networks, but to do it through conventional publishing channels, and to keep "company confidential information confidential."

According to the National Labor Relations Act, which gives workers the right to organize, unionize, and bargain collectively, some of these widely shared guidelines might be illegal. In response to Tryon's case, Poynter.org published a memo issued by the National Labor Relations Board that ruled the following social media policy provisions unlawful:

- "Avoid harming the image and integrity of the company."
- "Do not express public opinions about the workplace, work satisfaction or dissatisfaction, wages, hours or work conditions."
- "Don't comment on any legal matters, including pending litigation or disputes."
- Instruction not to "reveal non-public company information on any public site."

"I really want to emphasize this—I think this is so important—is that this is not an effort for me to slam the *Gazette*, to slam Freedom Communications, to slam the new owners, 2100 Trust. That's not what I'm doing," Tryon told the *Colorado Springs Independent*.

"I'm standing on principle that what I posted absolutely was not breaking any type of social media policy; I didn't interject any opinion. And the fact of the matter is it was on my personal account; I have a vested interest in what's happening with the new owner; and like anyone else in the country, if they were getting bought out by a new company would damn well do your research—as a reporter, or not—to look into that new company."

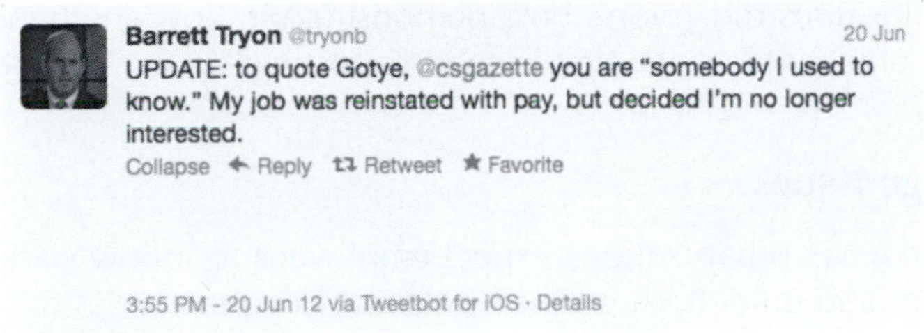

Figure 4.3. Twitter.com/tryonb

Figure 4.4. Twitter.com/tryonb

On June 19, 2012, about a week after Barrett Tryon posted the *Los Angeles Times* story to his Facebook page, his bosses at Freedom Communications called him with an offer to reinstate him. Tryon resigned from the newspaper instead. He announced his decision to followers on Twitter, referencing a hit song by the musical group, Gotye.

"I think after I realized there was support from so many people locally and nationally that I'm not really interested in working for an organization [where] we would even have this conversation; that there was never a dialogue to begin with—and that's unfortunate," he told the *Colorado Springs Independent*. "I hope that the takeaway is that people realize that, if you do have a social-media policy in place, it's important that you know what it is, and how it can be interpreted or misinterpreted."

Micro Issues

1. Did Barrett Tryon violate Freedom Communications' social media policy?
2. Was Freedom Communications within its right to demand Tryon remove the post from his Facebook page?
3. What risks do employees take when posting about their employer on social media? A competitor? A news story that has already been published or broadcast?

4. What loyalties did Tryon's boss demonstrate in how she handled her initial objections to the first Facebook posting?

Midrange Issues

1. Should news organizations expect employees to follow social media policies and guidelines on their personal accounts?
2. Evaluate the social media policy that suggests that news should not be broken on social media but through more traditional channels.
3. What, if any, types of social media posts should be fireable offenses for a journalist?

Macro Issues

1. Should news agencies publish their social media policies for public view?
2. Is there such a thing as "private" social media presence for a journalist? Should anything published under a journalist's name uphold all journalistic standards?
3. Tyron said he had a First Amendment right to publish on his Facebook page. Evaluate this claim ethically. Does the First Amendment trump professional loyalty in this case?
4. Do news organizations that promote their websites and encourage employees to use social media set themselves up for these sorts of conflicts? How might they be avoided?

CASE 4-F

WHERE EVERYBODY KNOWS YOUR NAME: REPORTING AND RELATIONSHIPS IN A SMALL MARKET

GINNY WHITEHOUSE
Eastern Kentucky University

Everybody is a source when you're covering an agricultural town with a population under 12,000.

But Sunnyside Police Sergeant Phil Schenck had not been a source for Jessica Luce when he asked her out for a date during a Halloween party in 1999. Luce had worked as a general assignment reporter at the *Yakima Herald-Republic* for almost a year. Sunnyside, Washington, was one of four communities she covered in this first job out of college. The two spent time together infrequently over the next two months.

"I was interested in him, we had fun, but if I had been asked what was going on I would have said we were friends," Luce said.

Nonetheless, a co-worker was incredulous. Luce remembers him saying, "You can't go out on a date with a source. It's one of the biggest taboos in journalism!"

The *Herald-Republic*'s four-page code of ethics advises staff to avoid conflicts of interest but offered no specifics on personal relationships that might cause conflicts of interest.

Luce decided to keep her relationship with Schenck quiet. She had never needed Schenck as a source and never thought the occasion would arise.

Schenck's boss, however, was another matter. Sunnyside Police Chief Wallace Anderson had been accused of shooting a great blue heron outside the police station, storing explosives at the station house, and of having a threatening temper. Following a lengthy and expensive investigation, Anderson resigned in November.

By New Year's Day, Luce and Schenck decided they were definitely dating. "I kept my relationship under wraps save for a few confidants at work. I felt the relationship would be perceived as something wrong," Luce said. "But I didn't see it interfering with my job. Phil and I didn't talk about work as much as normal couples might. We knew it wasn't fair to either one of us."

In mid-February, Schenck was named acting captain, the number two position in the Sunnyside police department, and the official media spokesman. Luce realized she needed to be pulled off the Sunnyside police beat immediately. Her editors agreed.

"It was hard to talk with them about my private relationship, and I was forced to define things about the relationship that I hadn't even done for myself," Luce said.

Craig Troianello, her city editor, sat her down for a long conversation. "Jessica made it easy because she was straightforward. We didn't ask intimate questions— that's irrelevant in this case," Troianello said. "By taking the proactive ethical stand that she did, it was easy for us to deal with this."

Luce said Troianello emphasized that he was not questioning her integrity. However, he had to make sure he hadn't overlooked something that could be perceived as a conflict by readers.

"This was a lesson on perception versus reality," Luce said. Luce's reporting did not affect Schenck's promotion, nor had Schenck ever implied that a story should or should not have been covered. Nonetheless, Schenck benefited from the chief's departure.

Troianello said he was never worried that Luce's reporting was compromised, but he wanted to make sure the newspaper was above suspicion. "Issues involving the police department were in the forefront of the news," Troianello said. "People could read anything into it—that she was protecting the chief, that she was trying to bring the chief down. Those kinds of spins drove my concern."

On the other hand, Schenck questions whether a strict conflict-of-interest standard is realistic in a small town. "Everybody is a potential source—even the clerk at the grocery store. We eat food. If her husband or boyfriend is a farmer, you could say she is promoting eating. This is an ideal that might be somewhat impractical," Schenck said. "If you can't be a real person, how can you report on real people?"

Luce says if she had to do it all over again she would not have kept the relationship a secret as long as she did. Nonetheless, it would still be hard to talk to a supervisor about dating. Troianello said he understands the complexities of a journalist's personal life but would rather Luce had brought the relationship to the newspaper's attention by New Year's Day, when the two began dating.

However, he understands the dynamic of the situation. "She's in a small town where the number of people with four-year degrees and professionals is small," Troianello said. "It seems like there will be some mixing at some point. Relationships could occur as naturally as it does in the newsroom. I married a copy editor."

Once their relationship went public (they were later engaged), Luce was surprised at how supportive the community and city officials were, including the new police chief (someone other than Schenck). "What we as journalists see as an ethical problem and conflict of interest isn't necessarily going to be seen as an ethical problem by the public."

However, Luce never heard comments one way or another from the former chief or his supporters. On several occasions, city officials have questioned whether Schenck leaked information to Luce or *Herald-Republic* reporters. Schenck simply explained that he had not. "I deal with stuff every day that Jessica would love to get her hands on," Schenck said. "But we just don't talk about it."

Luce now covers education in the city of Yakima.

Micro Issues

1. Did Luce have a responsibility to tell her editors about her relationship with Schenck? If so, when should Luce have informed them?

2. What responsibility did the *Yakima Herald-Republic* editors have to explain expectations on conflicts of interest? Is spelling out those expectations necessary or appropriate in a code of ethics?
3. How would the ethical questions have changed if Schenck worked in another capacity for the city, such as being a teacher?
4. How would the ethical questions have changed if Luce and Schenck had remained only friends?

Midrange Issues

1. What aspects of their lives should journalists be able to keep private?
2. Is public perception of an ethical problem truly relevant?
3. Journalists spend most of their time with two groups: their sources and their co-workers. Considering those limitations, is dating possible or advisable?
4. Recently, NBC "Dateline" correspondent Maria Shriver took a leave of absence as her husband, Arnold Schwarzenegger, ran a successful race for governor of California. As she returns to her duties, what limitations, if any, should be imposed on her reporting? Justify your decision.

Macro Issues

1. Can journalists cover communities effectively if they are expected to remain remote and removed?
2. How specific should codes of ethics be on conflicts of interest?

CASE 4-G

QUIT, BLOW THE WHISTLE, OR GO WITH THE FLOW?

ROBERT D. WAKEFIELD
Brigham Young University

Anyone who spends sufficient years in public relations will face a crisis of conscience. Practitioners are trained for the tenuous task of balancing institutional advocacy with the "public interest" (Newsom, Turk, and Kruckeberg 1996). Yet this role can lead to personal conflict, as it did in my case.

The setting was an urban school district with about 40 schools and more than 35,000 students. Its superintendent had a national reputation for innovative community outreach, and he was a media favorite. I worked with him for five years before he accepted a statewide position. His replacement was a quiet man with conservative views who, along with the administrative team he brought with him, believed that educators were trained to run the schools and could do so best with minimal interference.

Like most inner-city school districts, the system was losing students as people moved to the suburbs. In the previous decade, a student population that once filled four high schools could now fill only three.

The seven-member school board had approached—and then abandoned—the question of closing one of the schools because the proposal aroused such strong feelings among students, faculty, and parents. However, the new administration, trying to balance those responses against the financial drain of supporting an additional high school on taxpayer dollars, decided to broach the question again.

Promised a tumultuous situation, the new administrators aggravated the problem by how they handled it. Rather than sharing the issue with the community or with school faculties to seek a mutually agreeable solution, they tried to resolve the entire problem behind closed doors.

I first learned about the closed-door approach at a "study meeting" with the school board. The new superintendent held these informal meetings during his earliest days in the district; they tended to be so boring and ambiguous that journalists seldom attended.

Before the meeting in question, the superintendent asked me whether any media would be present. I told him one reporter might come late. As the meeting began, I was surprised to hear him tell the board and the few staff members, "If any reporter shows up, I will change the subject—but today we're going to talk about closing a high school." He then outlined the results of meetings he had already held on the issue, discussed a proposal from a local community college to buy the building so it would not be abandoned, and sought the support of the four high school principals.

Thus began my ethical conundrum. I agreed that the enrollment problem was serious and that closing a school was probably the best alternative, but I opposed the administration's method of resolving the issue. As public relations officer, I believed that public institutions must be open and that involving those affected by the closure in the actual decision-making process would eventually generate long-term support for whatever decision was made. I was appalled at the attempts to exclude the public, but I said nothing.

Closed doors can quickly swing ajar, and it took less than one day for news of the decision to leak. The school targeted for closure was one of the oldest in the state. It had recently received a US Department of Education award as an exemplary inner-city school, but its community was the least affluent and arguably the least politically powerful.

The day after the "study session," and with a regular board meeting scheduled for the same evening, reporters called to verify what they were hearing. (Chief executives often forget that supervisors of individual units within the system have their own allegiances. In this case, one of the high school principals left the "study meeting" and informed his teaching staff that they would be receiving transfer students "from that inner-city school." The rumors began.)

After the phone calls, I asked the superintendent what he planned to say at the board meeting and was told, "We will discuss space utilization needs." I told him about the calls and that our jobs would be threatened if we were not truthful with the community. To his credit, he responded quickly and openly. The evening meeting unfolded as expected. The room was jammed with district patrons and with the media. The expected lines were drawn. Underlying the fervor was a common theme: closing a traditional high school was awful enough, but the secretive way in which the administration had reached its conclusions was unforgivable.

The next several weeks were an intense period of work for a young public relations officer. I did media interviews, talk shows, and forums to explain the situation. I also met with dozens of teachers, parents, and citizens, both to hear their comments and to take their suggestions. I had to be careful that my words represented the district instead of myself. I had worked with some local reporters for several years and felt comfortable giving them background so they could seek additional materials without revealing me as the original source. It was a personal risk, but the reporters never betrayed my trust.

Two additional incidents epitomized my ethical struggles. The first occurred after the initial board meeting, when a top administrator said the community misunderstood why decisions were made behind closed doors. I lobbied for openness. The administrator admonished me to remember who paid my salary, a rebuke that confirmed the new administration did not share my own values.

The second incident occurred when I was asked to meet with a man who had been chosen to speak on behalf of the community. I had taken only a few steps into his office when he said to me, "You don't agree with your administration, do you?" My response was silence while he explained his position.

For some reason, it was this encounter that forced my crisis of conscience: Do I quit, blow the whistle, or keep quiet? I had a wife and child to support; the employment picture at the time was not robust.

Right or wrong, I surmised that the various relationships I had developed could appease many angry feelings. I also believed in the importance of education. So, I decided to stay through the crisis, then seek new employment.

About one month into the crisis, the board retained a consultant who, like me, believed in open communication. Two weeks later, four board members came to my office and requested a meeting. Because this constituted a majority of the board, such an assembly violated the law requiring the meeting be made public. I violated the law and invited them to stay. They said they were worn down by the constant tension and asked what I, as a public relations practitioner, thought they should do.

To me, the answer was straightforward. Relying on basic public relations formulas and common sense, I suggested that they could diffuse the tension by reverting to what should have been done in the first place: Announce that selected representatives from throughout the city would form a committee to help review the situation and come to a decision that would then be discussed by the board.

To my surprise, the board members took this advice to the administration, and much of what I recommended was done. A few months later, the school was closed in a tearful farewell. And, five weeks after the school closed, I accepted a job with a local public relations firm.

Micro Issues

1. What sort of press releases or other talking points should Wakefield have prepared once the rumors began?
2. Should Wakefield have gone off the record with reporters he trusted?
3. Are there some sorts of decisions governmental bodies make that really should be kept from the media and hence the public? Is this one of them?
4. How should Wakefield have responded to the racial subtext of some of the protests about the closing of the school?

Midrange Issues

1. Should Wakefield have "blown the whistle" on the board members who requested an illegal meeting?
2. Was it appropriate for Wakefield to advise the board to take an approach different from that suggested by the superintendent?

3. How much does Wakefield's previous experience with a different superintendent influence his understanding of how the district works? How did this "workplace" socialization influence his ethical thinking?

Macro Issues

1. To whom should Wakefield be loyal?
2. Should he ever have told members of the community of his own personal views?
3. How does Wakefield's job compare with that of a press secretary for a political figure?
4. Is it ever appropriate to keep journalists in the dark about how political decisions are made?

CASE 4-H

HOW ONE TWEET RUINED A LIFE

PHILIP PATTERSON
Oklahoma Christian University

On Dec. 20, 2013, Justine Sacco boarded a plane in New York headed for South Africa via London to spend the holidays with her family. By the time the final plane landed, her life would change forever.

Sacco had a dream job. At the age of 30, she was senior director of corporate communications at IAC (NASDAQ: IAC), a 20-year-old company that billed itself as "a leading media and Internet company comprised of widely known consumer brands such as Vimeo, Dictionary.com, Dotdash, The Daily Beast and Investopedia." Among IAC's other holdings at the time was their popular "dating portfolio" that included Match and Tinder and their home services sites such as HomeAdvisor and Angie's List. Headquartered in New York City's Chelsea neighborhood, with offices worldwide, IAC called itself "a trailblazer at the crossroads of e-commerce, media and the Internet, with brands and products that delight and engage millions of people all over the world."

On this day, Sacco took to Twitter to share with her 170 followers the struggles of travel. The first couple of posts were aimed at fellow passengers and observations from her layover. One such tweet said:

Weird German Dude: You're in First Class. It's 2014. Get some deodorant. Thank God for pharmaceuticals.

Another during her layover in London's Heathrow airport read:

Chilly—cucumber sandwiches—bad teeth. Back in London!

Then one additional tweet written just before she boarded the plane for Cape Town took things to a whole different level. That tweet read:

Going to Africa. Hope I don't get AIDS. Just kidding. I'm white!

Sacco boarded the plane for her 11-hour flight—the last leg of her long journey home—and would not realize until landing in Cape Town that her tweet had gone viral. Without her being aware, Sacco's Twitter feed had quickly filled with tweets from others labeling her a racist. Thousands of social media enthusiasts were counting the hours until Sacco's plane landed to observe her pain via social media. The hashtag #HasJustineLandedYet tracked Sacco's whereabouts and allowed other users to post their thoughts as well. One Twitter user drove to the airport to tweet her arrival live. And even though Sacco's friend deleted Sacco's Twitter account, the tweet lived on.

As her plane was taxiing the runway in Cape Town, Sacco noticed texts from people she had not spoken to in years. Many were offering her condolences for some reason that she couldn't even surmise at the time. The confusion continued until her best friend reached her and explained to Sacco that her tweet was the No. 1 worldwide trend on Twitter. Enraged tweets and blatant threats were among the many responses that shot Sacco to the top of the social media world. Even though Sacco released an apology statement, she was forced to cut her vacation short as workers threatened to strike at the hotels she had booked if she showed up. She was told no one could guarantee her safety if she stayed.

In an article entitled "How one stupid tweet blew up Justine Sacco's life," author Jon Ronson (2015) recounted how Justine, with a Twitter following of 170, had been "outed" and become an international phenomenon in less than a day. In that article for the *New York Times Magazine*, Ronson reported that blogger Sam Biddle was the first to retweet Justine's misguided attempt at humor. Biddle was then the editor of "Valleywag," Gawker Media's tech-industry blog. He retweeted it to his 15,000 followers and eventually posted it on Valleywag accompanied by the headline, "And Now, a Funny Holiday Joke From IAC's P.R. Boss." While doing his research for the article, Ronson received an email from Biddle in January 2014 explaining his reasoning: "The fact that she was a P.R. chief made it delicious. It's satisfying to be able to say, 'O.K., let's make a racist tweet by a senior IAC employee count this time.' And it did. I'd do it again." In that same email, Biddle later claimed to "certainly never hope to ruin anyone's life" and ended by saying she'd be "fine eventually, if not already."

After issuing an apology statement and losing her job, Sacco still struggled with the mistake she had made. In the only on-the-record interview she gave on the topic, she told Ronson (2015), "I cried out my body weight in the first 24 hours. It was incredibly traumatic. You don't sleep. You wake up in the middle of the night forgetting where you are." Later, she sent an email to Ronson that read, in part, "Unfortunately, I am not a character on 'South Park' or a comedian, so I had no business commenting on the epidemic in such a politically incorrect manner on a public platform," she wrote. "To put it simply, I wasn't trying to raise awareness of AIDS or piss off the world or ruin my life. Living in America puts us in a bit of a bubble when it comes to what is going on in the third world. I was making fun of that bubble."

Micro Issues

1. Of the millions of tweets sent daily, many of them far more controversial than this, why do you think this one went viral?
2. Is Biddle's motivation for what he did justified? Is his motivation relevant to determining whether his actions were ethical?

Midrange Issues

1. Do you agree or disagree with Biddle that those who work in the field of public relations or as a publicist be held to a higher standard given their background and training? Justify your answer.
2. Do you agree or disagree with Sacco that the tweet would have been acceptable had she been a comedienne? Do those who seek to make us laugh have a larger license when it comes to offensive words or offensive statements?

Macro Issues

1. Part of the appeal of certain social media sites such as Snapchat is the anonymity factor. Should free speech be absolute on such sites? Why or why not? What are the consequences of your decision?
2. Sacco later said: "Living in America puts us in a bit of a bubble when it comes to what is going on in the third world. I was making fun of that bubble." If the tweets are viewed in the light of social commentary, is the sarcasm expressed in the tweet any less racist?
3. What is the major lesson, if any, to be learned from Justine Sacco's story?

5

Privacy

Looking for Solitude in the Global Village

By the end of this chapter, you should

- appreciate the difference between the right to privacy and a need for privacy
- distinguish between the law and ethics of privacy
- understand the concepts of discretion, right to know, need to know, want to know, and circles of intimacy
- understand the contextual nature of privacy, particularly when social media are involved
- understand and apply Rawls' veil of ignorance as a tool for ethical decision-making

WHY PRIVACY IN THE NEW MILLENNIUM?

Gawker.

The name itself is meant to tantalize and tease. In fact, Gawker was the lead property in a stable of seven web-only sites, including the avowedly satirical and feminist website Jezebel. So, in 2015, when Gawker published a sex tape of professional wrestler Hulk Hogan in a tryst with the wife of his best friend, for many, it was simply business as usual. However, Hogan himself insisted that his professional wrestling persona was distinct from the human being who made intimate connections. He sued Gawker, bankrolled by conservative billionaire and Facebook board member Peter Thiel. Theil, by the way, had been the subject of an unflattering Gawker profile in 2007. When the courtroom battles settled, a Florida jury awarded Hogan $115 million in compensatory damages despite the fact that Hogan admitted in court that the sex tape was true. The damages awarded were so large that Gawker was forced into bankruptcy.

As the Gawker case, as it became known in media circles, worked its way through the court, many saw the verdict as an assault on the legal protections historically provided by the First Amendment. Some described it as a revenge verdict and worried about what would happen if the uber-rich began to bank-roll similar lawsuits over news stories that offended them. Your editors take a different view. We think Gawker is a privacy case emblematic of emerging shifts in thinking about the concept itself. For starters, the case represents the largest jury award by far for the truthful publication of what are arguably very private facts. That award drove a profitable media organization out of business. The case also speaks to the increasingly influential role that the internet is playing in how we think about and respond to "outing" or "pub-lication" on the web. It also illustrates the way that law and philosophy, at least in the American context, are beginning to inform one another about the increasingly nuanced way we understand privacy—depending on the role we hold at any given time. Helen Nissenbaum, one of the foremost scholars on the subject, argues that social media and many other forms of technology have erased the public/private dichotomy. Nissenbaum's sophisticated thesis is that privacy is neither a right to secrecy nor a right to control information but rather a right that individuals have to "control . . . the appropriate flow of personal information" in a variety of contexts (Nissenbaum 2010, 127).

The individual history and professional roles of the parties potentially affected by any decision to release information illustrates what scholars call "context-relative informational norms." That analysis will seldom result in a rule that fits all cases and all eventualities. But, before you can begin to conduct such an analysis on a complicated issue, it's important to understand some of the history and vocabulary of the term "privacy" and some contempo-rary criticisms of how modern culture understands these important concepts.

PRIVACY AS A LEGAL CONSTRUCT

The modern legal notion of privacy began in the 1960s with a taxonomy worked out by the late William Prosser, dean of the University of California, Berkeley, School of Law. Because of the work done by Prosser, today the tort of privacy is manifest in four distinct ways:

1. Intrusion upon a person's seclusion or solitude, such as invading one's home or personal papers to get a story.

2. Public disclosure of embarrassing private facts, such as revealing someone's notorious past when it has no bearing on that person's present status.
3. Publicity that places a person in a false light, such as enhancing a subject's biography to sell additional books.
4. Misappropriation of a person's name or likeness for personal advantage, such as using Hollywood megastar Julia Roberts' image to sell a product without her permission.

Problems still exist. Not every state recognizes every tort—particularly "false light." Also, our notion of privacy is dynamic, subject to change. Out-of-wedlock pregnancies, cancer diagnoses, substance abuse struggles, which less than 100 years ago were intensely private, are now casually mentioned, sometimes celebrated, and the focus of important public awareness and health campaigns. At the same time, information once available for the asking, such as a student's telephone number or the address of an individual based on driver's license registration, is now closed by a maze of privacy legislation enacted at the end of the last century.

The law further clouds the issue by rulings that different sorts of people have different sorts of privacy claims. Public figures, for example, are subject to a different standard than are others. There are "limited" public figures and even "accidental" public figures thrown into the spotlight by chance. Just exactly who the courts will consider a public figure fluctuates, leaving a journalist doing a story in a vulnerable position. As the newspaper lawyer in *Absence of Malice* told the young reporter played by Sally Field, "They never tell us until it's too late." The law provides unsatisfactory guidance to both journalists and citizens. However, there is an ethical commonality in the wealth of legal reasoning: the law links violating privacy and harm to the individual. In almost every instance, ethical thinking prior to broadcast or publication is preferable to a court battle and a potential monetary award.

One of the major problems of thinking of privacy through this legal lens is a misleading connection between privacy and money. Marketing personal information—through social media and search engines—is an example of reducing ethical thinking to a cost benefit analysis lodged in the market. Philosophers assert that the commodification of private information erodes the core of both individual autonomy and authentic community. While the law may be a place to begin, it does not provide a satisfactory framework in which is make ethical choices.

Journalists have often been caught between what the law allows and what their consciences will permit. This confusion has led to ethical bungling on a scale that undermines the profession's credibility and feeds the stereotypical notions that journalists will do anything to get a story, and that audiences will

---

The Need for Privacy

The so-called *right to privacy* has been widely debated and written about, but the arguments are made more problematic by the fact that the term never appears in the US Constitution. Relatively little has been written about the "need for privacy." Philosopher Louis W. Hodges writes on the *need for privacy*, saying that "without some degree of privacy, civilized life would be impossible" (Hodges 1983).

Both a personal and societal need for privacy exists, Hodges claims. First, we need privacy to develop a sense of self. Constance T. Fischer (1980) states that people need privacy to "try out" new poses, future selves, and so on, without fear of ridicule by outsiders. If we are to become the person we wish to be, we need a certain degree of privacy to develop that person apart from observation. Religious cults that seek cognitive control over their members do so in part by depriving the members of any real degree of privacy, restricting both growth and reflection.

Second, society needs privacy as a shield against the power of the state. As the state gains more information about its citizens, it is increasingly easy to influence, manipulate, or control each one. Precisely because the state is feared, limitations on the power of the state, such as the Bill of Rights, were established to protect private life (Neville 1980). Throughout history, totalitarian regimes have used extensive government surveillance—the near absence of privacy—as a major component of any attempt to create a uniformly subservient citizenry, a subject that dominates Orwell's *1984*. Third, society needs privacy as a shield against internet sites such as Facebook and others that demand large sums of data about you to enter into their site.

Therefore, while much of the debate focuses on the *right to* privacy, an equally compelling argument must be made for the *need* for privacy. *Privacy is not a luxury or even a gift of a benevolent government. It is a necessary component of a democracy.*

---

willingly consume anything the journalist delivers. And, the audience itself can be part of the problem. Most people simply are not aware of the storage and use of their personal data online (Raab and Mason 2004). As a result, internet users focus on the benefits of their online transactions and believe they can take necessary precautions to minimize any anticipated risks despite multiple data hacks of institutions as disconnected as big-box retailers to the IRS (van de Garde-Perik, Markopoulos, de Ruyter, Eggen, and Ijsselsteijn 2008). Internet users seem to view disclosure differently in social contexts such as blogs (Lee, Im, & Taylor 2008) and social networking sites.

As Nissenbaum notes,

> Learning that privacy is not as interesting to most people as learning that it has been "threatened," "violated," or "invaded." In short, people want to identify the moral and political significance of any given instance of diminished privacy;

they want to know in general terms when privacy claims are justified. Since a right to privacy imposes obligations and restrictions on others, it is important that the right be circumscribed in a non-arbitrary manner" (Nissenbaum 2010, 72).

Nonarbitrary is the key here—journalists, strategic communications professionals, and their audiences need some systematic ways of making privacy decisions. For Americans, some of that systematic analysis begins with the law.

PRIVACY AS AN ETHICAL CONSTRUCT

The ethical basis for privacy is much older than the legal one and appears throughout literature, asserting that privacy is a "natural right," that we possess by being human. Privacy is considered a need, a way of protecting oneself against the actions of other people and institutions. Privacy carries with it the notions of control, limited access, and the context within which that information is presented. Communitarian thinking links privacy and community instead of seeing them as competing forces. "A credible ethics or privacy needs to be rooted in the common good rather than individual rights" (Christians 2010). "Communitarians see the myth of the self-contained 'man' in a state of nature as politically misleading and dangerous. Persons are embedded in language, history, and culture, which are social creations; there can be no such thing as a person without society" (Radin 1982). In the communitarian view, the community itself—the larger society—benefits from maintaining individual privacy.

However, there is a tension between the self and the community, a tension that Radin (1982, 1993, 1996) explains using the theory of contested commodities. The debate begins when theory of the self—articulated by philosophers David Hume, Thomas Hobbes, Kant, J. S. Mill—and feminist philosophy engage traditional market economics where the concept of personhood and private property that can be bought and sold are inextricably joined.

> When the self is understood expansively so as to include not merely undifferentiated Kantian moral agency but also the person's particular endowments and attributes, and not merely those particular endowments and attributes, either, but also the specific things needed for the contextual aspect of personhood, then this understanding is a thick theory of the self (Radin 1996, 60).

Radin embodies the community in the self but also situates the self within community, noting that a thick theory of the self and the traditional concepts of market-driven economics do coexist within contemporary culture, but that there is a group of "goods"—contested commodities—for which market economics does not provide complete explanatory power. Private information that emerges from human beings acting within a cultural context constitutes a contested commodity, one that market forces may intrude upon but that are incompletely accounted for by examining only market transactions.

Privacy as a contested commodity fits well with 21st-century lived experience at the individual level—that privacy is an *a priori* right that individuals can chose to trade away, or to retain, based on individual needs and desires. The concept of contested commodity also notes that the "contest" takes place not just within an isolated individual but within an individual who is also embedded in a cultural and economic system. Finally, that "contest" is in the service of human capabilities—capabilities that can be actualized in a community and within certain sorts of markets, but are also separable from them in individual circumstances. Combining Radin's thinking with the communitarian approach would mean that corporate demands would be every bit as subject to restriction as government for the same reason—the health of the community that, in turn, supports the flourishing of individuals. Christians considers control over commercial data banks, along with government surveillance and invasive news coverage of victims of tragedy, as the most important privacy questions emerging in the 21st century. And, scholars note that although privacy is related to human experience, the concept itself is not relative. "Privacy's moral weight, its importance and a value, does not shrink or swell in direct proportion to the numbers of people who want or like it or how much they want or like it," (Nissenbaum 2010, 66). Perhaps the best example of this is Article 12 of the Universal Declaration of Human Rights.

Responsibility for keeping things private is shared: individuals have to learn when to share or withhold information, while the community has to learn when to avert its eyes. Legal scholar Jeffrey Rosen notes that this attention to the role of the community in avoiding "the unwanted gaze" (the title of his book) stems from Talmudic law. He writes:

> Jewish law, for example, has developed a remarkable body of doctrine around the concept of *hezzek re'iyyah*, which means "the injury caused by seeing" or "the injury caused by being seen." This doctrine expands the right of privacy to protect individuals not only from physical intrusions into the home but also from surveillance by a neighbor who is outside the home, peering through a window in a common courtyard. Jewish law protects neighbors not only from unwanted observation, but also from the possibility of being observed. . . . From its earliest days, Jewish law has recognized that it is the uncertainty about whether or not we are being observed that forces us to lead more constricted lives and inhibits us from speaking and acting freely in public (Rosen 2000, 18–19).

The last sentence is important: fear of being observed causes us to partially shut down our lives where we are celebrating, mourning or just going about our daily pattern. The law is detailed and strict. If your window looks into your neighbor's private courtyard, you are morally obligated to avert your gaze.

The central role of technology also influences contemporary theory. Scholars note that individual control over the bits and bytes of private information is much more difficult to accomplish (some assert impossible) for the average individual, particularly if that person is coerced by economic or political necessity (Marx 1999). European scholars have linked privacy with a capitalist market economy on the one hand and the interventions of the welfare state on the other. "What does privacy mean to the homeless and the unemployed? Is there a point to privacy if people do not have the means and the power to enjoy freedom?" (Gutwirth 2002, 52).

Some outside of academia have suggested that in modern society the very notion of privacy is impossible. "Privacy is dead" headlines have been appearing since the 1990s. In 1999, Scott McNealy, the then-CEO of technology developer Sun Microsystems, called consumer privacy issues a "red herring," according to *Wired*. "You have zero privacy anyway," he said. Donald Kerr, deputy director of the US Office of National Intelligence, told *Newsday* in 2007, "In our interconnected and wireless world, anonymity—or the appearance of anonymity—is quickly becoming a thing of the past."

Taken into a media context, the "injury caused by being seen" gets thorny. Part of the problem with a "shoot first, edit later" philosophy for photographers and videographers at the scene of a tragedy is that the "injury caused by being seen" has already been exacerbated by the camera. That injury was something the jurors in the Gawker case understood intuitively. Like the philosophical approach developed by the Greeks, privacy is linked to our ability to "become" human and retain some element of dignity while doing it. "Only citizens who respect one another's privacy are themselves dignified with divine respect" (Rosen 2000, 19).

Grcic (1986) asserts that privacy can be negated by more compelling rights. In simpler times, the right to invade privacy belonged almost exclusively to the government. For the survival of the entire political community, the government demands that its citizens provide it with certain information that is otherwise private. However, specific rules govern such disclosure. The government cannot legally give your tax return information—which under penalty of law must include much private financial information—to other interested parties. Such a check on government power theoretically allows the maintenance of some level of individual privacy.

However, the government is not the only institution today that can demand and receive private information. Banks, credit companies, doctors, and attorneys all request (and usually receive) private information, the bulk of it willingly disclosed. Inevitably, such disclosure is one-directional. While you are expected to provide your physician with your medical history to ensure proper treatment, your physician might be surprised if you inquired about her success rate with a particular surgical procedure, and she certainly is not required to give it to you. Doctors in states where laws requiring such information be made available to patients have been debated usually go on record as being against disclosure, saying that the information devoid of context can be deceiving or outright wrong.

Computers and databases have become tools for gathering and storing private information. Huge industries have cropped up selling private information. When you buy a house or apply for a job, the information industry disgorges huge amounts of legal and financial information about you with about a 40 percent chance of some error, according to some industry figures. The tensions over what should or should not remain private are not resolved; they are merely accounted for in today's complex society. And even when consumers are given a free chance to look at and correct their credit information, only a small percentage do, despite the financial advantage to do so.

Thinking about privacy philosophically has prompted scholars to develop four different types of potential harms when privacy is invaded. They are:

- informational harm such as identity theft;
- informational inequality, such as governments and corporations amassing large amounts of data about individuals without their knowledge or consent;
- informational injustice, for example, transferring data from your financial records to the local newspaper without appropriate contextual information; and
- encroachment on moral autonomy, "the capacity to shape our own moral biographies, to reflect on our moral careers, to evaluate and identify with our own moral choices, without the critical gaze and interference of others" (van den Hoven 2008, 49).

Contrast these sorts of harms with those outlined in American constitutional law and see if you find the philosophical approach more or less satisfactory in our data soaked information age. More importantly, thinking philosophically about privacy will encourage you to consider what justice might demand—a more positive and future-oriented approach to privacy—than focusing exclusively on harm that is almost always dealt with after the injury has occurred.

DISTINGUISHING BETWEEN SECRECY AND PRIVACY

People tend to think of private information as something they would like to keep secret, but such thinking confounds the two related but separable concepts of privacy and secrecy.

Secrecy can be defined as blocking information intentionally to prevent others from learning, possessing, using, or revealing it (Bok 1983). Secrecy ensures that information is kept from *any* public view. Privacy, however, is concerned with determining who will obtain access to the information. Privacy does not require that information never reach public view, but rather who has control over the information that becomes public.

Secrecy often carries a negative connotation. But secrecy is neither morally good nor bad. Privacy and secrecy can overlap but are not identical. "Privacy need not hide; and secrecy hides far more than what is private. A private garden need not be a secret garden, a private life is rarely a secret life" (Bok 1983, pg. 11).

The law has given us an interesting metaphor for the ethics of privacy. In *Dietemann v. Time*, jurist Alan F. Westin viewed privacy as the ability to control one's own "circles of intimacy." In the case, two reporters for the former *Life* magazine lied to Dietemann to enter his California home and later expose him as a medical quack practicing medicine without a license. While the courts saw some social utility in exposing such behavior, Dietemann had a reasonable expectation of privacy in his own home, so the court ruled against the media in the civil suit that followed.

Philosopher Louis W. Hodges has used the concept of circles of intimacy to develop a working concept of privacy for journalists and other professionals. If you conceive of privacy as a series of concentric circles, as figure 5.1 illustrates, in the innermost circle you are alone with your secrets, fantasies, hopes, reconstructed memories, and the rest of the unique psychological "furniture" we bring to our lives.

The second circle you probably occupy with one other person, perhaps a sibling, a spouse, a parent, a roommate, or a loved one. You might hold several "you plus one" circles simultaneously in life and the number and identity of these you plus one circles might change at various times in your development. In that circle, you share your private information, and for that relationship to work well, it needs to be reciprocal—based on trust.

The third circle contains others to whom you are very close—probably family or friends, perhaps a lawyer or clergy member. Here, the basis of relationships is still one of trust, but control over the information gets trickier. It's the nature of information. As the ripples in the pond of intimacy continue to spread, what you reveal about yourself becomes progressively more public and less intimate, and you lose progressively more control over information about you.

Using this model, privacy can be considered control over who has access to your various circles of intimacy. Invasion of privacy occurs when your control over your own circles of intimacy is wrestled from you by people or

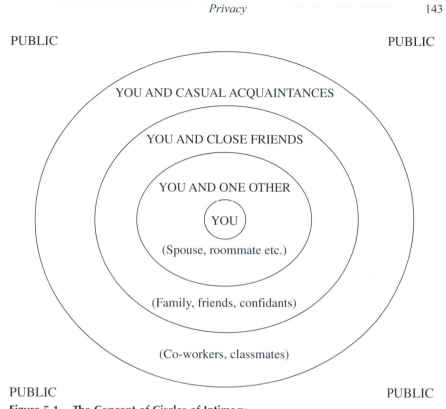

PUBLIC   PUBLIC

YOU AND CASUAL ACQUAINTANCES

YOU AND CLOSE FRIENDS

YOU AND ONE OTHER

YOU

(Spouse, roommate etc.)

(Family, friends, confidants)

(Co-workers, classmates)

PUBLIC   PUBLIC

Figure 5.1. The Concept of Circles of Intimacy

institutions. Rape victims who unwillingly see their names in print or their pictures broadcast frequently speak of the loss of control they felt during the experience as being similar to the loss of control during the rape itself.

Journalists sometimes invade circles of intimacy either accidentally or purposefully. Awareness of the concept will allow you to consider the rights and needs of others as well as the demands of society, particularly when the issue is newsworthy. Under at least some circumstances, invasion can be justified, but it's not under other circumstances. Part of the ethical growth of a journalist is to know when the rule applies and when the exceptions should occur.

DISCRETION: WHETHER TO REVEAL PRIVATE INFORMATION

With the distinction between privacy and secrecy in mind, the next problem confronting the ethical journalist is "discretion"—a word not usually associated with journalism. Bok (1983, 41) defines discretion as "the intuitive ability to discern what is and is not intrusive and injurious."

We all decide at times to reveal private information, and doing so wisely is a mark of moral growth discussed in the final chapter of this book. Discretion demands moral reasoning. Once a source decides to reveal private information, a reporter's discretion remains the sole gatekeeper between that information and a public that might need the information or might merely want the information. Take, for instance, the journalist covering the scene of a tragedy who gets answers to the posed questions, but the interviewees are clearly in shock and in no condition to be making complex decisions like the cost and benefits of granting an interview. Indeed, within a few hours, the family has hired an attorney to do the talking for them and you, for the time being, have the only interview. In times like these, the journalist is forced to rely on discretion to decide if he is feeding the voyeur or the citizen in each of us.

What is a journalist to do with information resulting from another's indiscretion? Kantian theory would suggest that the journalist treat even the indiscreet source as the journalist herself would wish to be treated, making publication of the indiscretion less likely. Yet many journalists claim that, in practice, everything is "on-the-record" unless otherwise specified. In situations like these, a return to Ross' list of prima facie duties could be helpful. What is my duty to an often vulnerable and sometimes unwitting source? To a curious readership or viewership? To a media owner who wants (and pays for) my story?

WHEN THE RIGHT TO KNOW IS NOT ENOUGH

Just as the distinction between secrecy and privacy is easily confused, there is also a misconception on the part of both journalists and the public among the concepts of "right to know," "need to know," and "want to know." However, the three concepts are distinct and not interchangeable.

Right to know is a legal term often associated with open-meeting and open-record statutes. These laws are a legal, not ethical, construct. Journalists have a legal right to the same information that other members of the public may obtain—for example, the transportation of hazardous materials through their communities.

Ethical problems can emerge from right-to-know information. Is it ethical to print everything a journalist has a legal right to know? For instance, police reports routinely carry the names of suspects, victims, and witnesses to a variety of crimes. If a reporter has information that might harm, on the local level, the right to a fair trial or, on the national level, national security, should it be withheld?

Need to know originates in the realm of philosophy. One function of the mass media is to provide information that will allow citizens to go about their daily lives in society, regardless of political outlook. Providing information the public needs to know includes within it the concept of journalistic tenacity and responsibility.

Too often, when journalists assert the public has a "right to know," what they mean is that citizens "need" the information to get along in their daily lives. For example, the average citizen cannot examine bank records—those records are specifically excluded from the Freedom of Information Act. But what happens when government fails? Consider the 2007–2009 turmoil in the financial sector. Investors lost billions in a New York–based Ponzi scheme. Major banks have written off billions of losses. Major investment banks faltered. Enron became a synonym for bad corporate management. Because of "carnage" left behind when these events happen, journalists could reasonably argue that at least some information about the health of financial institutions and the character of those who run them is needed by the public to make informed economic decisions. Need to know requires a tenacious journalist, as the law is not a tool for such stories.

Need to know is the most ethically compelling argument of the three. Need to know demands that an ethical case be constructed for making known information that others wish to keep private. Need to know also means that a case be made that the journalism is not engaging in mere voyeurism. When an argument is framed in terms of right to know, it reduces the journalist to ethical legalism: I will do precisely what the law allows. When an argument is framed in terms of need to know, however, it means that counterbalancing forces have been weighed and that bringing the information to light is still the most ethical act.

Finally, there is the issue of **want to know**, which speaks to the curiosity in all of us. Want to know is the least ethically compelling rationale for acquiring and disseminating information. We all want to know a lot of things—what our neighbors do in the evening hours, how much money other people earn and who in Hollywood is sleeping with whom. While we may want that information, we don't really need it and most certainly have no right to it.

Journalists—especially bloggers—have become sources for much "want to know" information. Nearly a century ago, *Police Gazette* titillated its readers with information they wanted to know that no other media outlet provided. Today that function is filled by slick websites and syndicated television shows such as "TMZ."

Consider the world of YouTube, where anything you "want to know" is probably available. Have a blooper at your wedding? There's an entire category for that. And if you need to be reminded what the "want to know" market is worth, in 2006, Google purchased YouTube for $1.6 billion.

Many of the most troubling individual cases that raise larger privacy issues are just like that described above—information brought to public notice not by strategic communications professionals or journalists but by average people who are computer literate and have something they believe is important to convey. Consider Matthew Creed of Shawnee, Kansas, who, in May 2012, developed the website blabbermouthkc.com. Creed said the website was a community service, but its content focused exclusively on the mug shots and addresses of people arrested in Johnson County. However, Creed's site contained no information on whether formal charges had been filed or on convictions. Some of the photos were of people arrested for infractions such as driving a car with an expired registration.

Superficially, Creed was operating on the principle of public shaming. "That was the biggest thing, to make others aware of those that were living around them that were breaking the law and to try to get those breaking the law to think twice about their future actions," Creed told the Associated Press. While numerous websites in the United States provide this sort of information, Creed added a new wrinkle. For $199.99, he would remove the listing immediately and for removal within a few days the fee was pegged at $149.99. "This guy is just a bottom-feeding vulture. The idea that he was trying to help the community is a total farce," said Jay Norton, a Johnson County attorney who represented some people featured on the website.

While Creed's approach to public shaming is perhaps uniquely market oriented, the fact that he is taking information made public by virtue of government (and hence paid for by taxpayers) and broadcasting it via the web to a larger audience is not unique. For instance, any aggregator can choose to carve out a niche on the web with Supreme Court opinions—free content thanks to the government. However, in the case of Creed and blabbermouthkc.com, what he is doing is philosophically important.

Some scholars are suggesting that ethical standards, which were once the exclusive purview of professionals, should in this age of the internet be open-sourced (Ward and Wasserman 2010). What that means is that ethical standards regarding important issues such as privacy would be arrived at through an open dialogue with audience members as well as journalists, public relations professionals, and others. Whether open sourced ethics is a good idea in philosophical terms, in practical terms, it may be the wave of the present where the consumer of information on the web is just as likely to be providing information—knowingly or not—in the transaction. Thinking through the implications of these rapidly shifting roles requires pointed and philosophically informed thought. It's either that or accepting that websites such as blabbermouthkc.com reflect professional norms.

JOHN RAWLS AND THE VEIL OF IGNORANCE

Preserving human dignity in times of crisis is a difficult task. Political philosopher John Rawls, an articulate proponent of the social contract theory of government, has provided a helpful exercise to make decisions about particularly thorny privacy issues (Rawls 1971).

Rawls's theory of "distributive justice" takes the best from utilitarian theory while avoiding some of its problems. It begins with the premise that justice should be equated with fairness. In order to achieve fairness, Rawls suggests an exercise he calls the "veil of ignorance." In the exercise, before a community can make an ethical decision affecting its members, the community must consider the options behind a veil of ignorance. Behind the veil, everyone starts out in an "original position" as equals. According to Rawls (1971) "no one knows his place in society, his class position or social status; nor does he know his fortune in the distribution of natural assets and abilities, his intelligence and strength, and the like."

Rawls suggests that, behind the veil, rational people would be willing to make and to follow decisions when individual distinctions such as gender or socioeconomic status are laid aside. For example, if the issue is whether to photograph or interview survivors at the scene of an airline crash, you could gather many people with diverse views behind the veil. Among them could be a reporter, a photographer, a survivor, a victim's family, an average reader or viewer, the management or owner of the media outlet, the owner of the airline, paramedics at the scene, the flying public, and others. Behind the veil, in the original position, none of the participants would know what their status would be when they emerged. *Their arguments would then be free of bias that comes from points of view.* The participants would argue the pros and cons of the public's need to know and the victim's right to privacy without knowing whether they would emerge as a reporter, a reader, or a victim.

When people begin their deliberations behind such a veil, Rawls suggests that two values emerge. We will first act so that *individual liberty is maximized*; however, we will also act so that *weaker parties will be protected*. We will look at each concept separately.

First, Rawls suggests the liberty of all will be valued equally. Behind the veil, freedom of the press (a liberty journalists cherish) becomes equal to freedom from intrusion into private life (a liberty readers cherish). How you retain both becomes a debate to be argued from all points of view, free of bias.

Second, behind the veil, the weaker party is usually protected. Few participants would make an ethical decision that might not be in the interest of the weaker party unless the evidence was overwhelming that it would better the lot of the entire group. Behind the veil participants would be forced to weigh the actual and potential harm that journalists, as powerful people representing powerful institutions, could inflict on people who are less powerful.

It is important to note that consensus is not required, and maybe even not expected, behind the veil. The veil of ignorance is designed to facilitate ethical discussions, not stymie them from lack of unanimity. Using the veil of ignorance, the ethical decision maker arrives at what Rawls calls "reflective equilibrium," where some inequalities are allowed. However, they will be the inequalities that contribute in some significant way to the betterment of most individuals in the social situation. For instance, the consensus of the group behind the veil might be to run a photo of a victim of tragedy if it might prevent a similar tragedy from occurring.

Reflective equilibrium summons what Rawls calls our "considered moral judgment." Balancing the liberties of various stakeholders while protecting the weaker party allows for an exploration of all of the issues involved, which utilitarianism sometimes fails to address.

Using the concepts of right to know, need to know, discretion, and circles of intimacy, along with Rawls's concept of distributive justice, will provide you with the ethical tools to begin the work of balancing conflicting claims of privacy. These tools will enable you to better justify your choices, to make decisions systematically, and to understand what went wrong when mistakes occur.

SUGGESTED READINGS

Alderman, E., & Kennedy, C. (1995). *The right to privacy.* New York: Alfred A. Knopf.

Bok, S. (1983). *Secrets: On the ethics of concealment and revelation.* New York: Vintage.

Grcic, J. M. (19860. The right to privacy: Behavior as property. *Journal of Values Inquiry* 20, 137–144.

Hixson, R. F. 1987. *Privacy in a public society.* New York: Oxford University Press.

Hodges, L. W. (1983). The journalist and privacy. *Social Responsibility: Journalism, Law, Medicine* 9, 5–19.

Nissenbaum, H. (2010). *Privacy on context: Technology, policy and the integrity of social life.* Stanford, CA.: Stanford Law Books.

Orwell, G. (1949). *1984.* San Diego: Harcourt, Brace, Jovanovich.

Rawls, J. (1971). *A theory of justice.* Cambridge, MA: Harvard University Press.

Rosen, J. 2000. *The unwanted gaze: The destruction of privacy in America.* New York: Random House.

Schoeman, F. D. (ed.). 1984. *Philosophical dimensions of privacy: An anthology.* New York: Cambridge University Press.

CASES

CASE 5-A

DRONES AND THE NEWS

KATHLEEN BARTZEN CULVER
University of Wisconsin

News outlets, along with a number of other kinds of businesses and organizations, are increasingly using unmanned aerial vehicles (UAVs) as part of their professional activities. Commonly known as "drones," UAVs are tightly regulated by the Federal Aviation Administration (FAA), especially for commercial uses, which the agency defines as including journalism. News organizations primarily use drones to capture video and still images but also can mount them with sensors to detect data, such as air pollution or water quality.

In 2016, the FAA issued the Small Unmanned Aircraft Rule—known as Part 107—and established an operator's certificate for commercial users. The certificate requires users to pass a test covering basics of airspace and aeronautics. According to the Center for Journalism Ethics at the University of Wisconsin–Madison, Part 107 also established specific restrictions, barring

- commercial use of UAVs weighing more than 55 pounds;
- UAV flight above 400 feet in most cases;
- night flight;
- flights over people not involved in the operation of the UAV;
- reckless or careless operation;
- flight in restricted airspace without permission (airspace restrictions vary based on size and location of an airport); and
- flight beyond the operator's visual line of sight (Culver and Duncan 2017).

As more newsrooms were exploring deployment of drones in compliance with FAA rules in 2017, Kentucky Gov. Matt Bevin used social media to challenge the ethics of such uses by Louisville news outlets. Bevin was under fire based on his purchase of a house and surrounding property that had been owned by a prominent campaign donor who also owned a company that did business with the state. Bevin bought the estate from Neil Ramsey in March 2017 for $1.6 million.

A county property evaluation estimated the property's worth far higher, at $2.97 million when including nine adjacent acres Bevin did not buy. The transaction prompted two ethics complaints, but a later ruling by an assessment appeals body cleared the governor.

In the midst of the controversy, the Board of Assessment Appeals inspected Bevin's home as part of the appeal he filed but denied access to reporters seeking to attend the inspection and report on it. The *Louisville Courier-Journal* later filed a complaint alleging the action violated the Kentucky Open Meetings Act (Loftus 2017a).

The day of the inspection, Bevin used Twitter to lash out at Louisville news media. He tweeted that two organizations—the *Courier-Journal* newspaper and the Wave3News television station—used a UAV to fly over the mansion and capture video of his children. "Drones again flying directly over and around my home filming my children . . . @wave3news @courierjournal #PeepingTom Loftus," Bevin wrote, referring to political reporter Tom Loftus as "Peeping Tom."

Staff from both named news outlets immediately responded that they did not, in fact, use a drone in reporting on the mansion assessment controversy, with the *Courier-Journal* editor tweeting that the paper neither owns nor operates drones in its reporting, and Wave3 News stating that it had not flown at the governor's property.

Just after these replies, the governor identified WDRB News as the responsible outlet:

News Director Barry Fullmer tweeted that his station had operated the drone in accordance with FAA requirements and did not capture video footage of the governor's children. The posted video bears this out with lofty images of the home, outbuildings, and lush green landscape (Andrews 2017).

The WDRB story quotes Bevin saying he bought the massive home so his nine children would have room and privacy. It's that latter

Governor Matt Bevin ✔
@GovMattBevin

Follow ⌄

Drones again flying directly over and around my home filming my children...@wave3news @courierjournal #PeepingTom Loftus

10:35 AM - 1 Aug 2017

Figure 5.2.

Governor Matt Bevin ✔
@GovMattBevin

(Follow)   ⌄

The drone that was just flying over my home
& filming my children was personally flown by
@WDRBNews Director

Barry Fulmer - Vice President & News Director
Contact Barry Fulmer
wdrb.com

11:11 AM - 1 Aug 2017

Figure 5.3.

Property dispute ensues over Kentucky governor's house

Figure 5.4.

consideration that appears to have prompted the governor to call
out news media outlets for their use of drones. In a recorded press
conference, he repeatedly critiqued outlets for "breathlessly" reporting
on the controversy and using drones and helicopters over his property
(Loftus 2017b).

Even though the news station appears not to have captured footage
of Bevin's children and certainly did not publish any, drones do have
vast capabilities to venture where reporters on foot cannot and to
record high-definition video that makes individuals easily identifiable.
Organizations such as the Center for Journalism Ethics, the Poynter
Institute, the Drone Journalism Lab at the University of Nebraska, and

the National Press Photographers Association encourage news outlets to consider privacy when developing ethics standards to guide their drone use. They highlight the Society of Professional Journalists' ethics code in noting, "Balance the public's need for information against potential harm or discomfort. Pursuit of the news is not a license for arrogance or undue intrusiveness."

Bevin said he sought out his home in part for the privacy it afforded his children and accused news media of intruding upon that privacy by using a new technology. News media instead argued they were covering an issue of public importance involving one of the state's most powerful political figures. In the balance between the public's need for information and the potential harm from privacy invasions, clearly the two sides came out seeing the weight on different ends of the scale.

Micro Issues

1. Is an assessment controversy involving a public official a valid public controversy requiring robust news media coverage?
2. Is it fair to fly a drone over private property to capture images of a home and surrounding grounds at any time? Does it matter that the property is owned by a public official or the subject of an assessment dispute?

Midrange Issues

1. Should privacy considerations differ when children are involved?
2. Use this case to contrast the concepts of right to know, need to know, and want to know.
3. Does the governor have a responsibility to the truth when using Twitter? If not, why not? If so, how does that apply to this case?

Macro Issues

1. Rawls considers justice as fairness. Was WDRB fair to the governor in this case? What other stakeholders should be considered in this case? Was the news outlet fair to them? Were the governor's actions fair?
2. Apply the veil of ignorance to this case. How would you articulate the positions of the journalists, governor, and public if you did not know in which condition you would end up?
3. What other ethical considerations beyond privacy are important in drone journalism?

CASE 5-B

CONCUSSION BOUNTY: IS TRUST EVER WORTH VIOLATING?

LEE WILKINS
Wayne State University
University of Missouri

By any measure, 2011 was a terrible year to be a New Orleans Saints fan. Less than two years after winning the Super Bowl, the team, its coach, and many of its players found themselves the subject of the most serious penalty the National Football league had ever levied. The reason: the team's defensive coordinator (who was subsequently suspended indefinitely from the league) had run a "bounty system" where Saints' players were rewarded financially for "cart offs" and exceptionally hard hits. Among the main targets were opposing players who had already sustained concussions.

Filmmaker Sean Pamphilon was working on a documentary about former Saint Steve Gleason, who has the neurological disorder ALS— Lou Gehrig's disease. In his research, he discovered the bounty system among defensive players in the Saints locker room. Pamphilon's more recent work includes a documentary about the NFL, *The United States of Football*, released in 2013. In his 2011 film, Pamphilon recorded defensive coordinator Gregg Williams urging players to target an opponent with a history of concussions before a playoff game. "The NFL's a production business," Williams said. "We'll never forget about it. . . . Kill the head and the body will die. Kill the head and the body will die. We've got to do everything in the world to make sure we kill Frank Gore's head. We want him running sideways. We want his *head* sideways" (Mooney 2012).

Pamphilon released the audio recording during the NFL's investigation of the bounty system over the objections of Gleason and despite heavy public criticism. Gleason opposed releasing the speech because he did not want to violate the trust of the Saints who had cooperated in making the documentary.

The conflict between Gleason on the one hand and Pamphilon on the other illustrates the confounding nature of contemporary discussions about privacy. In earlier times, privacy was often binary—it was something you had or something you did not. Today, that binary world is full of greys.

First, keeping the audio record of the speech "private" could be considered ethically appropriate if maintaining the trust of essential sources is the primary goal. But, there were other interests to consider, among them the physical well being of the players who became the focus of the cart offs and hard/illegal hits, the integrity of the documentary film itself, and the NFL investigation, which had potential criminal overtones.

Micro Issues

1. What, if anything, should Pamphilon have said to Gleason after he made the decision to release the tape over Gleason's strenuous objections?
2. Saints' management knew that Pamphilon was filming the documentary although not the specific footage. What difference, if any, does that make in Pamphilon's choice?
3. Saints' quarterback Drew Brees urged Pamphilon to wait to release the tape. How should Pamphilon have responded to this argument?

Midrange Issues

1. How does the decision to release the tape fit the concepts of right to know, need to know, and want to know?
2. Would a sports journalist, as opposed to a documentary filmmaker, have a different set of obligations? If so, what would they be? If not, why not?
3. *Sports Illustrated*'s Peter King blasted Pamphilon in his widely read "Monday Morning QB" column. "Pamphilon betrayed the wishes of a dying man and a former very close friend by releasing the tape; that much we know," King wrote. "This is one of those cases where what's legally right shouldn't matter. What's morally right should. What's morally right is that Pamphilon, who never would have heard what Williams said without being attached to Gleason, shouldn't have released the tape without Gleason's permission . . . I cannot find it in my heart to quite call Pamphilon a rat, but I cannot call him a hero either." How would you respond to King's evaluation?

Macro Issues

1. The NFL is a multi-billion-dollar-a-year business. How does that influence your thinking about risks that Pamphilon took in making this decision?
2. Apply Ross' theory of duty to the ethical issues this cases raises.

3. Pamphilon continues to be an active documentary filmmaker. How do you think this decision will influence his ability to make films? To the relationships he will need to develop with the sources for his documentaries?

CASE 5-C

JOE MIXON: HOW DO WE REPORT ON DOMESTIC VIOLENCE IN SPORTS?

BRETT DEEVER
Oklahoma Christian University

In 2014, Joe Mixon was a five-star football recruit who had signed on to play for the Oklahoma Sooners football program. During the summer of 2014, Mixon was in Norman, Oklahoma, for offseason workouts and practices with his new college team.

In July, Mixon was out with some of his teammates at the Campus Corner restaurant in Norman. According to witnesses, Mixon and his teammates were harassing one female student, Amelia Molitor, and one of her friends before they followed them into the restaurant. Mixon and Molitor exchanged words, with the incident escalating after Molitor shoved Mixon and then slapped him in the neck.

Mixon, a 6-foot-1 running back, punched Molitor in the face, knocking her to the ground and causing her to hit her head on a table nearby. Mixon then left the restaurant while someone helped Molitor get back on her feet. Molitor suffered broken bones in her jaw, cheekbone, and face. Molitor had to have her mouth wired shut and claimed that for six months she could not feel the left side of her face.

Following the incident, Mixon was charged with a misdemeanor but agreed to a plea bargain of a one-year probation, cognitive-behavior counseling, and 100 hours of community service. Mixon also was suspended by the team for the 2014 season. In effect, his suspension ended up becoming a redshirt year, a normal event in the lives of many athletes at major universities, where a player gets five years of education for four years of competing.

After Mixon fulfilled the terms of his plea, he was allowed to return to the team in 2015. Mixon performed well on the field, and the Sooners won the Big XII Conference championship in 2015 and 2016.

Nearly two years after the incident, Molitor filed a lawsuit against Mixon. In it, Molitor accused Mixon of negligence, willful and wanton misconduct, and intentional infliction of emotional distress. The courts threw out the first two charges but allowed the later charge to proceed.

On Dec. 16, 2016, Mixon decided to allow the video of his attack be released to the public. The video can be seen on YouTube. The Oklahoma Supreme Court had ruled earlier in December that the city of Norman had to release the video of Mixon's attack before Dec. 26, 2016, or file an appeal. Mixon decided to release the video himself before the deadline.

Following the release of the video, Sooners head coach Bob Stoops changed his stance on Mixon, saying the initial suspension was not severe enough and dismissal from the program would be the response if the incident occurred today. However, he did not bench Mixon.

The release of the video, combined with the comments from Stoops, led to numerous sports journalists and broadcasters commenting on the situation. Legendary broadcaster Brent Musburger, while calling the Sooners Sugar Bowl game against Auburn a few days after the release of the video, commented on Mixon's situation early in the game. He quoted the OU coaching staff as saying that Mixon was "doing fine." He then added a comment about Mixon's future, saying "let's hope that this young man makes the most his chance and goes on to have a career in the National Football League."

Musburger was immediately challenged on social media. He was deemed as "tone-deaf," and his response was seen as "troubling." Some tweeted that it was time for him "to sign off" after his comments. By the third quarter of the Sugar Bowl, Musburger was forced to respond, and he took an adversarial stance with his critics, saying "I happen to pull for people with second chances."

A long-time sports anchor for the ABC affiliate in Dallas, Dale Hansen, responded to Musburger's comments with his own "Unplugged" segment. In it, Hansen dismissed the criticism of Musburger saying "What was he supposed to say?" Hansen, referencing the NFL's early mishandling of domestic violence cases, claimed: "We've already decided that hitting a woman is bad, just not *that* bad if you're good and Joe Mixon is really good." He added that the Auburn fans who booed Mixon would have cheered for him if he were on their team.

Micro Issues

1. The major charges against Mixon were dropped, in part when video indicated that Molitor was a participant in the violence that ended

with the punch. If he did not break the law, is this a story? Justify your answer.
2. Was Musburger right to bring up the incident and suspension in the context of a major bowl game? Second, should he have responded to the public criticism live on the broadcast or waited until after the game was over?
3. Should the local media have been more aggressive in seeking out the video?

Midrange Issues

1. Dale Hansen's comments included him saying that supporting Mixon because he had made only a single mistake was like supporting "someone who kills someone—but only once." Critique this comment.
2. Does it make a difference that Hansen's "Unplugged" segment is clearly editorial commentary? Would your answer be different if it were in the regular sports segment?
3. In this case, Twitter responses clearly changed the narrative in the third quarter. Should audience reaction during a news or sporting event be allowed to influence the direction of the coverage?
4. At what point does Mixon's past cease to be newsworthy to sports reporters? At the end of his suspension? At the end of his collegiate career? When he turns professional?

Macro Issues

1. *USA Today* called Musburger "tone deaf," basing that charge mainly on the fact that Musburger doubled down on his comments in the third quarter when he had the chance to walk back the words. Were they correct? Justify your answer.
2. There is constantly a debate in sports about giving players who run afoul of the law a second chance. Does the media decrease the likelihood of these "second chances" working if the original story stays alive?
3. Discussions about Mixon's act and Stoops's handling of the situation covered thousands of hours of sports talk programming. What role does the 24/7 all sports network play in the coverage of Mixon?

CASE 5-D

LOOKING FOR RICHARD SIMMONS

LEE WILKINS
Wayne State University
University of Missouri

Beginning in 2016, one of the most popular "new media" was actually a reboot of some of the most popular programming long before television was invented.

The radio serial—weekly adventures of everyone from the Lone Ranger to the Shadow—attracted huge audiences during the 1920s and 1930s. President Franklin Roosevelt reassured a nation on the brink of war with his fireside chats, broadcast on the radio. Edward R. Murrow began his career as a radio reporter covering World War II before he became one of the early giants of the "new" medium of television. And Orson Welles's radio program "The War of the Worlds" gave rise to the first empirical research on media effects and is still broadcast today in places such as Boulder, Colorado, as part of annual Halloween celebrations.

Podcasts were the next generation radio serial. They combined the intimacy of radio with the on-demand qualities of computers and smartphones. Even the best were relatively inexpensive to produce. Podcasts provided a way for media organizations, including news organizations such as National Public Radio (NPR), to repurpose content, and they were becoming increasingly popular. Downloaded from places such as iTunes, the most popular podcasts of 2017, for example "This American Life," could net more than $50,000 per episode.

Fitness guru Richard Simmons, who led exercise classes that were televised in the 1970s and 1980s, was an early crusader for weight loss at a time Americans were beginning to expand to unhealthy proportions. With an on-air personality that combined some natural shyness with ebullience, Simmons had been a celebrity for more than three decades.

And then he decided he wanted a quieter life. A life out of the public spotlight. Simmons no longer wanted to be a celebrity.

Enter former *Daily Show* producer Dan Taberski, who said he was an acquaintance of Simmons and a regular at Simmons' Beverly Hills workout studio. Taberski said he was concerned enough about Simmons' three-year absence from mediated life that he wanted to find out what had caused him to withdraw to the backstage.

In February 2017, Taberski's podcast "Missing Richard Simmons" debuted. The six episodes were framed as a mystery. Simmons refused to be interviewed for the podcast, but Taberski interviewed—or tried to interview—friends and relatives. After the podcast began, and because some of the content focused on Simmons's physical and mental health, the Los Angeles Police Department, based in large part on the speculations about Simmons' condition included in the podcast, made a wellness check at Simmons' home. He was fine.

In the second episode of the podcast, Taberski urged listeners to drive to Simmons' home for a "stakeout." The *New York Times* reported that Taberski justified the tactic this way: "I don't want him to feel like I'm invading his privacy. On the other hand, I'm Richard's friend."

During the time the podcast was being produced and aired, Simmons called NBC's "Today Show," saying that he was fine. He also disparaged the podcast's claims on his Facebook page.

However, Taberski encouraged podcast listeners to call in with "any theory you think we missed." Those tips included assertions that Simmons was bereaved from the loss of his pets or that he was depressed. (Simmons had acknowledged previously that he had suffered from depression.) At one point, Taberski intimated that Simmons was transitioning to a woman, only to discard the idea in the next episode.

The podcast topped the iTunes charts for four straight weeks.

Ultimately, if there was a mystery surrounding Simmons, Taberski didn't solve it. As of this writing, Simmons remains alive and living a more private life.

Micro Issues

1. Using the concepts of privacy, secrecy, right to know, need to know, and want to know, analyze whether the podcast invaded Simmons's privacy.
2. Would your answer be different if the wellness check by the Los Angeles police had found Simmons in some sort of physical danger or suffering from a physical illness?
3. Should Taberski have spiked the project when Simmons refused to speak with him?

Midrange Issues

1. Taberski's podcast told a narrative of a "missing person." Evaluate this narrative for truthfulness. Are there times when "telling a story"

is not the most accurate way to provide readers and viewers with information about events and people?

2. How would you categorize podcasts such as "This American Life"? Are they journalism, entertainment, some new genre?
3. How do you think Taberski's background on Comedy Central influenced the narrative choices he made?

Macro Issues

1. The *New York Times* called the show the "morally suspect podcast." How do you evaluate the critic's characterization?
2. Can celebrities such as Simmons have privacy? Can public figures such as Attorney General Jeff Sessions have privacy? If your answers are different for different categories of people, explain.
3. Should iTunes or programs such as TMZ be responsible ethically for content such as that provided in the "Missing Richard Simmons" podcast? How should that responsibility be exercised?

CASE 5-E

CHILDREN AND FRAMING: THE USE OF CHILDREN'S IMAGES IN AN ANTI-SAME-SEX MARRIAGE AD

YANG LIU
University of Wisconsin

The brief ballot measure read, "Only marriage between a man and a woman is valid or recognizable in California" (www.voterguide.sos. ca.gov, 2008) but it was packed with potential for conflict. So when the parents of some San Francisco first graders recognized their sons' and daughters' faces in an advertisement promoting California's controversial 2008 Proposition 8, which successfully sought to outlaw gay marriage in the state (www.protectmarriage.com, 2008), they were shocked.

The ad picked up two scenes from a website news video clip originally produced by the San Francisco *Chronicle* for a news story that described 18 students attending their lesbian teacher Erin Carder's wedding (www. sfgate.com, 2008). The newspaper story was a feature piece that took no position on Proposition 8. The story included an account of the wedding, which was held on Oct. 10, 2008. In the newspaper piece, and on the 80-second accompanying video, the children's participation was described as "tossed rose petals and blow bubbles . . . giggling and squealing as they mobbed their teacher with hugs" (www.sfgate.com, 2008). The story noted that it was a parent who suggested the trip, and that because every student needed parental permission to attend, two students did not accompany their classmates to the wedding.

However, the central message of the advertisement was, "children will be taught gay marriage unless we vote Yes on Proposition 8" using two scenes with the children's images. The first showed the children in a group, and their faces are somewhat difficult to distinguish. The second showed a single child looking into the camera. The ad did not include the scenes of the children hugging their teacher that were part of the original news story. In addition, the creators of the ad altered the color tones in the scenes with children to be somewhat darker than the original news story as posted on the *Chronicle* website. The ad featuring the video clip of the wedding was one of several similar ads run in support of Proposition 8.

After viewing the ad, four of the parents of the children involved wrote a letter to the Yes-on-Proposition-8 campaign, demanding that the campaign stop running the ad. Their request was denied. The *Chronicle* did not question the use of the copyrighted material in the ad nor did it make a request that the ad be discontinued.

Micro Issues

1. How would you evaluate the truthfulness and accuracy of the video accompanying the political advertisement?
2. Three days after the ad began airing, law professor Lawrence Lessig said in an NPR interview that the law "should not stop the ability of people to use material that has been publicly distributed." Evaluate this statement using ethical theory.
3. Do children constitute a vulnerable audience when it comes to privacy?

Midrange Issues

1. All advertisements, by virtue of their brevity, engage in selective use of facts. Evaluate whether this ad is within that professional mainstream in an ethical sense.
2. What should the *Chronicle* do about the use of news material for the purpose of political persuasion, regardless of the specific issue?

Macro Issues

1. How would you evaluate the statement that this ad constitutes protected political speech?
2. It has been argued that the children do not have the ability to reason about the politics of same-sex marriage in this wedding, so they were not expressing consent to the same-sex marriage but only expressing affection for their teacher. Is their participation in the wedding a private matter without political meaning or not? Justify your answer.

CASE 5-F

MAYOR JIM WEST'S COMPUTER

GINNY WHITEHOUSE
Eastern Kentucky University

The quiet, conservative city of Spokane, Washington, woke up to a surprise on Thursday, May 5, 2005, as residents opened their newspapers. They discovered that Mayor Jim West had used his city computer to solicit young men in gay chat rooms and that two men claimed West had sexually molested them as children.

In the months prior, West had been e-chatting on Gay.com with someone he believed to be an 18-year-old recent high school graduate and offered him a city hall internship, sports memorabilia, help getting into college, and excursions around the country. In reality, he had been corresponding with a forensic computer expert hired by the *Spokesman-Review*.

Reporter Bill Morlin had spent two years along with reporter Karen Dorn Steele tracking down allegations from the 1970s that West had sexually molested boys while he was a county sheriff's deputy and a Boy Scout leader. West had been close friends with fellow deputy David Hahn and fellow Scout leader George Robey, who both committed suicide after sexual abuse allegations were brought against them in the early 1980s.

In 2002, the reporters discovered links to West while investigating abuse by local Catholic priests. West was at that time Republican majority leader in the Washington state senate and was considering running for what he called his "dream job"—being mayor of his hometown, Spokane. During the campaign, the reporters did not believe they had enough information to confirm any allegations. Eventually, they received tips from both anonymous sources and sources who would later go on the record and swear in depositions that West had abused them. One man, Robert Galliher, said West molested him at least four times as a child and that he was assaulted repeatedly by Hahn. Galliher, who says he has struggled with drug addiction as a result of the molestations, said he was in prison in 2003 when West visited him and sent him a message to keep his mouth shut. In addition, other young men reported that they had had sex with West after meeting him on gay chat lines and had been offered favors and rewards.

Spokesman-Review Editor Steven Smith and his staff spent days agonizing over creating a fictional character to go online at Gay.com and consulted with ethics experts at the Poynter Institute and elsewhere as they considered options. Smith told Spokane readers that the newspaper would not ordinarily go to such lengths or use deception, "But the seriousness of the allegations and the need for specific computer forensic skills overrode our general reluctance." Most important, Smith said the *Spokesman-Review*'s decisions were based on concerns about abuse of power and pedophilia, and not whether the mayor was homosexual.

The forensic expert, who previously worked for the US Customs Office, followed strict guidelines. The expert posed online as a 17-year-old Spokane high school student and waited for West to approach him. The expert did not initiate conversation about sex, sexuality, or the mayor's office. In the months that followed, the high school student supposedly had an 18th birthday. West then requested meetings with the fictional young man and arrived in a new Lexus at an agreed-upon spot—a golf course. His picture was taken secretly and the forensic expert broke off contact.

West was told about the forensic investigator in an interview with *Spokesman-Review* staff the day before the story broke. He admitted to the offers made within the chat room but denied abusing or having sex with anyone under age 18. When asked about the abuse allegations from the two men, West told the *Spokesman-Review* editors and reporters, "I didn't abuse them. I don't know these people. I didn't abuse anybody, and I didn't have sex with anybody under 18—ever—woman or man."

West insisted that he had not abused his office and that he was not gay. After the story broke, local gay rights advocate Ryan Oelrich, a former member of the city's Human Rights Commission, told the newspaper that he had resigned after coming to the conclusion West appointed him in an effort to pursue a sexual relationship. Oelrich said

West offered him at one point $300 to swim naked with him in his swimming pool. Oelrich declined.

A conservative Republican, West blocked antidiscrimination provisions in housing for homosexuals, and voted against health benefits for gay couples while he served in the Washington state legislature and as mayor. He supported legislation barring homosexuals from working in schools or day care centers and called for bans on gay marriage. He told "The Today Show" that he was merely representing his constituents' views.

West asserted a message that he would repeat eventually on CNN, MSNBC, and in a host of other national broadcasts: "There is a strong wall between my public and my private life."

Many political scientists disagreed with West's interpretation. Washington State University political science professor Lance LeLoup said using an elected position for personal benefit is both unethical and "a misuse of power." Gonzaga University Political Science Professor Blaine Garvin told the *Spokesman-Review,* "I think it's a pretty bright line that you don't use your command over public resources to earn personal favors. That's not what those resources are for."

At the same time, some media critics criticized the newspaper's choice to use deception. The public cannot be expected to believe journalists and the veracity of their stories if lies are told to get at information, said Jane Kirtley, director of the Silha Center for Media Ethics and Law at the University of Minnesota. Speaking at a Washington News Council Forum on the *Spokesman-Review'*s coverage, Kirtley asserted that police officers can practice deception as part of their jobs but journalists should not.

"It's one thing for the police or the FBI to pose as a 17-year-old boy," William Babcock, journalism department chair at California State University-Long Beach, told the *Seattle Post-Intelligencer.* "It's another for a journalist to take on the role of junior G-man and do something that essentially is considered police work." Babcock insists that the *Spokesman-Review* should have gotten the information through traditional reporting methods, but he agreed that no one, particularly a city mayor, should expect privacy in an online chat room.

Poynter ethicist Kelly McBride, who previously was a reporter at the *Spokesman-Review,* said deception should not be normal practice but that the newspaper considered key ethical obligations: that the issue is grave and in the public interest, alternatives are explored, the decision and practice are openly shared with readers, and the mayor is given the opportunity to share his story.

Jeffrey Weiss, a religion reporter for the *Dallas Morning News,* said he rarely believes the ends should justify the means, "but some do."

The FBI investigated West on federal corruption charges but did not find his actions warranted prosecution. Special Counsel Mark Barlett said in a media conference, "Our investigation did not address whether Jim West's activities were ethical, moral, or appropriate. . . . We did not attempt to determine whether Jim West should be the mayor of Spokane."

In December 2005, Spokane voters ousted the mayor in a special recall election. West later said the newspaper had created a "mob mentality" and that considering the accusations, even he would have voted against himself. On July 22, 2006, West died following surgery for colon cancer, a disease he had been fighting for three years. He was 55.

Micro Issues

1. Do you agree that police officers are ethically permitted to use deception but journalists are not?
2. Was the *Spokesman-Review* justified in using deception? Under other what extreme circumstances do you believe deception might be justified?

Midrange Issues

1. Some critics claimed that West's story only would come out in a provincial, conservative community, and that his story would not have been news had he been the mayor of Chicago or Miami. Do you agree?
2. Sissela Bok says deception might be permitted if the act passes the test of publicity. Does the *Spokesman-Review* meet that standard?
3. Should the use of a forensic computer expert in this case be characterized as the ends justifying the means? Why or why not?

Macro Issues

1. Should there be a wall between the public and private lives of public officials? At what point do public officials' private lives become public concern? Are public officials' sexuality always part of their private lives?
2. The *Spokesman-Review* is locally owned by the Cowles Publishing Company. The family business includes a downtown mall with a parking garage, which was developed in financial partnership with the city of Spokane. The garage has been subject to repeated lawsuits and controversy. Some critics believed that the *Spokesman-Review*'s delay in reporting about the mayor was due to a conflict of interest. Editor

Steve Smith insists that the story was reported as the facts became evident. How do locally owned media companies manage covering their own communities without incurring conflicts of interest?

CASE 5-G

POLITICS AND MONEY: WHAT'S PRIVATE AND WHAT'S NOT

LEE WILKINS
Wayne State University
University of Missouri

When the Supreme Court in 2011 decided that corporations and unions could contribute an unlimited amount of money to political campaigns—what is referred to as the Citizens United decision—most political pundits and scholars agreed that the opinion had the potential to alter the democratic election process.

The Supreme Court decision renewed journalistic emphasis on covering campaign finance. It was a story that had been around for at least 50 years but, with the new ruling, received new urgency. The journalistic reasoning was fairly straightforward: If wealthy individuals (who were not themselves candidates for public office) were willing to write checks to politicians they supported for millions of dollars, shouldn't the public know something about these donors?

Because of campaign finance laws that were not altered by the Supreme Court ruling, most large and even unlimited donations went to "SuperPacs" or outsized political action committees that were not legally required to report donations in the same way as an individual politician-based fundraising effort. What happened nationally with campaign finance was also evident at the state and sometimes the local level. Even state supreme court justices were not immune from the attacks levied by outside interests. When a mid-level state-elected official coming up for reelection encountered an opponent funded by a SuperPac, the resulting tsunami in cash overwhelmed these traditionally underfunded campaigns.

In the early months of the 2012 presidential campaign, the *New York Times* reported the following:

- Billionaire Harold Simmons gave $1 million to Newt Gingrich's political action committee, another $1.1 million to Texas Governor Rick Perry's SuperPac, and $10 million to American Crossroads, a Republican-oriented SuperPac advised by controversial GOP strategist Karl Rove.

- Peter Thiel, PayPal co-founder and a self-identified libertarian, gave Congressman Ron Pauls' Pac $2.6 million.
- Multiple news organizations reported that Gingrich's largest financial supporter, Sheldon Adelson, had donated more than $10 million to the SuperPac Winning Our Future.
- Millionaire Rex Sinquefield, of St. Louis, donated more than $1 million to various campaigns in the state, including campaigns focusing on public education and conservative political candidates.

While the bulk of million dollar donations went to Republicans, President Barack Obama's campaign also received

- at least $1 million in support from the Service Employees International Union; and
- $2 million from film industry executive Jeffrey Katzenberg.

The US Chamber of Commerce, both nationally and locally, endorsed candidates, often accompanied by sizeable donations from individual members.

Many of the large-dollar donors were on record with controversial political opinions or business decisions. Simmons, for example, had clashed with the Environmental Protection Agency over compliance with regulations for a Texas radioactive waste dump, and Thiel had blamed giving women the right to vote on the rise of the welfare state.

When the Obama campaign placed a list of million-dollar GOP donors on its website, Frank VanderSloot, who had contributed more than $1 million to the Mitt Romney SuperPac, characterized Obama's list as an "enemies list," borrowing the term from the Nixon presidency when such a list did exist. Both VanderSloot and the billionaire brothers, Charles and David Koch, who had bankrolled many political campaigns, claimed that the publication of their names and their donations had made them subject to attacks and a loss of business.

On June 20, 2012, in a report by NPR's Andrea Seabrook, VanderSloot was quoted as saying that he had lost customers, received negative press, and been the target of unsavory e-mails. VanderSloot refused to talk with NPR in its series on millionaire donors—not a single donor was willing to be interviewed on the record—but had spoken earlier with Fox News about the response to his donation after it became public.

As might be expected, the publicity and reporting surrounding these donations made its way to Congress. There, Republican Mitch McConnell said that the coverage was infringing on the donors right to free speech. "This is nothing less than an effort by the government itself to expose its critics to harassment and intimidation. That's why it's critically important for all conservatives, and indeed all Americans, to stand up and unite in defense of the freedom to organize around the causes we believe in."

Democrats and their supporters shot back by, among other things, quoting conservative Supreme Court Justice Antonin Scalia, who said that publicity is part of the price of getting involved in the adult and consequential game of politics.

NPR, in its series on millionaire donors, also asked the large-dollar contributors why they were unwilling to be interviewed by NPR for the story. The question was met with universal silence.

Micro Issues

1. Most Americans think of money—how they earn it and how they spend it—as very private. Should campaign contributions be treated the same way as salary information or income tax returns for private citizens?
2. Using ethical theory, justify the current state of reporting campaign donations. Should those who give a great deal of money be treated differently? Why or why not?
3. Using ethical theory, justify the current state of reporting how much candidates contribute to their own political campaigns.

Midrange Issues

1. Apply Nissenbaum's concept of control over the contextual flow of information to the subject of covering campaign finance.
2. Does journalistic reporting on the individual political beliefs and agendas of donors—both large and small—make the ethical mistake of guilt by association?
3. Did NPR make the correct decision in broadcasting that no one would speak on the record about their campaign contributions?

Macro Issues

1. Should news organizations be required to report the source of their income, particularly when it comes from airing campaign commercials?
2. How do you think Americans should define political speech? Connect your thinking to the privacy of the secret ballot, the notion of the marketplace of ideas, and your views about the relationship between money and politics.

6

Mass Media in a Democratic Society

Keeping a Promise

By the end of this chapter, you should

- know how "fake news" can influence politics and a checklist for spotting it
- understand the various institutional roles the media play in governing and why the First Amendment is central to them
- be able to evaluate all forms of political communication through a single, ethically based framework

THE WITHERING FOURTH ESTATE

Media organizations are expected to act as a watchdog on government. Edmund Burke, in a speech in Britain's House of Commons during the late 1700s, first called the media the "Fourth Estate" (Ward 2004) because it performed this role. The Founders protected the press in the Bill of Rights as the guardian of the public's interest despite the bitter, partisan nature of the press in 1789.

With this history, it's hard to know how much has really changed in 250 years. In October 2017, one national poll found that 46 percent of registered voters believe that the news media fabricate stories about President Donald J. Trump. Only 37 percent believe the news media do not make up stories. The Politico Morning Consult poll of almost 2,000 Americans also found that a mere 51 percent of them believe that the federal government should not be able to revoke the broadcast licenses of those news organizations who promulgate fabricated news (Shepard 2017).

"Voters, particularly Trump supporters, have become disenchanted with the national media," said Kyle Dropp, chief research officer and co-founder of Morning Consult. "Even 20 percent of Democrats think that the national media fabricate stories on President Trump and his administration. That being said, many are still not willing to let the federal government censor the media."

It's tempting to blame it all on the current tempestuous US president, but the poll results come as part of a decades-long decline in trust in government and other institutions by US citizens. That trend is global. Also in 2017, and for the first time in 17 years in a survey that spanned thousands of people and dozens of countries, a majority of citizens said they did not trust government, the media, nongovernmental organizations, and business "to do what is right."

For one institution to check the power of another, belief in the institution itself and what it represents is essential. Yet, journalists today are working in an environment where the general public is skeptical to the point of cynicism not only about whether the news media can get stories "right," but whether individual journalists and the news organizations for which they work are motivated by professional norms that stand apart from partisan strife.

There are, of course, multiple reasons for this, but in keeping with the focus of this book, we would like to suggest two philosophically based roots of the problem:

First, an Enlightenment vision of truth, reviewed in chapter 2, has not found a ready replacement in the 21st century. Humanity finds itself in the middle of an epistemological shift, and while we know that truth is complex, we do not have a grasp on how to summarize that complexity in a way that spans points of view, methods of inquiry, or the causes that such complexity must serve.

Second, and unique to American culture, is the First Amendment itself. While other nations have turned to the government as a way of checking the power of the news media, particularly the economic power that media organizations represent in the current multinational economic environment, Americans outlawed such a partnership at the beginning of the republic. In fact, efforts to protect free speech have added an almost wild west quality to what is said on the internet while erecting profound economic disincentives to actually control some of what is produced and said there. Furthermore, the US Supreme Court in its decision on Citizens United equated money with speech. In a country that constitutionally cannot regulate speech by governmental means, economic means becomes not just the driver but the decider of who speaks and how big a microphone that person wields. The autonomy from government that the founders sought to protect is now threatened by

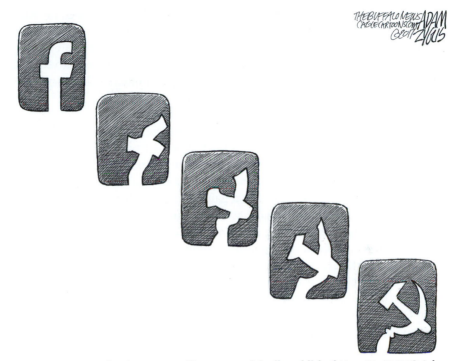

Figure 6.1. "Facebook News Feed" cartoon originally published Nov. 12, 2017 © Adam Zyglis.

powerful economic interests, some of which own media organizations that could be expected to counterbalance government power, the historic role of the fourth estate.

We will take on these challenges one at a time.

FAKE NEWS: THE TRANSFORMATION TO JUNK NEWS

In chapter 2, we defined fake news and linked it to philosophical definitions of lying. We also connected fake news to a drive for profit. Sissela Bok (1978), in her definition of lying, notes that the reason people lie is to gain power; lies allow liars to define situations in ways that give them advantage. In 2016, the lies became a particular kind of political framing. Fake news became news that you didn't like, and the term became so ubiquitous that it lost precise meaning. For example, various affinity groups used the internet to promote a "story" that Hillary Clinton was running a child-sex operation out of a pizza restaurant in Washington, DC. One enraged voter grabbed his AR-15, traveled to Washington, and fired three shots inside the restaurant injuring no one, all the while claiming that he was there to investigate the charges. Edgar Welch, 28, of Salisbury, NC, was ultimately sentenced to four years in jail on weapons charges. The internet groups that promulgated the story were never held to legal account. They remain active and searchable.

It's only a small step from whole cloth fabrication to the concept of junk news—news that isn't exactly a total fabrication, but that can be a sensationalization of some facts, the substitution of trivial content for more important and consequential information, or an attempt to provide opinion without a weighing of *all* the evidence. Junk news is alternate facts, stories that ignore evidence, often for political gain, or content that functions as click bait rather than providing a genuine attempt to inform.

Lies that demonize and degrade for political ends are pernicious for citizens as individuals and the political community as a whole. Junk news is the "bad" content that takes up so much bandwidth on the internet and so much journalistic effort to debunk that it closes the professional "window" on the production of quality, evidence-based content.

On Oct. 30, 2017, Facebook executives told Congress that they believed as many as 126 million Americans had received fake news stories initiated by Russia as part of their Facebook newsfeeds (Fiegerman and Byers 2017). A study conducted by the Oxford University Computational Propaganda Project found that in 11 of 16 swing states, including Wisconsin, Michigan, and Pennsylvania that provided President Trump with his electoral college victory margin, Twitter users received more fake and junk news than authentic political coverage in the two weeks before the November election (Woolley and Howard 2017).

The congressional testimony marked both a watershed and an about-face for the builders and owners of social media platforms and the corporations that have emerged from them. In the weeks before the 2016 election, the then president Barack Obama warned Facebook CEO Mark Zuckerberg about the potential impact of political disinformation only to be countered by Zuckerberg's insistence that the problem was not widespread. Facebook executives continued to downplay the problem until their congressional testimony more than a year after the Obama-Zuckerberg conversation. When Zuckerberg finally did testify before Congress, he admitted to "mistakes" but sidestepped the pointed questions about how the platform was going to counteract them.

Scholars who have begun to study the effect of widespread junk news have concluded that junk news did make—and will continue to make—a difference in how Americans frame politics and hence think about political problems.

"Adding fake news producers to a market has several potential social costs," say economists Hunt Allcott and Matthew Gentzhow (2017). Readers who mistake a junk-news outlet "for a legitimate one have less accurate beliefs and are worse off for that reason. Second, these less accurate beliefs may . . . undermine the ability of the democratic process to select high-quality candidates. Third, consumers may also become more skeptical of legitimate news producers. . . . Fourth, a reduced demand for high-precision, low-bias reporting will reduce the incentives to invest in accurate reporting and truthfully report signals."

While we would change the word "consumer" to citizen, the analysis provides an accurate description of some of the problems that currently characterize how citizens interact with the news media, at least if current polling data are correct. The scholars note that junk news, while "comforting" to some people because it does not challenge—and indeed may reinforce—pre-existing beliefs, is outweighed by long-term problems. The most significant of those problems is an ethical one; junk news undermines a belief in truth and the willingness to side with political truth, even when it is uncomfortable and contradicts personal belief.

Unearthing Fake News

One of the most basic tenants of journalism is "check it out." In previous eras, that has meant double checking what human sources say with other human sources, seeing if documents support or contradict what human sources say, and, more recently, making sure that documents are both authentic and complete. But, "fake news" calls for a different kind of checking, first by journalists and then by readers, viewers, and listeners. It calls for skepticism about every element of a news story—from the headlines, to the visuals, to the origin of the words themselves.

And, in what is sure to be an affirmative change in role, journalists need to educate their viewers, readers, and listeners on how to "check it out" for themselves. If veracity can be considered an ethical news value, something we suggest in chapter 2, then this sort of investigation of news stories themselves can become part of your journalistic routine.

Here is a checklist we think you should consider as you develop your own methods for verifying facts, sources and images.

- Look up sources before posting or publishing.
- Check the URL. Can you tell where the story is from?
- Read the "About" page.
  Warning: If there is no "about" page or if it is not clear who is running the site, be skeptical and double check everything.
  Warning: A URL pretending to be a news site, for example ABCNews. com.co, is a tipoff for bogus content.

- Analyze the headline.
  Do the facts in the story match the headline?
  If there is a quote from a prominent/famous person, put the quote in a search engine and see what turns up.
  Are the quotes in the story in context?
  No quotes in the story—be very cautious. Journalists quote their sources.
- Does the story attack a general enemy, for example "Washington," "the media," or "Trump supporters"?
- Check the author—stories with no author or written under a pseudonym deserve extra scrutiny.
- What's the support?
  Click the links on the story and see where they lead; links that don't exist or don't link to credible sources indicate a problem.
- Check the photos through a search engine such as Google images—who is really pictured?
- Check the date.
- Check your sense of humor—are you sure this isn't a joke?
- Check your biases.
  Is the story so outrageous you don't believe it?
  Is the story so good you must believe it?
  Stories that are too perfect, too good to be true, or provoke an immediate and intense emotional reaction deserve a second and then a third look.
- Are other, reputable news sources reporting on the story?
  If you Google the URL and get a report back from Politifact or Snopes, the claim you searched is false.

We also encourage you to beware of sudden popularity. Five years ago, going viral was a sort of gold standard for journalistic reports. But with bots, hackers, and troll farms at work, viral popularity is just as likely to be fool's gold.

This checklist also can be made a prominent part of every news organization's website.

THE MEDIA'S POLITICAL ROLE

In a less complicated time, Americans viewed the written word as essential to political society. The First Amendment to the US Constitution states:

> Congress shall make no law respecting an establishment of religion, or prohibiting the free exercise thereof; or abridging the freedom of speech, or of the press; or the right of the people peaceably to assemble, and to petition the government for a redress of grievances.

Scholars such as John C. Merrill (1974) assert that the First Amendment should be interpreted purely as a restriction on government, emphasizing

Figure 6.2. *Mother Goose & Grimm* (New) © 1999 Grimmy, Inc. King Features Syndicate.

freedom of expression and downplaying any notion of reciprocal journalistic responsibility. *In other words, freedom of speech is not extended to only speech written or uttered by "mainstream" media. Free speech also extends to minority voices, even those who are decidedly unpopular.*

But others, including Alexis de Tocqueville (1985), who studied our democracy about 175 years ago, viewed the press of the day as an essential antidote to a culture that valued liberty over community. The press, de Tocqueville said, was an incubator of civilization, an idea that political philosopher John Dewey would further for the mass media of his day just under a century later.

Madison, Hamilton, and Jay in the *Federalist Papers* expected citizens to be informed and to participate in politics. They knew that political debate, including what was printed in the press, would be partisan and biased rather than objective, but they also believed that from this "noisy" information the rational being would find the truth. Unfettered communication was essential to building a new nation. Citizens had an obligation to read such information; the press had an obligation to provide it.

> The founders were thinking about the press of the day as an important institution in the emerging democracy. At this level, it is not the individual story or single ad but the aggregation of all of them that matters. The media—here considered an aggregation of individual media outlets—is analyzed in terms of the media's relationship to the state and specifically to the political system (Christians, Glasser, McQuail, Nordenstreng, and White 2009).

Recent scholarship outlines four normative roles for the media in democratic political systems. Normative used in this way means a description of how the media ought to behave. In real life, and in real theory, individual organizations can fulfill multiple roles simultaneously. These roles are as follows:

- The *radical role* operates when the media provide an alternate vision to the current political and social situation in a country.

- The *monitorial role* is what citizens most often think of when they speak of the watchdog function of the news media.
- The *facilitative role* is perhaps best captured by news coverage of elections and political advertising about candidates and public issues. Both news and ads can facilitate governing, although how well that role is accomplished is the source of much analysis and debate.
- The *collaborative role*, where the media promote the views of the state. Broadcasting weather forecasts can serve this role as can much less benign forms of collaboration.

The way a nation governs is reflected in its media and in the role the media play. In authoritarian regimes, the media need to obey the strictures of the state in order to continue to function at the organizational level. At the individual level, promoting the goals of the state keeps individual journalists out of jail at the most extreme or allows them to maintain a license to continue to practice professionally. How a democracy develops depends, in part, on the conversation the media have with other, important institutions in that democracy. How citizens, professionals, and scholars evaluate media performance depends significantly on the role expectations of a particular media system. Thinking about role provides a somewhat abstract but certainly achievable set of standards.

THE PROPER ROLE OF THE MEDIA: GUARD DOG OR LAP DOG?

One of the ironies of democratic politics is that, in order to accomplish something, you first have to get elected, but it is accomplishing something, not getting elected, that is the major work of politics. Journalists fuel the irony by covering politicians more at the time of their elections or re-elections and paying much less attention to their policy making between elections. Regulatory agencies, cabinet offices, and the courts are not considered glamour beats by the national press corps. Most news organizations can no longer afford to staff reporting on state legislatures.

Yet the national press corps, particularly, is often a player in the policy process by reporting "leaks" and granting "off-the-record" interviews. Political scientist Martin Linsky (1986) describes how leaks have become part of the Washington policymaking process. Government officials, both elected and appointed, use the mass media to leak a story to find out how others will react to it—floating a "trial balloon" in the press. Other times, policymakers will leak a story because they wish to mount support for or opposition to a cause.

Sometimes leaks take the form of whistleblowing when a government employee honestly believes the public good is not being served by the system.

Watergate's famed (and now named) source, "Deep Throat," apparently was so motivated when he leaked key parts of the government investigation into the Watergate break-in to *Washington Post* reporters Bob Woodward and Carl Bernstein, who wrote a set of stories that ended in the resignation of President Richard Nixon. More recently, the initial information about the Abu Ghraib prison abuse scandal in Iraq came to journalists in emails from service men and women who were alarmed at the treatment of Iraqis held at the prison and of the military command's unwillingness or inability to change the system.

More than three decades ago, Linsky (1986) wrote about the role of the media in the policymaking process and raised two important points regarding ethical journalistic practice still relevant today. First, leaks are an acceptable way of doing government business, and policymakers are using them skillfully. Second, leaks can alter the outcome of the policy process itself.

Of fundamental importance for journalists is the question of whether reporters, editors, and their news organizations should become consciously involved in the process of governing by participating in the leaking process, and if so, in what manner? Wikileaks provided the first such test, and this rebellious organization has existed for long enough that its original stated intention—to confront power—seems compromised by its apparent cooperation with Russia during the 2016 US presidential election. Edward Snowden's leaks revealed secret policy decisions in the United States that were designed to forestall additional terrorist attacks by making everyday communication the subject of government surveillance. Scholar Elizabeth Stoycheff's work has documented that the act of surveillance is more detrimental to free speech than government censorship (Stoycheff 2016). And, in 2017, the release of the Paradise Papers, reported by a consortium of more than 150 news organizations worldwide, revealed the breadth and depth of individual, corporate, and institutional efforts to "stash" money in offshore accounts, thereby dodging tax laws in dozens of countries and inflating earnings in everything from retirement accounts to university endowments. Based on the history of the past decade, it is difficult to assert that the journalists who undertake to report such leaks do so unaware of the potential those leaks have to change everything from individual lives to political and economic policy at the national and international level.

Most ethicists agree that the media's primary function is to provide citizens with information that will allow them to make informed political choices (Hodges 1986; Elliott 1986). The watchdog media, set apart by custom and by law, also have a "guide dog" function to help citizens make their way through the political process. However, when the press covers politics as a constant "food fight" by competing interests, both journalists and citizens are soured to the process. Political reporter E.J. Dionne, in *Why Americans Hate Politics* (1991), argues that defining news as conflict (as virtually every journalism text does) inevitably reduces political debate into a shouting match. And, in the world of "fake news" and "alternative facts," there is always the chance that critical coverage of government will be labeled "unpatriotic," particularly by those in power. This is not a problem exclusively confined to the US system, as documentaries such as *Control Room*—in an in-depth look at the Al-Jazeera newsgathering operation—make clear.

Dionne agrees with Plato, who said that democratic politics, while a "degenerative" form of government, was probably the best available system considering that human beings were its primary components. And the same can be said of the humans who cover the governing process. Media critic James Fallows (1996, 7) goes one step further. He holds journalism directly responsible for voter apathy, congressional gridlock, and government via opinion polls rather than political leadership. In a quote that rings just as true today as it did when he made it before the turn of the century, Fallows claims:

> The harm actually goes much further than that, to threaten the long-term health of our political system. Step by step, mainstream journalism has fallen into the habit of portraying public life in America as a race to the bottom, in which one group of conniving, insincere politicians ceaselessly try to outmaneuver another. The great problem for American democracy . . . is that people barely trust elected leaders or the entire legislative system to accomplish anything of value. . . . Deep forces in America's political, social and economic structures account for most of the frustration of today's politics, but the media's attitudes have played a surprisingly important and destructive role.

Media critic Kathleen Hall Jamieson (1992) has suggested that, when it comes to politics, journalists should get themselves a new definition of news. Instead of emphasizing events and conflict, Jamieson believes news stories could equally revolve around issues and multiple policy perspectives. Fallows and others insist that implicit in the right to report on politics is that successful governing is an outcome for which the media are partially responsible. The cynical assumptions that government can never act for the public good, and that journalists and the media are somehow outside and perhaps even above the political system, are almost nihilistic. Ethical practice allows journalists and their media consumers to become more conscientiously involved in the American democratic political system.

And, there is at least one more crucial question: Are Facebook and Twitter simply technology platforms, governed exclusively—and profitably—by the rules of an intensely capitalistic marketplace, or are they media organizations with obligations beyond those owed their stockholders?

Although the history is recent, Facebook, which is marketed as a way to stay "in touch" with friends, actually began as way for men to evaluate women based on their physical appearance. Its architecture allows users to divide themselves into "friends" and "not friends." In almost any other setting—and certainly in one focused on ethics—this structure of "in group" vs. "out group" would be considered problematic. It would raise questions about how "friends" can form a political community with those who are "not friends." For the Greeks, the answer was political debate, and for much of the history of British and US democracy, it was a republican government serving an increasingly better informed and more active electorate. The media had an institutional role in governing and in the United States that institution received protection that was afforded no other institution and shared with only one other group: citizens. However, Zuckerberg, particularly, has resisted having Facebook labeled a media company, insisting as late as August 2016 that it was a technology platform and nothing else. Later in 2016, he conceded that Facebook was a media company, just not a traditional one. To many, this seemed like stating the obvious: Facebook's institutional role had become that of a media company; it facilitated discussion about government, and it collaborated with those in power and those who sought power. Facebook took advantage of protections afforded only to citizens and media organizations in the United States, specifically, the First Amendment. But, by maintaining that Facebook was not a media organization, the corporation was able to dodge the ethical obligations and legal strictures incumbent on journalists and news organizations.

In a world of "fake news" and too comfortable information bubbles, allowing any organization to ignore the obligations of citizenship seems careless at the least and perilous at worst. It certainly raises the following question: Until technology platforms—and those who own and operate them—concede that the role they play in political society is one of mediating information through a combination of narrowcasting and broadcasting, should friends continue to let friends get their news on Facebook?

GETTING ELECTED

For any politician to enact change, he or she must first be elected, and in our mass society, that means turning to the mass media to reach the electorate. In one classic study, voters admitted learning more about candidates' stands on issues from advertising than they did from news (Patterson 1980). And considering that modern presidential campaigns place ads only in contested states, many voters get little exposure to even the limited and one-sided information coming from ads unless they access them online.

In the past few presidential campaigns, websites have become increasingly important. But because they are under the control of the candidate and not bound by any constraints of objectivity or completeness, they too qualify as advertising. So today, more than 30 years after the first studies indicated it to be true, advertising is still the leading source of information for most people in most campaigns.

Because ads are a leading source of campaign information, factual accuracy, therefore, must be the starting point for ethical political advertising. As philosopher Hannah Arendt has noted, "Freedom of information is a farce unless factual information is guaranteed and the facts themselves are not in dispute" (Arendt 1970).

News stories about elections emphasize strategy and tactics rather than stands on issues, forcing voters who want to become informed about the candidate's policy choices to get their information from ads, often "negative" or "attack" ads framed by the other side. Policy analysis, when it is present at all, is more frequently found on candidate websites, where spin and incomplete data are the foundation for content.

Contemporary voters can discern the various types of political ads, according to election studies. Comparative ads, ones that contrast candidate positions on specific issues, were viewed as information rich, and voters view them as an appropriate part of political discourse. Attack ads, ones that are personal and negative, that contain no "positive" or "issue-oriented" information, were disliked and distrusted in the studies. A few years ago, a majority of political ads were either positive or contrasted stances of the candidates (Benoit 1999). Another study from the same time showed that voters were able to distinguish among negative, comparative, and positive or biographical ads (Jamieson 2000).

Today, "ad watches," put the claims in political ads to the tests of truthfulness and context. Anecdotal evidence suggests that aggressive journalism focusing on attack ads and negative campaigning can have an impact on the voters' knowledge of particular candidates. Under the social responsibility of the press, it is the responsibility of journalists to evaluate political advertising as legitimate news and to hold candidates publicly accountable for the advertising sponsored by a campaign or, in the grayer areas, advertising paid for by political action groups, even those disavowed by the candidate.

Ideally, political advertising would be factual and rational. The use of emotional arguments designed to stir listeners or viewers "to set aside reason" is a "violation of democratic ethics" (Haiman 1958, 388). There may, however, be times when valid issues have strong emotional content, such as the ongoing debate over immigration, gun control, and the need for government to insure health care for all. The melding of emotion and issue in such cases is not unethical, but totalitarian regimes have historically used emotional rather than rational appeals to either gain or retain power.

Figure 6.3. Ed Stein © The Rocky Mountain News. Reprinted by permission of Andrews McMeel Syndication for UFS. All rights reserved.

Such ads usually lack any evidence to support the claims. Seeking the evidence behind political assertions has historically been the role of the news media. When this sort of journalism is lacking, it begins a cycle that was foreseen by Walter Lippmann: "In the absence of debate, restricted utterance leads to the degradation of opinion . . . the more rational is overcome by the less rational, and the opinions that will prevail will be those which are held most ardently by those with the most passionate will" (Lippmann 1982, 196).

If political advertising is indeed a "special case" (Kaid 1992), then journalists and their audiences should demand higher standards, more regulations, or both. While some of the solutions to the current problems have both First Amendment and financial ramifications, they are worthy of discussion. They include the following:

- Allot limited amounts of free time to qualified candidates for major office to level the playing field for candidates.
- Strengthen state regulations against corrupt campaign practices and find ways to enforce those regulations.
- Encourage journalists to stop covering the "horse race" aspect of campaigns and focus on problems and solutions.
- Hold candidates accountable for their ads and for the ads of political action committees or other groups such as moveon.org.
- Teach journalists to read and report on the visual imagery of a campaign, and to ask candidates questions about it.
- Allow attack ads only if they include the image of the candidate directing the attack.
- Reject unfair or inaccurate ads created by political action committees.

- Conduct ad watches as part of media coverage of a campaign, analyzing the ads for omissions, inconsistencies, and inaccuracies.

It takes money to buy ads, and in contemporary democratic societies that means the candidate with the most money often has the loudest voice. Many argue the influence of money in the political system is pervasive and corrosive. In the 2012 election cycle, following the Citizens United decision, the Supreme Court essentially allowed supporters of candidates—including corporations and unions—to collect and spend unlimited amounts of campaign funds. While the impact was most noticeable at the presidential level, Senate and House races, and even state legislative races, also were influenced by an influx of campaign cash, much of it from supporters outside the geographic boundaries of specific legislative districts. Off-year elections in 2017 provided evidence that the trend was accelerating. It can be argued that money buys elections, especially in the light of evidence that the most heavily-funded campaign wins more often than not. However, it also can be argued that monetary gifts are merely precursors to votes, and the most popular candidate in gifts is often the most popular in votes as well. Whether the money brings the votes or popularity brings the money, the lower level the race (state legislators, judges, etc.) the more impactful these outside gifts can be.

How to deal with the influence of money in elections is an important policy question, but there seem to be few answers. Politicians are too tied to the existing system to be seek change, and the media that could presumably investigate political money and its negative influence are compromised by the act of receiving so much of the cash. The problem cannot be "solved" in this brief chapter, but it is worth considering whether a media system in a democracy might not be able to be a part of the solution rather than a part of the problem.

LEARNING ABOUT LEADERS AND THEIR CHARACTER

Today, a pressing political issue is whether people can become acquainted well enough and deeply enough with any candidate to acquire an opinion. After all, a representative democracy rests on the Greek concept of *adios*, a concern for the good opinion of others. Except for a small group of insiders, the mass media have become the primary source of political information, including information about character. In addition to providing voters with facts, something that is generally assumed to be the role of news, the media also provide citizens with a framework to understand those facts.

Candidates have been quick to utilize a variety of media outlets. For example, former California Governor Arnold Schwarzenegger announced his candidacy on the "Tonight Show." Because journalists cover national campaigns in a pack, there is seldom any really distinctive political reporting during elections (Crouse 1974; Sabato 1992). However, for journalists, campaign assignments hold the opportunity for personal prestige. The person who covers the winning candidate for a network will almost assuredly become the White House correspondent for the next four years. Journalists covering a national election have almost as much at stake as the candidates they cover.

Journalists treat frontrunners differently than they do the remainder of the candidate pack (Robinson and Sheehan 1984). Frontrunners are the subject of closer scrutiny, but those examinations are seldom about issues. Candidates and their paid consultants have developed strategies that will allow them either to capitalize on frontrunner status and image or to compensate for a lack of it. In the movie *The Adjustment Bureau*, Matt Damon portrays a young and good-looking candidate who uses his concession speech early in the film to poke fun at the absurd amounts his staff paid to test his shoes, his ties, etc. But the movie makes a good point: TV-friendly candidates are more likely to receive free media—the Sunday morning programs, the 5 p.m. news, the higher-rated cable news shows, etc. Candidates have mastered the "photo opportunity" and, for incumbents, the "Rose Garden strategy" designed to thwart anything but the most carefully scripted candidate contact with the voting public.

At the same time candidates try to script their every move, the media have the right, and the responsibility, to get "behind the curtain" (Molotch and Lester 1974) to the real candidate. What happens after the curtain is down often makes news in ways the candidates could not have foreseen, often including sexual scandal or financial wrongdoing. Just because the information is available and even accurate does not automatically mean that it is relevant and ethical to broadcast or print it.

Conceptualizations of character have changed significantly since the founding of the republic, when character was defined in Aristotelian terms—an observable collection of habits, virtues, and vices. Freudian psychology has altered that definition to include motivation, the subconscious, and relationships that help to form all of us as people. What journalists cover is "political character," the intersection of personality and public performance within the cultural and historical context. Character is dynamic—the synergy of a person within an environment (Davies 1963). Journalists who explore character often do so for an ethical reason, despite apparent invasions of privacy.

Political figures are powerful people. Ethicist Sissela Bok (1978) has noted that when an unequal power relationship is involved, it is possible to justify what would otherwise be considered an unethical act. To paraphrase Bok, investigation of the private character of public people is validated if the person investigated is also in the position to do harm. In those cases, invading privacy in an attempt to counter that threat is justified. However, that invasion also needs to meet some tests (Schoeman 1984):

- The invasion must be placed in a larger context of facts and history and must include context to provide meaning.
- The revelation of private facts about political figures should meet the traditional tests of journalism and needs to be linked to public, political behaviors before publication or broadcast becomes ethically justifiable.
- The invasion of privacy must further the larger political discourse and must meet the most demanding ethical test: the "need to know."

Even reporting that passes the three tests above must be filtered through discretion—a word usually used in moral development theory. In ethics, discretion means having the practical wisdom not to reveal everything one is told, even if facts or events would be of casual interest to many. Journalists have the difficult problem of being discreet in their news coverage, even when candidates, their handlers or supporters, and opponents have been indiscreet—sometimes deliberately so. Reporters covering political character should be aware that there are several building blocks of character, including the

- politician's development of a sense of trust;
- politician's own sense of self-worth and self-esteem;
- development of a politician's relationship to power and authority;
- early influences on adult policy outlook;
- way a politician establishes contact with people;
- flexibility, adaptability, and purposefulness of mature adulthood; and
- historical moment.

The media's current emphasis on covering political character provides the best illustration of the need to balance the demands of governing with privacy. No culture has ever expected its leaders to be saints; in fact, some cultures have prized leadership that is decidedly unsaintly. In American culture, the concept of public servant—which is the work of politics—has been replaced by the epithet "politician"—synonymous with "crook," or "liar," a caricature reinforced in popular culture by iconic films such as *Mr. Smith Goes to Washington* or *All the King's Men*. However, Americans were reminded that public service can be a high calling, as shown by the first responders to the 9/11 tragedy, many of whom lost their lives. The late senator Edward Kennedy described his job as public service. Such service, dating as far back as Athens, was considered the mark of a life well lived.

EVALUATING POLITICAL COMMUNICATION

For the Greeks, where democracy was born, the art of politics was considered a gift from the gods, who provided men with *adios*, a sense of concern for the good opinion of others, and *dike*, a sense of justice that makes civic peace possible. In the ancient myth, these gifts were bestowed on everyone, not just some elite. All men were able to exercise the art of politics through rhetoric and argument in the assembly, a form of direct democracy that survived for only a few years in Athens. The Greeks called it *polity*, which translates as community.

Greece was also the last place that direct democracy was practiced, and considering the contemporary cacophony, that's not such a big surprise. Fake news has become a stalking horse for negative campaign commercials, and it amplifies opinion masquerading as analysis on cable television. A 2004 study by the Pew Charitable Trusts found that more than half of Americans under age 50 get their news about politics "regularly" or "sometimes" from late-night comedians. But these respondents were also among the least likely to know basic facts about candidates. Even on the lowest level, politics, for most, is a mass-mediated event.

Evaluating all this political information is a problem for both media consumers and journalists. Furthermore, as news blends into entertainment and persuasion leaches into both genres, providing a consistent way of examining every political message becomes essential in ethical analysis. Political scientist Bruce A. Williams (2009) has begun this process with a four-part test he believes will help you determine when information has political relevance:

- First, is the information **useful**—does it provide citizens with the kind of information that helps individual and collective decision-making?
- Second, is the information **sufficient**—is there enough of it and at enough depth to allow people to make informed choices?
- Third, is the information **trustworthy**?
- Fourth, **who is the "audience"**—the political "we" on which the ancient Greeks placed so much emphasis?

Information that meets these criteria should be considered politically relevant, mediated information regardless of genre or source, Williams says.

Under this test, a John Oliver newscast or a Stephen Colbert monologue would be considered politically relevant communication every bit as much as a campaign ad or an investigative piece. Under this sort of analysis, cable news programming, which often features dueling opinions by talking heads talking over each other (often unsubstantiated by evidence) *would actually fare less well* than the comedy monologue.

In a famous dust-up with cable news personality Tucker Carlson, Comedy Central comedian Jon Stewart took on the entire genre of punditry. Stewart suggested that his show was more truthful and politically relevant. Interestingly, Stewart has made that claim in other arenas—that Comedy Central actually has political clout—and adds that it personally frightens him—which gets a good laugh but makes a poignant point.

Putting all political communication into the same arena also has another virtue—every message can be evaluated along the same standard. Here, again, Williams (2009) suggests four criteria.

- **Transparency**—Does the audience know who is speaking? This has become a major problem in recent elections with the rise of PACs and groups not bound by campaign finance rules and rarely bothered with the total accuracy of their claims.
- **Pluralism**—Does the media environment provide an opportunity for diverse points of view, either in different messages that are equally accessible or within a single message? Does every side have access to the engines of information that are now the modern equivalent of the face-to-face rhetoric of ancient Greece?
- **Verisimilitude**—Do the sources of the messages take responsibility for the truth claims they explicitly and implicitly make, even if these claims are not strictly verifiable in any formal sense?
- **Practice**—Does the message encourage modeling, rehearsing, preparing, and learning for civic engagement? Does it encourage activities such as voting or less direct forms of political activity such as thinking about issues, looking at websites, blogging, or talking to neighbors face-to-face? Is the ad or article empowering, or does it contribute to the cacophony that has dominated recent political campaigns?

We acknowledge that this framework places a premium on rationality and fact. But, it also acknowledges context and point of view. It also assumes autonomy—not just in the voting booth but in choosing what to access through various web portals—while requiring community. Its foundation is an ethical one, and like the Greeks, it asserts that politics is essential to human flourishing.

SUGGESTED READINGS

Christians, C. G., Glasser, T., McQuail, D. Nordenstreng. K., & White, R. A. (2009). *Normative theories of the media: Journalism in democratic societies.* Champagne: University of Illinois Press.

Dionne, E. J. (1991). *Why Americans hate politics.* New York: Simon & Schuster.

Fallows, J. (1996). *Breaking the news: How the media undermine American democracy.* New York: Pantheon.

Fry, D. (1983). *The adversary press.* St. Petersburg, FL: The Modern Media Institute.

Jamieson, K. H. (2000). *Everything you think you know about politics . . . and why you're wrong.* New York: Basic Books.

Linsky, M. (1986). *Impact: How the press affects federal policymaking.* New York: W. W. Norton.

Madison, J. S., Hamilton, A., and Jay, J. *The Federalist papers.*

Ward, S. (2004). *The invention of journalism ethics.* Montreal: McGill-Queen's University Press.

CASES

CASE 6-A

REPORTING ON RUMORS: WHEN SHOULD A NEWS ORGANIZATION DEBUNK?

LEE WILKINS
Wayne State University
University of Missouri

The Oct. 2, 2017, shooting at the Mandalay Bay Resort and Casino in Las Vegas posed a number of problems for journalists. However, even as local reporters were trying to uncover the facts of the incident and of the resulting investigation, rumors began to circulate on the internet.

Within hours, there were internet reports that the gunman, Stephen Paddock, was associated with ISIS or had been radicalized by that group. Authorities were able to establish no such connection despite a claim from ISIS that the statement was true. Writing under the username Jack Sins, another internet troll tweeted (and asked for retweets) that his father was missing after the shooting. The photo accompanying the tweet was of a well-known porn star.

In yet another interaction of a debunked internet meme, an internet comedienne also was linked to the shooting—and every mass shooting in the United States for the 12 months preceding the Mandalay Bay tragedy in which 58 people were killed and more than 480 injured. This particular rumor was promoted by the group 4chan, which has a history of attempting to frame members of that internet community as mass shooters.

Both Hillary Clinton and Jimmy Kimmel, who began to speak in favor of additional federal gun control regulations soon after the shooting, were mocked on a variety of internet sites, including Breitbart. Musicians and other entertainers who also began to lobby for additional gun control legislation were also the subject of malicious posts.

Within four days of the event, multiple news organizations provided a different approach to the story. In the *New York Times*, reporter Linda Qui debunked the rumor that there was a second gunman involved in the shooting. The blog Punditfact outed the website Nelson Nettle, which described itself as "free and independent news" for falsely claiming that an eyewitness had seen multiple gunmen dressed as security guards at the resort. Abby Ohlheiser in an Oct. 3 story in the *Washington Post* rounded up multiple fake stories including the images that were published with them and promised continued postings as the viral misinformation morphed into additional bogus accounts.

Television station KUSA in Denver took the debunking approach one step further: Its report advised viewers how to spot erroneous information that reached them through the web. That story urged viewers to check images by using Google Chrome and the instruction "Search Google for this image." The news account also urged viewers to think critically about internet posts, noting that people who were truly searching for loved ones in the wake of the tragedy were unlikely to be "bragging about the response they were getting to their tweets." The story concluded, "In a life-and-death situation, false information is at best a distraction from efforts to help and at worst dangerous. But, it's all too easy to spread in the world of instant sharing. Pranksters prey on your emotions to get clicks and shares, which only compounds the problem. But there are easy steps you can take to avoid falling for these hoaxes—they just take a few seconds more."

Micro Issues

1. Do stories such as the ones noted above support journalism's commitment to truth telling? Why or why not?
2. How would you distinguish between the concepts of fake news and internet hoaxes?
3. Evaluate the approach of the KUSA story in trying to provide viewers with tools to independently verify internet content. Compare that with the approach employed by the *New York Times* and the *Washington Post*. Which do you think is the better approach? Justify your choice using philosophical theory.

Midrange Issues

1. Many news organizations have a standing policy of not reporting things such as bomb threats to schools because they are so frequent and are often pranks. Analyze this approach in light of the most recent mass shooting in the United States. When is it inappropriate to report a rumor?
2. Many critics noted that Stephen Paddock, the gunman in the Mandalay Bay shooting, was Caucasian and that he was treated differently by journalists because of his race. Evaluate this criticism.

3. News organizations that spend time debunking rumors shift resources from other stories to provide this sort of coverage. How would you justify assigning a reporter to such a story? What elements of craft—for example, proximity—and ethical news values—for example transparency—might support your decision?

Macro Issues

1. Alexis S. Madrigal, writing in the *Atlantic* on Oct. 2, 2017, blamed the problem on Google and Facebook, and their corporate managers, for refusing to put more human beings in the loop to decide whether particular posts and shared stories are bogus. "The truth is that machines need many examples to learn from. That's something we know from all the current artificial-intelligence research," Madrigal wrote. "They're not good at 'one-shot' learning. But humans are very good at dealing with new and unexpected situations. Why are there not more humans inside Google who are tasked with basic information filtering? How can this not be part of the system, given that we know the machines will struggle with rare, breaking-news situations?" Analyze these comments. What philosophical theory supports your analysis?

CASE 6-B

DOXXER, DOXXER, GIVE ME THE NEWS?

MARK ANTHONY POEPSEL
Southern Illinois University Edwardsville

Tiki torches blazed in the night on Aug. 11, 2017, in Charlottesville, Virginia, and images of screaming white supremacists burned paths through our social media consciousness. Cable and online news outlets covered the story as evidence of the rising threat of white nationalism in the context of a broader protest to maintain Confederate monuments in Charlottesville and elsewhere.

Monuments to the Confederacy and to white supremacy were being removed or relocated across the country as various groups, in particular those representing people of color, objected to their prominent display. Opponents also argued that the monuments maintain a narrative of white supremacy that was particularly threatening as the rhetoric of then-candidate and now-president Donald Trump seemed to support white supremacist ideas and nationalist rhetoric that threatens safety and security.

The tiki-torch protest, startling enough for many Americans, grew into an even bigger story on Aug. 12. On that day, James Alex Fields allegedly drove his car into a group of counter-protestors in Charlottesville, killing Heather Heyer, 32, of Charlottesville (Caron 2017).

President Trump sent signals of tacit support to white supremacists after Heyer was killed. He stated that blame rested "on both sides" of the Charlottesville protest—a claim he maintained a month later (Landler 2017). To many, the president's comments were reinforcement of a narrative that white nationalists, also known as neo-Nazis, are only as threatening as those who oppose them. While there had been acts of violence on the part of anti-fascist protestors, they note, in their defense, that they must prepare for violence because white supremacists would attack even peaceful protestors (Shihipar 2017).

Heather Heyer was one such peaceful protestor standing up in her home city against those who wield torches and shout hateful speech. Her killing added urgency to efforts to "dox" the white supremacists who had made Charlottesville a battleground.

Ethicist David M. Douglas (2016) defines doxxing as "the intentional public release onto the Internet of personal information about an individual by a third party, often with the intent to humiliate, threaten, intimidate, or punish the identified individual." The practice is used by, and against, members of extremist groups to exact a form of vigilante justice. Not all doxxers are extremists, but they are generally interested in punishing those they feel are not being punished, or are not being caught fast enough by existing institutional law enforcement agencies.

The Twitter account @YesYoureRacist, run by Logan Smith of Raleigh, North Carolina, published photos highlighting the faces of white supremacist demonstrators in Charlottesville (Cain 2017). According to *Wired*, he gained more than 300,000 followers in a single weekend. By implication, it invited doxxing of those depicted. Smith argued it was necessary to expose participants in the white supremacist rally.

"And these people aren't afraid anymore. They're not hiding behind their hoods like they did before the civil rights era. They are out and proud. I think if they are so proud of their beliefs and proud to stand shoulder-to-shoulder with neo-Nazis and KKK members and white supremacists of all stripes, then I think their communities need to know who they are. They're not random faces in the crowd, they're your neighbors, they're your coworker, they're the people you pass in the grocery store," Smith said, according to the *Raleigh News & Observer* (Cain 2017).

The problem, of course, is that Smith and those who use the photos he publishes, can and do make mistakes. *Wired* reported:

> Kyle Quinn was more than 1,000 miles away from Charlottesville at the time of the protest—a case of mistaken identity that brought a wave of threats and accusations of racism so large that Quinn felt unsafe in his home (Ellis 2017).

Again from *Wired*:

> [A]s doxing continues to evolve as the preferred tactic of both far right and left wing internet factions, it's important to take a hard look at what each side is trying to accomplish. While the two sides use different logic to justify their actions, the true result is the same and even cumulative—leading to an arms race of financially incentivized, shame-slinging vigilantes.

Using crowdfunding tools, doxxers, and those who organize them, often seek financial assistance from the public. This opens the opportunity for a digital war on identity that journalists must be aware of when reporting on doxxers and information they develop and disseminate.

Micro Issues

1. Is doxxing, as it was used in this case, ethical? Justify your answer.
2. Is your answer based on whether you feel that the ones doing the "doxxing" are on *your* preferred side of the issue? If, as *Wired* points out, doxxing becomes the "preferred tactic" for both sides of an issue, does your opinion change on the ethics of doxxing?
3. Critique this statement by Smith: "I think their communities need to know who they are."

Midrange Issues

1. Many communities have seen tabloids crop up where people who are arrested on violations such as drug possession or DWI have their "mug shot" put into a tabloid for sale near the cash register of a convenience store even before they are formally charged with a crime. In what way, if any, does doxxing differ from this practice?
2. What could be the "greater good," if any, that would justify doxxing in a case such as this?

3. Logan Smith is a private individual who runs a Twitter site. Should the Raleigh newspaper have given his decision to publish photos of bystanders in the Charlottesville crowd a larger audience through an article in their pages? Does their article imply endorsement of what he did?

Macro Issues

1. The Charlottesville protest was one of the biggest news stories of 2017. After you look up this incident online, critique the "blame on both sides" statement by President Trump.
2. The author of the *Wired* quote says that the two sides of the racial divide use "different logic" to justify their use of the tactic. What, exactly, are the two sides, and what would be the logic that each would use in reaching a decision to use doxxing as a tactic?

CASE 6-C

THE TRUTH ABOUT THE FACTS: POLITIFACT.COM

LEE WILKINS
Wayne State University
University of Missouri

You would think journalists—the folks who write the "first draft of history"—would have better memories about accepting political claims at face value. However, early in 1950 when Wisconsin Republican Senator Eugene McCarthy stood at a podium in Wheeling, West Virginia, and claimed to have a list of 205 State Department employees who were members of the Communist Party, news organizations reprinted the statement without further corroboration. The news coverage destroyed lives and reputations, despite the fact that McCarthy had no such list nor was he ever able to produce one. Journalists learned that facts, what people say, and truth are not always closely connected. From that point forward, political journalists emphatically did not want to repeat the mistake.

Tampa Bay Times Washington, DC, bureau chief Bill Adair, who came to the nation's capitol in 1997 during the era when acid political rhetoric and partisan shilling were gaining a national platform on cable television and becoming more and more common in Congress, did have a journalist's instinct for truth. More than that, he felt professionally compelled to help his readers distinguish among political claims, no matter who was making them, and discoverable facts. It was in this context that he developed the website Politifact.com, which was initially supported by his newspaper *Tampa Bay Times* (formerly the *St. Petersburg Times*) and produced in conjunction with *Congressional Quarterly.*

Fact checking itself is not new. The *New Yorker* magazine earned much of its journalistic reputation for its fact checking: a not-always perfect process where a separate group of journalists checked the facts in *New Yorker* stories before they were printed. What made Politifact distinct—and memorable and marketable, according to Adair (personal communication 2012)—was the invention of the Truth-O-Meter, a visual representation of whether a statement was completely true to "pants-on-fire," a reference to the chant many Americans grow up with: "liar, liar, pants on fire."

When Politifact.com researched the truth behind political statements, it ranked them, from truthful, to mostly true, to mostly false, to whoppers. Adair believes it was the Truth-O-Meter that separated his fact checking site from many others. His own research shows that most readers look at the Truth-O-Meter first; many do not investigate further into the actual reporting and analysis that fuels the individual ranking.

Other elements also separated Politifact.com from its competitors. Beginning in 2009, the site awarded the "Lie of the Year" which, that year, went to former Alaska governor Sarah Palin for her utterly mendacious statement that the Patient Protection and Affordable Care Act would lead to death panels deciding whether elderly Americans would live or die. In 2011, the "Lie of the Year" went to the Democratic National Committee for its statement—carried in political ads as well as new stories—that the Republican budget approved by the US House of Representatives would repeal Medicare. The website has fact-checked sketch comedy ("Saturday Night Live") and Jon Stewart—himself a fact checker of some repute. Adair says that he does not pay attention to whether one political party or the other is found to be lying more often (as some studies have shown) but that the site is even-handed in selecting claims to be checked. Politifact.com is potent enough that those who are accused of lying—or even not telling the complete truth—contest its claims in the media, often vociferously.

And, in an era when website hits matter in terms of revenue, Adair is also forthright about the impact of the Truth-O-Meter on the site's popularity and hence profitability.

The *St. Petersburg Times* and Politifact.com were awarded the Pulitzer Prize for national reporting in 2009, for "its fact-checking initiative during the 2008 presidential campaign that used probing reporters and the power of the World Wide Web to examine more than 750 political claims, separating rhetoric from truth to enlighten voters."

Micro Issues

1. Is what Politifact.com does reporting? Is it objective reporting?
2. How would you evaluate the truthfulness of the Truth-O-Meter?
3. Why is the truthfulness of a statement examined in a separate news story instead of becoming part of continuing coverage? Is this approach ethically defensible?

Midrange Issues

1. Should individual journalists be responsible for checking the political claims of public officials, or is that job best left to "fact checkers" and websites such as Politifact.com?
2. Should there be a parallel website to check the claims of commercial messages? What would be the ethical rationale for such a site?
3. Adair has said that he believes the site would not be as successful without the Truth-O-Meter, even though he acknowledges that truth is often subtler than a simple rating would indicate. Do such sites need a gimmick to cut through the clutter of political speech today? Can such gimmicks be ethically justified?

Macro Issues

1. Based on the theories of truth outlined in chapter 2, what is the standard of truth Politifact.com employs? What are the dangers and benefits of employing this standard as opposed to others?
2. Evaluate this James W. Carey statement in light of the efforts of Politifact.com: "There is no such thing as a fact without context."
3. Provide an ethical rationale for fact checking "Saturday Night Live" or "The Daily Show."

CASE 6-D

WIKILEAKS

LEE WILKINS
Wayne State University
University of Missouri

In her book about secrets, ethicist Sissela Bok maintains that there are only two professions that regard keeping secrets as morally questionable at the outset: psychiatrists and journalists. Had she written the book about three decades later, Bok would at least have had to consider one additional, if non-traditional profession: computer hackers.

Australian-native Julian Assange, who describes his profession as hacker, has made the assertion multiple times that secret keeping, when done by nation states, is bad. Assange means this characterization in a moral/ethical sense. Thus, in 2005 and 2006, he created an organization—his title there was CEO and editor—that had the goal of releasing state secrets that were leaked to the nonprofit group.

While Assange was interested in all secrets, he was particularly interested in those kept by the most powerful nation on earth and its allies: the United States. In those early years, Assange began emailing the British publication the *Guardian* with unsolicited tips that led the *Guardian* to some remarkable stories, among them the Kroll report, which detailed how former Kenyan President Danile Arap Moi had stashed hundreds of thousands of pounds in foreign bank accounts—a story of political corruption most news organizations would have been proud to publish.

Assange first came to media attention in the United States in 2010 when Wikileaks published the video footage of Iranian civilians, including journalists working for Reuters, being gunned down by a US Apache helicopter. The US military had denied this version of events, and continued to do so until the video emerged. The resulting news coverage, coming as it did when the United States was bogged down in what became a decade-long conflict, catapulted Assange to international media attention.

But Assange had a great deal more information to offer. In 2010, Wikileaks published more than 400,000 documents—everything from raw reports of foreign service officers to military accounts of specific incidents—about the US prosecution of war in Iraq and Afghanistan. Collectively called the "war logs," these documents and their release raised central ethical questions for news organizations.

Those questions began with how individual news organizations cooperated with Assange in the release and verification of the documents. In addition to the *Guardian*, the *New York Times* and the German publication *Der Spiegel* entered into collaborative arrangements with Assange that allowed the individual news organizations to verify the facts in the documents and, when necessary—for example, when life might be at stake—to redact elements of the documents (most often names and locations) in news accounts.

These collaborative arrangements were unprecedented, in part because they involved multiple news organizations and were international in scope, and, in part because these documents—unlike the Pentagon Papers, which had set the standard for leaks that questioned the US government's international political policies—were about events that were ongoing and had the potential to upset or even end decades of diplomatic efforts. In addition, Assange himself proved exceptionally difficult to work with (Leigh and Harding 2011). He was often impossible to contact, unreliable in terms of keeping agreements, and, by 2011, embroiled in a criminal sex scandal in Sweden.

The various collaborative arrangements Assange developed with news organizations, particularly the *New York Times*, fell apart in the months after the publication of the war logs. Ultimately, Assange placed the documents—unredacted and unverified—on the web. In April 2011, Wikileaks began publishing secret files about the prisoners in the notorious Guantanamo Bay prison camp. How journalists treated all these files became the focus of one element of the ethical debate surrounding this complicated series of events.

A second focus of ethical debate was how Wikileaks obtained its information. Wikileaks did no independent reporting. Instead, it relied on others to provide "leaked" information. In the case of the war logs, that source was 23-year-old Bradley Manning, an army private, who was court-martialed for violating the Espionage Act, later pardoned by President Barack Obama, and now lives as a woman calling herself Chelsea Manning.

After Manning's arrest, it was widely reported that the private had an access to classified information in his role as a communication specialist, that he was bright, interested in technology and computers from an early age, and gay at a time when the US military still operated under the policy of "don't ask, don't tell." Servicemen and women who "came out" were dishonorably discharged. As more details about Manning emerged, Wikileaks critics questioned whether Assange had taken advantage of a vulnerable young man who did not understand the magnitude of the charges that could be leveled against him and would lack the personal resources to mount a vigorous defense if his role in the war logs were discovered.

Finally, there was Assange himself, a complex, mercurial figure even before the war logs were released. Assange was concerned about whether powerful governments—particularly the United States—would extradite him to the United States to face a multiplicity of charges emerging from his role in the release of classified documents.

Micro Issues

1. Is Assange a journalist? A hacker? An information middleman? A whistleblower? In an ethical sense, does his occupation matter?
2. Sophisticated news organizations entered into agreements with Assange before they published documents. Based on an ethical analysis, what should those agreements have focused on? Why?
3. When presented with documents such as those in the war logs, what specific steps should news organizations take to confirm them? Does this include asking government officials to verify or explain the contents?
4. How should news organizations treat both Wikileaks and Manning? After you have reviewed coverage, how would you evaluate the journalists' relationship with these two sources?

Midrange Issues

1. At one point, Assange hid in *Guardian* reporter David Leigh's house. Is this an appropriate thing for a journalist deeply involved in the story to do for a source? Does your answer change if Leigh were a documentary filmmaker?
2. How would you respond to the previous questions if the leaked documents came not from government but from a private for-profit organization such as a chemical or pharmaceutical firm?
3. In an ethical sense, contrast the process of "going under cover" from publishing leaks.
4. Strategic communication professionals often have access to corporate strategy documents and similar sorts of information? Evaluate whether strategic communication professionals have the same sort of whistleblower responsibility as those who uncover government wrongdoing.

5. Does Assange's personal character matter in how a journalist or new organization should evaluate his actions?

Macro Issues

1. What role do organizations such as Wikileaks fulfill in democratic societies? How is that role like and unlike that of news organizations?
2. Governments frequently claim that some of what they do needs to remain secret to be effective. Evaluate this claim from the perspective of a citizen, a journalist, and a diplomat.

CASE 6-E

CONTROL ROOM: DO CULTURE AND HISTORY MATTER IN REPORTING THE NEWS?

LEE WILKINS
Wayne State University
University of Missouri

Almost a decade before the 2011 Arab Spring, there was Al-Jazeera, a fledgling Middle Eastern television network with 40 million viewers predominantly in that region. (Currently, Al-Jazeera includes a staff in Washington, DC, and the network itself is available worldwide including a strong cable and internet presence.)

Journalists routinely cite the expression that "truth is the first casualty of war," but those in charge of Al-Jazeera also know that modern war cannot be waged without an intense propaganda effort on all sides of the conflict. Thus, when the United States was getting ready to invade Baghdad, director Jehane Noujaim requested and received permission to film the work of Al-Jazeera journalists as they covered the conflict. The 86-minute film, *Control Room*, won numerous awards.

Noujaim said that his goal was to produce a documentary about how truth is gathered, delivered, and ultimately created by those who deliver it. By telling the story of the coverage of the Iraqi invasion through the eyes of Arab journalists—many of whom had worked for news organizations such as the BBC before they worked for Al-Jazeera—the documentary provides an insider's view of how journalists report a complicated story, often questioning the conventional wisdom of one of both sides involved.

One focus of the film is Captain Josh Rushing, a military public information officer, who is shown trying to explain the American side of the story to the Al-Jazeera journalists. Rushing maintains that Iraq has weapons of mass destruction, that the Iraq invasion was not an attempt by the United States to capture oil resources, and to—from his point of view—provide a truthful account of these early days of the conflict. The film also shows the journalists questioning Rushing's facts, asking him to provide proof of what he says. For his part, Rushing says that he believes that the Al-Jazeera journalists are biased toward the regime of Saddam Hussein, noting that Al-Jazeera did not document the atrocities that regime perpetrated on Iraqi citizens.

Other elements of the film are tough to watch. They include footage of injured and dead Iraqis who died as the result of US bombing. Also included are images of US prisoners of war as they are questioned by Iraqi troops. Journalists working for Al-Jazeera are shown debating what they should show in terms of gory images. And, the journalists from Al-Jazeera are also shown discussing their personal opinions of American foreign policy that led to the invasion—they opposed it—and their belief that the American public will demand that the US government embark on a course other than invasion. The impact of images is also debated in the film—particularly the colliding of images about Israel with public opinion in the Middle East and how the images of Israeli aggression are linked to US foreign policy and this particular decision to invade Iraq.

The film also shows US officials, from the Secretary of Defense Donald Rumsfeld to former vice president Dick Cheney, claiming that Al-Jazeera journalists were lying and their network's coverage was entirely propagandistic. These segments are juxtaposed against Al-Jazeera journalists saying that they define their role as showing the human side of war. Interspersed are actual images from Al-Jazeera broadcasts that include interviews and press conference footage from former president George W. Bush—coverage the network broadcast that was vociferously criticized by Middle Eastern governments. The network was equally harshly criticized—predominantly by American officials—for broadcasting the images of American POWs. Journalists from Al-Jazeera are asked if they can be objective about the conflict; those same journalists ask American correspondents the same question. Rushing himself notes that Al-Jazeera's coverage is powerful precisely because US news organizations were not showing these images domestically.

The film also shows the shock of the Al-Jazeera journalists as Baghdad is overthrown. And, the biggest emotional punch of the film comes when one Al-Jazeera journalist who elected to stay in Baghdad to report on the invasion is killed in a US airstrike on the hotel in which hundreds of journalists were staying. The United States says the airstrike was a mistake; journalists from many nations disputed this claim. Through it all, the film documents the journalists doing what they believe is their job under difficult physical and emotional conditions.

Micro Issues

1. How do you think the journalists working for Al-Jazeera define their jobs? Is their definition of journalism different from your own?
2. How do you think the public information office for the military defines its role? How do you see its role as supporting or impeding the work of gathering the news? Would you say the same thing about the public information officer for your local police department or public health department?
3. Contrast the public statements by government officials about Al-Jazeera during this era of history with the statements made about the network during the Arab Spring. What do you think has led to this change in public perception about the network?

Midrange Issues

1. Should US television networks have shown the same sort of footage about the invasion as Al-Jazeera? Justify your decision in terms of the institutional role of the media in a democracy.
2. Al-Jazeera journalists were not embedded with US troops during the invasion. How might the process of embedding have changed coverage, both for embedded and non-embedded journalists?
3. The head of Al-Jazeera says, "I have plans for my children. I will send them to America to study, and they will stay there." Rushing says that he believes his role is to promote understanding between the Western and the Arab cultures. Evaluate both these statements in light of ethical theory.

Macro Issues

1. What is the difference between propaganda and news in war time?
2. Are there certain journalistic values that cross culture and language?
3. What are common frustrations—regardless of employer—that the journalists in the film appear to share?

4. You are being asked to evaluate this film more than a decade after it was first produced. Knowing what you now know about recent political history, evaluate the job that Al-Jazeera did in covering the Iraq invasion. Evaluate the job that American journalists did.

CASE 6-F

VICTIMS AND THE PRESS

ROBERT LOGAN
National Institute of Medicine, Washington, DC

Alice Waters' daughter, Julie, 7, has leukemia. Her illness was diagnosed in its early stages in March 2000. Julie's physicians believe her condition can be successfully treated.

Ms. Waters, 37, lives in a mobile home in an unincorporated area a few miles from Metroplex, a city of 1.5 million. Ms. Waters' street is the only residential section in the area. At the north end of the street—which has 12 mobile homes on each side facing one another—are four large gas stations that catch traffic off the interstate that runs a quarter mile away to the west. At the south end of the street (about a quarter mile away) are two large tanks that are a relatively small storage facility for Big Oil, Inc. Next to this—starting almost in her backyard—is the boundary of a successful, 700-acre grapefruit orchard, which borders on a municipal landfill. About a quarter mile away are large well fields that are the principal source of drinking water for Metroplex.

In July 1999, a 6-year-old boy in the household two doors down from Ms. Waters was diagnosed as having leukemia. He was not as lucky as Julie; his diagnosis was late in the progression of his disease, and he died in December 2000. In 2001, an infant girl became the second baby born with birth defects in the neighborhood within seven years. Both families moved before Ms. Waters came to the neighborhood in 1999. Internal medicine specialists Dr. Earnest and Dr. Sincere met Julie soon after she was admitted to the hospital in October 2000. They were instrumental in getting funding for Julie's care when her mother was unable to pay. They are members of Worried M.D.s for Social Responsibility, a self-proclaimed liberal, national public interest group that gets actively involved in national political issues.

The physicians told Ms. Waters that they were suspicious about the causes of Julie's illness. Three cancer and birth-defect incidents on the same street, the physicians said, were not a coincidence.

In November 2001, they began to collect water samples from the wellhead at Ms. Waters' house. They sent the samples to a well-regarded testing lab in another city. Since then, they have tested the water at a professional lab every four months. Every test revealed traces of more than 10 human-made and natural chemicals often associated with oil storage tanks, pesticides, grapefruit orchards, gas station leaks, lead from automobile emissions, and a large landfill.

However, each chemical occurs consistently at 6 to 15 parts per billion, which is considered safe for drinking water based on standards set by the US Environmental Protection Agency (EPA). At higher levels these chemicals are associated with carcinogenic risks or increases in birth defects, but the levels found at Ms. Waters' wellhead are within safety thresholds set by the EPA. There is no evidence the chemicals are associated directly with the health problems found in Ms. Waters' neighborhood.

At a fundraising party last night for mayoral candidate Sam Clean, Drs. Earnest and Sincere privately told Clean what they had found. Clean is a well-known public figure, has a reputation as an environmentalist, owns a successful health food restaurant chain, is media wise and looks good on television. He is a long shot to become mayor and needs fresh issues to draw attention to his candidacy.

At 11 a.m. today, KAOS news radio begins running as the top story in its 20-minute news rotation "Clean Attacks City Lack of Cleanup." In the story, Clean gives a soundbite attacking city officials for "ignoring cancer-causing agents in water in a neighborhood where children have died, which is next door to the city's water supply." He describes the neighborhood's medical problems and describes (without naming) Julie and Alice Waters. The news report explains that water from the neighborhood has several "toxic agents believed to cause cancer at higher levels" and points out that the city's water wells are within a quarter mile of oil tanks, gas stations, a grapefruit orchard, a landfill, and septic tanks. County officials are said to be unavailable for comment. The report runs throughout the day at 20-minute intervals.

By 2:30 p.m., calls to the switchboard have jammed the newsroom. The callers who get through are frightened about their drinking water. City Hall's switchboards are jammed. The callers sound upset and ask whether their water is safe to drink.

By 4 p.m., reporters from the local ABC affiliate are already knocking on doors in the trailer park and sending live reports from the scene. Neighbors tell them where Alice and Julie Waters live.

At 4:15 p.m., your managing editor gives you the story. You are an ambitious reporter for *Metroplex Today*, the only morning newspaper in

Metroplex. Both of you realize this is clearly Page 1 potential, but you have only a few hours before deadline for the next morning's edition. After a few phone calls, you discover that the mayor, the city council, and most city and county officials are all out of town at a retreat and are unavailable for comment. The regional EPA office is not answering the phone.

A trusted spokesperson for Regional Hospital tells you that Drs. Sincere and Earnest are furious at Clean for releasing the story and have no comment. She fills you in with all of the above information. The same Regional Hospital spokesperson says Ms. Waters does not want to be interviewed. She suddenly realizes that her husband, whom she walked out on several years before, might see the story and return to town.

Sam Clean is more than happy to talk to you.

Micro Issues

1. Is Clean a reliable enough source for KAOS radio to base its reports on?
2. Should KAOS have broadcast the story?
3. Should you respect Ms. Waters' wishes and leave her and her daughter out of the story?
4. Are Dr. Earnest and Dr. Sincere reliable sources?
5. What do you tell the public about whether the water supply is safe?

Midrange Issues

1. Would you be working on the story if KAOS and ABC had ignored it?
2. Would you be working on the story if there was little public reaction after the KAOS broadcast?
3. If Ms. Waters decides to do an interview on ABC later today, do you then include her in your story?
4. If city and county officials remain unavailable, how do you handle their side of the story? Does that delay publication until you can get more information, or do you go with what is available?
5. Are there unbiased sources you can contact about risk assessment? Whom?

Macro Issues

1. How do you handle the discrepancy between the information from the EPA and the skeptical scientists and environmentalists?

2. What is the public's probable reaction to reporting this story? Should your newspaper take any precautions to prevent public panic? If so, what should they be?
3. How risky is the water compared to risks we take for granted, such as traveling by car? Can you think of a relevant comparison for your article comparing the relative risk of the water to a well-known risk?
4. Is it the media's role to speak for a society that is averse to many risks? How might the media accomplish this function?

CASE 6-G

FOR GOD AND COUNTRY: THE MEDIA AND NATIONAL SECURITY

JEREMY LITTAU
Lehigh University

MARK SLAGLE
University of North Carolina—Chapel Hill

The ethical issues involving the intersection of the media and national security typically revolve around the question of duties and loyalties. Those questions, as the following three-part case demonstrates, are long-standing. They also allow journalists to evaluate the consistency of their reasoning over time—something good ethical thinking is supposed to promote. How journalists respond to these cases also may depend on the differing philosophies individual journalists and their news organizations adhere to.

With this introduction, decide each of the following three cases, all of which have an important role in the history of journalism ethics. As you resolve the various issues in each case, ask yourself whether you have been consistent in your decision-making and what philosophical approach or approaches best supports your thinking.

CASE STUDY 1: THE BAY OF PIGS

In 1961, an anti-communist paramilitary force trained and supplied by the CIA was preparing to invade Cuba and topple Fidel Castro. Although the desire of the American government to overthrow Castro was no secret, the specifics of the invasion plan were not known to the public. On April 6, a *New York Times* reporter filed a story with his editors that declared the invasion was "imminent." The paper prepared to run the story with a page-one, four-column slot using the word "imminent" in the text and the headline.

After much discussion, *Times* managing editor Turner Catledge and publisher Orvil Dryfoos decided to remove the word "imminent" from the story and shrink the headline to a single column. These changes were made, in part, in response to a phone call from President John F. Kennedy, asking the paper to kill the story. On April 17, the anti-Castro forces landed at Cuba's Bay of Pigs, where all group members were either taken prisoner or killed. The botched invasion was a major embarrassment for Kennedy, who later told Catledge that if the *Times* had run the story as planned, it might have prevented the disastrous invasion (Hickey 2001).

Micro Issue

1. Did the *Times* act ethically in downsizing and downplaying the story?

Midrange Issue

1. Are there certain categories of information, for example, troop movements or the development of new weapons, that journalists as a matter of policy should either downplay or not publish as all?

Macro Issue

1. How should journalists respond if government officials request that specific "facts" (which are not true) be printed as part of a disinformation campaign to confuse our enemies?

CASE STUDY 2: OSAMA BIN LADEN

Since the 9/11 attacks until his death at the hands of the US military in 2012, Osama bin Laden and his deputies released a series of video and audio tapes containing speeches about their ongoing operations. Many of them first aired on Al-Jazeera, the Arabic-language news channel that broadcasts in the Middle East but also can be received in many American and European markets. The US government, specifically President George W. Bush, urged the US media not to rebroadcast these tapes, arguing that they might contain coded messages to al-Qaeda "sleeper cells" and could result in more attacks. Most broadcast networks acquiesced to the request, although it was never made clear whether any of the tapes, in fact, contained such messages (Spencer 2001).

Micro Issue

1. How is this request like and unlike President Kennedy's request to the *New York Times*?

Midrange Issues

1. Does the fact that other news agencies in other countries broadcast the tapes have any bearing on what US broadcasters should do?
2. Should US broadcasters have agreed to this request in October 2001? Should they agree to the request today? Why or why not?

Macro Issue

1. How would you respond to a viewer who says that broadcasting the tapes is unpatriotic and puts American lives at risk?

CASE STUDY 3: MAKE NEWS, NOT WAR?

In 1991, CNN correspondent Christiane Amanpour arrived in the Balkans to cover the breakaway of Slovenia and Croatia from Yugoslavia. After witnessing several brutal battles, including the siege of Dubrovnik, she moved on to Bosnia to cover the hostilities there for almost two years. Troubled by the lack of coverage the war was receiving, Amanpour encouraged her editors to devote more time to the issue. In 1994, Amanpour appeared via satellite on a live television broadcast with President Bill Clinton. She asked the president if "the constant flip-flops of your administration on the issue of Bosnia set a very dangerous precedent." Amanpour's pointed questions embarrassed the administration and generated more coverage of the war and of American foreign policy. Amanpour later admitted she wanted to draw more attention to the plight of the Bosnian Muslims (Halberstam 2001).

Micro Issues

1. Should Amanpour consciously have tried to influence US foreign policy in this way?
2. If she had not tried to influence US policy, would she have been complicit in the genocide that followed?

Midrange Issues

1. Are some issues, such as genocide, so ethically reprehensible that journalists should speak out as citizens in addition to fulfilling their professional responsibilities?
2. Is it appropriate for journalists to testify at war crimes trials when they have witnessed and reported on atrocities?

Macro Issue

1. Is it naive for journalists to continue to say that "we just let readers make up their minds" on these issues? If you answer yes, what does that say about the ethical dilemmas that come with the power we have as journalists?
2. Media theorist Marshall McLuhan predicted more than a half century ago that wars of the future would be fought with images rather than bullets. How true has that prediction become in the ongoing war on terror?

7

Media Economics
The Deadline Meets the Bottom Line

By the end of this chapter you should be familiar with

- the economic realities of the social responsibility theory of the press
- the economic and legislative initiatives that have combined to place control of information in the hands of fewer and larger corporations
- how various mediums have coped with the current economic and technological realities of media
- the "stakeholder" theory of economic success

OF MARKETS AND MORALS

Let's say you're a famous Broadway producer—Joe Papp—and in the mid-1970s decide that while Broadway productions are terrific, it would be even better if the average New Yorker could see classics for free. Shakespeare in the Park was born. Each summer, New York City's Public Theater puts on free outdoor Shakespeare performances in Central Park, subsidized by taxpayer dollars. All New Yorkers have to do is stand in line—and sometimes it's a long one—to get the tickets.

Enter Craigslist and services that will wait in line for you: at a cost of $125 per hour. Suddenly, the free tickets weren't so free. New York is not the only place you can hire someone to stand in line. Washington, DC, has an industry fueled by Linestanding.com where surrogates will stand in line for seats to US Supreme Court arguments or at Congressional hearings. Homeless people are often hired to do the work. And, of course, if you want to move to the front of the line at Disney World, you just have to pay more for the tickets.

Or, if you want to drive in the high occupancy lane in some metropolitan areas—without benefit of a car pool—you can pay for the privilege, even if there is no one in your vehicle but you.

What's wrong with that? In a market economy, goods and services change hands and no one really gets hurt. Or do they? In the case of Shakespeare in the Park, New York's attorney general (later governor) Andrew Cuomo pressured Craigslist to stop the ads, arguing that selling tickets that were meant to be free deprived New Yorkers of one of the more unusual benefits of their political community.

The chance to stand in line for a chance to see Al Pacino play Shylock is something that should not be for sale, according to Harvard political philosopher Michael Sandel. In his bestselling 2012 book *What Money Can't Buy: The Moral Limits of Markets*, Sandel argues that in this century, economic language—where literally everything has to be marketed and incentivized—has not only crowded out moral thinking but has sometimes changed our conception of what it means to have a good life in the sense that Aristotle meant it—to have a life with authentic flourishing. Whether it's paying kids to get good grades, the naming opportunities for everything from sports stadiums to national parks to newborns, to the selling of everything from blood to kidneys, Sandel argues that there are places and areas of life where the market simply doesn't belong.

Sandel notes two sets of basic objections to thinking that everything should be the subject of commerce. The first is the notion of fairness, which is highlighted by the example of hiring someone to stand in line for a free ticket. Those with money move to the front. Shakespeare might have objected (after all, he wrote jokes for the groundlings who couldn't afford the expensive seats); Sandel most certainly does. Line jumping just is not fair. In addition, it's coercive—those involved in the case, the citizens of New York, haven't given their permission for "free" tickets to be sold to the highest bidder. And, they have no recourse to change the system that emerges, unless they become unwilling participants.

The second set of objections to thinking about everything in terms of a market begins with the capacity to fuel corruption. This objection is not new. Paying money for priestly indulgences in the Roman Catholic Church, a corruption of the concept of forgiveness of sins, is one of the reasons for the Protestant reformation more than 500 years ago. God, and forgiveness, simply could not and should not be bought—even though they were for sale. As Sandel notes, you can buy sports memorabilia or even a sports team. What you cannot do is buy the actual experience of hitting a home run in the World Series or scoring the winning touchdown in the Super Bowl. Moneyball will take you only so far, and the experiences are not equivalent.

In many areas of life, money does not incentivize better behavior. Students who were offered a monetary incentive to raise money for a charity raised less money than those who were offered nothing. Citizens of a community in Switzerland volunteered to become the locus of a nuclear waste repository. In 2012, Alvin Roth won the Nobel Memorial Prize in Economic Sciences in part for his pioneering work that created an efficient and moral market for kidney donors moved by altruism but lacking a specific person in their lives who needed the kidney at that time. The New England Program for Kidney Exchange was born. However, when the same problem was presented to them with an economic inducement, they turned the same proposal down. Traditional economists tend to think that qualities such as altruism, generosity, solidarity, and civic duty are scarce. Sandel argues that they are like a muscle: they grow with repeated use. They speak to notions of the good life, and when market language is substituted for the language of morals, our concept of the good life itself is degraded. Corruption and degradation are the second set of reasons that market thinking fails to capture what human beings truly want and need.

Sandel concludes his book with the following:

"The disappearance of the class-mixing experience once found at the ballpark represents a loss not only for those looking up but also for those looking down. Something similar has been happening throughout society. At a time of rising inequality, the marketing of everything means that people of affluence and people of modest means lead increasingly separate live. . . . Democracy does not require perfect equality, but it does require that citizens share in a common life. . . . For this is how we learn to negotiate and abide our common differences, and how we come to care for the common good" (Sandel 2012, 203).

A LEGACY OF RESPONSIBILITY

The *social responsibility theory of the press* was developed in the 1940s by a panel of scholars, the Hutchins Commission, with funding from Henry Luce, the conservative founder of *Time* magazine. The social responsibility theory envisioned a day when an active recipient of news and information was satisfied by a socially responsible press. According to the Hutchins Commission, media have the following five functions in society:

1. To provide a truthful, comprehensive and intelligent account of the day's events in a context that gives them meaning.
2. To serve as a forum for exchange of comment and criticism.

3. To provide a representative picture of constituent groups in society.
4. To present and clarify the goals and values of society.
5. To provide citizens with full access to the day's intelligence.

But social responsibility theory has a fundamental flaw: it gives little attention to modern media economics. This omission occurred in part because multinational corporations and chain ownership were still on the horizon when the Hutchins Commission worked. Because the theory was developed early in the McCarthy period, there was also an unwillingness to link economic and political power for fear of being labeled Marxist. This omission means that *the social responsibility theory does not deal with the realities of concentrated economic power*, particularly in an era when information has become a valuable commodity.

As the mass media became enormous, economically powerful institutions, they joined what political scientist C. Wright Mills (1956) called the "power elite," a ruling class within a democratic society. Time has proved Mills right. Power is found not only in the halls of government but also on Wall Street. And power is found not only in money or armies, it is also found in information. Media organizations, precisely because they have become multinational corporations engaged in the information business, are deeply involved in this power shift.

Today, the media are predominantly corporate owned and publicly traded, with media conglomerates among the largest (and until recently, the most profitable) of the world's corporations. The corporate owners of the average news operation are more insulated from contact with news consumers than virtually any other business owner in America. And, there are fewer of them. Most local media outlets in the world are owned by six multinational corporations and each has become increasingly large in an attempt to gain market efficiencies.

A handful of media conglomerates—NewsCorp, CBS, Comcast/NBCUniversal, Viacom, Bertelsmann AG, Time Warner, and the Walt Disney Corporation—own the vast majority of media, including newspapers, broadcast and cable television networks, radio stations, movie and music studios, and book publishers. Other media organizations have a virtual stranglehold on various mediums—from the Sinclair Broadcast Group in local television to Clear Channel Communications in commercial radio. This consolidation of voices might limit the marketplace of ideas, especially when ownership has a decided partisan and political bias.

These corporations typically adhere to market philosophies (Barnouw 1997). Commercial news organizations concurrently trade in four markets: the market for audience, competing for readers and viewers; the stock market because most firms trade stock and desire higher valuations; the advertising market because firms compete for advertising revenue; and a market for sources, competing for information to disseminate (McManus 1994). According to market theory, these four markets should operate efficiently and consistently to produce high-quality news that aligns with public interest; however, a focus on profitability and serving the market often conflicts with serving the public (Barnouw 1997; McManus 1994).

This emergence of media as economic and political power brokers leads to the question of how a powerful institution such as the mass media, which traditionally has had the political role of checking other powerful institutions, can be checked. Can the watchdog be trusted when it is inexorably entwined with the institutions it is watching? For instance, ESPN reportedly pulled out of a joint documentary with PBS's *Frontline* about the effects of concussions in football after NFL commissioner Roger Goddell directly pressured the network, which routinely shows NFL highlights and has a $15 billion contract to broadcast *Monday Night Football*.

Similarly, what news organization can be trusted to take a critical look at the FCC's loosening the ownership rules meant to protect local ownership and diversity of media voices when the conglomerate that owns individual outlets stands to profit from the changes? Similarly, how should such conglomerates cover other FCC decisions, such as repealing net neutrality, which prohibited broadband providers such as AT&T, Comcast, and Verizon—all major advertisers as well as news distribution competitors—from blocking or slowing down websites or charging for certain content? As media corporations expand in the pursuit of profit, who will watch the watchdog? Perhaps as important, who will watch the new kids on the block, Google and Facebook, both of which have "projects" that include news and both of which also attempt to monetize every hit?

When the social responsibility theory was framed in the 1940s, the primary informational concern was scarcity: people might not get the information they needed for citizenship, and until recently, government agencies such as the FCC were still basing policy decisions on the scarcity argument when any consumer with cable or a satellite dish knew otherwise. Today, however, the primary informational concern is an overabundance of raw data: people might not filter out what they need through all the clutter. Media and their distribution systems changed, but the theory remained silent, especially about the role of profit.

The clash of large, well-financed institutions for control of information is a modern phenomenon. Classical ethical theory, which speaks to individual acts, is of little help in sorting out the duties and responsibilities of corporations larger than most nations that control the currency of the day: information.

Americans are unwilling to accept government as the solution to counter the concentrated economic power of the media, and government has been hesitant to break up the large media conglomerates. Europeans have taken a different view, in many cases using tax dollars to support a government controlled broadcast system. In some cases, such as the Scandinavian countries, tax dollars also support newspapers—with the goal of sustaining multiple, distinct voices in the public sphere (Picard 1988).

HYPER-COMPETITION AND ITS IMPACT ON NEWS

Legacy journalists, those journalists who did not come of age as "digital natives," and the news organizations that employ them, face a huge shift in the assumptions about what makes news media profitable and praiseworthy. Legacy journalism emerged from an era of low-to-moderate economic competition. Even though specific rivalries were often intense, they were local and definitely not across media platforms. Individual organizations competed for consumer satisfaction and time, consumer spending, content, advertisers, and employees. More than 30 years ago, media scholar Steve Lacy (1989) predicted these low-to-moderate competitive environments would produce a quality news product based on individual organizations' financial commitment to news, which in turn was perceived useful by audience members and sustained by a journalistic culture that valued excellence and public service.

But, low-to-moderate competition no longer exists in the contemporary media marketplace. Instead, you now live in an era of hyper-competition, much of it provided by web access. In hyper-competition, *supply substantially exceeds demand so that a large percentage of the producers in the market operate at a financial loss*. Classical economic theory holds that hypercompetition cannot exist permanently. However, news and information are not traditional economic commodities; they are called "experience and credence" commodities, meaning that a consumer cannot judge whether the product actually meets his or her individual needs until he or she has invested in and spent time with the product. News also is linked to social welfare, a category of products with significant external values not readily captured by price point or profit margin.

John McManus argued that, beginning in the 1980s, news organizations began moving toward making news "explicitly a commodity" (1994, 1). Journalists in a market-driven newsroom, McManus argued, would select stories for the "issues and events that have the greatest ratio of expected appeal for demographically desirable audiences" (1994, 114). In other words, the first goal of journalists would not be informing the public. Instead, it would be providing news that could entice more readers or viewers. More readers or viewers, in turn, would lead to increased profitability. Journalism, historically, aims to inform citizens and assist in strengthening democracy. Market-driven journalism, however, was not a service to the public. Instead of informing readers or viewers, market-driven news organizations entertain while possibly informing.

The current state of media financial affairs can be summarized as an emphasis on corporate responsibility to the stockholders of publicly traded corporations. In stockholder theory, corporations and their leaders have a single, overriding, and legally binding promise to those who purchase stock: increase the share price. Milton Friedman, who first articulated the theory, suggests that increasing the share price is *the* promise that managers make. Whatever is legally done to promote that end is ethically right.

Business ethicist Patricia H. Werhane (2006) has a different vision of the traditional stakeholder map. She says that some sorts of businesses—such as health care—have a public responsibility that extends beyond individual stockholders. These companies, she says, should operate from an "enriched stakeholder" model as opposed to a "profit-driven stockholder" model. The enriched stakeholder model puts something other than the corporation at the center of the "stakeholder" map (for health care, she suggests the patient) and rings that central stakeholder with government, investors, the court system, medical professionals, insurance companies, managed care plans, and others. By changing the stakeholder map, Werhane suggests that other "promises" surface and that other measures of success emerge.

The stakeholder model of media economics has much to recommend it. At the center of the map are citizens and community. Around the center is a ring including audiences, creative artists, stockholders, governments, nongovernmental organizations, journalists, strategic communication professionals, corporate managers, and employees. By asking what benefits citizens living in communities the most, media corporate managers would begin to use a different gauge of success that does not place profit first in every situation. Media corporations would no longer search for a one-time "hit" that can be packaged, imitated, and mass reproduced. Instead, they would make smaller investments in a variety of experiments, allowing creativity and connection to community to help determine what works for both stakeholders and stockholders and what does not.

From the level of the individual journalist or strategic communications professional to the organizations that employ them, today there are multiple experiments with "new" business models. While it is difficult to categorize them, they share an attempt to shift the costs of producing and distributing

Figure 7.1. *Non Sequitur* © 2008 Wiley Ink, Inc. Distributed by Andrews McMeel Syndication. Reprinted with permission. All rights reserved.

content to the individual listener/reader/viewer rather than to advertisers. New business models are producing some efforts that, just a few decades ago, were seen as an unprofitable backwater or completely ethically forbidden. Documentary films were once a staple of art film houses attracting small audiences. Today, they take on issues of public importance, combining traditional news gathering efforts with Hollywood-style cinematic techniques. Some are financially successful, and some, such as Josh Fox's *Gasland*, have influenced public policy. Podcasts thrive as well in outlets such as NPR, where consumer suggestions are sometimes the starting point for NPR documentaries, a polar opposite of the "agenda setting" role of the press that media theorists wrote about in the latter part of the 20th century.

Other examples are all across the media landscape. The *New York Times* now has an "Op Docs" section attached to the more traditional opinion page. Niche sites such as Five Thirty Eight and Jezebel have become successful enough that they have been purchased by mainstream news organizations, often with little change to content or frequency from the days before they found financial security. Popular YouTube stars such as Felix Arvid Ulf Kjellberg (better known as PewDiePie) make salaries rivaling those of the most successful Hollywood actors, and comedians such as Aziz Ansari of *Master of None* and Derek Waters of *Drunk History* launched their careers with internet-based short films. And almost everyone, from the folks who sell you household products to the stodgiest of the "old guard" newsrooms, is experimenting with reader/viewer/listener engagement. From allowing consumers to comment on stories, to pre-testing news programming, or developing ad messages, the public now has a say in what "news" is.

The result is what at least one scholar has called "liquid journalism" where "traditional role perceptions of journalism influenced by its occupational ideology—providing a general audience with information of general interest in a balanced, objective and ethical way—do not seem to fit all that well with the lived realities of reporters and editors, nor with the communities they are supposed to serve" (Deuze 2008, 848).

When news organizations, and even individual journalists, worry about their "brand" rather than the public they serve, something essential has changed. Perhaps the most troubling element in this strand of research in media economics is that the public appears not to value—or even sometimes recognize—that quality is declining. In hypercompetitive situations, ethics takes a back seat to survival and the common good becomes the loser in the process.

TELEVISION: CONGLOMERATION, CONSOLIDATION, AND SURVIVAL

Television, a medium that began its existence as a free service brought to the public by willing advertisers, has morphed into something that nine out of ten Americans now pay for twice—once with their cable or satellite bills and, for most, twice with their attention to advertising. Yet, television, particularly at the network or cable level where programming is produced, is always in search of more efficiency and revenue streams.

Take the two entities that are the original television networks: NBC and CBS. In the past decade, both have acquired more assets from publishing houses to cable networks to content distributors. The goal of all this financial activity is not only to find profit centers but also to create vertically integrated companies with diverse sources of income. Consider this scenario:

- By acquiring production facilities, networks can now own the shows they broadcast, a new phenomenon cutting deeply into the old system of buying programs from independent producers who took the risks in order to reap the possible rewards if shows were picked up.
- By acquiring cable stations such as Bravo (owned by NBCUniversal), networks control outlets for their shows as they go into the lucrative phases of syndication, taking advantage of legislation that ended the FCC's old "fin-syn" rule prohibiting networks from being syndicators.
- By acquiring the maximum number of local television stations owned by law, networks have a built-in advantage for uploading news when it happens in a market where they own a station, something that Rupert Murdoch's Fox brand has perfected even after getting a late start in the market.
- By acquiring the rights to broadcast major and minor sports, amateur and professional alike, both of the traditional two, NBC and CBS, launched their own 24/7 cable sports networks to rival EPSN, which is owned by another traditional network, ABC.

- By acquiring aftermarket distributors, networks make money on rentals and sales of boxed DVD sets of popular series after their original airing. Even series that were closed after two or three seasons find an afterlife in boxed sets.
- By licensing shows to streaming services such as Netflix, Amazon Prime, and Hulu (partially owned by NBCUniversal), networks have yet another revenue stream to make money from popular (and sometimes unpopular) television programs. Some cable networks, including HBO and Showtime, have launched their own streaming services. Of course, the major streaming services also program original content, including series such as *Arrested Development* and *Longmire* that failed to find more than a cult following when they originally aired on broadcast and cable networks.

The result of vertical integration is a pair of companies that have survived in the broadcasting industry for nearly a century and that can now control a product from the filming of the pilot episode to the last airing of the syndicated show or personal download, sometimes decades from now. And it must be emphasized that much of what is now possible in the bullet points above has only recently been made possible by FCC and court rulings as well as generous anti-trust rulings. And NBC and CBS are but two "legacy" media corporations to have acquired their way to financial success.

Media consolidation allows for a diversification of income. In the case of NBC, after the acquisition of Universal, revenues went from 90 percent advertising-based to 50 percent, with the remainder coming from subscriptions, admissions, licensing, and other ancillary income. By weaning away from advertising, media companies have hedged against the vagaries of recession.

Conglomeration, consolidation, and the aftermarket added more revenue streams and made things more predictable for stockholders. But not everyone is happy with the direction media ownership is taking. Groups as diverse as the National Organization for Women and the National Rifle Association criticized and challenged changes in ownership limits proposed by the FCC. *Columbia Journalism Review* Editor at Large Neil Hickey (2003) summed up the fears of many when he concluded,

> What we risk over the long haul is ownership creep that may eventually see the end of the few remaining rules, and with them, the public's right to the widest possible array of news and opinion—at which point, robust, independent, antagonistic, many-voiced journalism may be only a memory.

NEWSPAPERS: WHAT COMES AFTER THE PENNY PRESS?

Financing the American media through advertising is so deeply ingrained in the system that it is hard to imagine any other way. Yet, newspapers in America were supported solely by their readers for more than a century. Incidentally, in 1920, the then-secretary of commerce Herbert Hoover argued for commercial-free radio, a funding formula that would have likely failed or at the least, changed the medium entirely.

The legacy funding formula for most newspapers was created more than 180 years ago when Benjamin Day, publisher of the *New York Sun*, started the "penny press" revolution by lowering the price of his newspaper to a penny at a time when his competition was selling newspapers for a nickel. He gambled that he could overcome the printing losses with additional advertising revenue—if circulation increased. When his gamble paid off, virtually every publisher in town followed his lead.

What Day did was farsighted. By pricing their products at or below the cost of printing, publishers cast their economic future with their advertisers. But advertisers demand "eyeballs" and paid circulation, guaranteed by the Audit Bureau of Circulation, was the standard. The system worked as long as circulation increased to cover the increasing costs of covering the news. But readership peaked more than three decades ago, and newspapers began shedding costs. Some sold to chains. Others combined with rivals in "joint operating agreements" (JOA) which were, in effect, a congressionally approved exception to antitrust laws. Under a JOA, rival papers could combine press operations, billing operations, etc. but act as rival newspapers in their quest for news. However, with more than 30 years of history to evaluate the impact of the JOA legislation, what scholars and stockholders now know is that no joint operating agreement has allowed both newspapers to survive under the new financial arrangement indefinitely.

Such consolidation efforts were not nearly enough to survive the onslaught of the web and a business model that provided news—an expensive commodity to produce—for free online. Layoffs and hiring freezes became a fact of life at large and award-winning papers such as the *Los Angeles Times*, the *Chicago Tribune*, and the *New York Times* and smaller community papers as well. National papers such as the *New York Times* and *Washington Post* have found some success with online subscription models; audiences are willing to pay for quality journalism. However, small- and medium-market papers continue to struggle to find a way to "monetize" the internet operation. Attempts to gain more readers by being more convenient eventually became a way for many to not pay for news content at all. Although ads were possible and even populous on newspaper websites, advertisers were loath to pay the same amount that audited readership had commanded. Major newspapers such as the *Rocky Mountain News* in Denver folded. Some, such as the *Wall Street Journal*, decreased their page size while most decreased their page count, beginning a cycle where smaller "news hole" required fewer journalists. Other papers, most notably the *New Orleans Times Picayune*, went to less-than-daily circulation in an attempt to survive.

At the time this book went to press, newspapering remained in serious trouble. The local newspaper in most communities had long been a monopoly operation with returns of greater than 20 percent annually common before the bleeding of circulation and advertising. Even after cutbacks, newspapers still boast a "name brand" in most communities and the largest reporting staff in any given local market. Economically, small market dailies are actually thriving financially. However, with readers decreasing, some newspapers are increasingly putting video segments on their websites in an attempt to siphon viewers from local nightly newscasts. How this even more expensive use of the web will play out is unknown, but it does demand that journalists be cross-trained for the new media reality as newspapers add video and sound and television stations add print stories to their websites.

MOVIES AND MUSIC: BLOCKBUSTERS AND PIRATES

While digital technology sent shock waves throughout all media industries, the strongest tremors were felt in the entertainment business. There, digital technology arrived at the same time a handful of global companies took control of about 85 percent of the record industry. The rationale for the consolidation in the music industry was that profits from established labels and artists would be used to promote new talent. However, the corporate approach meant that managers now focused on quarterly profits and selling records rather than making music and promoting art.

Corporations wanted blockbuster hits. They were difficult and expensive to make and promote and impossible to predict. Walmart, the largest retailer of music in America, wanted to make its profits from the industry while carrying only about 2 percent of all releases available in a single year (Anderson 2006).

Chris Blackwell, who began a small record label in the 1970s and sold it to PolyGram in 1989, said,

> I don't think the music business lends itself very well to being a Wall Street business. You're always working with individuals, with creative people, and the people you are trying to reach, by and large, don't view music as a commodity but as a relationship with a band. It takes time to expand that relationship but

most people who work for the corporations have three-year contracts, some five, and most of them are expected to produce. What an artist really needs is a champion, not a numbers guy who in another year is going to leave (Seabrook 2003, 46).

Other industries are affected by the new economic realities as well. Major studios no longer want to make medium-budget films—from $40 million to $80 million. Instead, they prefer smaller films for $10 million or less and "blockbuster" films with budgets of $100 million or more. Films in the middle—particularly the $40 to $60 million range—are now considered too risky to make by many producers and some studios.

Plus, investors want films with a built-in audience, so a huge percentage of the nation's screens are filled with sequels, comic book heroes, and action-adventure movies known to be big in foreign distribution. For instance, in 2017, nine of the top 10 grossing movies was either a sequel of a previous movie, a remake of an earlier film, or a tie in with a fictional book or comic book character. Most of these top 10 will eventually see yet another sequel as long as audiences are willing to pay. So the surprise 2014 hit *Guardians of the Galaxy* (grosses of $333 million) becomes *Guardians of the Galaxy Vol. 2* (grosses of more than $385 million), while the live-action version of the oft-told love story *Beauty and the Beast* raked in more than $500 million. The urge to create a sequel is irresistible for Hollywood. Such movies, regardless of their merit, consume a huge proportion of available screens leaving art films, indies, and the like pushed aside. In addition, promotional budgets for potential blockbusters have become so bloated that smaller films with more modest budgets tend to get lost in the noise. These promotions created large opening weekends that are typically followed by drop-offs in attendance of up to 70 percent as the word of mouth got out that some films were not that good.

The effect of this trend was that mid-priced, independent films, with fewer explosions and with no-name actors, have less chance of being made than ever before. True, there was the occasional medium budget breakout but the entertainment industry, focused as it was on the "blockbuster" business model, continued to play it safe. The same mentality is true of music and book publishing as well, where fewer producers meant fewer outlets for artists and a dumbing down of content to please a mainstream audience.

Meanwhile, another threat to the digital entertainment industries emerged. Piracy and sharing of digital files sent music CD sales plummeting and threatened movies as download speeds and storage space allowed for the transfer of very large files. Those who did buy their music legally through iTunes, Rhapsody, or some other source opted to pay less than a dollar for a tune they like instead of nearly twenty dollars for the corresponding CD. Many music fans forego purchase altogether and stream music through sites such as Pandora or Spotify. In 2002, the industry shipped 33.5 million copies of the year's 10 best-selling CDs, barely half the number it had shipped in 2000. Today, that number has been halved again, with a "best-selling" CD often registering sales in the tens of thousands compared to chart-topping "albums" in the early rock era that routinely sold millions of copies.

The music industry—from producers to radio station owners—was slow to realize that consumers had forever changed the way they would buy and listen to their music. Sir Howard Stringer, the chairman of the Sony Corporation of America, called downloaders "thieves" and compared them to those who shoplift from stores. The recording industry initially filed suit against some select downloaders and was successful in shutting down the very popular, but ultimately illegal, file-sharing site Napster. But, eventually, a pricing structure that made downloading inexpensive, combined with the emergence of popular devices to play it on such as the iPod (itself now obsolete due to advances to the iPhone), seemed a more effective—and more profitable—remedy. But recording's gain was radio's loss as iPods and then iPhones became the equipment of choice for the under-40 audience to access music. A look at the top 10 formats in radio, available at several industry websites, validates the fact that it is a medium with an aging audience.

Meanwhile, the movie industry, not yet hurt as deeply as the music industry, raced to find its own equivalents of the dollar download, especially after the DVR made high quality copying easy. By making legal movies readily available through streaming services such as Netflix (which also ships DVDs to your home), Amazon Prime, and Hulu, as well as retail kiosks at as low as a dollar per night, the industry got at least some money from the movie aftermarket at the same time that domestic and foreign box office held strong.

On an industry-wide level, new artists, especially those who don't fit the corporate view, will find the internet to be a two-edged sword. It will give them the publicity they need at an affordable cost, but it will allow for file sharing or dollar downloads that make it virtually impossible to make significant sums of money. As is often the case in the mass media, the development and adoption of a new medium or delivery technology has unanticipated consequences for existing media and formats. For music, the solutions are elusive and the stakes are high. Will creative people, who find their energies unusable in the music industry, turn to other mediums, or will the industry—and most importantly—consumers find a way to reward the creators of this most personal of medium?

NEW MEDIA, OLD ISSUES

Publishers, editors, and reporters at legacy news organizations long have argued that the current crisis is economic, not journalistic. Financial woes, they argue, are the result of Craigslist and Monster siphoning off classified ads, Match and eHarmony taking personal ads, and car dealerships and grocery stores realizing that it is more cost beneficial to create their own websites than advertise in print or on television. The hope was that a new generation of online media companies would help fill some of the void left by shrinking newsroom budgets.

However, new media companies are facing many of the same issues as their legacy counterparts. BuzzFeed and *Vice*, for example, both missed 2017 revenue targets by 15–20 percent. Mashable, once valued at $250 million, sold in November 2017 for only $50 million. Univision is trying to sell part of its Fusion Media Group, which includes major online media sites such as Deadspin, Jezebel, and Gizmodo. The DNAinfo-Gothamist network was shuttered by its publisher after journalists there voted to unionize.

One major issue facing new, and legacy, media is that consumers, especially in the desired 18–29 age demographic, increasingly are getting their content online. Network and cable television now compete with internet media from Amazon Video, Hulu, iTunes, Netflix, Sling TV, and YouTube. Cable subscriptions have decreased quarterly since 2010. In 2017, 196.3 million US adults paid for traditional television, though that number represents a drop of 2.4 percent since 2016 (Spangler 2017). This loss of viewership, and by extension revenue, has led to massive layoffs at cable behemoths such as ESPN.

Platforms such as Facebook and Google compete with publishers for advertising content, so, in essence, online publishers (much like their legacy counterparts before them) are paying to produce content while Facebook and Google reap most of the monetary rewards. The display-advertising model, which led to a destructive race for "clicks," is outdated and ineffective. Some sites—from Mashable to MTV News—pivoted to video on the hope that video ads would be more appealing, and, therefore, lucrative, than their display counterparts. All must find a workable revenue model, with subscriptions, memberships, events, nonprofit status, and venture capital—or some combination of all of the above—being the most likely economic fix, at least in the short term.

SOCIAL RESPONSIBILITY IN THE NEW MEDIA WORLD

But stakeholder theory is far from a reality in the media universe. Good jour-nalism is expensive, and in an era of declining subscriptions and ad revenues, few newsrooms enjoy budgets as large as in past years. The television networks have closed entire bureaus, and many newspapers have pulled back on overseas correspondents, leaving coverage of foreign news to the wires and CNN. The current era of cutbacks and consolidations has been noted by media researcher Robert McChesney (1997), who makes this analogy:

> Imagine if the federal government demanded that newspaper and broadcast jour-nalism staffs be cut in half, that foreign bureaus be closed, and that news be tai-lored to suit the government's self-interest. There would be an outcry that would make the Alien and Sedition Acts, the Red Scares and Watergate seem like child's play. Yet when corporate America aggressively pursues the exact same policies, scarcely a murmur of dissent can be detected in the political culture.

The effect of cutbacks is lost news for the consumer. One photojour-nalist, Brad Clift, told the authors that he went to Somalia months before US troops were dispatched, using his own money because he felt the starvation there was an under-reported story. Only an occasional network crew and a handful of newspapers pursued the Somalia story before former president George H.W. Bush committed US troops to the region in December 1992. Most news organizations, such as this photojournalist's employer, declined to cover the emerging story, pleading that they had depleted their international budgets by covering Operation Desert Storm. However, other approaches and organizations are emerging—funded by cooperative agreements among news organizations and sometimes foundations. They have produced excel-lent journalism. Some, such as ProPublica, have won prestigious awards, including the Pulitzer Prize.

In reading the code of ethics of the Society of Professional Journalists, two of the "guiding principles" of journalism speak directly to the ethics of media economics: (1) seek truth and report it as fully as possible and (2) act independently. Seeking the truth can be personally and financially expensive, something that stakeholder theory demands and stockholder theory avoids.

Some media companies *have* learned the lesson. McKinsey and Company (National Association of Broadcasters 1985) studied 11 of the nation's great radio stations, such as WGN in Chicago and reported what made an excellent radio station. Their findings were as follows:

- The great radio stations were audience-oriented in their programming.
- The great radio stations were community-oriented in their promotions.

Great radio stations had a knack for becoming synonymous in their communities with charitable events and community festivities even without an immediate return on investment. The attitude is summed up by WMMS (Cleveland) general manager Bill Smith:

> If you want a car to last forever, you've got to throw some money back into that car and make sure that it's serviced properly on a continual basis. Otherwise, it's going to break down and fall apart. We know that we're constantly rebuilding the station one way or another. We throw the profit to the listening audience . . . to charities, to several nonprofit organizations, to free concerts or anything to affect the listeners of Cleveland as a whole . . . because they identify us as being community-minded.

Uplifting examples are far too rare. Entry-level salaries for journalists in both print and broadcast are far too low—under $30,000 in one survey, draining the industry of the talent that might solve some of the seemingly insoluble problems. But a strong democracy requires a strong media and valid solutions must be found.

The stakes could not be higher.

SUGGESTED READINGS

Auletta, K. (1991). *Three blind mice: How the TV networks lost their way.* New York: Random House.

Bagdikian, B. H. (2000). *The media monopoly.* 6th ed. Boston: Beacon Press.

Cranberg, G., Bezanson, R., & Soloski, J. (2001). *Taking stock.* Ames: Iowa State University Press.

Mills, C. W. (1956). *The power elite.* New York: Oxford University Press.

Mcchesney, R. W. (1991). *Rich media, poor democracy: Communication politics in dubious times.* Urbana: University of Illinois Press.

Picard, R. G. (2010). *The economics of financing media companies.* New York: Fordham University Press.

Spence, E. H., Alexandra, A., Quinn, A., & Dunn, A. (2011). *Media, markets, and morals.* London: Wiley-Blackwell.

CASES

CASE 7-A

MURDOCH'S MESS

LEE WILKINS
Wayne State University
University of Missouri

It may have begun as an instance of "watching the watchdog." For two years, *Guardian* reporter Nick Davies had been doggedly investigating whether Britain's tabloid press—particularly the Rupert Murdoch owned *News of the World*—had been engaging in unethical activities to report the news. Specifically, Davies was investigating whether the voicemail messages left on cellphones had been accessed in order to gain information. In most instances, such practices would be illegal. A 2005–2007 investigation concluded that celebrities, the royal family, and politicians had been the subjects of phone hacking and that the hacking had been conducted by a single reporter. The rest of the British press dropped the story, and the public didn't seem to care.

Murdoch, who was born in Australia but became a US citizen, continued to build his media empire, which included a sizable financial stake in BSkyB, the most lucrative broadcast holding in the United Kingdom. During this same period, Murdoch purchased the *Wall Street Journal*, adding it to his US holdings that include several other newspapers and, most prominently, the Fox network including both its news and entertainment divisions.

Davies worked for *The Guardian*, an unusual publication on any continent. *The Guardian* is owned by a trust; it is not a traditional profit-making enterprise and its exemplar journalistic status is a relatively recent phenomenon. *Guardian* employees are required to take public transportation to cover most stories, and the paper itself conducts and publishes an ethical audit once a year that includes the paper's impact on the environment and its role as a citizen of its local community. In the British media market—almost all of which is focused in London—*The Guardian* competes fiercely with Murdoch publications, both tabloid and more traditional news organizations.

In July 2011, Davies reported that phone hacking extended beyond a single journalist and those usual and seemingly acceptable suspects.

Voicemail messages to families of British soldiers serving in Afghanistan, victims of the July 2007 London tube bombings, and, most grievously, the voicemails of murdered British schoolgirl Milly Dowler also had been hacked. In fact, according to Davies and subsequent investigations, Dowler's voicemail had not merely been hacked, it had been altered, leaving her family with the impression that the child remained alive after she had been murdered. Davies' later reports also revealed that the journalists involved appeared to have bribed Scotland Yard as part of the newsgathering effort. The outrage was immediate; major advertisers withdrew from the *News of the World* and many others threatened to follow. On July 10, 2011, the 168-year-old paper published its last edition. About 200 journalists lost their jobs, and James Murdoch, Rupert Murdoch's son and heir apparent, conceded that the paper had been irrevocably "sullied by behavior that was wrong."

On July 13, Murdoch announced he was withdrawing his bid to take over BSkyB. The announcement was made just a few hours before the British Parliament was scheduled to debate a resolution, supported by all political parties, calling on Murdoch to withdraw from the process. Despite the announcement, the House of Commons unanimously passed the resolution. On July 16 and 17, Murdoch published full-page apologies to the British public for the scandal and its impact. The next month, Wireless Generation, a NewsCorp subsidiary, lost a no-bid contract with the state of New York to build an information system to track student performance. New York State Comptroller Thomas DiNupoli said the revelations of corporate and individual malfeasance had made awarding this bid to Wireless Generation "untenable."

The elder Murdoch was politically influential on both sides of the Atlantic, but his power reached to the highest levels in Britain. At the time the phone-hacking scandal broke, a former Murdoch employee was serving as Prime Minister David Cameron's chief communications officer.

Rupert and James Murdoch were called before Parliament. Both admitted that the hacking had occurred, but each denied, in different terms, the existence of a corrosive organizational culture that could have led to a wide-spread ethical and legal breach. Rupert Murdoch testified that he was a victim of a cover-up. Concurrently, there were high level resignations throughout the Murdoch empire, including that of long-time Murdoch employee Wes Hinton, who had been serving as the chief executive of Dow Jones, owner of the *Wall Street Journal*. Hinton had testified to Parliament that there was never any evidence of phone hacking beyond the actions of a single employee.

However, as the scandal continued to unfold, it became apparent that other Murdoch-owned news organizations had engaged in similar news gathering tactics. The FBI opened an investigation into whether any phone hacking had occurred in the United States, with potential targets the victims of the 9/11 bombing among others.

About a year later, a British inquiry ruled that Murdoch was not a "fit and proper" person to be allowed to own or acquire media outlets in the United Kingdom. In the meantime, multiple lawsuits were filed over the scandal—and the Murdoch empire has paid more than 1 million pounds to settle them. As of this writing, there have been more than 30 arrests of current or former Murdoch employees.

Rupert Murdoch has been called the last of the media barons and the criticisms of him and his business practices parallel those leveled against Joseph Pulitzer and William Randolph Hearst at the height of the Yellow Journalism era in the United States. All were accused of building media empires that lacked an ethical foundation. Journalism professor Karl Grossman, State University of New York at Old Westbury, accused Murdoch of building the most "dishonest, unprincipled and corrupt" media empire in history and turning the notion of public service journalism on its head. He also accused Murdoch of changing the newsroom culture at his most recent acquisitions, among them the *Wall Street Journal*. *Newsweek* in July 2011 quoted one of Murdoch's top executives as follows:

> This scandal and all its implications could not have happened anywhere else. Only in Murdoch's orbit. The hacking at *News of the World* was done on an industrial scale. More than anyone, Murdoch invented and established this culture in the newsroom, where you do whatever it takes to get the story, take no prisoners, destroy the competition, and the end will justify the means. . . . In the end, what you sow is what you reap. Now Murdoch is a victim of the culture that he created. It is a logical conclusion, and it is his people at the top who encouraged lawbreaking and hacking phones and condoned it.

While many were willing to blame Murdoch personally, other critics noted that the 24/7 nature of competitive news on the internet had created the sort of atmosphere in which hacking was not merely tolerated but encouraged. These critics noted that hidden cameras, lurking on websites, publishing stories before checking facts—all in the drive to increase web hits—were merely less illegal, but not less ethically questionable results, of the 24/7-celebrity driven news cycle.

Micro Issues

1. Phone hacking is illegal, but is it unethical? Why?
2. How would you, or could you, justify Davies' pursuit of this story about one of his major competitors?
3. In most of the phone hacking cases, none of the victims have said that the information collected about them was untrue. Is how a journalist collects information a component of the truthfulness of the story?
4. Contrast phone hacking to the other deceptive techniques evaluated by Investigative Reporters and Editors. How are they alike and different in an ethical sense?

Midrange Issues

1. What is the role of competition in the concept of "watching the watchdog"? Does the same sort of thinking apply to the media's watchdogging of other major institutions in society?
2. Does the 24/7 nature of the news cycle—and the sometimes wild west nature of the internet—encourage working at the very edge of acceptability? If you answer "yes," then what sort of rules, guidelines, or training might encourage contemporary journalists to stay on the "right" side of the ethical boundaries?
3. In light of this case, how do you respond to those who say that all journalists will do anything to get a story?

Macro Issues

1. What should be the role of democratic governments in policing the ethical behavior of corporate media owners?
2. Evaluate the notion of an ethical newsroom culture. Contrast the culture of *The Guardian* with that of the *News of the World*? What makes the ethical difference?
3. One role for the mass media as an institution is that of collaboration. Yet, journalists have historically been suspicious of the sort of collaboration and political influence Rupert Murdoch has had. Analyze what you believe is the most ethically defensible role relationship between the mass media as an institution and powerful political and economic institutions.

Fast Forward to 2018

In June of what was already a tumultuous news year, "Fox and Friends" news anchor Gretchen Carlson was apparently fired from her job with the conservative network. Fox News, which had supported the campaign of the then-candidate Donald J. Trump, was the flagship of the Murdoch empire in the United States.

Within a month, Carlson filed suit against the network, alleging that she had been fired because she refused the sexual advances of network chairman Roger Ailes. Within a week, six additional women came forward with similar stories, although only two were willing to go on the record. Fox and Ailes responded to the suit by saying that Carlson's firing had nothing to do with sex and everything to do with ratings.

The Carlson suit was only the latest in a series of public allegations against various managers at Fox properties, dating back to 2004 when Bill O'Reilly was sued for $60 million by one of his former producers for sexual harassment. In 2009, a former managing editor at the *New York Post*, another Murdoch property, sued her boss for racial and gender discrimination.

But with this history, and with allegations of sexual harassment becoming the focus of then candidate Trump's campaign, Carlson's allegations and those of the 25 women who ultimately came forward in the case struck a societal nerve. The network was forced to dismiss Ailes, who originated the tagline "fair and balanced" that the network had used to characterize its news operation, although that dismissal came with a reported $40 million settlement. Rupert Murdoch, who shared a vision with Ailes about the potential financial and political impact of a conservative television network, continued to praise Ailes. Known as one of the most powerful, and vindictive, of media managers, Ailes died within a year of the Carlson suit, which the network settled for $20 million including a rare public apology. O'Reilly's departure came within a month of Ailes' death.

The revelations about the various sexual harassment claims also came at a time when the Murdoch and the Fox corporation has renewed its efforts to purchase Sky TV for $15 billion. In September 2017, UK culture secretary Karen Bradley ordered a thorough review of the process because of a "genuine commitment to broadcasting standards," a review that postponed any purchase until at least 2018. However, in October 2017, the *New York Times* reported that O'Reilly had paid former news analyst Lis Weihl $32 million in a settlement of a sexual harassment suit. Further, James Murdoch, Murdoch's son and now chief executive of 21st Century Fox, said that the size of the settlement "was news to me."

Then, on Nov. 20, 2017, *The Guardian* and a number of other news organizations reported that Fox had entered into potential talks with the Disney Corporation, a much larger corporation even than Fox. Disney was interested in the Fox movie studios and its television networks—in other words, Fox's assets that produce content in an era of streaming video. Disney reached a $52.4 billion deal in December 2017 to combine two of the biggest studios in Hollywood.

Macro Issues

1. Evaluate the impact of leadership on the Fox organization. Do you think that the standards set by managers and owners can make a difference in how individual employees behave? Why?
2. What are some of the potential corporate reputation problems that the now merged Disney and Fox studios might face? Are those problems surmountable?
3. In November 2017, John Lasseter, the creative force behind Pixar and Walt Disney animation studios, announced he would take a six-month leave of absence after allegations of inappropriate behavior towards women surfaced. In light of these continuing revelations, how should these potential financial deals be covered by media outlets such as NPR, *Variety*, the *Wall Street Journal*, or the *New York Times*?

CASE 7-B

WHO CONTROLS THE LOCAL NEWS? SINCLAIR BROADCAST GROUP AND "MUST RUNS"

KEENA NEAL
Wayne State University

Americans take for granted that the news they watch on their local NBC, ABC, CBS, or Fox affiliate is local. But what if what we watch on our local news is produced at the corporate headquarters of the broadcaster rather than by local reporters and producers?

In May 2017, Sinclair Broadcasting Group brokered a $3.9 billion deal to buy Tribune Media's 42 television stations. Sinclair, the largest owner of local television stations in the United States, would subsequently reach nearly three out of four homes in the country (Zhou 2017). Sinclair has largely operated in small to medium markets, often owning multiple stations within one market. The addition of Tribune

Media's stations gives Sinclair access to the three largest markets in the nation: New York, Los Angeles, and Chicago (Folkenflik 2017). A look at the holdings of each company also reveals that the new group would own at least two television stations with fully staffed newsrooms in many small- to mid-sized markets. Under the deal, Sinclair also would assume $2.7 billion in Tribune Media's debt. (Note: At the time of this writing, the deal was pending approval.)

Critics argue Sinclair uses its television stations to promote right-wing propaganda. After the 9/11 attacks, Sinclair required its anchors and reporters to read positive messages supporting the then-President George W. Bush's campaign against terrorism. In 2004, when ABC's *Nightline* devoted an entire episode to soldiers killed in the Iraq war, Sinclair barred its local ABC affiliates from airing the program. Nationwide, local anchors read a segment in April 2018 denouncing "the troubling trend of irresponsible, one-sided news stories plaguing our country" in which "the media use their platforms to push their own personal bias and agenda to control 'exactly what people think.'"

The company produces "must-run" content it distributes to its 173 stations. For example, the "Bottom Line with Boris" feature commentary from Boris Epshteyn, Sinclair's chief political analyst and former staff assistant to President Donald Trump, must air nine times per week. Epshteyn "reliably parrots the White House on most issues" including claiming that former FBI Director James Comey's Capitol Hill testimony "was more damaging to Hillary Clinton and former Attorney General Loretta Lynch than to the president" (Gold 2017). Sinclair denies any partisan tilt to its programming and defends its "must-run" practice, stating, "We stand by our approach to sharing content among our stations to supplement the excellent work our newsroom staffs do every day in service to their communities" (Gold 2017).

Consumer advocate groups oppose the merger because the combined company would surpass the federally mandated maximum reach of 39 percent of national TV homes (Snider 2017a). If approved, Sinclair-Tribune would own and/or operate more than 200 stations and reach 72 percent of US households. The increase in stations could permit Sinclair to demand larger payments to pay-TV operators that want to retransmit their programming, the cost of which ultimately could be passed down to the American consumer (Snider 2017b).

Democratic Sen. Dick Durbin of Illinois urged the FCC to block the proposed purchase, writing that the deal would "threaten diversity and localism in broadcasting, ignore the unique concerns and interests of local audiences and harm competition" (CBS 2017). Additionally, the attorneys general in four states (Illinois, Maryland, Massachusetts, and Rhode Island) announced their opposition, contending the merger would increase market consolidation, reduce consumer choice, "and threaten the diversity of voices in media" (Johnson 2017a). The proposed merger came at a time when four other huge media outlets were attempting mergers of their own. Both AT&T and Time Warner (Kang and de la Merced 2017) as well as Disney and 21st Century Fox (Delk 2017) were running into congressional resistance in their attempts to merge into two more media behemoths.

Recently, the Republican-led FCC has relaxed several long-established rules designed to protect against monopoly and ensure diverse content in local media. In April 2017, the FCC reversed a 2016 rule which limits the number of television stations a broadcaster can buy (Shepardson 2017), and, in October 2017, it "rescinded a 78-year-old rule that required broadcasters to maintain a local studio in communities where they're licensed, overturning a requirement to deliver strong local content" (CBS 2017). In November 2017, the FCC voted to allow broadcasters to own newspapers in the same market and two of the top four stations in a city (Johnson 2017b).

Micro Issues

1. What are the advantages and disadvantages of local ownership for television stations? What are the advantages and disadvantages of a broadcast company producing content for stations across the United States?
2. Critics charge that Sinclair censors alternative viewpoints, requires its stations to air conservative content, and exercises corporate control over local news content. How might these arguments influence your answer from the previous question?

Midrange Issues

1. Evaluate Illinois senator Dick Durbin's statement that the merger would "threaten diversity and localism in broadcasting, ignore the unique concerns and interests of local audiences and harm competition."
2. What is the value of local autonomy for journalists and producers? Discuss using the concepts of public service, credibility, and trust.

3. Do you see a difference in mergers that involve journalism, such as the Sinclair merger with Tribune, and mergers that are largely about entertainment such as AT&T/Time Warner and Disney/Fox?

Macro Issues

1. Who are the stakeholders in the proposed merger? How should their interests be weighed by the FCC?
2. Would Immanuel Kant approve the merger? Would John Stuart Mill?
3. The "39 percent" rule is designed to limit monopolization of news. Should this rule still be enforced in the digital age when citizens can access virtually any news media via the Internet? Why or why not?

CASE 7-C

AUTOMATED JOURNALISM: THE RISE OF ROBOT REPORTERS

CHAD PAINTER
University of Dayton

Traditionally, workers considered most at risk of being replaced by machines performed physical jobs in predictable environments such as operating machines in a factory or preparing fast food. Today, however, another kind of worker is at least partially replaceable: news reporters.

News organizations including the Associated Press, Reuters, the *Los Angeles Times*, the *Washington Post*, and *USA Today* have begun experimenting with automated content-generating systems for fairly boilerplate stories such as earning reports and simple sports recaps.

Content-generation systems such as Narrative Science and Automated Insights can produce short articles with structured data. These systems comb data feeds for facts and trends, then meld that information with historical and contextual data to form narrative sentences (Keohane 2017). For example, the *Washington Post* uses a program called Heliograf. Editors create narrative templates for stories and then tap Heliograf into a source of structured data such as VoteSmart.org. Heliograf can identify relevant data, match it to corresponding phrases from the narrative template, merge the data and the phrases, and publish the resulting story across different platforms (Keohane 2017). There is a better-than-average chance that you have read a Heliograf-created article; the program wrote and published more than 850 articles in 2016 about the Rio Olympics, congressional and gubernatorial races, and Washington, DC, area high school football games.

The rise of robots does not mean the fall of reporters, however. Heliograf, for example, includes a function to alert reporters if it finds data anomalies such as a wider margin of victory than expected in a gubernatorial race (Keohane 2017). In 2014, Reuters created News Tracer, a program that tracks social media, specifically Twitter, for breaking news. The program can track 500 million tweets daily in real time, and it alerted Reuters reporters to hospital bombings in Aleppo and terrorist attacks in Nice and Brussels before other media outlets were aware of the stories (Stray 2016). Similar programs can scan data and documents to make connections for complex investigative projects and evaluate the truthfulness of statistical claims (Stray 2016).

In these cases, automation creates leads, not stories. In other words, robots can report a figure but cannot interpret its meaning. Humans still have to do the in-depth work of talking to sources, piecing together data points from multiple inputs, and drawing evidence-based conclusions. Robots can write formulaic stories, but at least so far humans are needed to write profiles, trend pieces, and analyses. As Kevin Roose writes, "Rather than putting us out of work, it might free us up to do more of the kinds of work we actually *like*." The Associated Press estimates that automation has reduced reporters time spent covering corporate earnings by 20 percent while also increasing accuracy (Moses 2017).

Still, reporters are unconvinced that robot reporters are good for journalism. In one recent study, journalists expressed concerns that robots could produce a high volume of stories that negatively impact the news agenda:

> We believe robo-journalism will be used more often to produce simple factual reports, increase the speed with which they are published, and to cover topics currently below the threshold of reportability. . . . However, the increased volume of news resulting from automation may make it more difficult to navigate a world already saturated with information, and actually increase the need for the very human skills that good journalists embody such as news judgement, curiosity, and skepticism (Scott 2017).

Micro Issues

1. Should news organizations identify stories generated by automated programs?
2. Ken Schwencke developed an algorithm called Quakebot for the *Los Angeles Times* to quickly write articles about any LA-area earthquakes. The program plugs in relevant data to an existing template and publishes the story under Schwencke's byline. Is this practice ethical reporting? Does it make an ethical difference that Schwencke wrote the algorithm? Why or why not?

Midrange Issues

1. Beginning reporters typically are assigned to write the formulaic stories. What are the advantages and disadvantages of having automated programs produce these stories instead of assigning them to beginning reporters?
2. How does your answer to question 1 change if and when automated programs advance to the point where they can write more complex pieces such as profiles, trend pieces, and analyses?
3. Do automated content systems prioritize information from certain kinds of sources? Evaluate how this kind of privilege might influence the news agenda or certain types of stories.
4. Programs such as this might allow media to get "hyper-local" in its coverage, for example, by producing news stories for each student on the honor roll. Is this a good use of the tool or does this just add to the clutter some predict will come from automated reporting?

Macro Issues

1. Evaluate the statement that the number of articles produced by automated journalism could "make it more difficult to navigate a world already saturated with information."
2. Most newsrooms experimenting with automated reporting are large, national organizations such as the Associated Press and the *Washington Post*. Does the use of automation give these organizations an unfair advantage over small- and medium-market organizations that cannot invest in similar programs?
3. At the end of chapter 2, there is a list of ethical news values. Examine how robot-generated stories might and might not fulfill those values.

CASE 7-D

CONTESTED INTERESTS, CONTESTED TERRAIN: THE *NEW YORK TIMES* CODE OF ETHICS

LEE WILKINS
Wayne State University
University of Missouri

BONNIE BRENNEN
Marquette University

In January 2003, the *New York Times* broke a lengthy tradition and published its new ethics code on the web. The *Times* decision was an important one, for ethics codes are often controversial in both their creation and their application. However, ethics codes can be an important marker of specific social practices created under particular social, economic and political conditions at distinct times in history.

For example, members of the American Newspaper Guild in 1933 crafted one of the first ethics codes developed by journalists rather than managers. That code suggested the "high calling" of journalism had been tarnished because news workers had been pressured by their employers to serve special interests rather than the public good. Conflict of interest was centered on the relationship between reporters and sources, and the code made a particular point that business pressures were putting undue stress on newsrooms. The code recommended that to combat business pressures the news should be edited "exclusively in newsrooms."

Ethics codes in general are controversial among professionals and scholars. Some maintain that ethics codes are nothing more than generalized aspirations—too vague to be of any use when specific decisions must be made. Others insist codes can be helpful to beginning journalists, photographers, and public relations practitioners; they provide some guidance in the form of rules that can be internalized as professional expertise and experience deepen. And still others see codes as a manifestation of the ideology of an era—more about power and politics than ethics.

The new *Times* code linked its creation to the public perception of the "professional reputations of its staff member(s)." The code was directed to "all members of the news and editorial departments whose work directly affects the content of the paper."

The code focused primarily on conflict of interest. In fact, the code did not mention accuracy and fairness and devoted only a single sentence to privacy. However, when addressing conflict of interest, the code was both specific and detailed. The *Times* code considered the impact that spousal relationships might have on news coverage. It also addressed whether journalists working abroad should abide by the ethics and mores of the countries in which they are stationed, most of which do not provide the equivalent of First Amendment protections.

The code required staff members to disclose yearly speaking fees in excess of $5,000 and prohibited staff members from accepting gifts, tickets, discounts, or other "inducements" from organizations the *Times* covered. Staff members could not invest in companies they covered, and payment for favorable or altered coverage was specifically forbidden.

However, staff members were allowed to do certain sorts of unpaid work—for example, public relations for a child's school fundraising event. But *Times* staffers were forbidden from giving money to candidates or causes, marching in support of public movements, or appearing on radio and television shows to voice views that went beyond those of the paper. When family members, such as spouses, participated in such activities, *Times* staffers were required to disclose those activities to management and recuse themselves from certain sorts of coverage.

The *Times* code was protective of the newspaper's place in the marketplace. Staffers were prohibited from disclosing confidential information about the operations, plans, or policies of the newspaper to other journalists. Such questions were to be referred to management. If readers asked such questions, *Times* staffers were encouraged to respond "openly and honestly." *Times* staff members also were prohibited from doing freelance work for any media outlet that competed with the *Times*. "Staff members may not appear on broadcasts that compete directly with the *Times*'s own offerings on television or the Internet. . . . As the paper moves further into these new fields, its direct competitors and clients or potential clients will undoubtedly grow in number."

Micro Issues

1. Should managers and owners be subject to a code of ethics, particularly for publications as influential as the *Times*?
2. Why is the notion of perception—as opposed to action—important in considering the issue of conflict of interest?
3. Should the *Times* code have addressed a variety of common journalistic issues—such as accuracy, fairness, and privacy?

Midrange Issues

1. Disclosure is often suggested as a remedy for conflict of interest. Evaluate this remedy.
2. Should conflict of interest rules be different at a small newspaper as opposed to the *Times*?
3. Does the *Times* code infringe on staffers' First Amendment rights? Do journalists give up some of their rights as citizens in order to do the work of journalism?
4. Are there instances when recusing oneself from an assignment is unsatisfactory? What should journalists do if such a case arises?
5. Should a conflict of interest extend as far as prohibitions against a journalist being an officer in the parent–teacher association (i.e., PTA or PTO) of his or her child's school? An officer in your local homeowners' association? Does the potential for those organizations to get involved in the news pages (i.e., teacher problems, zoning protests) influence your decision?

Macro Issues

1. What are the specific historical developments in the field of journalism that may have promoted the development of this particular version of the *New York Times* code?
2. Research indicates that codes that are developed by the newsroom have a much better chance of influencing behavior than codes that are superimposed by management. If the *Times* had used this approach, would it have "discovered" the actions of reporters such as Jayson Blair (details of the Blair case may be found on the internet)?
3. Does the *Times* code place the organization's financial health on equal footing with the public trust? Is that appropriate?

The *New York Times* Social Media Policy: Everything We Do Is Public

In October 2017, the *New York Times* expanded its existing ethics policies to cover social media. *Times* executive editor Dean Baquet, himself a prize-winning investigative reporter, presaged the change with some comments at a George Washington University forum where he said that *Times* reporters should not be able to say anything on social media platforms that they would not be able to say in the pages of the newspaper.

In a preface to the changes, Baquet wrote:

Social media plays a vital role in our journalism. On social platforms, our reporters and editors can promote their work, provide real-time updates, harvest and curate information, cultivate sources, engage with readers and experiment with new forms of storytelling and voice.

We can effectively pull back the curtain and invite readers to witness, and potentially contribute to, our reporting. We can also reach new audiences.

But social media presents potential risks for *The Times*. If our journalists are perceived as biased or if they engage in editorializing on social media, that can undercut the credibility of the entire newsroom.

We've always made clear that newsroom employees should avoid posting anything on social media that damages our reputation for neutrality and fairness.

The guidelines applied to all *Times* employees, including those who do not cover government. They specifically require the following:

- In social media posts, our journalists must not express partisan opinions, promote political views, endorse candidates, make offensive comments or do anything else that undercuts the *Times'* journalistic reputation.
- Our journalists should be especially mindful of appearing to take sides on issues that the *Times* is seeking to cover objectively.
- These guidelines apply to everyone in every department of the newsroom, including those not involved in coverage of government and politics.

The new social media policy also offered advice to *Times* journalists, particularly the women on the staff, about how to handle trolls who, in the heat of the 2016 election, suggested through internet memes that rape would be an appropriate response to *Times'* stories written by women that readers might disagree with.

The decision by editors to try to damp down social media posts by *Times* reporters dated at least to September 2016 when the public editor, the *Times'* version of an ombudsman, wrote that *Times* editors had cautioned reporters about stating opinions about then-candidate Donald Trump's tweets.

Some media outlets, among them Fox News, called the guidelines a "fig leaf" that could not obscure what Fox and others have called the *Times's* left-leaning reporting.

In an article in the *Columbia Journalism Review*, reporter Mathew Ingram noted the changes at the *Times* were connected to Trump's continuing campaign against "the failing New York Times." However, the article noted that such restrictions were unlikely to convince readers that journalists were "objective." The piece also noted that the such restrictions would not allow *Times* journalists and others to use social media to its fullest potential. However, Ingram also noted there were financial implications:

> This flawed approach is even more dangerous for publishers who, like the *Times* and the [Wall Street] *Journal*, are relying increasingly on subscriptions, membership fees, and other relationship-based models for their continued economic survival.
>
> How do you convince people to support you in such a way? By building a relationship with them, one that encourages them to believe you share a worldview, or at least that you can be trusted. And how do you do that? Not by pretending you have no opinions, but by being as honest as possible—asking for feedback and admitting when you make a mistake. In other words, by being human.

Micro Issues

1. How is the *Times'* social media policy like or unlike its general ethics policy?

Midrange Issues

1. Should journalists, in order to practice journalism, give up their First Amendment rights on social media platforms?

Macro Issues

1. Is objectivity the appropriate professional standard in a century increasingly dominated by social media and where fact and opinion continue to blur? If your answer is no, what do you think might be an appropriate preliminary substitute?

CASE 7-E

TRANSPARENCY IN FUNDRAISING: THE CORPORATION FOR PUBLIC BROADCASTING STANDARD

LEE WILKINS
Wayne State University
University of Missouri

In chapter 2, we asked you to consider the implications of transparency as a guiding ethical standard in the collection and dissemination of news. We linked that issue to the US Corporation for Public Broadcasting's (CPB's) efforts to develop a new code of ethics that would apply to all aspects of the organization.

When CPB developed the code, applying the concept of transparency to news was accepted—at least in terms of discussion. What was groundbreaking was CPB's attempt to apply the same ethical standard to its fundraising activities and, within that, the relationship the corporation has between its donors and its news and entertainment content.

The transparency in funding document opened with this general statement of principles: that trust is the foundation of the relationship between the public and public media. Every year, thousands of Americans support their local public radio and television stations. These donors don't require a contract and rarely even make specific requests about how their money is to be used; they simply have faith in the integrity, expertise, and goodwill of their local station. The importance of this trust is magnified whenever a station takes on a journalistic role.

The standard notes that the relationship between public broadcasting stations and donors should not be merely financial—that donors represent a significant element of political support and social capital in their own communities. The transparency standard emphasizes that transparency should not apply only to donors—stations themselves need to become more transparent about their financial operations, obligations, and potential entanglements. However, the standard also calls for a "firewall" between donors and the various local news organizations associated with public broadcasting, most often National Public Radio and local NPR programming.

The standard also suggests that stations make fundraising information available and publicly accessible, including gift acceptance policies, guidelines governing the use of challenge grants, donor rights, appropriate donor acknowledgement, conditions of acceptance of anonymous gifts, and guidelines for seeking and accepting foundation grants. The policy also includes sections that outline the rules public broadcasting must comply with promulgated by the FCC and IRS.

CPB's transparency fundraising standard is probably the most radical attempt by a media organization to rethink, and to make public, what is a non-advertising based business model. It is unique because it is based on an ethical concept.

Micro Issues

1. In an ethical sense, distinguish between advertising and CPB sponsorship.
2. Do newspaper display ads provide a kind of transparency of financial support for a specific publication? Is such advertising ethically distinct from the CBP transparency standard?
3. If you were a CPB or NPR donor, would you be willing to have your name announced on the air? Placed on a website? Why or why not?
4. If you helped to run a foundation, do you think you would be willing to provide funds to a news organization knowing that your support would become public in this way?

Midrange Issues

1. CPB receives about 2 percent of its budget from taxpayers in the form of a congressional allocation. Should the transparency standard also speak to taxpayer support?
2. CPB is a nonprofit organization. Discuss the ethical implications of a transparency standard for for-profit news and entertainment organizations.
3. Compare the transparency standard with the published guidelines for personal or foundation support of organizations such as Investigative Reporters and Editors, The Pulitzer Center, or ProPublica. Which do you find the most ethically justifiable?

Macro Issues

1. Using the concepts of stakeholder and stockholder theory, evaluate the transparency fundraising standard.
2. Public broadcasting television and radio stations have on-air fundraising drives during the year. How would you compare these

fund drives with traditional advertising placed in newspapers, magazines, or on television and commercial radio?

3. One ethically based justification of paid advertising is that many advertisers dilute the influence of any single advertiser. Evaluate this claim ethically. Do you believe the same evaluation applies to public broadcasting sponsors?

4. In an age when media finances are difficult, are firewalls a luxury that can no longer be afforded?

CASE 7-F

NEWS NOW, FACTS LATER

LEE WILKINS
Wayne State University
University of Missouri

Supreme Court decisions are always eagerly awaited, but none more so than the court's summer 2012 ruling on the constitutionality of the Patient Protection and Affordable Care Act. The facts of this case are taken from Tom Goldstein, publisher, of SCOTUSblog, a website that covers the US Supreme Court and is sponsored by Bloomberg Law. The blog post is used with permission of the author.

News organizations prepared for the release of the court's decision in a variety of ways. CNN worked for weeks on ways to make certain that the decision, as reported by CNN, reached as many Americans as possible through as many portals as the network has access to. It had spent a great deal of time thinking through its internet strategy with an emphasis on getting the story first. Fox News made a similar effort, although its internet strategy is not as well honed. Megyn Kelly, a former lawyer turned television personality, was assigned to the story for Fox. CNN was using an established team including a producer and on-air reporter.

The Supreme Court also had been active on the internet front. The court's technical staff was prepared to load the eagerly anticipated opinion on to the court's website where it will be accessible to everyone from average Americans to the White House. Before 2012, the court routinely emailed copies of opinions to parties involved in litigation, but in 2012 began to rely only on the website. One week before the opinion was handed down, the court denied a request from SCOTUSblog to email the decision to that organization. In practical terms, what this meant was that the only people with access to the decision itself would be those in the courtroom when the decision was announced and those accessing the website. The court made every effort to ensure that the website itself would remain in working order on this important day.

But, in the face of unprecedented demand for information, the court's site crashed. That meant that the entire country relied on the news media for the story with no way to independently confirm news accounts.

The first reports of the decision, as carried by CNN and Fox, were that the Supreme Court had ruled the act unconstitutional. Those accounts were broadcast about seven minutes after the decision was handed down. In the case of CNN, the initial account of the ruling was broadcast even while its onsite producer was on a conference call with network executives. The CNN social media team published tweets and RSS feeds stating unequivocally that the Supreme Court has struck down the act.

Fox, just a few seconds later, published a banner on the network saying "Supreme Court finds health care individual mandate unconstitutional." Bill Hammer, one of the network's most experienced journalists, was assigned to lead the coverage. A few seconds before 10:08, he stated on air that the individual health care insurance mandate has been overturned. Fox commentators begin to discuss the impact of the ruling on the 2012 presidential election.

President Barack Obama saw both reports. He also has access to the SCOTUSblog conference call on speaker phone and SCOTUSblog on his computer. NPR picked up the CNN and Fox reports, saying the law had been struck down, as did the *Huffington Post*. The *Huffington Post*'s social media team also ran with the story, neglecting to note the source of its information.

Tom Goldstein, SCOTUSblog publisher, is in charge of the coverage for the website, which is highly respected within the DC Beltway, including the journalistic community, for its Supreme Court coverage but little known to the average American. Goldstein, who was in the Supreme Court chambers when the decision was handed down, filed an initial post that merely said the Supreme Court had produced the decision.

About 90 seconds later, Goldstein had skimmed the decision. He does this by reading the first sentence of every paragraph in the opinion, and then he confers with colleague Lyle Denniston, who has written the majority of the blog's coverage, and Denniston and Goldstein agree: The court has upheld the act based on the tax clause of the US Constitution. SCOTUSblog then reported that the law has been upheld.

That information is picked up by the NPR News Blog, which attributes it to the website. At about 10:20 a.m.—less than 20 minutes after journalists received the decision—CBS also accurately reports that the law had been upheld.

At the White House, the president's advisers, after conferring with Goldstein about the focus of the ruling, conclude they need to tell the president that his signature legislative act has been ruled constitutional.

Soon after SCOTUSblog publishes its version of events, CNN and Fox have the unenviable job of walking back their initial reports. Because it had put such effort into social media as part of the reporting process, the false reports broadcast by CNN reached many more people than had the Fox News coverage. CNN's seamless news network had, in this instance, become a serious disadvantage.

Goldstein, in his own blog about the events, said that CNN and Fox made three mistakes: first, they treated a complex decision as a breaking news story, even though the law itself would not have taken effect until 2014; second, the networks did not put "sufficiently sound procedures in place" to deal with what many believed was going to be a complicated decision; and third, the networks appear to have failed to look at the consensus view of the wire reports, which, in this instance, were accurate.

Micro Issues

1. Should this have been considered a breaking news story?
2. What should the journalists with access to the opinion have told their editor?
3. What should the editors have asked the journalists who were reporting the story?

Midrange Issues

1. What sort of stories should CNN and Fox have broadcast once they discovered that their initial reports were incorrect?
2. Is this the sort of story that general assignment reporters should not be assigned to? In other words, should only journalists with serious expertise be assigned to report stories such as this?
3. Evaluate Goldstein's statement that all journalists should have put more faith in the accuracy of the wires on this story? How would— or would you—distinguish this from pack journalism?
4. If you were a manager, how would you—or would you—discipline the on-scene reporters whose initial reports were inaccurate?

Macro Issues

1. Fox News leans to the political right. Many said they believed the initial reports because they coincided with Fox's political ideology. Critique this statement.
2. Less than two months after the event, the head of CNN resigned. Is a mistake of this sort a resigning offense?
3. How do you think the website crash of the Supreme Court itself influenced these events, if at all? Do you think the Supreme Court itself bears some responsibility for the inaccurate reporting?
4. Contrast the conflicting values of speed, profit, and accuracy in this case. Using ethical theory, construct a policy for your local television station on the reporting of breaking news that accounts for all three—speed, profit, and accuracy.

CASE 7-G

CROSSING THE LINE? THE *LOS ANGELES TIMES* AND THE STAPLES AFFAIR

PHILIP PATTERSON AND MEREDITH BRADFORD
Oklahoma Christian University

The *Los Angeles Times*, in a "special report" on Dec. 20, 1999, called attention to an event its editors perceived as a breach of journalism ethics. The multistory report was entitled "Crossing the Line." What made this report extraordinary is that it was the *Times* itself that had crossed the line that triggered this journalistic exposé.

A few weeks earlier, the Staples Center, a $400 million sports and entertainment arena in downtown Los Angeles, had opened to great fanfare. Most observers shared the hope that the facility, which would house two basketball franchises and one hockey team, would spark a revitalization of downtown. Staples Inc. had won the naming rights to the arena by paying $116 million.

Tim Lieweke, president of the Staples Center, left with $284 million more to raise, had initiated talks with McDonald's, Anheuser-Busch, United Airlines, Bank of America, and others to become "founding partners." He was eager to have the *Los Angeles Times* as a founding partner because of previous joint successes and because he thought the paper could contribute value beyond cash.

The Staples arena already had a promotional arrangement with the *Los Angeles Times* in exchange for cash payments from the *Times* and free advertising in the paper. "The arrangement is similar to that many big-city papers have with their local professional sports teams," said David Shaw, the *Los Angeles Times* Pulitzer Prize–winning media critic, in an investigative piece on the controversy (Shaw 1999). "But for the Staples Center, Lieweke wanted more. He wanted the *Times* as a founding partner."

Since the Staples Center could be a major contributor to the revitalization of downtown Los Angeles, *Times* executives were "eager to participate," Shaw said. The price for founding partners ranged from $2 million to $3 million per year for five years. Jeffrey S. Klein, the then-senior vice president of the *Times*, who supervised early negotiations on the Staples deal, "didn't think it was worth what they were asking." Negotiations stalled for several months in 1998 until a "Founding Partner Agreement" was accepted on Dec. 17, 1998, between the L.A. Arena Company and the *Los Angeles Times*. Part of the language in the agreement stated the two companies "agree to cooperate in the development and implementation of joint revenue opportunities."

"Although all of the principals in the negotiations say that the precise terms of the Staples deal are confidential," Shaw reported, "information from a variety of sources shows that in effect the *Times* agreed to pay Staples Center about $1.6 million a year for five years—$800,000 of that in cash, $500,000 in profits and an estimated $300,000 in profits from what Lieweke had called 'ideas that would generate revenue for us.'"

This latter part of the deal was clarified in a clause of the final contract that said, in part, that the *Times* and the L.A. Arena Company would agree to cooperate in the development and implementation of joint revenue opportunities such as a special section in the *Los Angeles Times* in connection with the opening of the arena, or a jointly published commemorative yearbook, Shaw said.

These "joint opportunities" were to create $300,000 of net revenue for each party annually. According to the contract, these opportunities would be subject to the mutual agreement of both parties.

On Oct. 10, 1999, the *Times* published a special 168-page issue of its Sunday magazine dedicated to the new Staples Center sports and entertainment arena.

Only after the section was published did most of the paper's journalists learn that the *Times* had split the advertising profits from the magazine with the Staples Center. Feeling that the arrangement constituted a conflict of interest and a violation of the journalistic principle of editorial independence, more than 300 *Times* reporters and editors signed a petition demanding that publisher Kathryn Downing apologize and undertake a thorough review of all other financial relationships that may compromise the *Times'* editorial heritage.

The petition, in part, stated "As journalists at the *L.A. Times,* we are appalled by the paper entering into hidden financial partnerships with the subjects we are writing about. The editorial credibility of the *Times* has been fundamentally undermined."

Less than two years before the episode, Downing had been named publisher by Mark Willes, the new chief executive of Times Mirror Corporation, parent company of the *Los Angeles Times*, despite having no newsroom background. Her previous experience had been as a legal publicist. Willes had moved from General Mills to Times Mirror in 1995. Willes had made no secret of his desire to "blow up the wall between business and editorial" (Rieder 1999). He was also on record as telling *American Journalism Review* in 1997 that "[the] notion that you have to be in journalism 30 years to understand what's important, I find rather quaint" (Rieder 1999).

Downing did apologize, calling it a "major, major mistake." After taking questions at a two-hour staff meeting on Oct. 28, she admitted that she and her staff "failed to understand the ethics involved" (Booth 1999). Downing meanwhile canceled all future revenue-sharing deals with Staples, promised to review all contracts with advertisers, and ordered up awareness training for the ad side.

For his part, Willes seemed to reverse his earlier stance when he said, "This is exactly the consequence of having people in the publisher's job who don't have experience in newspapers" (Rieder 1999).

On the business side of the paper, the arrangement was widely known and discussed openly for most of 1999. Downing says she deliberately withheld the information from Michael Parks, the paper's editor, but did not direct her subordinates on the business side not to talk about it to him or to anyone else in editorial, according to several reports.

Shaw reports that Willes argued that the absence of such discussion only shows the need for "more communications, not less. . . . The profit-sharing deal happened not because the wall came down," Willes says, "but because people didn't talk to one another when they should have."

In an interesting argument, Downing claimed that if the editorial side of the paper did not know about the profit-sharing deal with the Staples Center before printing, then the Sunday magazine devoted to the Staples Center would be unbiased. The uninformed editorial staff would have no reason to be biased.

Many critics from inside and outside the newspaper agree with Shaw that "readers have no reason to trust anything the *Times* wrote about

Staples Center, or any of its tenants or attractions, anywhere in the paper, now or in the future, if the *Times* and Staples Center were business partners." He adds that readers will wonder whether other improper arrangements, formal or informal, might also exist or be created in the future with other entities, agencies, and individuals covered by the *Times*.

Whether connected to the Staples affair or not, massive changes were in store for Willes, Downing, Parks, and the *Times*. The newspaper was bought by the Tribune Company, publisher of the *Chicago Tribune*, in March 2000. All three employees were gone within a year.

Micro Issues

1. Critique Willes' early and late statements about journalistic experience in newspaper management positions.
2. Is the actual loss of credibility as disastrous as the reporters felt, or does the public really have the same sensibilities as those in the profession?
3. How does entering into the contract with the Staples Center differ from the sports department accepting press passes for the events held in the arena?

Midrange Issues

1. If one acknowledges that "the wall" is good and necessary, how does that affect media engaged in advocacy journalism?
2. Shaw entitled his article "Journalism Is a Very Different Business." In what ways do you think journalism differs from other businesses?

Macro Issues

1. In the new information age, where so many competing views can be found on most issues, is "the wall" still relevant?
2. When a newspaper is a publicly traded company, do the loyalties of the paper shift from the public to the shareholders? If not, how can you justify a move that might be counterproductive to profits?

8

Picture This

The Ethics of Photo and Video Journalism

By the end of this chapter, you should be familiar with

- the pros and cons of citizen journalism
- the legal and ethical issues involved in photojournalism in the area of privacy
- the legal and ethical problems of file footage and "eyewash"
- the conundrum of open source journalism

In the years leading up to the American Revolution, press owners, post-masters, pamphleteers, etc. controlled the words that filtered to the people where the notion of being for or against the impending war would be made. In the decades that followed, the currency of persuasion was the written word. But by the time of the Civil War in the 1860s, photography had left the studio and had entered the battlefield. The haunting images of war by Matthew Brady had an effect on a nation raised on words. The impact of the image was on the rise, and with it came unique problems not foreseen when both freedom of "speech" and "press" were given clauses in the First Amendment.

Although it would take a few more decades to develop, one of the earliest notions of privacy was the freedom from having one's image "stolen." At the end of the 19th century, during a period of journalism history commonly referred to as "yellow journalism," two Boston lawyers, Samuel Warren and Louis Brandeis (who would become the first Jewish US Supreme Court Justice), had seen enough. The snooping, prying Boston press photographers had disrupted the society wedding of Warren's daughter. The two men aired their views of this early type of "tabloid journalism" in an 1890 *Harvard Law Review* article entitled "The Right to Privacy," marking the first time this new "right" had been suggested in public debate.

From the earliest days of our national notion of privacy, freedom to be secure that one's own image would be under their control was a part of the debate. Just over a decade after the Warren and Brandeis article, in 1901, a pre-teen, Abigail Roberson, found her image on posters and even painted on barns advertising a brand of flour—all without her permission. Although she didn't win her case because there was no law against what happened, New York soon passed the nation's first privacy law a year later focusing specifically on the unauthorized use of one's image. Other states followed, and within the first decade of the 20th century, people were suing successfully for the misappropriation of their own image.

There is something personal about images. They are intimate; they are subjective. What some see as obscene, others see as artistic. Images have power—from personal to commercial to political. The iconic images of Sept. 11, 2001, evoke strong images in many Americans. So do images of the fall of Baghdad several years later, only these images mean something quite different depending on whether the viewer is American or Iraqi. Since that time, images of hurricanes from Hurricane Katrina that hit New Orleans in 2005 to Hurricane Sandy in 2012 that battered the east coast as far as New York in 2012 to the back-to-back hurricanes of 2017 in Texas, Florida, and Puerto Rico have not only moved the nation at a time of national grief but also aided in spurring the public to help in the recoveries.

Marshall McLuhan said more than half a century ago in his book *Understanding Media* that there will come a time when images would replace bullets in warfare. He went on to add that "all technology can plausibly be regarded as weapons" (McLuhan 1964). One needs only look at the large number of riots in the wake of the release of videos of police brutality to see the power of this statement. With the ubiquity of police body and dashboard cameras, as well as bystander videos, the number and the horror of the images increases each year. The video of a defenseless detainee being beaten or shot long after being subdued by police sears into the mind and the national psyche much deeper than words.

The power of images is so overwhelming that the George W. Bush administration banned the presence of press photographers at the Air Force base where flag-draped coffins containing the remains of soldiers killed in action in Iraq and Afghanistan came in almost daily. One military contractor and her husband lost their jobs in Kuwait for leaking such a photo and ultimately allowing it to be run in the *Seattle Times*. Today, the battle for the lasting image of any armed conflict is an important one with enormous stakes. So, the lone man facing down a tank in the middle of China's Tiananmen Square may not have won the war (and indeed he didn't), but the image of that man did win a major battle, so much so that today any totalitarian government has to control a nation's images as well as its missiles.

THE CITIZEN AS PHOTOJOURNALIST

Nowhere is the concept of citizen-journalist more accepted than in photography, where devices such as cellphones have made virtually everybody a photographer and most a videographer. Add in the hundreds of thousands of video cameras that businesses employ for security, and virtually no event—from one child stomping on another in a soccer match to a would-be terrorist buying household chemicals to make a bomb—falls outside the realm of cameras. Citizen photographers often have the earliest and sometimes the only footage of tragedies such as mass shootings that have become all too common in the United States today. Today's editorial question is rarely "Do we have art?" It's more likely "Which photo or video do we use?"—often from sources whose day job is not journalism.

The availability of video and photos from a variety of sources ranging from freelancers to amateurs to official sources such as police has caused turmoil in the newsroom. Cutbacks in photo budgets became a common way for traditional print media to cut costs. Nowhere is this better illustrated than at the *Chicago Sun-Times* where the entire full-time photography staff—including one Pulitzer Prize winner and about 28 photographers—were all laid off in May 2013. In their press release discussing the move, the *Sun-Times* explained it this way: "Today, *The Chicago Sun-Times* has had to make the very difficult decision to eliminate the position of full-time photographer, as part of a multimedia staffing restructure."

The statement went on to say that "the business is changing rapidly," and audiences are "seeking more video content with their news." The paper would later train its reporters in the basics of cellphone photography, create mechanisms for readers to submit news photos to be considered for publication, and increase the number of wire service photos used even for local Chicago stories.

Other issues with submitted photos soon emerged. The rise of social media outlets has dramatically shortened the time between the occurrence of a news event and the dissemination of photos or video to the public. Photos and video are posted to the internet almost instantaneously. For instance, when a man drove a car into a group of activists in Charlottesville, Virginia, killing one and injuring 19 others, the raw and unedited video of the racially charged violence was available almost immediately online—well before the families of the victims had been notified. In the past, the most instantaneous ethical decision in photography was "Shoot or don't shoot?" Today, the question has added layers: "Post or don't post?" Or: "Go live or not?" Or: "Can we trust this amateur video?"

Because of this, decisions that once could be made in the relative calm of the newsroom after a dramatic tragedy now must be made in the field in an increasingly competitive media environment. And making the right decision can be the difference between being applauded for ingenuity or being criticized for insensitivity.

The contributions of citizen journalists have already changed history. Back in 1992, it was amateur video, aired first on local and then on national television news, of African-American Rodney King being beaten by a uniformed Caucasian police officer that set off a rash of riots in Los Angeles. Since that date, amateur video has been both an influencer and a chronicler of history. The number of events captured first or captured solely by amateur photographers include the 2004 scandal over the conditions at the Abu Ghraib prison, the 2007 assassination of Prime Minister Benazir Bhutto of Pakistan, protests in Tunisia in 2010 that became the catalyst for the Arab Spring movement, and the assassination of Libyan leader Muammar Gaddafi in 2011.

Perhaps the most noteworthy case of amateur photography aiding law enforcement came immediately after the 2005 subway bombings in London when the perpetrators were identified in part through the use of the more than 1,000 images passengers on the city's underground captured with their cellphones and forwarded to police. Richard Sambrook of the BBC noted (Reuters Institute for the Study of Journalism 2015), "People were participating in our coverage in a way that we had never seen before. By the next day, our main evening TV newscast began with a package edited entirely from video sent in by viewers. From now on news coverage is a partnership." Those images, together with sophisticated face recognition technology, became a tool of law enforcement, and the trend continues today.

Recently, video of Midwestern tornados—taken at great personal risk by amateurs who aren't paid for their efforts and accepted by media outlets well aware that the weather garners the highest ratings during the traditional local television news show—have themselves become news. The practice gained attention in the popular culture following the 1996 Hollywood movie *Twister*. It came under extreme scrutiny in 2017 when three storm chasers were killed in a car accident while pursuing a tornado in West Texas. Parties in both cars were chasing the same storm, including two of them contracting for the Weather Channel and its show *Storm Wranglers*. Later that year, another storm chasing fatality was recorded in Oklahoma involving a Weather Channel reporter.

Before the internet opened the possibility of "open-source journalism" to thousands of bloggers and videographers, the government could and did exercise control over the media by denying access to information or battlefields or by selectively granting access or leaks to those in favor with the administration. But the web changed all that, as *Newsweek*'s David Ansen writes in his review of the 2006 film about World War II propaganda, *Flags of our Fathers* (Ansen 2006, 71):

> What the Pentagon didn't foresee, and couldn't control was the rise of new media—the unfiltered images popping up on the Web, the mini-TV cams put in the hands of soldiers that emerge in the recent documentary, *The War Tapes*. We don't see much of the real war on network TV, but the unauthorized documentaries—*The Ground Truth, Gunner Palace* and many more—come pouring out. Just as many people think they get a straighter story from Jon Stewart's mock news reports than from traditional outlets, it's been the "unofficial media" that have sabotaged the PR wizards in the Pentagon. The sophistication of the spinners has been matched by the sophistication of a media-savvy public.

The emerging ethic of open source journalism has forced some interesting compromises with the emerging ethic of the blogosphere (for a more detailed discussion, see chapter 10). However, open-source journalism—particularly if it is managed by a more traditional news organization—faces the same ethical tests as more traditional photography. The premiums are accuracy, fairness, and originality. Editors at open-source cites realize that they must subject amateur content to the same journalistic standards as work by their own professionals. For instance, contributed video cannot be staged or re-enacted and then presented as news. Editors must be able to verify the accuracy, and sometimes the context, of citizen contributions.

PROBLEMS IN THE PROCESS

Your grandparents had sayings such as "the camera never lies" and that "seeing is believing." Yet, as Arthur Berger (1989) points out in *Seeing Is Believing*, because of the many variables in photography—camera angles, use of light, texture, and focus, a picture is always an *interpretation* of reality, not reality itself. He adds that a dozen photographers taking pictures of the same scene would produce different views of the reality of it.

Not only does the camera differ from the eye in its ability to manipulate angle, light, and focus, but cameras also capture an isolated reality by presenting us with a slice of life, free from context. In *About Looking*, John Berger (1980, 14) says:

> What the camera does, and what the eye can never do, is to fix the appearance of that event. The camera saves a set of appearances from the otherwise inevitable supersession of further appearances. It holds them unchanging. And before

the invention of the camera nothing could do this, except in the mind's eye, the faculty of memory.

The role of journalism is to place context back into the ubiquitous images created by professionals and amateurs alike. It's not enough, from an ethical standpoint, to say "Here's what happened" to an audience who probably knows the news before the newscast airs or the newspaper story goes live online. The audience also knows that photos are easily manipulated on any laptop computer and video is only marginally harder to change. Because of those two facts, journalism must say, "Here's why we believe this happened the way you are seeing it." Otherwise, the news does nothing for the consumer that YouTube can't do better.

TO SHOOT OR NOT TO SHOOT?

Arriving on the scene of a newsworthy event, the photographer must make several decisions. The most basic is whether or not to shoot the photo of a subject who is in no position to deny the photographer access to the event. Often these vulnerable subjects are wounded, in shock, or grief-stricken. In that newsworthy moment, the subject loses a measure of control over his or her circles of intimacy (see chapter 5 for a description of this concept). That control passes to the photographer, who must make a decision.

Goffman (1959) claims people possess several "territories" they have a right to control. Included in Goffman's list are the right to a personal space free from intrusion (i.e., by a camera lens) and the right to preserve one's "information," such as a state of joy or grief from public view.

By its very nature, photojournalism is intrusive and revealing—two violations of Goffman's sense of self. Someone else's misfortune is often good fortune for the photojournalist. In the last century, more than half of the winning images in top photography contests were pictures of violence and tragedy. Most of the amateur images that make the news are of violence and tragedy. Eventually, every photojournalist happens on an assignment that intrudes on a subject's privacy. Garry Bryant (1987), a staff photographer with the *Deseret News* of Salt Lake City, offers this checklist he goes through "in hundredths of a second" when he reaches the scene of tragedy:

1. Should this moment be made public?
2. Will being photographed send the subjects into further trauma?
3. Am I at the least obtrusive distance possible?
4. Am I acting with compassion and sensitivity?

To this list Bryant adds the following disclaimer:

> What society needs to understand is that photographers act and shoot instinctively. We are not journalists gathering facts. We are merely photographers snapping pictures. A general rule for most photojournalists is "Shoot. You can always edit later" (1987, 34).

The line between newsworthiness and intrusiveness, between good pictures and bad taste, is often blurry. Donald Gormley, the general manager of the *Spokane Spokesman-Review,* offers some insight into the difference between photos that are universally offensive and photos that are simply tough to view:

> Compassion is not the same as good taste. If a reader knows the person pictured in a very dramatic photograph, he may find it offensive. That's a sin against compassion. If he is offended whether he knows the person or not, the sin is probably one against good taste. (1984, 58)

Editors argue that decisions cannot be made concerning photos and videos that do not exist. Not every picture of grief needs to be ruled out just because the subject is vulnerable or grieving. Where to draw the line is a decision best made in the newsroom rather than at the scene; however, that is increasingly no longer the norm. The "new normal" for the decision to air video from the scene of a tragedy is made in the field, and your first time to have to make such a decision will come surprisingly early in your career, making the suggestion of Sissela Bok in chapter 1 become all the more relevant.

Because this ethical dilemma is almost inevitable in any market, Bok would suggest discussing ahead of time what you will do when the situation arises. The photographer who attempts to perform an ethical triage at the scene of a tragedy might find his career in jeopardy if the assignment fails to capture the pathos of the event when all other photographers succeeded. In addition, the photographer who fails to capture some of the event, for whatever reason, fails to capture some of the truth for the reader or viewer.

Essentially, the photographer who is deciding whether and how to photograph a tragedy is wrestling with the dilemma of treating every subject as an end and not merely a means to an end. We can agree that powerful images of accident victims may cause some drivers to proceed more safely, but if that message comes at the expense of an accident victim's privacy, is it a message that needs to be told?

Warren Bovée (1991), in an essay entitled "The Ends Can Justify the Means—But Rarely," offers this set of questions to help the photographer find the answer.

1. Are the means truly morally evil or merely distasteful, unpopular, etc.?
2. Is the end a *real* good or something that merely *appears* to be good?
3. Is it probable that the means will achieve the end?
4. Is the same good possible using other means? Is the bad means being used as a shortcut to a good end when other methods would do?
5. Is the good end clearly greater than any evil means used to attain it?
6. Will the means used to achieve the end withstand the test of publicity?

STAGING PHOTOGRAPHS AND VIDEO

Photographer John Szarkowski (1978) writes of "mirror" and "window" photographs and his 1978 Museum of Modern Art show was entitled "Mirrors and Windows." The two types of photos are also roughly analogous to realistic and romantic photography. According to Szarkowski, window photographs should be as objective a picture of reality as the medium will allow, untouched by the bias of the lens or the photographer. On the other hand, the mirror photograph attempts to subjectively re-create the world in whatever image suits the photographer. Anything can be manipulated: light, proportion, setting, even subject.

Each type of photography has a function. A large percentage of the government-commissioned Dust Bowl–era photographs that have seared our memories of the Depression would fit into the mirror category. Photographers searched for settings, posed people, and shifted props to achieve the maximum effect. On the other hand, the photos that show us the horrors of war and famine, and arouse public opinion, are windows, where the photographer captures the moment with no attempts to alter it.

The problem comes in the substitution of one for the other. When a photograph has been staged for greater effect yet is passed off as a window on reality, the viewer has been deceived. Iconic photos such as the Marines raising the flag on Iwo Jima or the young girl crying over the body of the dead student shot by the Ohio National Guard on the campus of Kent State College have been debated for decades about whether they were spontaneous and contextually correct photos. Again, the rise of citizen photojournalists has exacerbated this problem as well because the competition to submit the definitive photo of a spot news event is intense among amateur photographers, many of them without training in or knowledge of any code of ethics for the profession.

"Your work sounds interesting." Francesca said. She felt a need to keep neutral conversation going.

"It is. I like it a lot. I like the road, and I like making pictures."

She noticed he'd said "making" pictures. "You make pictures, not take them?"

"Yes. At least that's how I think of it." That's the difference between Sunday snap-shooters and someone who does it for a living. When I'm finished with that bridge we saw today, it won't look quite like you expect. I'll have made it into something of my own, by lens choice, or camera angle, or general composition or all of those.

"I don't just take things as given; I try to make them into something that reflects my personal consciousness, my spirit. I try to find the poetry in the image."

—Robert James Waller, *The Bridges of Madison County*

ELECTRONIC MANIPULATION

The largest story of 2011 was the killing of Osama bin Laden at his compound in Pakistan by Navy Seals who helicoptered in under the cover of darkness. In a now-iconic photo, many of President Obama's team who knew of and signed off on the attack can be seen gathered in the Situation Room listening to the activities half a world away. Secretary of State Hillary Clinton is shown in the middle of the photo, her hand covering her mouth. However, for the readers of *Di Tzeitung*, she was never there, having been manipulated out of the photo before it went to the presses of the Brooklyn-based Hasidic newspaper. In keeping with their religious beliefs on modesty, she had been removed along with another female participant, counterterrorism director, Audrey Tomason.

When the deception was uncovered, the Jewish paper issued an apology (Bell 2011) that read in part: "In accord with our religious beliefs, we do not publish photos of women, which in no way relegates them to a lower status. Because of laws of modesty, we are not allowed to publish pictures of women, and we regret if this gives an impression of disparaging to women, which is certainly never our intention. We apologize if this was seen as offensive."

The Clinton disappearance was not the initial use of photo manipulation by the press and certainly not the last. The history of photo manipulation is long, beginning with such crude drawing-board techniques as cropping with scissors and paste, and darkroom techniques such as "burning" and "dodging" and airbrushing. Today, technology allows increasingly sophisticated changes to be made to an image after it has been captured with relative ease. Technology has, in fact, made the word "photography"—it literally means "writing with light"—obsolete, as a lighted reality no longer need exist in order for a "photograph" to be created.

For decades now, photos and video have been what photography researcher Shiela Reaves (1987) called a "controlled liquid" more than a quarter century ago. Writing in the infancy of computer manipulation of photography, Reaves foresaw a time when photos would lose their "moral authority" while Don Tomlinson (1987) wrote in that same year that photos could lose their legal authority as well—something that has also occurred in many jurisdictions. As a more sophisticated audience of visual media has grown up with computers, today's viewers bring with them a skepticism about the authenticity of photos and visuals not present in previous generations of consumers.

Most editors and photographers agree that manipulation or staging of *news photos* is generally more culpable than manipulation or staging of *feature photos*. During the 2003 war in Iraq, Brian Walski, a photojournalist for the *Los Angeles Times* was fired for combining two similar photographs into one more aesthetically pleasing one. Today, you can find the original photos and the blended composition online. While the resulting photo was so similar to the "real" ones that the difference originally escaped the eye of the *Times* photo editor, a line had been crossed, and the photographer was dismissed. Walski later told a colleague that "I went from the front line for the greatest newspaper in the world, and now I have nothing. No cameras, no car, nothing" (Irby 2003).

The reason for the different standard for news photography is a presupposition that *while art may be manipulated, information may not* (Martin 1991). The problem for audiences is compounded by the fact that both advertising and non-news sections of the newspaper make frequent use of these techniques. Confusion over what is appropriate in one context and not another is bound to occur, but we suggest that the same standard of visual truth telling can and should be applied to advertising as well.

SELECTIVE EDITING

Another ethical question centers on the video editing process: whether editing itself renders a story untrue or unfair. Actually, the term "selective editing" is redundant. *All* editing is selective. The issue is who does the selecting and what predispositions they bring to the process.

A dual standard has emerged between words and photos. The writer is allowed to reorder facts and rearrange details into an inverted-pyramid story on the rationale that the reader wants the most important facts taken out of sequence, and even out of context, and placed first in the story for more efficient reading. The result is praised as good writing and is taught in every journalism program.

However, should a photographer attempt to do the same thing with a camera—rearrange reality to make a more interesting photo or video—the result is called "staged." Our unwillingness to allow visual journalists the same conventions as print journalists says something fundamental about the role of visuals in the news. When a writer edits, it makes for a more readable story, and the act is applauded. When a photographer or video editor does the same thing, he or she is open to accusations of distortion.

That is because we evaluate news photos according to print standards: linear and logical. Yet video and photographs are neither. They have a quality Marshall McLuhan called "allatonceness" that we are not quite comfortable with as a technology. Just what the photographer can do with the visual truth the camera uncovers is still a topic of debate.

However, as long as readers think that "seeing is believing," that view—whether based in reality or not—becomes a promise between the media and their audiences that photographers and videographers should be hesitant to break. While many photojournalists argue that "seeing is believing" should have never been a cultural truism (Lester 1992), others argue that we must work within our readers' or viewers' predispositions about the truth of what they see. Steve Larson (quoted in Reaves 1991, 181) director of photography for *U.S. News & World Report*, summarized this viewer-based rationale:

> The photo is a record of a moment in time. We're on shaky ground when we start changing that. We must maintain this pact. Catching a moment in time has history. When you look at a Matthew Brady photo there is that sense "this really happened." I believe strongly that's where photography draws its power.

In the wake of a large number of entries at the World Press photo competition in 2015 being disqualified for being discovered to be manipulated photos, including the revocation of one first prize, the *New York Times* interviewed several leading photographers in an essay entitled "Staging, Manipulation and Truth in Photography (New York Times 2015). Their questioning of several of the nation's leading photographers revealed a substantial gap between the various codes of ethics that govern photojournalists and photojournalism contests and what happens in the real world. Stanley Green, a photojournalist and co-founder of Noor Images told the *Times*, "Setting up photos, where they are completely staged is very widespread. I've seen it done by very well-known photographers." He added, "It seems the honor system is not working."

A 2015 survey answered by more than 1,500 photographers worldwide for the Reuters Institute for the Study of Journalism and the World Press Photo Foundation (Hadland, Campbell, and Lambert 2015) showed an interesting mix of results on the major ethical questions in the industry. While just over three-quarters of those responding said that manipulating or altering photos is wrong and an equal number claimed to have "never" done it, more than half of all those responding say they "sometimes" manipulate photos such as asking people to do actions again or wait to do actions until the photographer is ready. Twelve percent said they did so "at least half the time." While virtually every respondent agreed that the ethical standards of the profession were important, the researchers concluded that they were not always followed in the field.

EYEWASH

Imagine a new government study that is released on compulsive gamblers that you are told to make into a video package for tonight's news. You might show a woman enjoying herself on a sunny afternoon at the races. Or a man sitting at a slot machine in a casino. While each of their actions takes place in public view, they might or might not be a victim of the syndrome addressed in the article, although the casual reader might infer that each is, indeed, a compulsive gambler. In this context, the photo is serving the purpose of "eye-wash," decoration for a story that bears no genuine relationship to it.

While the courts have been ambiguous on the matter of eyewash, the media have created divergent policies to cover the issue. Some newspapers and television stations, for instance, will use no picture not directly related to the story. Others limit the use of file or stock footage to that which is clearly labeled. Others limit the shooting of eyewash only by insisting that it occur in public view.

The issue is exacerbated by the voracious appetite that both television and the print media have for visuals. Virtually all surveys have shown that the presence of a photo adds to the number of readers for a newspaper story, while television news consultants insist that viewers will watch "talking heads" for only a few seconds before diverting their attention elsewhere. The

Figure 8.1. *Calvin and Hobbes* © 1992 Watterson. Reprinted with permission of Andrews McMeel Syndication. All rights reserved.

answer to the question "Have you got art?" often means the difference in running or killing a story. Good visuals can often get a story better placement in whatever news medium they appear in.

Given the importance of visuals, it is not surprising that ethical lines blur. A. D. Coleman (1987) tells the story of his young son falling off a horse and breaking his arm. A photographer friend took a picture of the boy "dirty, tear-stained, in great pain, slumped in a wheelchair with his arm in a makeshift sling" on his way to the operating room. About a year later, a textbook publisher ran across the photo and wanted it as an illustration for a book on child abuse. Coleman denied the request but added that the photo could have easily been selected if he had not been easily available for the publisher to ask. The public would have been deceived by a photograph of a boy who had been a victim of nothing more than a childhood accident.

AESTHETICS AND ETHICS

Taste in spot news photography has been an issue almost from the very start of field photography during the Civil War. For years, newspapers and morning television news shows used the "Post Toasties Test," to determine the photos or video that accompanied early morning news stories. The test gets its name from a popular breakfast cereal and is a sensitivity test for media that might be at the breakfast table from newspapers to television and even websites. The test asked the question "Does this need to be shown at breakfast? Or "Should children see this over their morning breakfast?"

However, according to Louis Hodges (1997), no photographer or photo editor has identified "what exactly what we mean by 'in bad taste.' The closest they come is to note that people do not want bloody pictures at the breakfast table." Hodges argues that many issues in visual journalism that appear to be lapses in ethics are actually differences in opinion over matters of aesthetics—the ancient Greek branch of philosophy that considered beauty and what is beautiful and also whether beauty could be objectified or codified so that everyone could agree on its qualities.

Oscar Wilde is widely quoted as having said, "There is no such thing as a moral or an immoral book. Books are well written, or badly written. That is all." Hodges would agree saying that many works that are considered "unethical" are often merely "unbeautiful" instead. He adds that the ethics questions are more easily identified and solved than the aesthetic ones. On the issue of how rational humans could differ on the aesthetics, or beauty, of an image, Hodges uses this illustration: "The mushroom cloud from the atomic bomb, for example, has always appeared beautiful to me. Those pictures led to moral rejoicing that the war was about over and my father would soon be coming home. For others, the cloud is symbolic of human evil, power and inhumanity."

An agreement on aesthetics is one of the most difficult in all of philosophy. Hodges states, "Philosophers, whose function is inquiry into the good (ethics), the true (epistemology) and the beautiful (aesthetics) have been far more successful and helpful in uncovering standards for the true and the good than for the beautiful." Modern philosopher Elmer Duncan (1970) claims that even if we agree on the principles of "goodness" in aesthetics in art (e.g., a "good" painting should have balance and unity), we would not be able to definitely call it "good" or "bad" without committing what philosophers call the "naturalistic fallacy," namely that the "good" is a simple, irreducible concept that cannot be defined in terms of any other concept. When a photo or video is called "unethical" by viewers, it is often based on an indescribable quality inherent to the viewer and is neither shared universally nor is it defensible logically. It really is a matter of taste.

CONCLUSION

The debate over visual ethics is emotionally charged and constantly changing with technology. Simultaneously, the consumer of news photography is sometimes presented with a product too raw to be watched and at other times too polished to be believable. Photojournalists should operate under this version of Kant's categorical imperative: *Don't deceive a trusting audience with manipulated reality and don't offend an unsuspecting audience with your gritty reality.* Photographers are dealing with a trust that readers and viewers have placed in them. If that trust is betrayed, it will be slow to return.

SUGGESTED READINGS

Berger, A. (1989). *Seeing is believing.* Mountain View, CA: Mayfield.

Berger, J. (1980). *About looking.* New York: Pantheon Books.

Journal of Mass Media Ethics. (1987). Spring–Summer. Special issue on photojournalism.

Lester, P. (1991). *Photojournalism: An ethical approach.* Hillsdale, NJ: Lawrence Erlbaum Associates.

Lester, P. (2003). *Images that injure.* 2nd edition. Westport, CT: Greenwood Press.

Newton, J. (2000). *The burden of visual truth: The role of photojournalism in mediating reality.* Hillsdale, NJ: Lawrence Erlbaum Associates.

Reuters Institute for the Study of Journalism (2015). How mobile phones are changing journalism practice in the 21st Century. http://www.reutersinstitute.politics. ox.ac.uk. Accessed on November 29, 2017.

CASES

CASE 8-A

KILLING A JOURNALIST ON-AIR: A MEANS/ENDS TEST

MITCHEL ALLEN
University of Oklahoma

On Aug. 26, 2015, broadcast journalist Allison Parker and cameraman Adam Ward of Roanoke (VA) CBS affiliate WDBJ were shot while filming a live television interview with Roanoke Chamber of Commerce Executive Director Vicki Gardner. In an instant, Parker and Ward were dead, shot by a disgruntled former employee of the station who caught the event on his cellphone as he perpetrated it.

The shooter was Vester Lee Flanagan, a former reporter at the station. He had been fired for "disruptive behavior" after working at the television station for a year. On a personal video Flanagan made of the shooting, he approaches the live interview holding a handgun and his phone. He shows himself walking up behind Ward. On the video, he raises his gun and unloads his clip on the three. He then went home and posted the video to Facebook. He would later shoot himself during a car chase with police and die in a local hospital.

After posting the video shot from his perspective, Flanagan faxed a document to the news station using his on-air name "Bryce Williams." In it, he expresses his growing anger because of the racial and sexual discrimination he claimed to have endured at WDBJ. He also included his admiration for other killers who have gone on killing sprees, including the shooters from Columbine High School. On the day the news station had fired Flanagan, police had escorted him out of the building. After investigating the killings, police concluded that Flanagan had been planning this attack for two years.

Soon, other media had to decide how to handle the video—both the video that aired live on WDBJ and the video posted by Flanagan. CNN's coverage is typical of how many outlets handled the delicate footage. At the top of their online news story was the live broadcast with a label at the beginning warning people of the graphic content. In the video, everything is normal until gunshots are heard. Parker stumbles backward as she screams for her life. The camera falls to the ground as Ward is shot in the back. More shots are heard on the audio as the camera lies on the ground until the broadcast cut back to the station.

CNN chose not to post the personal video made by Flanagan. A search on the internet shows the video from the shooter's point of view available on several websites. This video is much more graphic and shows the gun in the frame as Flanagan shoots the journalist and cameraman.

Critics of the story expressed concern that the video was posted. They felt the video was not needed to successfully tell the story. The video shows a woman screaming as her life comes to an end. Some critics posted that this video goes beyond a graphic image and becomes a form of voyeurism.

Others countered that hearing and seeing this woman at the end of her life, and seeing the camera fall to the ground, is much more powerful and captures the horror more than any story or still photo could. They feel that the warning graphic at the beginning of the video is enough to warn anyone who does not want to watch it. Still others say the video by Flanagan was significant enough to the story that it should have been put in the coverage too.

Micro Issues

1. Does the decision of CNN to post the video matter because it was already broadcast live when it happened and quickly became available online?
2. Did the use of a warning graphic before the video starts make a difference?

Midrange Issues

1. Did the end of telling a tragic story justify the means of showing the live video as the journalist gets shot?
2. Does the public have a need to see graphic content that happens in the world they live in or should they be sheltered from it? What ethical reasoning supports your view?
3. Parker and Ward were the seventh and eighth US journalists killed while doing their jobs since 1992, according to statistics from the Newseum. In light of this, should incidents such as this make stations rethink how many live shots they do and how they handle their reporters in the field?

Macro Issues

1. What do you see as the difference, if any, between the live video and the shooter's personal video? Do you air one? Both? Neither? Justify your decision.

2. Flanagan applauded previous mass murderers in his posting. Address the criticism that airing video such as this might possibly give motivation to others considering violent acts. If the news outlets show these graphic videos, are they giving the killers what they want?

3. About eight children are shot somewhere in the United States each day. Would your decision be different if the victim of a shooting captured on video was a juvenile? What are the ethically relevant distinctions and the philosophical theory that support your decision?

CASE 8-B

REMEMBER MY FAME: DIGITAL NECROMANCY AND THE IMMORTAL CELEBRITY

SAMANTHA MOST
Wayne State University

In 2013, Universal Pictures put the production of its film *Furious 7* on hold after Paul Walker, one of the film's stars, died. Two years later, the movie was released to solid reviews while grossing more than $1 billion worldwide. To complete Walker's scenes, Universal asked Walker's brothers to fill in the role, using computer-generated imagery (CGI) to fuse Walker's facial image over body doubles. Walker's brothers provided voiceover for the character.

This concept actually wasn't new. Universal began using celebrity images posthumously in 1966 when the corporation sold merchandise depicting deceased actor Bela Lugosi in his portrayal of Count Dracula (Petty and D'Rozario 2009). In the 1990s, Coca-Cola used a variety of dead celebrities such as Cary Grant and Groucho Marx to promote Diet Coke and dance onscreen with a living Paula Abdul. That commercial generated a Nova episode to explain how computers were used in the effort.

Digital necromancy is the term used to describe the use of a deceased celebrity's likeness in many kinds of mediated messages. Films such as *Furious 7* and the *Star Wars* "backstory" *Rogue One* successfully resurrected the images of deceased actors, in those cases Walker and Peter Cushing, respectively. In 2013, an ad for the whiskey brand Johnnie Walker Blue employed the image of Bruce Lee, more than 40 years after his death, to promote the product. Marilyn Monroe's image is widely used in ads.

Scholars note that the use of such images—which some have termed "Delebs"—raises ethical questions. They note that the likeness of a dead celebrity is often less expensive to acquire and is a safe bet for maintaining a sound reputation that, in turn, means less potential blowback for a brand that inadvertently uses the image of a living celebrity who becomes caught up in some sort of scandal.

Ethical issues abound.

Micro Issues

1. Is there an ethical difference if the celebrity's family refuses to consent to the use of the image rather than cooperating with the effort as was the case in *Furious 7*?
2. Should creative projects such as films be treated differently regarding the use of deceased celebrity images compared to commercial projects such as ads? What philosophical theory justifies your response?
2. Is there an ethical distinction between selling a still image and an image that moves and speaks? Justify you answer.

Midrange Issues

1. In *Furious 7*, the producers justified the use of Walker's CGI image by noting that the use allowed the multi-episode plot to be brought to a conclusion, which fans expected. Evaluate this justification.
2. If the use of a "delebs" image was done poorly in a technological sense—in other words, if the use of the image was not made a seamless part of the film or advertising content—would that change your ethical evaluation?
3. Dead celebrities are cheaper to employ. Should this economic reality be a part of the justification for using such images?

Macro Issues

1. Digital necromancy raises issues of truth telling. Discuss those issues, from the point of view of content creators and from the point of view of audience members. Refer to the conceptualizations of truth outlined in chapter 2.
2. Can a deceased celebrity make an authentic claim for the selling of a particular product?

3. In 1984, California passed the Celebrity Rights Act, which protected the right of the deceased celebrity up to 50 years after his or her death (Petty and D'Rozario 2009). Should the use of these sorts of images be legally constrained? Why?

CASE 8-C

PROBLEM PHOTOS AND PUBLIC OUTCRY

JON ROOSENRAAD
University of Florida

Campus police at the University of Florida were called on a Saturday to a dorm to investigate "a large amount of blood on the floor of a women's bathroom," according to police reports. They determined that the blood "appeared to have been from a pregnancy miscarriage" and began searching the dorm area. Some time later a police investigator searching through a trash dumpster behind the dorm found bloody towels, plastic gloves, and a large plastic bag containing more towels and the body of a 6- to 7-pound female infant.

Police discovered no pulse. Rigor mortis had set in. After removing the body from the bag, the police briefly placed the body on a towel on the ground next to the dumpster. The photographer for the student paper, the *Independent Florida Alligator,* arrived at this time and photographed the body and dumpster.

Later on Saturday, the 18-year-old mother was found in her dorm bed and taken to the university's hospital. The hospital exam revealed "placenta parts and the umbilical cord in her" and she was released later in good health. A local obstetrician contacted about the case said that judging by the size of the infant, it was likely a miscarriage and not an abortion. The infant was determined to be about 7 months developed.

The story began on the front page of the Monday issue, across the bottom of the page, under the headline "UF police investigate baby's death at dorm." It jumped inside to page 3 and was accompanied by the photo.

It was a dramatic photo, contrasting two well-dressed detectives and one uniformed policeman with the naked body and contrasting the fragile human form with the harsh metal dumpster filled with pizza and liquor boxes. The photo was played 7 by 5 inches.

The story was well written and the photo dramatic but likely offensive to many—potentially so offensive that the newspaper's staff debated

Figure 8.2.   Photo courtesy of the *Independent Florida Alligator*. Used with permission.

most of Sunday about how to use it. The editor decided to run it, but in an unusual move she wrote an editor's column explaining why that appeared on the opinion page of the same issue. It showed a scene one readers would not expect but not on a college campus. It showed that supposedly sexually educated and sophisticated college students still need help. The editor wrote:

> Even with these legitimate reasons we did not run the picture on the front page. This is partially in response to our concern that we do not appear to be exploiting this picture to attract readers. . . . We also examined the photographer's negatives to see if there were any less graphic prints. . . . Is the message perceived by the reader worth the shock he or she experiences? After pondering what we feel is a very profound photo, we decided there is. This was a desperate act in an area of society where it is not expected. The picture shows it.

The local daily covered the story Monday in a police brief. No photo ran. It was determined that the body was from a miscarriage. The woman involved left school. The campus paper got several letters critiquing its coverage of the story. Many chose to criticize the editors for running the photo, while some praised the staff for pointing out the problem and for listing places on campus where sex and pregnancy counseling was available. Some letters did both.

An example of some of the outrage over the running of the photo by the *Alligator* came from a female student who called the coverage "the most unnecessary, tactless piece of journalism I've ever encountered." Another letter from a male student called the photo "in poor taste and extremely insensitive." The writer added, "There are times when good, sound judgment must override 'hot' copy."

Perhaps the most pointed comment came from a female writer who added 24 other names to her letter. The letter stated:

> The incident *could* have been used to remind people that they need to take responsibility for their own sexuality. The story *could* have been used as a painful reminder that there are many un-educated, naïve people out there who need help. But, unfortunately, the *Alligator* chose to sensationalize the story with a picture, completely nullifying any lesson whatsoever that might have been learned.

Micro Issues

1. Should the photographer have taken the picture? Justify your answer.
2. Is this a legitimate story, and if so, does it belong on page 1?
3. If this was the only photo available, did the paper then have to run it?
4. Various letters to the editor called the photo "unnecessary," "tactless," and "insensitive." What would you say to those charges if you were on the staff?

Midrange Issues

1. Does running the photo inside lessen any criticism of poor taste? Did its placement mitigate any ethical criticism?
2. If the staff was so unsure, was the editor correct in writing a same-day rationale for its publication?
3. Critique the reasoning stated by the editor in running the photo. What moral philosophy, if any, would lead one to agree with the action?

Macro Issues

1. Should a paper play a story and photo such as this to crusade about a problem?
2. Is the perceived social value of such a picture worth more than the shock and criticism?

3. Was the writer correct in her assessment that the shock of the photo negated any good that might have been done by the story?
4. Should a campus newspaper have a different standard—of taste, play, news value—than a "regular" daily?

CASE 8-D

ABOVE THE FOLD: BALANCING NEWSWORTHY PHOTOS WITH COMMUNITY STANDARDS

JIM GODBOLD, MANAGING EDITOR
Eugene Register-Guard, Eugene, Oregon

JANELLE HARTMAN, REPORTER
Eugene Register-Guard, Eugene, Oregon

Author's Note: *On Nov. 10, 1993, a nightmare unfolded in Springfield, Oregon, a quiet town adjoining the university community of Eugene, as Alan McGuire held his 2-year-old daughter, Shelby, hostage in their house. By the end of the standoff, both were dead, and the media had captured some horrific photos.*

Seven children had died as a result of child abuse in Lane County, Oregon, in the 20 months prior to that day, and the media had just witnessed the eighth. Jim Godbold was the assistant managing editor of the Eugene Register-Guard *at the time. The remarks below are from an interview with him months after the event.*

Godbold: The call came over the police scanner shortly after noon. We responded to a hostage situation, a man holding someone at knifepoint in a Springfield neighborhood. We knew it was probably 20 minutes from the *Register-Guard* in the best of possible circumstances, so we really scrambled. Photographer Andy Nelson and police reporter Janelle Hartman went as fast as they could to the area.

We got there when the police were trying to set up a perimeter to get people away from the area. It was real pandemonium right when Andy arrived. The situation didn't unfold for more than a few minutes before there was a burst of flame inside the house that caught the attention of the police officers, and they immediately made the decision that they were going to have to go inside.

A group of officers ran at the door, and then all of a sudden Alan McGuire, the man who was in the house, came hurtling through the front window on fire. I am not even sure if police officers knew how many people were in the house at the time. His wife had escaped from the home. She had been held at knifepoint and bound, and she had somehow gotten out, and she let police know that their 2-year-old daughter, Shelby McGuire, was in the house.

Shelby was a hostage and being held at knifepoint. Police saw her and tried to set up a telephone line so they could negotiate with McGuire, but the events unfolded rapidly, and after Alan McGuire jumped through the front window, police broke down the door. Two officers hauled McGuire's flaming body to the ground and tried to douse the flames with a garden hose. Inside the house, one of the officers saw Shelby McGuire sitting upright on the couch. She had a plastic grocery produce bag over her head, and it apparently had been duct-taped in some fashion, maybe around the neck.

They immediately tore the bag away. A detective picked Shelby up and sprinted out of the house with her. It was at that moment that Andy Nelson snapped his picture of one of the officers with Shelby's body in his

Figure 8.3. **Photo courtesy of the *Eugene Register-Guard*. Used with permission.**

arms, running out, two other officers standing on the side of the doorstep, another officer with a hose near Alan McGuire, and Alan lying on the ground. The flames were now out, but the charred and still-smoking body was present in the viewfinder as Andy snapped the picture.

At that moment, the officer with Shelby McGuire, the 2-year-old, began mouth-to-mouth resuscitation on the front lawn. Andy subsequently took a photograph of that. Then they rushed both Alan and Shelby McGuire to the hospital. We did not know Shelby's condition. The police didn't respond about whether she was able to be resuscitated.

We have a standing policy at the newspaper that as a general rule we don't run photographs of dead bodies of children. That immediately triggered the kind of review that we would go through to determine where this particular incident was going to stand up on our policy, whether or not anyone was going to argue for publication or against publication.

We began to talk about the policy and the potential community reaction that we might face. The discussion was pretty brief. The photo was so compelling and the situation that it sprang from so horrifying that we began looking at the photograph and saying,

"Well, I don't know, but look at what the photo has captured." "People are going to be upset." "This is potentially a photograph of a dead 2-year-old child." "Look at the concern and the expression on the police officers' faces. This is an example of what they deal with day in and day out. They are up against this kind of domestic violence hostage situation and people don't realize that."

So, the debate was intense and yet pretty short. We prepared a selection of pictures, and we brought those to the then-managing editor Patrick Yak and made the case that this is going to be a tough photograph for us to run. This is going to be one that we are going to have to be prepared to defend. But we believe it's that kind of exception to the rule that we look for.

The public response to the publication of the Shelby McGuire photograph was unprecedented in my 22 years in journalism and unprecedented at this newspaper. I have not come across a case, having been shown a number of them subsequently, that is of the magnitude per capita of reader response to a single photographic image. We received on the order of 450 telephone calls that began the moment people got the newspaper, which started at 6 a.m. First they came into our circulation department. The circulation department switchboard became overloaded and gave them the main newsroom switchboard, which didn't open until 7:30. At 7:30 when they threw the switch, all 20 of our incoming phone lines lit up, and the calls began to roll over into a holding pattern that had never been utilized by our switchboard before.

I was called at home by Al Gimmell, the corporate controller, who said, "We are inundated with telephone calls. We need some help." So I immediately came in to try to handle telephone calls, and I tried to find the time in between phone calls to call other editors in, but the calls were coming so rapidly that every time I hung up it rang again. When I picked up my voicemail messages, I had 31 unanswered messages, and that was probably 7:45 in the morning.

The range of responses weren't monolithic, except in their anger. But the anger came from different places. For some people, the anger came from a belief that we had simply stooped to a tremendously sensational graphic crime picture trying to sell newspapers. For others, the anger came from the terrible sense of violation that the surviving mother and brother of Shelby McGuire would have to wake up to the morning after their ordeal and see this on the front page of the hometown newspaper.

Another component argued that this was wholly inappropriate for the kind of newspaper the *Register-Guard* has been and continues to be. That 5-year-olds and 6-year-olds were sharing the newspaper at the breakfast table, and parents were finding themselves in a position of having to explain this horrifying incident and having the question "How is the little girl?" asked again. And there was also a range of responses from people who were themselves victims of domestic violence or spouses of victims or had family members who were involved in it. For them, it was a combination of anger and pain.

I spoke with literally dozens of people through tears. It was an emotional response that was overwhelming and people were extremely upset by the picture. Most asked the question "Why? I need to understand why the newspaper published this picture."

Figure 8.4. Photo courtesy of the *Eugene Register-Guard*. Used with permission.

We were really, I think, at a loss initially to respond to that question. I think a lot of that had to do with being, in a very real sense, out of touch with a substantial number of readers. The kind of reaction that we had was not anticipated by anyone in the news department.

If we were presented with a similar situation and a similar photograph today, we would absolutely not do it the way that we did it in the Shelby McGuire case. Thousands of our readers have defined for us a boundary in this community and for this newspaper that I don't think until we began to see it materialize we had any sense of exactly where it was.

Micro Issues

1. Look at the photos that accompany this text. The photo of the officer carrying out Shelby McGuire ran in full color above the fold, two-thirds of the page wide and 6 inches tall. Does a photo of that size over-sensationalize the story?
2. The photo of Sergeant Swenson's attempts to resuscitate Shelby ran below the fold in a small two-column photo. Why do you think the decision was made to run this photo smaller and lower?

Midrange Issues

1. Does the fact that Shelby died influence your decision on whether to run the photos? If so, in what way?
2. Does the fact that at least one television station and the local Springfield newspaper were there with photographers influence your decision to run the photos? If so, in what way?
3. Does the fact that seven other children had died in Lane County in less than 2 years affect your decision to run the photos? If so, in what way?
4. The biweekly *Springfield News* chose to run a front-page photo of Alan McGuire falling out of the front window of his home, his badly burned flesh still in flames. However, they covered the front page with a wrapper that read "Caution to Readers" and explained the content of the stories and photos underneath the wrapper. Critique that approach to handling the story.
5. A local television station showed a few seconds of the scene described above after warning viewers of the violent nature of the video that followed. The station got fewer than 20 complaints. How do you explain the vast difference in the reaction to the broadcast and print photos?

Macro Issues

1. What are the privacy rights of:
   a. Shelby McGuire?
   b. Shelby McGuire's mother and 4-year-old brother?
   c. Sergeant Swenson?
2. Critique the argument that these photos should be shown because they illustrate the type of tragedy that law enforcement officers are often called upon to handle.
3. Critique the argument that these photos should be shown because they illustrate the horror of domestic violence.
4. Critique the statement that "if we were presented with a similar situation and a similar photograph today, we would absolutely not do it the way that we did it in the Shelby McGuire case." In your opinion, is that based on sensitivity to reader concern or caving in to reader pressure?

CASE 8-E

HORROR IN SOWETO

SUE O' BRIEN, FORMER EDITORIAL PAGE EDITOR
The Denver Post

On Sept. 15, 1990, freelance photographer Gregory Marinovich documented the killing, by a mob of African National Congress supporters, of a man they believed to be a Zulu spy.

Marinovich and Associated Press reporter Tom Cohen spotted the man being led from a Soweto, South Africa, train-station platform by a group armed with machetes and crude spears. Marinovich and Cohen continued to witness and report as the man was stoned, bludgeoned, stabbed, doused with gasoline, and set afire.

It was one of 800 deaths in two months of factional fighting among blacks as rival organizations vied for influence in the declining days of apartheid.

The graphic photos stirred intense debate among editors. In one, the victim, conscious but stoic, lies on his back as a grinning attacker poises to plunge a knife into his forehead. In the final photo of the series, the victim crouches, engulfed in fire.

As the series was transmitted, several member editors called to question what the photographer was doing at the scene—could he in any way have stopped the attack? In response, an advisory went out on the photo wire, saying Marinovich had tried to intervene and then, when told to stop taking pictures, had told mob leaders he would stop shooting only when they "stopped hurting that man."

Decisions on what to do with the photos varied across the country, according to a survey. If any pattern emerged, it was that newspapers in competitive markets such as Denver, Minneapolis-St. Paul, and New York were more likely to go with the harsh graphics.

The burning photo was the most widely used, the stabbing the least. Several editors said they specifically rejected the stabbing as too extreme. "It showed violence and animalistic hatred," said Roman Lyskowski, graphics editor for the *Miami Herald*. Another editor, who agreed that the stabbing was much more disturbing than the burning, said he recalled immolation pictures from the Vietnam era. "That's not as unusual an image as that knife sticking right out of the skull."

When the Soweto series cleared at the *Miami Herald*, the burning photo was sent to Executive Editor Janet Chusmir's home for her approval. At her direction, the immolation picture ran on the front page, but below the fold and in black and white. The detail revealed in color reproduction, Chusmir and her editors agreed, was too graphic.

At the *Los Angeles Times* and *Dallas Morning News*, however, the burning photo ran above the front-page fold—and in color.

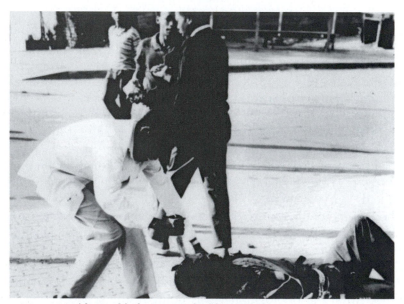

Figure 8.5.   AP/Wide World Photos. Used with permission

The *St. Paul Pioneer Press* chose the stabbing for front-page color. "I look at the moment that the photo freezes on film," said News Editor Joe Sevick. "Rarely do you see a photo where a knife is about to go into somebody." The photo ran in color on the *Pioneer Press* front page, accompanied by the story Cohen had written on the attack and a longer story on the South African government's attempt, announced that day, to crack down on black-on-black violence.

In Denver, at the *Rocky Mountain News*, Managing Editor Mike Madigan wanted to run a comprehensive package on the Soweto story. The tabloid's only open page was deep in the paper, but a page 3 box referred readers to the story with a warning the photos were "horrific and disturbing." Inside, stories on the attack and government crackdown and an editor's note on Marinovich's intervention accompanied three photos: the victim being led away from the train station, the stabbing, and the burning.

Most papers that ran the more challenging photos involved top management in the decision. Frequently, top editors were contacted by telephone, or came in from home, to give the photos a final go-ahead.

In most newsrooms, the burning or stabbing photos made it to the news desk for approval or rejection. But there, they sometimes were killed abruptly. "The editors at that point said no," one picture editor reported. "They would not take the heat."

Several editors deferred to the so-called breakfast test. "The question is 'Which of those photos would help tell the story without ruining everyone's breakfast?'" asked Rod Deckert, managing editor of the *Albuquerque Journal*. One editor said his paper is especially likely to de-emphasize disturbing material in the Sunday paper, which children often read with their parents. But many editors who rejected the more brutal pictures said the "breakfast test" is irrelevant. "If you're putting out a paper in New York and don't have something that's going to cause some discomfort over breakfast, then you're probably not putting out the full paper you should," said Jeff Jarvis, Sunday editor at the *New York Daily News*. "I don't think the breakfast test works for [today]."

Others cited distance tests. Some newspapers, in deference to victims' families, are less likely to use death photos from within their own circulation areas. Another editor, however, said his paper is *less* likely to run violent photos unless they are local and have a "more immediate impact on our readership."

Newspapers also differed widely on how they packaged the Soweto story. Some accompanied a photo series with the Cohen and crackdown stories, and a note on Marinovich's intervention. Some ran a single photo, often the burning, with only a cutline and a brief reference to the train-station incident in the "crackdown" story. Two respected big-city dailies, which omitted any reference to the Soweto attack in their accompanying stories, ran cursory cutlines such as "Violence continues: A boy runs away as an ANC supporter clubs a Zulu foe who was beaten, stabbed and set ablaze."

Although 41 papers used at least one of the Marinovich photos, only four—the *Charlotte Observer*, *Akron Beacon-Journal*, *Rocky Mountain News* (Denver), and *USA Today*—told the story of Marinovich's attempt to halt the attack.

Among collateral considerations at many news desks was the coverage of South African troubles that had gone before. At least one editor said the Soweto photos, which followed several other beating and killing photographs from South Africa that had been used earlier in the week, were "just too, too much."

With only three exceptions, editors said race did not figure in their considerations. One white editor said the fact that both attackers and victim were black deprived the series of clarity: "You don't have a sense of one side against another. You don't have a sense of right or wrong." Two editors who identified themselves as African-American, however, argued for aggressive use of the photos. Both work in communities with significant black populations. "I think black readers should be more informed about this," one said. "Across the board, black Americans don't realize what's going on with the black-on-black violence."

Figure 8.6.   AP/Wide World Photos. Used with permission.

Front-page placement and the use of color frequently triggered reader objections, but the adequacy of cutline information and accompanying copy also appear significant. The *Albany Times Union* was flooded by phone protests and subscription cancellations. Two other papers perceiving significant reader unrest—the *Dallas Morning News* and *Los Angeles Times*—ran the burning photo in color on their front pages. But each of the three papers also ran the front-page photos with only cutline accompaniment, referring readers inside to the stories that placed the images in context.

In retrospect, *Rocky Mountain News'* Madigan said he was very pleased with the final Soweto package and readers' reaction to it.

> It wasn't so much the idea that "yeah, we ran these really horrific pictures and, boy, it knocked people's socks off." I don't think that was the point. I think it was more the way we handled it. Just one word or the other can make a terrific difference in whether the public starts screaming "sensationalize, sensationalize," or takes it as a thoughtful, important piece of work, which is what we were after.

Micro Issues

1. In all but the most important stories, would you support a ban on dead-body photos in your newspaper or newscast?
2. Some editors believe it is their ethical duty to avoid violating readers' sense of taste or compassion. Others argue that it is their duty to force society to face unpleasant truths, even if it means risking reader anger and rejection. Whose side would you support?
3. Many readers suspect that sensational photos are chosen to sell newspapers or capture rating points by appealing to morbid tastes. Do you believe they're right?

Midrange Issues

1. Editors sometimes justify running graphic photos by saying they can provide a "warning bell," alerting people to preventable dangers in society. What values might the Soweto photographs offer readers?
2. Is the desire to avoid offending readers an ethical consideration or a marketing consideration?
3. Is it appropriate to base editorial decisions on what readers are likely to be doing at home: to edit newspapers differently, for instance, if they are likely to be read at the breakfast table, or present newscasts differently if they are to air during the dinner hour rather than later in the evening?

4. As an editor, would you be more likely to run a photograph of someone being murdered if the event happened in your own community, or if it happened thousands of miles away and none of your readers would be likely to know the victim or his family?
5. Do you see any distinction in:
   a. whether a violent photo is run in color or black and white?
   b. whether it is run on the front page or on an inside page?

Macro Issues

1. Is aesthetic, dramatic, or photographic value ever reason enough to run a picture, regardless of how intrusive it may be or how it may violate readers' sensitivities?
2. Is it your responsibility as an editor to find out if a photographer could have saved a life by intervening in a situation rather than taking pictures of it? Is that information you need to share with your readers?
3. Is it your responsibility as an editor to find out if the presence of the camera at the scene in any way helped incite or distort an event? Is that information you need to share with your readers?
4. When dramatic photographs are printed, how important is it for readers or viewers to be told all the background of the story or situation?

CASE 8-F

PHOTOGRAPHING FUNERALS OF FALLEN SOLDIERS

PHILIP PATTERSON
Oklahoma Christian University

Editor's note: *In 2012, the war in Afghanistan became the longest-running war in US history, and that August was one of the bloodiest months in the history of that conflict. With American soldiers dying weekly, the case below about their funerals is repeated across the nation.*
On May 11, 2004, an improvised explosive device struck the vehicle in which Army Spc. Kyle Adam Brinlee, 21, was riding in Iraq. He was killed in the explosion, the first combat-related death of an Oklahoma National Guard member since the Korean War. On May 19, more than 1,000 people gathered in the Pryor (OK) High School Auditorium for his funeral. Guests included the governor of Oklahoma, who spoke

at the ceremony. Members of the media were allowed to attend but confined to a sectioned-off area. Most of the media were reporters from Oklahoma City and Tulsa media outlets.

In attendance also was photographer Peter Turnley, who was shooting a photo essay for *Harper's Magazine*. It was to be the first of four "major eight-page photo essays" of Turnley's work that *Harper's Magazine* would showcase in 2004, according to a press release on the National Press Photographers website. Turnley was a well-known photographer whose work had been on the cover of *Newsweek* more than 40 times according to Turnley's own website. His photos had appeared in such publications as *Life*, *National Geographic*, *Le Monde*, and *The London Sunday Times*, among others. He had also covered wars in such locations as Rwanda, South Africa, Chechnya, Haiti, Afghanistan, and Iraq.

In August 2004, three photos from Brinlee's funeral appeared in *Harper's* in a photo essay entitled "The Bereaved: Mourning the Dead in America and Iraq." The essay focused on both American and Iraqi funerals with several pictures of grieving families, a photo of doctors unable to save a 10-year-old Iraqi boy, and a stark scene of Iraqis passing by a corpse lying on the street in Baghdad. In an interview given before the essay was published (Winslow 2004), Turnley said, "This first essay speaks in images about a very important theme touching our world today in a way that I don't think has been seen much before elsewhere."

One of the photos shows Brinlee in an open casket at the rear of the auditorium with several mourners still seated in the background. As of 2018, this photo does not appear on a website of all the Turnley photo essays for *Harper's Magazine*. It was not available for printing in this book, but can be found on page 47 of the August 2004 edition of the magazine.

Brinlee's family filed suit against Turnley and the magazine claiming a variety of torts including intentional infliction of emotional distress, invasion of privacy, and unjustly profiting from the photos. In their filing, the family claims that despite the large crowds in a public school, the funeral was a "private religious ceremony." They added that the photos went "beyond all bounds of decency."

The family claimed that Turnley had been told by the funeral director to abstain from photographing the body of the soldier. In a response to the court, Turnley denied he had received the instructions and claimed the body was placed near the media section for access. In a later interview with CNN, Turnley claimed, "It seems to me that the responsibility of a journalist today is to tell as much as possible about the true realities of what is taking place in the world. My desire is to simply try to dignify the reality of what people experience in war by showing the public what does happen there."

"The casket was open for friends and family—not to gawk at and take pictures and publish them. Not for economic gain," the lawyer for the family argued in an interview with the Associated Press.

The family sought $75,000 in actual damages on complaints including publication of private facts, appropriation of Brinlee's photo for commercial purposes and intrusion. In December 2005, a federal judge ruled that the family privacy was not invaded by the photos. "[P]laintiffs appear to have put the death of their loved one in the public eye intentionally to draw attention to his death and burial," Judge Frank Seay ruled in granting summary judgment to the media defendants. Elsewhere in the ruling, Seay pointed out that the plaintiffs lost their right to privacy during the funeral by choosing to publicize the event.

Harper's Magazine publisher John R. MacArthur echoed the ruling of the judge. "For me, from the beginning, it was a First Amendment issue and it was also a matter of our integrity. I have not met anyone yet who thought that photograph was disrespectful in any way."

Micro Issues

1. Can a funeral that is held in a public place be considered a private event?
2. Does it make a difference that Turnley and other media were given permission to attend the funeral?
3. Does it make a difference that the photos taken were of images in plain view of those attending the funeral?

Midrange Issues

1. Is newsworthiness a legal defense to the claim of invasion of privacy? Is it an ethical defense?
2. Does the fact that the family allowed media coverage of the funeral prevent them from suing for the distress that the Turnley photos allegedly caused? If the family had not allowed media coverage of the funeral, would your opinion of Turnley's photos be different?
3. In what way, if any, would video of the funeral differ from the still photographs of Turnley? 4. Are open-casket photos of soldiers a reality that journalists should be covering as Turnley contends or "beyond all bounds of decency" as the family contends? Can the two sides be reconciled?

Macro Issues

1. Is this a First Amendment issue as the judge and the media maintain? When other rights, such as the right to privacy, come into conflict with the First Amendment, how is the conflict best resolved?
2. What is the role of the media in covering conflicts such as the war in Afghanistan or the Arab Spring, which turned genocidal in Syria? Do wounded soldiers or civilians have any privacy rights that trump the public's right to know?

9

Informing a Just Society

By the end of the chapter, students should

- be able to explain why social justice can be understood by examining institutions as well as individuals
- be able to outline four ways of thinking about social justice
- understand how diversity can influence coverage of issues such as crime and the reporting process
- understand the concept of fault lines and how they can aid in evaluating professional performance

COVERING POVERTY IN DETROIT

By the time you've read the subtitle of this chapter, you've probably already developed a preliminary frame. After all, Detroit has been the locus of nationally significant news stories in the past five years—the city declared bankruptcy, its nearby neighbor Flint is now notorious for its lead-tainted water, it is repeatedly among the most violent cities in America, four years ago it elected its first Caucasian mayor in more than 90 years, and suburban voters in the metropolitan area gave President Donald J. Trump a narrow victory in Michigan, one of three states whose voters provided his victory margin in the electoral college. Go back 50 years, and Detroit erupted in civil unrest that included tanks on the city streets, the devastation of many neighborhoods, the Kerner Commission Report that examined the causes of those disturbances, including the role played by the media, and a continuing debate about whether that 1967 civil unrest is best termed a "riot" or a "rebellion."

But among the things you probably think you know about Detroit is that it is a city with a high poverty rate and that it is predominantly African-American. You would be right—about Detroit (where the population is about 80 percent African-American) but not about the rest of Michigan or the rest of the United States. And, that is the root of the problem. Covering poverty in Detroit represents a singularly difficult problem for journalists: how to cover poverty without racializing it. In other words, how can contemporary news stories break the unfounded connection between race and poverty that has characterized news coverage for the past 50 years?

Indeed, in total numbers, there are more Caucasians in poverty than any other racial group. The overall poverty rate—calculated as those earning less than $24,600 for a family of four—was 12.7 percent, or 40.6 million people in 2016 (Census.gov 2017).

One popular misconception is that poverty is a mainly urban problem. However, 48 of the 50 US counties with the highest child poverty rates are in rural America, according to the Annie E. Casey Foundation. Further, almost one in five rural kids is poor, and rates of rural child poverty are higher than urban child poverty for all kids and every minority group.

Many low-income families, especially those in high-poverty communities, pay too much for life's necessities, a phenomenon the Annie E. Casey Foundation dubs "the high cost of being poor." For example, families in low-income rural communities often pay nearly 20 percent more than the USDA-recommended budget for basic food items. The same upcharge is true for clothing, furniture, and appliances. This surplus charge occurs because small-scale local businesses operate outside of the economies of scale that allow larger businesses such as Walmart or Target to offer more options and charge less for products.

Still, "from 1964 to 1965, the percentage of African-Americans who appeared in news pictures of the poor jumped from 27 to 49 percent, at a time when the actual percentage of African-Americans among those whose income placed them among the poor was about 30 percent," wrote Martin Gilens almost 20 years ago (1999). He argues that "distorted coverage found in newsmagazines reflects a broader set of dynamics that also shapes images of the poor in the more important medium of television news." Gilens' study also found that the tone of that coverage changed beginning in the mid-1960s. In his study, stories about mismanaged welfare programs included more visual images of African-Americans as sometimes corrupt and often lazy and undeserving, a concrete symbol of the "Welfare Mess." However, stories that focused on the economic downturns of those decades, which also threw middle-class workers into poverty, were more sympathetic in tone and feature visual images of Caucasians.

The trends that Gilens and other scholars have been documenting for more than four decades still accurately describe many news stories. "Most journalists," Gilens wrote, "consciously reject the stereotype of African-Americans as lazy. But in the everyday practice of their craft . . . these same journalists portray poor blacks as more blameworthy than poor whites," (Green 1999). Some scholars directly connect public attitudes about the poor and changes in public policy about poverty to media coverage and images of the poor (Rose and Baumgartner 2013).

COVERING CRIME: MORE THAN A MATTER OF BLACK AND WHITE

Crime is one of the most prevalent issues in news, and the media's constant reporting of crime cultivates widespread fear and concern (Gross and Aday 2003; Iyengar 1991). Crime reporting, however, also perpetuates racial stereotypes and biases because African-Americans most frequently are depicted as criminals, victims, or dependents on society (Leshner 2006). In contrast, most news stories and entertainment programming feature Caucasians, so audiences tend to associate Caucasians with a variety of topics, including business, technology, and science (Dixon and Linz 2000). Local news also often over-represents African-American criminals while under-representing Caucasian and Latino criminals, as well as African-American victims (Dixon and Linz 2000). Further, African-Americans are more often shown in handcuffs, and African-American mug shots, often without names included, were shown four times more than Caucasian mugshots (Entman and Rojecki 2000; Leshner 2006). This lack of identifying information could cause audiences to categorize all African-Americans as criminals instead of noticing characteristics of individual perpetrators (Entman and Rojecki 2000).

This emphasis on African-Americans as criminals, especially men, has real-world consequences. Seventeen-year-old Trayvon Martin was shot and killed by a self-proclaimed neighborhood watch volunteer in 2012. When George Zimmerman later was acquitted for that shooting, Alicia Garza went on Facebook and wrote a post that ended, "black lives matter." A movement was born. It gained further prominence after the deaths of Michael Brown in Ferguson, Missouri, in 2014; Tamir Rice in Cleveland in 2014; Eric Garner in Staten Island, New York, in 2014; Freddie Gray in Baltimore in 2015; and Philando Castile in suburban St. Paul, Minnesota, in 2016. The *Washington Post* began an interactive database of people shot and killed by police in 2015; in 2017, the number of fatalities reached 987. One major change from even a decade ago is the extensive use of cellphone and surveillance cameras allows citizens to video-record many of these incidents and compare that footage with information provided by police officials.

If you've made it this far, you are probably thinking to yourself, "there's a lot going on here." Suddenly we are no longer concerned with the actions of an individual journalist or public relations practitioner, but how those actions contribute to the ideals and assumptions of society at large. You are probably also thinking that race may not be the only issue worth thinking about in these terms. What about women? Or members of the LBGTQ community? Or the elderly? Or the mentally ill? Don't they face some of the same problems, and aren't those problems awfully big for a single editor or videographer to take on?

PHILOSOPHICAL APPROACHES TO SOCIAL JUSTICE

These questions all center philosophically in the broad area of social justice, that branch of philosophy and political philosophy that connects individual acts to their societal consequences and the societal understanding to a range of possible individual actions. It's a philosophical feedback loop that places community on an equal footing with the individual. Thinking about social justice, unlike issues of truth telling or privacy, requires understanding the following foundational assumptions.

Social justice is comparative. It asks not just about the individual but about all the others as well. In the opening illustration, if African-Americans are portrayed inaccurately as poor and lazy in a preponderance of news reports about poverty, how does that portrait influence all individuals in a community and their access to the "goods" that living in that community may provide?

Social justice is relational. While it can speak to individual decisions, it also can speak equally well to policies that cover a number of decisions. Take, for example, the Associated Press' decision about how the word "terrorist," "Islamist," and "migrant" are to be appropriately used in news stories. Contrary to what some critics have alleged, the Associated Press made these style decisions in an attempt to equalize and destigmatize certain groups of people. The folks at the Associated Press had read and understood the research about stereotyping, stigma, and the racialization of poverty that has emerged in the past 20 years. They have decided to provide an alternative view—one based on a concept of social justice—literally one word at a time.

"Justice is the first virtue of social institutions, just as truth is of systems of thought," writes philosopher John Rawls. "A theory however elegant and economical must be rejected or revised if it is untrue; likewise laws and institutions no matter how efficient and well-arranged must be reformed or abolished if they are unjust. . . . An injustice is tolerable only when it is necessary to avoid a greater injustice. Being first virtues of human activities, truth and justice are uncompromising" (Rawls 1971, 3–4).

Thinking about social justice explores—and attempts to connect—distinctive ethical questions to one another. The three Enlightenment-based approaches to justice, philosopher Michael Sandel notes, begin in different places.

One branch of theory examines the maximization of welfare—something you were introduced to in chapter 2. Utilitarianism is deeply connected to this approach—doing the greatest good for a community of your fellows does maximize the welfare of all. In 2017, the US government, after decades of litigation, required US tobacco companies to develop and then pay for the broadcasting and printing of advertisements that informed consumers of the negative health effects of cigarettes and other tobacco products, as well as admit that those same firms used just enough nicotine in cigarettes to make them addictive. This act maximizes public health and welfare through the use of media messages. Even though the tobacco firms might be financially hurt by this advertising campaign, the larger good of the community—fewer deaths through tobacco-related illness—was promoted. As contentious as the decision is, it is fundamentally grounded in a sense of social justice that speaks equally to both the community and the individuals within it.

A second branch of social justice theory focuses on freedom and individual rights, and Americans particularly are familiar with the broad range of the individual rights debate. On the one hand, some who examine social justice through the individual rights lens assume a sort of laissez-faire position, that justice consists of respecting and upholding the voluntary choices made by consenting adults. This argument is often, but not exclusively, framed in economic terms, and most Americans would connect this way of approaching social justice with the contemporary Libertarian political movement. However, freedom and individual rights may also be thought of as the need for there to be some rules so that all individuals would have access to the "goods"—material and otherwise—available to those living in the community. For those who subscribe to this approach to social justice, markets are not always the best regulators of individual welfare and may apportion the "goods" of society in a decidedly unfair way. I may be "free" to drive down the left-hand side of the road, but that choice could have disastrous consequences for myself and others depending on whether I am driving in London or New York. Some rules are needed to govern my access to and use of the highway system—again, so that all may have access and that the "good life" will be more widely available to all.

Finally, a third way of thinking about social justice is to connect it to the virtues. A just society affirms certain virtues, whether they are arrived at through contemplation or religious instruction. But, it is not difficult to imagine that certain sorts of societies might make upholding the virtues easier—or more difficult—than others.

Rawls' concept of justice as fairness is among the most widely applied to issues of social justice. His approach, because it combines utilitarian thinking with the concept of freedom of access for societal "goods," provides a way of thinking about social justice that melds both utilitarianism and freedom and, through the veil of ignorance, devises a way of coming up with some institutional policies that might speak to social justice issues before specific questions occur.

In the Catholic intellectual tradition, social justice requires facing the intellectual and moral challenges of cultural and religious differences both nationally and globally (Hollenbach 2010). The challenge of pluralism, Hollenbach argues, produces a need to wrestle with questions that reach across boundaries between diverse traditions. For example, Thomas Aquinas incorporated ideas from Aristotle, a pagan, Moses ben Maimon, a Jew, and Ibn Sina and Ibn Rushd, both Muslims, to transform both Western Christianity and Aristotelian ways of thinking. For Aquinas and Aristotle, justice calls for commitment to social solidarity and mutual responsibility for each other. The term "social" is used here to assert that justice is not concerned with relations between individual members of society but to the economic and political structures that determine our communal lives.

More recently, Indian philosopher Amartya Sen has provided a distinctive insight into theorizing about social justice. Sen argues that much of Western philosophy has been preoccupied with questions of what is the *most* just society. "If a theory of justice is to guide reasoned choice of policies, strategies or institutions, then the identification of fully just social arrangements is neither necessary nor sufficient," (Sen 2009, 15).

Sen bases much of his thinking in social choice theory, a political theory that focuses on a rational and often mathematical comparison among alternatives. Sen's approach employs practical reason as the tool for comparison and requires that reasoning be "public." His theory stipulates that thinking about social justice requires accepting the "inescapable plurality of competing principles," encourages re-examination of existing arrangements, allows for partial solutions, and accepts a diversity of interpretation. By diversity of interpretation, Sen acknowledges that different principles and individual preferences may yield different specific results, but that all such results should withstanding clear and precise logical inquiry (Sen 2009, 106–111). For Sen, behavior—not some theoretical ideal—is the goal of justice.

Thinking about social justice using this approach would allow for multiple solutions to questions of justice, solutions that, for example, could take both culture and history into consideration without allowing them to determine any specific outcome. Under this reasoning, the very different professional norms and laws that govern how crime and the courts are covered in the United States and Great Britain, both developed democracies, could be equally just without descending into relativism. One approach is not better than the other, and both can be re-examined in the light of new information, policies, laws, and regulations.

These four approaches to justice speak deeply to moving a society from a less just to a more just set of institutions, including government and the media. Feminist philosopher Martha Nussbaum provides an affirmative vision of what such a society might look like in her books *Creating Capabilities: The Human Development Approach* (2013), *Political Emotions: Why Love Matters for Justice* (2015), and *Upheavals of Thought: The Intelligence of Emotions* (2001). Nussbaum is a capabilities philosopher. "Thus the capabilities approach feels free to use an account of cooperation that treats justice and inclusiveness as ends of intrinsic value from the beginning, and that views human beings as held together by many altruistic ties as well as by ties of mutual advantage" (Nussbaum 2006, 158). Many of Nussbaum's 10 capabilities focus on the communication that must occur to allow groups and individuals to develop and flourish. This most certainly would include news, persuasive messages, and the communication inherent in art and entertainment. These capabilities include the development of emotions that allow people to attach to others outside themselves; affiliation—being able to live in a group and show concern for others; play and creation; and control over one's environment, particularly political control, including the right to political participation, free speech and association. Nussbaum argues that careful attention to "language and imagery" (Nussbaum 2006, 413) allows individuals to re-conceptualize their relationship—both actual and metaphoric—to others. She acknowledges that her capabilities approach includes the affirmative—things that people should do, ways that people might be encouraged to imagine and act—that contrast markedly with other articulations of justice that focus more on prohibitions and restrictions.

Nussbaum's affirmative vision of justice would support in-depth reporting of issues such as poverty and race, two contemporary problems she has written about extensively. Her capabilities approach also would encourage journalists to experiment with coverage, a recommendation that would apply equally to documentary filmmakers and strategic communication professionals. The creativity inherent in journalism and strategic communication finds a home in the capabilities approach, providing it is used in the service of the moral imagination.

SOCIAL JUSTICE IN A DEMOCRATIC SOCIETY

Just as there are members of a power elite, there also are those who feel excluded from political society. One popular interpretation of US history has been to track the gradual extension of power to ever more diverse publics. But the process has been uneven and contentious. All minority groups seek access to the political process and, because mass media have become major players in that process, they seek access to media as well.

Journalists say diversity matters. The marketplace of ideas—conceptualized by John Milton, John Locke, and John Stewart Mill, and then Americanized by Thomas Jefferson and Oliver Wendell Holmes—is incomplete and inadequate when and if voices are left out of the discussion. One component of seeking and reporting truth, according to the Society of Professional Journalists code of ethics, is to tell "the stories of diversity and magnitude of the human experience. Seek sources whose voices we seldom hear." That statement echoes a similar one made by the Hutchins Commission in its report *A Free and Responsible Press*, which included the charge to project a representative picture of the constituent groups in society." More contemporary thought, from the facilitative role in which media seek to promote dialogue among constituent groups (Christians, Glasser, McQuail, Nordenstreng, and White 2009) to the mobilizer role where media incorporate citizens into the news process (Weaver and Wilhoit 1996) also incorporate ideas of diverse voices.

Further, journalists should care because diverse voices help both the byline and the bottom line. Journalists need to appeal to a wide variety of populations, and this is true whether you write for newspapers, magazines, or online; broadcast on radio or television; or work in advertising, marketing, or public relations. Economically, journalists cannot eliminate segments of the audience by appealing to one gender, race, class, or age group. For example, while Caucasians are still the majority population in the United States (with 63.7 percent of the population, according to the 2010 Census), they represent the only major racial or ethnic group with a declining population (down from 75.1 percent in the 2000 Census). Similarly, while advertisers typically target the 18–44 year-old demographic, 63.5 percent of the US population either is younger or older than that age group.

Byline diversity also could aid in improving coverage. For example, women generated only 37.7 percent of news at 20 of the nation's top news outlets in 2016 (Women's Media Center 2017). The thoughts, feelings, and experiences of women are not monolithic, so greater numbers of women in the newsroom, for example, might ensure greater diversity by allowing various women's perspectives to be represented while also better reflecting culturally diverse communities (Harp, Bachmann, and Loke 2014; Len-Ríos,

Hinnant, and Jeong 2012). A more robust representation also could influence editorial content, framing, sources, format, tone, and newsroom culture. Similarly, greater racial and ethnic diversity could influence a wide range of topics, from immigration to gun violence. For example, scholars found that media focused on the 2007 Virginia Tech shooter's Korean ethnicity and immigration status. Asian-American journalists were among the first to alert the public and the journalism community of potentially excessive racialization of the shooting. With more common representations of Asian-Americans, they argued, the shooter's race might have escaped the reporters' attention (Park, Holoday, and Zhang 2012). The race of the 1999 Columbine High School shooters, by contrast, were virtually absent from media coverage (Zillman 1999). The internet also enhances the number of differing opinions available in the marketplace of ideas. For a legacy news organization, then, it's better to have those voices represented in your news coverage than to be competing against them.

Media ethicists suggest these political and social outgroups provide mass media with a further set of responsibilities. They assert that mass media, and individual journalists, need to become advocates for the politically homeless. Media ethicist Clifford Christians suggests that "justice for the powerless stands at the centerpiece of a socially responsible press. Or, in other terms, the litmus test of whether or not the news profession fulfills its mission over the long term is its advocacy for those outside the socioeconomic establishment" (Christians 1986, 110).

Christians' argument can be amplified beyond democracy's racial, ethnic, and economic outgroups. In contemporary democratic society, clearly some "things" also are without political voice. The environment, ethnic issues, poverty, and human rights violations beyond American shores all have difficulty finding a powerful spokesperson.

Communitarian thinking urges that justice is the ethical linchpin of journalistic decision-making. If justice becomes the fundamental value of American journalism, then the media have the goal of transforming society, of empowering individual citizens to act in ways that promote political discussion, debate, and change (Christians, Ferré, and Fackler 1993).

What makes journalists uneasy is that this role shift smacks of a kind of benevolent paternalism. If individual human beings carry moral stature, then assigning one institution—in this case, the mass media—the role of social and political arbiter diminishes the moral worth of the individual citizen. Mass media become a kind parent and the citizen a sort of wayward child in need of guidance. Such a relationship does not promote political maturity. On the other hand, linking justice and truth as the two irreducible ethical values as Rawls does provides a kind of philosophical alignment that may help journalism as a profession develop a rationale beyond objectivity that would justify its central, and protected, place in American democracy.

While the weight of recent scholarly opinion sides with Christians, the view is not without risk. If accepted, it means a thorough change for the mass media in the US political system. That change would bring about other changes, some of them not easy to anticipate. As Thomas Jefferson said, being a citizen of a democracy is not easy—to which journalists might well add, neither is covering one.

INTERNET INFLUENCE ON SOCIAL JUSTICE

The original journalists in America were citizens who stepped into the role of pamphleteers or publishers based on a desire to shape an emerging nation. Most of them, such as Benjamin Franklin or Thomas Paine, had sources of income outside of their role as citizen journalists, and many lost money in their publishing pursuits. During the next 100 years, the role of professional journalist emerged in the new democracy and for the next century, the delivery of information was primarily considered the role of the full-time professional.

However, no formal education or license is required to be a journalist. Toward the end of the 20th century—propelled by the internet—it became evident that the role of "journalist" no longer belonged exclusively to the trained writer working at a recognizable institutional media outlet.

And even institutionally employed journalists today often step out of their institutional roles through their tweets and blogs—some out of passion, others by contract with their employers. Citizen journalists who have never been in a newsroom now create websites, write blogs, and gain Twitter followings whose readers rival in numbers the readers of the mainstream press and whose stories often break important national and international news. Videos on YouTube often receive a number of "hits" that would rank them among the top-rated television programs if they had been measured by the Nielsen ratings. While the delivery methods are new, the concept is old: Citizen journalists as the eyes and ears of the public. And as they point their cameras at increasingly serious topics, the results are often dramatic.

The most dramatic of these events internationally is the 2011 Arab Spring, a country-by-country revolution in the Middle East that owed its emergence to social media and the ability of cellphone users to congregate to protest dictatorships that, in the ensuing months, collapsed, sometimes peacefully but often through the use of military force. New York University professor Clay Shirky predicted something like the Arab Spring in his 2009 book *Here*

Come's Everybody when he noted that the internet gave individuals the power to organize as never before. While Shirky was prescient in his analysis of one kind of organizational capacity the internet makes more possible, he and many others failed to grapple with the specific kind of organizational tool the internet itself constitutes.

The web is very good for getting people together in a common cause, whether it's overthrowing a government or tracking down a stolen bicycle by asking "friends" to keep an eye out for it. Social media is particularly adept—it appears—in separating people into groups. In fact, as the film *The Social Network* makes clear, the original impetus for the site was all about what sociologists call in-groups and out-groups—a way of giving everyone access to the sort of social status as "cool kids" that too many geeks and brainiacs were denied in high school and college. Getting rich in the process didn't hurt, either.

Social media, however, does not appear to be an effective organizing tool in the sort of activities, such as forming a government after a revolution, that require face-to-face interaction over a long period of time with people who are like and unlike "you" in significant ways. The internet is great for that initial burst of energy; the sustained commitment to building a "new" social and political structure of almost any sort demands time and face-to-face interaction. While social media can promote some of that effort, the technology itself appears to make some sorts of human activity no more possible than has been the case in other eras.

In-groups and out-groups are also ethically problematic. Indeed, if philosophical theory is taken seriously, then one of the intellectual goals of ethical thinking is trying to lessen and, where possible, eliminate the in-group–out-group divide. In a democracy, listening only to "friends" can lead to the sort of political structures that the Arab Spring successfully overcame. Professionally, some of the best journalism and advertising emerges not when you are thinking "just like" everyone else, but when you succeed in making others take a look at things from a point of view that is unlike their individual experiences.

In the early 21st century, social media seems to be separating two roles that about 400 years of media history had previously blended. The role of information provider and collector—what some scholars and professionals now refer to as the "first informer" role—can be done by citizens as well as journalists. But citizen journalism lacks one important component that traditional media had: information verification. It is this second role—verifying information and placing it in a social, political, and cultural context—that is becoming more and more the work of journalism.

The "first informer" role values speed. The information verification role is what makes the initial fact into something reliable and accessible to all. The information verification role values truth, context, and equality. It can and does employ social media as a corrective—and sometimes an essential one. But, it is the ethical values of truth and inclusive access that will continue to fund professional performance in this internet age. Indeed, if professionals lose their adherence to these values, there will be little to separate them from "first informers" and less to separate the institution of the mass media from its role as check and balance on the other powerful actors such as the modern nation state and the multinational market.

EXCELLENT JOURNALISM AND FAULT LINES

Once journalists understand why social justice and diversity is important in their work, they next turn to how to incorporate the concepts into their stories, packages, and campaigns. Two useful tools are excellent journalism, developed by Keith Woods at the Poynter Institute, and Robert C. Maynard's fault lines.

Woods argues that journalists need to ask four questions when writing stories: First, does it provide context? The story needs to provide enough historical context—time, place, environment, social and cultural background, political history, legal history, and economic implications—for the audience to be able to make sense of what is happening. Second, does it embrace complexity? Woods argues that stories need to rise above one-dimensional explanations and polarized framing to reveal gray truths. By moving past black-and-white frames, journalists uncover multiple layers to people and their actions, develop fuller opinions, and expose a fuller picture of a story. Third, do we hear the voices of the people? Stories should bring the voice of people to the listener, reader, or viewer; quotes and sound bytes should be purposeful, clear, and should advance the story by conveying character and personality or revealing new truths. And, finally, does it have the ring of authenticity? The reporting needs to be broad and deep enough, the details fine enough, and the opinions open enough to provide insight.

One tool to develop authentic stories is through the use of fault lines. Maynard originally conceived of five fault lines: race and ethnicity, class, gender and sexual orientation, geography, and generation. Subsequent scholars have expanded the list to include religion, disability, and political affiliation as potential fault lines. Maynard argued that we, both as journalists and as society, cannot and should not pretend that differences do not exist. The key, then, is providing context and history. That context and history occurs through understanding and utilizing fault lines. For journalists, fault lines can better help them reflect the interests, decisions, and actions of sources in a different social group. They also can provide a way to identify missing cultural voices, as well as story angles and perspectives that could offer a way to reframe a story or add complexity. The questions to ask are what fault lines are reflected in my sources, and how do those fault lines affect their comments, interests, decisions, or actions? Arguably more importantly, what fault lines are missing, and are they needed to help readers better understand the relevance of the information?

SUGGESTED READINGS

Jewkes, Y. (2011). *Media & crime: Key approaches to criminology.* Thousand Oaks, CA: Sage.

Len-Ríos, M., & Perry, E. L. (eds.). (2016). *Cross-cultural journalism: Communicating strategically about diversity.* New York: Routledge.

Morgan, A. L., Woods, K., & Pifer, A. E. (2006). *The authentic voice: The best reporting on race and ethnicity.* New York: Columbia University Press.

Nussbaum, M. (2015). *Political emotions: Why love matters for justice.* Cambridge, MA: Belknap Press.

Shirky, C. (2009). *Here comes everybody: The power of organizing without organizations.* New York: Penguin Group.

CASES

CASE 9-A

SPOTLIGHT: IT TAKES A VILLAGE TO ABUSE A CHILD

LEE WILKINS
University of Missouri
Wayne State University

The process of investigative reporting has been the focus of two classic Hollywood films—*All the President's Men* in 1976 and the 2015 Oscar-winning Best Picture *Spotlight*. *All the President's Men* recounted the story of the *Washington Post*'s Watergate coverage, focusing on the external obstacles, specifically corruption in the White House, that journalists Bob Woodward and Carl Bernstein encountered in their reporting.

Spotlight dramatized the investigative reporting process, but instead of focusing on the external obstacles, *Spotlight* focused on the way that community and individual biography shape journalism. And, in the case of the *Boston Globe*'s investigation of the Catholic Church pedophile priest scandal, the film explores how the history of specific journalists covering specific stories in specific communities shapes those stories—from the "discovery" of a decades-long problem to how the newspaper reported and published what it found.

Early in the film and at the outset of the investigation, one of the characters notes that "your best shot is to try these cases in the press," meaning that it was impossible to challenge the historic and pervasive institution of the Roman Catholic Church and its leaders in Boston without the help of other powerful institutions. Those powerful institutions, including prominent Boston lawyers, made sure that the scandal left a minimal paper trail and, when there were documents, that they sometimes vanished—including from official court records and legal proceedings.

However, if the press was unable or unwilling to take on other powerful institutions over the issue, then the injustice would continue. In the initial phases of the reporting process, multiple characters tell the journalists involved that they believe the *Globe* will simply lack the courage to cover the story in anything other than an episodic fashion, as the paper had for several decades before the investigation uncovered the systemic roots of the scandal itself.

The *Globe*, despite its big-city circulation, envisioned itself as a community newspaper. Within the *Globe*, the six-member Spotlight team (reduced to a four-member team for the film) identifies itself as the oldest continuously operating newspaper investigative unit in the United States, with a high degree of autonomy over both story selection and journalistic methods. The staff members, including Spotlight team leader Robbie Robinson and the other team members who reported the story, were raised in the Roman Catholic Church, attended Catholic parochial schools, and had deep roots in the community of Boston.

From that personal history emerged a respect for the church itself, its leadership, and a skepticism about the scope of the story that ultimately fueled the reporting of it. Connections to the community also made it possible for powerful people to try to exert pressure on the journalists involved to abandon the story or to downplay it. How that pressure was exerted, and ultimately resisted—what some critics referred to as nongovernmental censorship—is one of the themes of the film.

A second theme is the ethical virtue of listening. The impact of listening as part of the interviewing process, and of doing so without judgment, emerges as the journalists interview the victims of the pedophile priests who recount the details of their molestation in explicit detail. The interviews include difficult questions, and because the victims are recounting events that occurred decades before, the viewer is able to at least superficially gauge the impact the molestation had on people throughout their lives. However, it is the act of listening that ultimately weaves trust among the journalists and the victims they interviewed.

The third theme that emerges is one of persistence, a theme also in *All the President's Men*. "Keep going" becomes the watchword of the reporting process in *Spotlight*, just as "follow the money" did for Watergate. However, the directive to "keep going" also meant that the reporters involved also questioned their own actions when pieces of the story had emerged years before anyone understood either the scope of the story or the problem. Their self-doubt about the quality of their journalism also distinguishes the film's portrayal of journalists in the midst of a big story that even they struggle to believe. Fictionalized though based on real-life executive editor Marty Barron, who kept the team focused on the systemic problem rather than the sensational individual stories of abuse, personified the maxim of "keep going until you've got the bigger story" that the *Globe* ultimately reported.

Critics of the film lauded it for its non-glamorized portrayal of journalism and journalists. "They got the journalism right" was one of the most frequent comments about the production.

Micro Issues

1. What are the specific instances in the film where listening without judging is important in reporting the story?
2. What role does family and friendship play in the reporting? Do you believe the journalists handled these conflicts appropriately?
3. At one point in the film, one of the characters says that only an outsider could have uncovered this story. Do you agree?

Midrange Issues

1. Did the Spotlight team do the right thing when it abandoned the story to report on 9/11? Why?
2. Use the theory of W.D. Ross to explore how the journalists viewed their duties as they reported the story. Did the ordering of those duties change during the reporting?
3. Evaluate the level of proof that the *Globe* reporters amass to make their story believable. Do you think this is a new standard of "proof" for journalists reporting instances of sexual assault and abuse?

Macro Issues

1. Does this film trivialize the harm of childhood sexual abuse for the sake of profitable entertainment?
2. At one point in the film, one of the characters urges Robinson to look around: "Robbie, this is the church . . . these are good people." Evaluate this rationale as a reason to curtail reporting on this story. Which philosopher would support your decision?
3. Evaluate how community shaped this story? Was it right for the journalists involved to tell their sources they "cared"?

CASE 9-B

12TH AND CLAIRMOUNT: A NEWSPAPER'S FORAY INTO DOCUMENTING A PIVOTAL SUMMER

LEE WILKINS
Wayne State University
University of Missouri

The documentary film *12th and Clairmount* debuted in March 2017, timed to coincide with the 50-year-anniversary of the most significant period of urban unrest in the history of Detroit and which continues to haunt the city five decades later.

Brian Kaufman, a reporter for the *Detroit Free Press* and one of the film's two editors, collaborated with a Detroit television station (Channel 7—WXYZ) and *Bridge* magazine to try to present a holistic portrait of the Detroit riots, which many Detroiters refer to as a rebellion. Those five days of unrest, in which 43 people died and hundreds were arrested, are credited by scholars and pundits alike with intensifying the Caucasian flight from Detroit proper to the city's suburbs and exurbs—housing patterns that continue to this day.

"What we tried to do was get to the heart of why this happened and it happened for several reasons, police brutality being one of them, housing segregation being another, and lack of jobs being the third," Kaufman said.

The narrative backbone of the film was the relationship between the city's African-American community and Detroit's police force which, at that time, was almost exclusively Caucasian. Through crowdsourcing, including notes from reporters working in the city at the time, archival news footage, and home movies that were first culled and then digitized to be edited into the film, viewers learned about the actions of a cadre of four Detroit police officers, known locally as the Big Four, who beat, intimidated, arrested on false pretenses, and terrorized African-American Detroiters for years before the riots broke out. The film's producers interviewed Detroiters who had encountered the Big Four, memories that remained vivid despite the decades.

Housing patterns in the city were examined, including the practice of redlining that meant, in Detroit, that African-Americans could not get traditional mortgages from banks and instead had to purchase homes on land contracts, a practice that meant that even one missed payment could, and often did, result in eviction with no recourse, including recovering the money that homeowners had paid for years. Kaufman noted that how

Detroiters of the time reacted to the riots was very much a function of where they lived. Neighborhoods in the northeast part of the city were untouched by the unrest; Detroiters alive today who lived in the city in 1967 say they were unaware of the riots at the time they were happening—depending on the neighborhood in which they grew up.

Footage from media coverage of the Detroit riots also moves the narrative forward. Prominent images in those stories include tanks on major thoroughfares in the city, looting and arson in the African-American neighborhoods most affected by the unrest, and footage of both local—including Michigan governor George W. Romney (father of 2012 Republican presidential candidate Mitt Romney)—and national political leaders calling for military force to quell the riots. In the larger context of the film itself, it is possible to examine whether journalists of the time really "got" and reported the deeper story of the problems of the people and the institutions of Detroit.

The filmmakers also took some risks. In order to keep the documentary visually engaging, they had to "find" images that either never or no longer existed. This included hiring an artist to provide sketches of important people and scenes—the only way the film's editor and producers found to maintain visual continuity.

In a review of the film by Owen Gleiberman, the *Variety* contributor, noted, "Kaufman lets us hear from people of every class and neighborhood: the melting pot of downtown, the whites in their secluded enclaves, the African-Americans who were kept out even when they could afford to buy a home, the way the practice of 'blockbusting' worked, with landlords indulging in greedy scare tactics like paying black children to throw a bottle through a window, thereby establishing a neighborhood as vulnerable to crime, at which point the landlord would snap up one house at a fire-sale price, then another, fomenting a wave of panicked sell-offs. This was the economic engine of white flight."

All of this, of course, occurred in a context of the history of Detroit, one of the most racially diverse cities in the United States in 1967. Detroit was led by Mayor Jerome P. Cavanaugh, a politician who spoke for integration, was sometimes compared with John F. Kennedy, and who, before the summer of 1967, may have had presidential aspirations of his own. The riots also occurred the same summer when thousands of Detroiters heard Dr. Martin Luther King give an earlier version of his "I have a dream speech" that, when delivered at the foot of the Washington Monument several months later, inspired the nation.

The film opened the *Detroit Free Press*' Freep film festival to sell-out audiences. It was aired on local television.

The film debuted within weeks of Hollywood director Katheryn Bigelow's *Detroit*, also timed to coincide with the summer of 1967. Bigelow won as Oscar for best director. In explaining her decision to make a film about the 1967 riots, she said: "James Baldwin said: 'Nothing can be changed until it is faced.' And in America, there seems a radical desire not to face the reality of race. So these events keep replaying."

Micro Issues

1. Successful documentary films often have a point of view. Is it appropriate for a newspaper to support and participate in such an effort?
2. Anniversaries are often used as a news peg to revisit significant events such as disasters or the 9/11 terrorist attacks. What is the role of such journalistic efforts?
3. The filmmakers said they made the film for those who did not live through the events. Evaluate this justification.

Midrange Issues

1. The use of crowdsourcing, and particularly the use of home movie footage, raised concerns about privacy and point of view. Evaluate those concerns in light of the theories of social justice reviewed in this chapter.
2. How do you evaluate the decision to employ an artist to provide sketches of significant actors in the Detroit unrest because no other visual images existed? Do you think this approach devalues the truthfulness of the message?
3. How would you describe the events in Detroit? A riot? A rebellion? A revolution? How might your choice reflect the five theories of social justice reviewed in this chapter?
4. Are such films fair to police officers serving in cities nationwide today?

Macro Issues

1. Compare the approach of *12th and Clairmount* to that of the narrative fiction film *Detroit*. Which do you believe does the better job of informing audience members about the factual events of that summer?

2. Do films such as *Detroit* and *12th and Clairmount* contribute
   to racial tension in the United States? Compare the portraits of
   the 1967 unrest with contemporary news coverage of protests in
   Ferguson, Missouri; Baltimore, etc.

CASE 9-C

CINCINNATI ENQUIRER'S HEROIN BEAT

CHAD PAINTER
University of Dayton

Heroin-related overdose deaths have more than quadrupled since 2010,
with nearly 13,000 people dying nationwide in 2015 alone. Some of the
greatest increases have occurred in women, the privately insured, and
people with higher incomes—demographic groups with historically low
rates of heroin use (Centers for Disease Control and Prevention 2017).
In response, the CDC added overdose prevention to its list of top public
health challenges, and President Donald Trump created the Commission
on Combating Drug Addiction and the Opioid Crisis to study "ways to
combat and treat the scourge of drug abuse, addiction and the opioid
crisis" (The White House 2017). This designation focused on raising
national awareness about the severity of the problem but stopped short
of providing additional funding for treatment and research about the
opioid crisis.

News media also have responded with new initiatives. Specifically,
the *Cincinnati Enquirer*, a daily newspaper covering Cincinnati and its
Northern Kentucky suburbs, established the nation's first heroin beat in
January 2016. While the heroin and opioid epidemic is a national problem,
Ohio—and, more specifically, Southwestern Ohio—is considered its
epicenter. Heroin is thought to be the most accessible drug in Ohio (Ohio
State Bar Association 2017), which leads the nation in both opioid and
heroin overdose deaths (Kaiser Family Foundation 2014).

Terry DeMio, the *Enquirer* reporter who heads the heroin beat, said in
an interview with the author that the *Enquirer* really is just responding to
the community's need for information:

> There's a recognition that, not only is this a crisis, it's a crisis that, even
> now, is not well understood. I have easily more than 100 and probably
> well over 100 individuals talking to me, reading my work, people

who have families who are addicted or people who are in recovery. In Northern Kentucky, which is where I started, one in three people knows someone addicted to heroin. So, these are our neighbors, and we want to be responsive to our community's needs.

DeMio covers the heroin and opioid epidemic from a public health angle, not as a crime beat. She often discusses issues such as the need for first responders to carry naloxone, a drug that can block an opioid overdose; medication-assisted instead of abstinence-based treatment; and needle exchanges to help prevent HIV and Hepatitis C in both addicts and non-addicts who can accidentally step on improperly discarded needles. DeMio wants her reporting to help provide solutions to a community that is facing a public health crisis:

> I think the urgency is pretty obvious as far as the fact that this is a public health crisis. I mean, we want to stop the dying and then turn it around. That's my primary focus, which is a public health issue.

In DeMio's coverage, she routinely talks to a wide variety of sources, including addicts and their families, doctors and healthcare experts, police officers, and local and state government officials. She said the key to doing this kind of beat is credibility and trust:

> They have to trust you and understand that you care. I think through the work of doing this it shows that we as a newspaper care and that I personally care. I report objectively by, just like any reporter, introducing both sides, being fact based, telling a story which shows the compassion and hopefully gives people clarity about what this really is like for someone to go through. But I don't hesitate to provide resources to people.

The *Enquirer* coverage gained widespread national attention when it published "Seven days of heroin: This is what an epidemic looks like" on Sept. 10, 2017. The 20-page special section, which was supplemented with additional online content, included contributions from more than 60 reporters, photographers, and videographers from the *Enquirer* and colleagues from 10 other news sites affiliated with the Media Network of Central Ohio. (Versions of "Seven days of heroin" appeared in those newspapers as well.) The special section focused on one week in July, a week that included 18 deaths, at least 180 overdoses, more than 200 heroin users in jail, and 15 babies born with heroin-related medical problems. The full story can be found at https://www.cincinnati.com/pages/interactives/seven-days-of-heroin-epidemic-cincinnati/.

Micro Issues

1. Evaluate the *Cincinnati Enquirer*'s decision to cover the heroin and opioid epidemic as a public health instead of a criminal issue.
2. How might the *Enquirer*'s reporting influence how the community understands and addresses the heroin and opioid epidemic?
3. How can a newspaper cover the heroin and opioid epidemic consistently without sensationalizing coverage or publishing "addiction porn"?

Midrange Issues

1. The *Enquirer*, like many medium-market newspapers, has made tough budget decisions, including newsroom layoffs and shuttering beats. How should a newspaper balance necessary beats (crime and courts, education, etc.) with important community issues in a time of shrinking newsroom budgets?
2. How should a reporter balance objective reporting with showing compassion and sharing treatment and other resources with sources and their families?
3. This ambitious series was labeled as being financially sponsored by a local hospital. Could this funding in any way have affected the coverage?

Macro Issues

1. In Cincinnati and Northern Kentucky, the majority of heroin and opioid users and overdose victims are middle-class, suburban whites. How would you respond to criticism that news organizations and other institutions began treating heroin and opioid as a disease instead of a crime once the racial and class demographics changed?
2. Projects such as these often win prizes and even sabbaticals for their authors. Prizes help quality storytelling get recognized, but they have also been the occasion for scandal. On balance, are awards good for the profession?
3. How might the *Enquirer*'s coverage serve as a template for other news organizations that want to start doing the same type of beat coverage in their communities?

CASE 9-D

FEMINIST FAULT LINES: POLITICAL MEMOIRS AND HILLARY CLINTON

MIRANDA ATKINSON
University of Oregon

On Sept. 12, 2017, Hillary Clinton released her memoir and eighth book, *What Happened*, detailing her account of the 2016 presidential campaign. The book was promoted as Clinton's attempt to "let her guard down" and to be candid about her life as a high-profile female political figure. The book offered a first-hand evaluation of the historic 2016 election. In it, Clinton assigns and accepts blame for the missteps and ultimate election outcome without partiality. But she also takes aim at Vermont senator Bernie Sanders, Russia, President Donald J. Trump, and former FBI director James Comey.

Media coverage of Clinton's book, and more specifically the fact that she chose to write it, was divided. Responses from news outlets that traditionally cover politics were overwhelmingly critical. Women's magazines, and other typically non-political outlets, published content supporting Clinton's choice to write her account of the 2016 election and lambasted the criticism she and the book received as a reflection and further confirmation of the inherent sexism she faced as the first female candidate to win a major party nomination.

Much like an episode of "Who Wore It Best," these opposing perspectives are illustrated by two articles, one written by Ruth Marcus, deputy editorial page editor for the *Washington Post*, and a second one by Michelle Ruiz, a *Vogue* contributing editor. Marcus' article, published on June 2, 2017, was one of the first to cover Clinton's memoir and offered harsh criticism of Clinton's book and her overall decision to share her experience.

Marcus argues that Clinton's book harms the Democratic Party and women in general. She writes: "Well, Hillary Clinton isn't going gently. That may be understandable, but it's not smart—not for Clinton, not for her party and not for other female candidates" (Marcus 2017). Marcus compares Clinton's response with those of former vice president Al Gore and former senator John Kerry, who "demonstrated little appetite for rehashing their loss in public." Clinton's concession, handled with "grace and optimism" the day after the election, was a much better response, according to Marcus.

While Marcus concedes that it's important to understand what happened in the election, she calls Clinton the "wrong messenger." She also writes that Clinton's book "doesn't help would-be glass ceiling-crackers. Publicly calling out misogyny is probably not the best strategy for combating it, or for encouraging other women to run for office."

Ruiz's article, published Sept. 11, 2017, responded to Marcus' assessment and other similar pieces by highlighting arguments that reinforce the sexism Clinton encountered when running.

"Hillary Clinton doesn't have to go out 'gently'—or be otherwise schooled on how she should or should not handle her particular, unprecedented situation," Ruiz wrote. "She's the first woman to win a major party's presidential nomination in American history; she definitely doesn't have to shut up about it, not now, not ever" (Ruiz 2017).

Arguments such as those from Marcus, Ruiz argues, normalize the election outcome and omit its historic nature—this was the first time a woman secured the nomination for president from a major party and then went on to win the popular vote. Ruiz wrote, "The attempts to silence Clinton are in fact just more proof that the misogyny she writes about in *What Happened* was not imagined, and is still working against her."

Ruiz also marvels at the argument Marcus and other critics present about Clinton's qualifications to provide an assessment of the events of the 2016 presidential election. Ruiz writes that it is ridiculous to label Clinton's first-person perspective "extraneous." Ruiz concludes, "There's something about a powerful woman using her voice—and in a way that is not gentle or measured but bold and pointed—that still doesn't sit well with the general public."

Micro Issues

1. Both the *Washington Post* and *Vogue* articles include the journalist's perspective. Evaluate this approach. Does this context make the articles more or less informative—or truthful—than they otherwise might have been?

2. In the *Post,* Marcus wrote, "Speaking out against the actions of the Trump administration is warranted, even imperative. . . . But enough already, with the seemingly never-ending, ever expanding postmortem. Sure Clinton was responding to questions, but if anyone knows how to duck a line of inquiry, it's her." Given that Clinton was consistently critiqued for "ducking" questions on the campaign trail, evaluate Marcus' critique of the book?

Midrange Issues

1. How does social justice reporting in women's magazines illustrate the fault lines between the second and the third wave of feminism? What influence does the age of the reporters—Ruiz is about 10 years younger than Marcus—have on your answer?
2. Because activism sells, magazines and other publications that rely on ad sales are now able to publish content focused on social justice issues. Should media outlets "sell" social justice? Justify your answer using the five theories of justice outlined in the text.

Macro Issues

1. Julie Wittes Schlack in *Not Your Mother's Feminism: Teen Vogue And The Next Wave of Activism* explains that "we as women have more important matters to discuss than whether we're selling out or preserving the patriarchy every time we apply mascara." In other words, the women's movement has moved past the oversimplification that fashion is bad for feminism. From the role as magazine editor, evaluate this statement.
2. Which is more important: unbiased reporting or using journalism as a social justice tool? Does this question set up a false dichotomy for news organizations?

CASE 9-E

GOLDIEBLOX: BUILDING A FUTURE ON THEFT

SCOTT BURGESS
Wayne State University

For more than 100 years, boys' toys have included Legos, erector sets, and Lincoln Logs—toys that help them build math and engineering skills. Girls, on the other hand, play with tiaras, Barbies, and ballet shoes. Debbie Sterling, the founder of the Oakland-based toy company GoldieBlox, sought to change this dichotomy. Sterling started GoldieBlox in 2012, the first girls-only toy company that also develops computer apps and publishes books that focus on keeping girls interested in science (GoldieBlox 2017).

GoldieBlox wants to "disrupt the pink aisle in toy stores globally" and challenge gender stereotypes "with the world's first girl engineering character," according to the company's website. The company began with $280,000 raised in a Kickstarter campaign after many people were inspired by the company's mission (Sterling 2013). For the next year, GoldieBlox received a small amount of favorable press as a fun, feminist-oriented business with strong ideals.

That changed in November 2013, when the company released the YouTube video "Girls." In the video, three girls get bored watching a television show where girls in pink taffeta dresses dance on a sofa. So, with a revised version of the Beastie Boys 1987 song "Girls" playing in the background, they grab work belts, safety goggles, and tools, and build an elaborate contraption using many of the pink toys in their house.

The video received more than 8 million views on YouTube and 100,000 shares on Facebook in a few days. The company and its founder were featured on news programs, magazines, and newspapers around the world. While the privately held company does not release sales reports, some estimates suggest that sales tripled immediately following the video. Sterling claimed the company sold every toy it made during the 2013 Christmas season (Li 2014).

One group, however, remained disappointed in the video: the Beastie Boys. GoldieBlox had not sought permission to use its song, and the band previously had never allowed its music to be used in commercials. Further, when Beastie Boy Adam Yauch died in 2012, he specified in his will that "in no event may my image or name or any artistic property created by me be used for advertising purposes" (Cubarrubia 2012).

The two remaining band members, Michael Diamond and Adam Horovitz, approached GoldieBlox about the use of their music in the advertisement and the toymaker responded with a lawsuit claiming fair use.

"As creative as it is," Diamond and Horovitz said in a statement, "make no mistake, your video is an advertisement that is designed to sell a product, and long ago, we made a conscious decision not to permit our music and/or name to be used in product ads. When we tried to simply ask how and why our song Girls had been used in your ad without our permission, YOU sued US" (New York Times 2013).

GoldieBlox, now facing a legal and public relations backlash to a dying man's wishes, took down the video and issued the following statement:

Although we believe our parody video falls under fair use, we would like to respect his wishes and yours. Since actions speak louder than words, we have already removed the song from our video. In addition, we are ready to stop the lawsuit as long as this means we will no longer be under threat from your legal team (Michaels 2013).

The Beastie Boys filed suit against GoldieBlox claiming copyright infringement (Michaels 2013). In March 2014, GoldieBlox settled with the Beastie Boys. The company issued an apology and agreed to pay a portion of its proceeds to the Beastie Boys, which in turn would donate that money to charities that furthered development of girls learning science and math (Itzkoff 2014). (The original video is still available via YouTube.)

Furthermore, the negative publicity from the legal battle with the Beastie Boys also may have put a brighter light on GoldieBlox, which was accused of "pink washing" its toys. Critics accused GoldieBlox of claiming to provide toys for girls that would inspire them to pursue careers in engineering while still perpetuating the very stereotypes the company says it wants to tear down. Pink is used as a primary color in GoldieBlox toys, and among their collection is a kit to build a parade float for princesses. Sterling has fought this criticism, saying in interviews that "girls should be able to design their own princess castles" (Miller 2013).

Micro Issues

1. Both versions of the GoldieBlox "Girls" video are widely available on the internet. How does the message in the advertisement change without the inclusion of the Beastie Boys song?
2. Compare and contrast the "Girls" advertisement with more traditional "girls' toys" advertising such as commercials for Barbie dolls.

Midrange Issues

1. Do companies claiming to take on social issues have more responsibility for transparency to their customers than companies that do not make such claims?
2. What are the ethical responsibilities of media outlets reporting this case? Should they show the original commercial that includes the Beastie Boys song?

3. Critique the final statement of Sterling above. Does the fact that girls are invited to design mitigate the fact that the project being designed deals in stereotypes?
4. GoldieBlox is a privately held company. Would any of your answers change if this company had stockholders? If so, in what way?

Macro Issues

1. Can a company such as GoldieBlox "disrupt the pink aisle in toy stores" and still use pink as a primary color in its toys?
2. Where should companies draw the line between advertising and activism?
3. Do the creators of the GoldieBlox ads have an obligation to follow the wishes of the Beastie Boys on the use of their music? What about filmmakers?
4. What are the responsibilities of consumers when they make decisions to purchase such products? Is it reasonable to expect the average consumer to be aware of the desires of the Beastie Boys with regard to how their music would be used?

10

The Ethical Dimensions of Art and Entertainment

By the end of this chapter you should be able to

- understand the link between aesthetics and excellent professional performance
- explain Tolstoy's rationale for art and apply it to issues such as stereotyping
- understand the debate over the role of truth in popular art

In the last century, the primary use of media shifted from distributing information to providing entertainment and popularizing culture. In this chapter, we examine the ethical issues from the field of aesthetics. We will apply these principles, plus some findings from social science, to the art and entertainment industries, focusing on the responsibilities of both creators and consumers of entertainment.

AN ANCIENT MISUNDERSTANDING

Plato didn't like poets. His reasoning was straightforward: poets, the people who dream, were the potential undoing of the philosopher king. They were rebels of the first order, insurrectionists on the hoof, and he banned them from the Republic.

Plato's skepticism is alive today. Few weeks elapse without a news story about an artist or entertainment program that has offended. You are probably familiar with at least some of the following:

- Late-night comedian Jimmy Kimmel made headlines with monologues about healthcare and gun control. In April and September, an exasperated and impassioned Kimmel discussed his infant son, who had open-heart surgery in April and whose medical coverage could be severely limited if the Affordable Care Act is repealed. During his Oct. 2 opener, a clearly emotional Kimmel focused on the mass shooting in his Las Vegas hometown, calling on politicians to pass "common sense" measures to limit similar catastrophes. Proponents applauded Kimmel for using his platform to discuss important national topics. Opponents said that he is an entertainer who should stick to making people laugh.

- The successful demand by British censors that the film *The Hunger Games* be shortened by seven seconds due to violent content. The deletion meant that children 12 and over could see the film in the United Kingdom.
- Producers on *The Ed Sullivan Show* asking the Rolling Stones to change the lyrics of "Let's Spend the Night Together" to "let's spend some time together" (which they did) and the Doors to change the "Light My Fire" lyric from "Girl, we couldn't get much higher" to "Girl, we couldn't get much better" (which they did not).
- Attempts to ban books, even classics such as *Catcher in the Rye* or *Lady Chatterley's Lover*, from public or school libraries for being too sexually explicit. Recently, Harry Potter books were the focus of the most successful and the most unsuccessful attempts to ban a book, a move led largely by conservative Christians.
- The controversy over government funding of art that some claim is obscene.
- Calls by conservatives and liberals to boycott television networks and their advertisers over allegedly objectionable content.
- The furor over rappers, television producers, and filmmakers whose homophobic, misogynistic, and sometimes clever content offend many while earning nominations for the industry's top awards.
- While these examples come from the West, other cultures and political systems show the same tendencies. In 2012, the Russian punk band Pussy Riot received a two-year jail term for its criticism of Russian President Vladimir Putin's policies.
- In China, architect and sculptor Ai Weiwei, a member of the team that designed the 2008 Olympic stadium nicknamed The Bird's Nest, was arrested and held without charge for more than 2 months in 2011 in response to his protests about the Chinese government's lack of action after devastating earthquakes and his allegations of government corruption.

Like Plato long ago, those who would restrict the arts do so because they mistrust the power of the artist or even the audience to link emotion and logic in a way that stimulates a new vision of society, culture or individuals.

OF TOLSTOY AND TELEVISION

Tolstoy was the sort of artist Plato would have feared. In his famous essay "What Is Art?" Tolstoy (1960) argued that good art had one dominant characteristic: it communicated the feelings of the artist to the masses in the way that the artist intended.

> To evoke in oneself a feeling one has once experienced and having evoked it in oneself then by means of movements, lines, colors, sounds or forms expressed in words, so to transmit that feeling that others experience the same feeling— that is the activity of art. . . . Art is a human activity consisting in this, that one may consciously by means of certain external signs, hand on to others feelings he has lived through, and that others are infected by these feelings and also experience them.

Tolstoy's standard was so demanding that he rejected the works of both Shakespeare and Beethoven as being incapable of being understood by the masses. Tolstoy's rationale is particularly pertinent to photographers and videographers who, through their visual images, seek to arouse emotion as well as inform. Haunting pictures of starvation from the Third World have launched international relief efforts. Televised images of Katrina's victims spurred the resignation of some of FEMA's top officials—and affected the 2006 election. Award-winning dramas such as the play *Angels in America*, the AIDS quilt, movies such as *Philadelphia* (in which Tom Hanks won an Academy Award for his portrayal of an AIDS victim), and obituaries of famous artists who have succumbed to AIDS have all aroused both our intellects and our emotions about the disease. Similarly, the opioid overdose deaths of Prince and Philip Seymour Hoffman, as well as great journalistic and fictional work about the spread of heroin and opioids across the United States, has both brought the epidemic to the public consciousness and helped frame it as a public health crisis instead of a law enforcement issue. They invite action. Television and film documentaries have made viewers more aware of the plight of the mentally ill and homeless, raised important public policy questions, and occasionally made us laugh, through a unity of purpose and craft.

Such work reminds readers and viewers of the moral power of art by putting us in touch with characters and situations sometimes more complex than our own lives. By thinking about these fictional characters, we enlarge our moral imaginations.

Unfortunately, Tolstoy's assertion that great art is defined by how it is understood by an audience also includes a genuine dilemma. Even if given Tolstoy's life experiences, many readers could not articulate the deep truths about human nature Tolstoy wrote about in *War and Peace*. Worse yet, it is

Figure 10.1. *Calvin and Hobbes* © 1990 Watterson. Reprinted with permission of Andrews McMeel Syndication. All rights reserved.

nearly impossible to sell those insights to a sometimes lukewarm public, or to produce them on demand for an hour a week, 36 weeks a year. The result is popular art that loses its critical edge and takes shortcuts to commonplace insight. In fact, some mass-communication scholars have argued that the unstated goal of popular art is to reinforce the status quo; popular culture, they say, blunts our critical-thinking abilities.

What Is Art?

Philosophers, sociologists, and artists have debated the meaning of art for hundreds of years. Prior to the Industrial Revolution, art was something only the well-educated paid for, produced, and understood. Mozart had to capture the ear of the Emperor to get a subsidy to write opera. Such "high" or "elite art" provided society with a new way to look at itself. Picasso's drawings of people with three eyes or rearranged body parts literally provided Western culture with a new way of seeing. Michelangelo's paintings and sculpture did the same thing in the Renaissance. But patronage had disadvantages. The patron could restrict both subject matter and form, a reality depicted in the film *Amadeus* where the Emperor informed Mozart that his work, *The Marriage of Figaro*, had "too many notes." Gradually, artists discovered that if they could find a way to get more than one person to "pay" for the creation of art, artistic control returned to the artist. The concept of "popular art" was born. Scholars disagree about many of the qualities of elite and popular art; some even assert that popular art cannot truly be considered art. While both kinds of art are difficult to define, the following list outlines the major differences between popular and elite art and culture:

1. Popular art is consciously adjusted to the median taste by the artist; elite art reflects the individual artist's vision.
2. Popular art is neither abstruse, complicated, nor profound; elite art has these characteristics.

3. Popular art conforms to majority experience; elite art explores the new.
4. Popular art conforms to less clearly defined standards of excellence, most often linked to commercial success; elite art is much less commercially oriented, and its standards of excellence are consistent and integrated.
5. Popular artists know that the audience expects entertainment and instruction; elite artists seek an aesthetic experience.
6. The popular artist cannot afford to offend its target audience; the elite artist functions as a critic of society, and his or her work challenges and sometimes offends the status quo.
7. Popular art often arises from folk art; elite art more often emerges from a culture's dominant intellectual tradition.

Today, mass media have become the primary cultural storytellers of the era. Nearly half a century ago, Jacques Ellul (1965) argued that, in a modern society, storytelling is an inevitable and desirable tool to stabilize the culture. This "propaganda of integration" is not the deliberate lie commonly associated with propaganda but the dissemination of widely held beliefs to the culture at large. Aesop's fables and the early *McGuffey Readers* influenced generations of Americans with subtle (or not) messages that reinforced the social structure. This is precisely where the entertainment media get their power—not in the overt messages but in the underlying assumptions that (if unchallenged) will become widely held societal values. For instance, entertainment content can reinforce the status quo by constantly depicting certain social groups in an unflattering and unrepresentative way, presenting a distorted picture of reality. Groups as disparate as Muslims and evangelicals have chafed under depictions (or omissions) that reinforce cultural stereotypes despite evidence to the contrary.

At least some such distortion is the natural outcome of compression. Just as substances such as rubber change form when compressed, so do media messages. Given only 15 seconds to register a message in a commercial, an advertising copywriter will resort to showing us the presumed stereotype of a librarian, a mechanic, or a pharmacist. Using stereotypes as a form of mental shorthand is a natural way media work and was noted as early as 1922 by Walter Lippmann in *Public Opinion*. Lippmann said that we are all guilty of "defining first and seeing second."

Soon, we expect reality to imitate art. Mass communicators know the power of stereotypes and deeply held notions and use them. According to Tony Schwartz (1973), advertising messages are often constructed backward. The communicator actually starts with what the receiver knows—or believes he knows—and then constructs a message that fits within that reality. Schwartz calls it hitting a "responsive chord." Time is saved in plucking the chords already deeply held by the public rather than challenging stereotypes. So pimps are African-American, terrorists are Middle Eastern, and no one challenges the unstated assumptions. The audience gets the idea of a pimp or a terrorist, but notions of racism and worse have been planted as well. While these images suit the artist's purposes, they are problematic.

TRUTH IN ART AND ENTERTAINMENT

No question in the field of aesthetics is more thoroughly debated with less resolution than the role of truth in art. Most philosophers seem to agree that artists are not restricted to telling the literal truth. Often artists can reveal a previously hidden or veiled truth, providing a new way of looking at the world or understanding human nature that rings deeply true.

But just how much truth should the audience expect from entertainment? And how entertaining should the audience expect truth to be? There are several opinions. At one point on the continuum is the argument that there is no truth requirement at all in art. At another point on the continuum is the belief that there must be one accepted truth for all. Compounding the problem is that often the audience doesn't care when the lines of truth and entertainment are blurred.

The Daily Show and Modern "Mock" News

We live in a society saturated with mock news programming. While a tradition of satirical news stretches at least as far back as the Greeks, the most famous example of modern satire is *The Daily Show*. Created as a spoof on local news with host Craig Kilborn in 1996, the show reached national prominence when Jon Stewart took over the anchor seat in 1998 and refocused content to concentrate on national affairs. Stewart's mock news footprint continues today with his hand-picked successor, Trevor Noah, at *The Daily Show*, as well as former correspondents Samantha Bee and John Oliver hosting similar shows on different networks.

The brilliance of *The Daily Show* and its ilk is that these programs so closely mimic the structure and substance of "real" news. *The Daily Show* features the same structure of headlines, special reports, breaking news, and correspondents "on location" as network and cable broadcast news (Barbur and Goodnow 2011; Hess 2011; McGeough 2011). "Mock" news programs also cover the same types of stories—politics and elections, foreign affairs, news media, and policy issues—as traditional news broadcasts while skewering political actors such as politicians, journalists, economists, consultants, and corporatists (Barbur and Goodnow 2011; Compton 2011; Spicer 2011). By playing the role of real reporters, and by playing that role so well to often be indistinguishable from their traditional counterparts, mock journalists suggest that "real" journalists also simply are playing a role (Baym 2005).

The overarching social critique of mock news programs is that the modern news industry, driven by commercial pressures, the quest for ratings, and the near impossibility of filling a 24-hour news hole with substantive programming, often eschews substance for style (Hess 2011). News networks, according to this critique, forgo hard news for the "infotainment" of popular culture and moralistic fights on highly contrived events (Hess 2011; McBeth and Clemons 2011).

Satirical programs, however, do more than critique. They also educate otherwise tuned-out citizens who come for the humor but stay for policy information and discussions of media and the electoral process (Caufield 2008). These mock television programs can influence viewers' evaluations of political candidates, perceptions of certain institutions, interest in campaigns, and support for specific policies (Compton 2011). That sort of civic engagement and media literacy is no laughing matter.

Should there be a truth standard in art? The tendency of the status quo to impose a specific moral "truth" on the masses has been common to many cultures and political systems across the ages. In *Republic*, Plato had Socrates argue against allowing children to hear "casual tales . . . devised by casual persons." The Third Reich burned books deemed unsuitable for reading. In the United States, the battle historically has raged over library books. Classics such as *Huckleberry Finn*, *Of Mice and Men*, *The Grapes of Wrath*, and *The Merchant of Venice* are but some of the long-revered and award-winning works that now face censorship by various school systems. The American Library Association reports that incidents of book banning now reach more than 1,000 instances annually, with little legal intervention. The US Supreme Court has not heard a book-banning case since allowing a lower court ruling to stand in 1982.

Protests began early in the history of television. The 1951 show *Amos n' Andy* was condemned by the National Association for the Advancement of Colored People for depicting "Negroes in a stereotyped and derogatory manner." In the 1960s, the United Church of Christ successfully challenged the license renewal of WLBT in Jackson, Mississippi, on the grounds that the owners had blatantly discriminated against African-Americans.

In the latter half of the 20th century, a variety of special-interest groups used subtler methods to influence entertainment programming. Some, such as the Hispanic advocacy group Nosotros, worked closely with network bureaucracies, previewing potentially problematic episodes of entertainment programs, often altering program content before it reached the airwaves. Not all protests involve censoring a program. Some want to make sure that programming airs, such as advocacy groups who lobby advertisers and affiliates to ensure the airing of certain shows or inclusion of certain controversial characters in prime time.

New York Times television critic Jack Gould framed the problem of artistic accountability in the early days of these advocacy groups arguing that such agreements held

> latent dangers for the well-being of television as a whole. An outside group not professionally engaged in theatre production has succeeded in imposing its will with respect to naming of fictional characters, altering the importance of a leading characterization and in other particulars changing the story line (Montgomery 1989, 21).

And for the artist trying to create in the medium, network attempts to "balance" competing advocacy-group interests had come close to recreating the patronage system, albeit a far more sophisticated one with government as the patron.

The struggle over content becomes even more acute when governmental sponsorship is at stake. Some argue that because tax dollars are extracted from all, the programs they fund should be acceptable to all. Federal support for programs such as the National Endowment for the Arts (NEA) has been repeatedly questioned in Congress. Conservatives objected to funding artists such as photographer Robert Mapplethorpe, whose blend of homoerotic photos and traditional Judeo-Christian symbols offended many. Eventually, the criticism was a factor in the resignation of one of the NEA's directors, John E. Frohnmayer.

The government also censors directly. On multiple occasions, Infinity Broadcasting was fined several hundred thousand dollars for disc jockey Howard Stern's on-air profanity and offensive racial slurs. Stern protested that the FCC's action amounted to an enforcement of political correctness. But others noted that Stern most often castigated disadvantaged people and groups. By 2006, Stern had left terrestrial radio and its rules for satellite radio, where he found a fat payday, artistic freedom, and a much smaller audience.

In 2006, with the Broadcast Decency Enforcement Act, Congress raised the fine for a single count of indecency from $27,500 to $325,000. Because of the potential liability for crippling fines, producers of live programming such as the Grammy awards and the Oscars were forced to put a delay on the broadcast to bleep out what the courts called "fleeting expletives" or nudity.

COP TV: ENTERTAINMENT, INFOTAINMENT, OR NEWS?

In his ingenious Academy Award-winning script, *Network*, the late writer-director Paddy Chayefsky envisioned a time when the lines would be blurred between entertainment and news, rendering them indistinguishable. However,

Chayefsky was wrong in one detail. News did begin to take on the look of entertainment (as he predicted it would, to great satirical effect) but he did not predict that entertainment would also begin to look like news with the two meeting somewhere in the middle.

Consider these current and former shows: *America's Most Wanted*, which ran for 25 seasons, in which audience members were encouraged to help police by calling in tips; *Unsolved Mysteries*, with its focus on the criminal and the paranormal; *TMZ on TV*, a celebrity gossip show heavy on mug shots, police reports, and drunken rants by the rich and famous; *Inside Edition*, a voyeuristic look at stories dubbed "too hot to handle" for traditional network news and which featured a pre-Fox News Bill O'Reilly and NBC and CBS reporter and anchor Deborah Norville as hosts; and others of the same breed, including *COPS*, *The First 48*, *Bait Car*, *America's Dumbest Criminals* and any number of other spin-offs. Or consider *Dateline*, which blurred the lines of entertainment programming and the apprehension of would-be child molesters duped on to the show's set.

And then came YouTube, where virtually no event was outside the range of cameras and videos shot by amateurs. These videos then often found their way into the mainstream media.

In what genre do these shows belong? Is it news or entertainment when Hawaiian police arrest the co-stars of *Dog the Bounty Hunter* for illegal detention and conspiracy? Which set of standards of truth should the producer of that show (and others like it) operate under—the artistic license of entertainment or the more rigorous truth standard of news? When *Dateline* sets up one of its "stings" with the internet promise of sex to would-be predators, have they crossed the line from entertainment to entrapment? Is it the truth that the television show prevented a crime or is it the truth that the show caused someone to act in a criminal fashion?

Currently, dozens of such pseudo-news, pseudo-cop, pseudo-court shows are in production simultaneously. Very little escapes our fascination. Dubbed "infotainment" by critics, these shows are hot with television programming executives and audiences alike. Producers love it because such shows are quite cheap to produce and deliver better ratings than reruns, news, or other syndicated programming. Audiences love it because such programming provides relief from reruns of situation comedies and the sameness of game shows. When produced by syndicators, the shows are prepackaged with ads embedded in them, making them attractive to station owners. In fact, local station owners who have found their station consistently at the bottom of the local news ratings can turn to a game show such as *Wheel of Fortune* and reclaim ratings that their news side never could.

The blending of facts and entertainment is not restricted to the small screen. Films such as *Ray*, *Walk the Line*, *The Alamo*, *The Social Network*,

Lincoln, and *American Sniper* reflect a particular artistic vision based on fact. That blending of fact and fiction becomes more pronounced in films such as *Moneyball* that includes characters such as Billy Beane and Art Howe, based on real people, and other characters, such as Jonah Hill's Peter Brand, that are composites of several real-life baseball executives. Such depictions simplify and overly dramatize historical facts, foregoing context and complexity in favor of a sharp focus on a few select individuals.

Based-on-reality films and reality-based television shows differ in format and content but they are alike in invoking the license allowed entertainment programming while retaining the authority of fact—a risky combination. By blending information and entertainment, the possibility for abuse of an unsuspecting audience exists. To understand how this happens, we look to the theory of "uses and gratifications." Phrased simply, the theory says audience members will use the media to gratify certain wants and needs. People bring something to the message, and what they bring affects what they take away.

For example, seeking news and information is a common use of the media, with an expected gratification of getting information necessary for living one's life from traffic to weather to news about government. Entertainment is another common media use, with its own gratification of laughter, crying, or any other emotion evoked by entertainment media—something Tolstoy said was the basic aim of the audience.

Infotainment keeps the look of news yet airs the content of lowbrow entertainment juxtaposing traditional uses and gratifications. With a look of authority (an anchor's desk, a courtroom, a police precinct) and the hype of their importance (e.g., "200 lives saved so far!"), these shows appear to be useful for acquiring information. However, by invoking their license as entertainment, such shows are free to bypass accuracy, fairness, balance, and other standards normally associated with news and to focus on more sensational elements to gather larger ratings.

Consequently, infotainment, while fundamentally flawed, gets widely accepted as fact. *New York Times* columnist A. M. Rosenthal (1989) compared airing these tabloid television shows to buying news programming "off the shelf." Stations should add the disclaimer, "We did not put this stuff in the bottle, whatever it is," Rosenthal added.

REALITY TELEVISION: OXYMORON, PROFIT CENTER, AND USING THE AUDIENCE

They eat cow's lips, let their families pick their mates, and routinely lie about their financial and physical assets. They are Americans with talent. They are seven strangers who stop being polite and start getting real. They race, they sing, and they dance. It's all part of the reality television craze that has made strong inroads into prime-time entertainment programming. The craze began with the wildly successful *Survivor* series, which ran first as a summer replacement show and garnered ratings that impressed network executives. *Survivor* quickly spawned other reality shows, among them *Amazing Race*, *American Idol*, *Big Brother*, *Dancing with the Stars*, and *Keeping Up with the Kardashians*.

Why the rush to reality programming? Ratings and money. For three decades, traditional network television programming lost audience share to cable television, TiVo, and the internet. At their height, the original three American networks, ABC, CBS and NBC, could count on attracting approximately 90 percent of American homes with televisions on any given evening; the rest tuned in a few fledgling independents playing reruns. Today, the audience for five broadcast networks (including Fox and CW) has plunged to less than half of all households, with the number slipping every season.

Then traditional cable outlets such as HBO, TNT, and USA—and later online streaming websites such as Netflix, Amazon Prime, and Hulu—got into original scripted programming, cutting further into the audience for scripted entertainment, often sweeping the industry's awards along the way. The reason for the immediate artistic success was a matter of sheer economics: it was easier to program a few hours of quality television a week than to try to program three hours every night as the traditional networks have done for years.

Compounding the problem, those who continued to watch the traditional networks were an older demographic not popular with advertisers. For the networks, reality television was a chance to pull viewers away from cable and computers and back to their programming at a cost lower than scripted television series. Not only did reality shows draw viewers, but the audience they drew centered on 18–49-year-olds, a ratings bonanza in the preferred demographic and a potent inducement to produce more reality programming.

Reality programming was not only popular but also cheap to produce. There was little need to pay writers, and the actors who populated them worked for scale or prizes. Unlike the *CSI* and *Law and Order* franchises where the popularity of the show caused cast salaries to skyrocket, programs such as *Pawn Stars*, *Ice Road Truckers*, and *The Deadliest Catch* got great ratings for minor networks with few of the traditional costs of scripted programming with sets to be built, outdoor permissions to be sought, etc.

However, using cheaply produced reality programming to garner ratings has had consequences. Quality shows such as *Modern Family* and *Breaking Bad* were expensive to produce, and it often took time to find an audience sufficient to sustain these shows. What the producers hoped for was a chance to air enough episodes—typically 60 or more—to make it to the lucrative syndication market and DVD, where they live on for years and produce a sizable return on the initial investment. What networks ordered were 12 episodes with options for more at a later date—a clause that kept writers, etc.

tied to the show and kept lives in limbo until the network exercised or failed to exercise the option.

By eating up entire chunks of the network schedule, reality television pushed many quality shows into an early retirement and kept many more out of production. The result now is fewer quality programs in syndication and fewer producers of quality shows able to get their product into the schedules of the major networks now infatuated with reality. Quality writers fled to the movies or the cable channels willing to try scripted television. For example, Netflix outbid HBO and AMC for David Fincher's *House of Cards* by guaranteeing to air two seasons and 26 episodes before a single episode was produced. The light-viewing months of the summer were once a time when networks took some chances on genre-defining shows to see if they could find an audience. Now that season is given over to "star-making" shows that turn immediate profits with no regard for the future.

If they didn't add to the nation's intellect, reality shows have added to American slang. Getting "voted off the island" became a catch phrase for everyone from politicians to news journalists. "You're fired" entered the American vernacular from *The Apprentice*, starring future president Donald Trump, who continued to use the line while commander in chief.

The "new" reality television was really a second pass at the genre. The first attempt took place in the 1950s with quiz shows such as *21* and *The $64,000 Question*. These shows were enormously popular and, as it turned out, could be rigged. Popular contestants were given the answers to general-knowledge questions beforehand. What the audience saw was a scripted contest with the winner predetermined. Winners came back from week to week and some gained a national following. Not surprisingly, the predetermined winner was the one the producers believed would sustain the ratings or increase them. The quiz show scandals, as they are referred to in media history, were followed by congressional hearings, ruined careers, and even legislation.

The new reality shows suffered from some of the same problems. When it was discovered that those who advanced on one or more popular reality shows had actually been determined in advance, it became national news. Soon after, audiences learned that participants in the various reality shows were not always novices to the medium but were often recruited from ranks of fledgling actors. Furthermore, the notion of spontaneity, crucial to getting the audience to believe the premise of the reality show, was false. The producers of shows such as *Survivor*, *The Real World* and the like most often shot hundreds of hours of video with a predetermined "story line" to edit into an allegedly spontaneous program.

Some reality shows were based on legally questionable premises, such as the series that proposed to capture men hiring prostitutes—the reality of "johns"—or cop shows that allowed media to capture arrests inside homes only to be successfully sued for invasion of privacy later. Some shows seemed notable for their complete lack of a moral compass or made us more like voyeurs than traditional viewers. There is little to nothing socially redeeming about TLC's freak show parade of *My Big Fat Fabulous Life*, *Sister Wives*, and many other similar series. *Temptation Island* put couples and relationships in physical and emotional jeopardy for the entertainment of the audience. ABC halted filming of *Bachelor in Paradise*, a spinoff of the popular dating game show, after allegations that the crew might have filmed one cast member sexually assaulting another. But, still, America watched even as lives were altered irreparably.

In June 2009, a record 10.6 million people tuned into the TLC show *Jon and Kate Plus 8* to learn that Jon and Kate Gosselin were calling it quits after 10 years of marriage, including several years that were documented on television. The concept was a reality series of two parents and their eight children on a $1.1 million Berks County, Pennsylvania, home built in part with television funds. At the time of their divorce, papers filed by the couple indicated that they had long lived separate lives, including the possibility that they had been misleading the public about their marriage for up to two years before the filing—a claim disputed by the lawyers as mere "legalese." In an interview with *People* magazine, Kate didn't blame the ubiquitous cameras for the failure of the marriage, saying that the divorce would have happened with or without the television show, which was consistently one of the top shows for the TLC network.

Reality television raises an important ethical question: What constitutes reality? Kris Bunton and Wendy Wyatt (2012) raise other important questions in their philosophical approach to the ethics of reality television. For example, do reality programs stereotype participants or activities? Even though participants sign legal waivers that are between 20 and 30 pages long, do reality programs invade privacy? Can contestants ethically give away the sort of access the shows require? Does reality television inspire us—particularly if we have talent or can create a team that functions well under original circumstances and stress? Suzanne Collins, whose successful book trilogy begins with *The Hunger Games*, takes on many of these same questions in fictional form, often with disturbing answers. Collins has said that she wrote the series, in part, as a response to reality television and that her early literary influences included George Orwell's *1984*.

The early part of this century has been a scary time, and watching bachelors and bachelorettes find "true love" is a lot easier than taking the chance of going out on a first date. However, that scary first date has the chance of turning into something wonderful or awful. Truth in relationships matters because it's how people form connections. Reality television was people, inside a box, having a planned and edited experience. That planning wasn't about truth. It wasn't even particularly personal.

THE DOCUMENTARIAN: ARTIST OR JOURNALIST?

"Perhaps no media genre blends art and journalism together as does documentary film. In fact, if you ask a documentarian—particularly a fledging one—to define a professional role, directors, producers, and editors are quite likely to say that they are producing art that sometimes looks like journalism. Yet, as recent scholarship and professional conferences suggest (Aufderheide 2005), documentarians share many of the same ethical questions as their journalistic first cousins. However, because many of them are either self-taught or the product of film programs, they stumble into the same ethical questions with relatively little guidance.

Documentarians generally agree that they are truth tellers, but that the truth they seek is not necessarily objective in the way that journalists traditionally have defined it. Rather, documentarians seek to tell truth from a point of view influenced by context. It is not unreasonable to suggest that multiple documentaries can be made about what is essentially the same subject—for example, Oregon's controversial assisted suicide law—each one taking a point of view. However, documentarians assert that the best documentary film is one that acknowledges, and sometimes deeply examines, views in opposition to the director's point of view. The *New York Times*, in 2011, began a new feature on its opinion pages: Op Docs, where citizens and professionals were invited to provide editorial commentary in the form of short documentaries on subjects of public importance.

Documentary links facts to beliefs and opinions in important ways. Documentarians also wrestle with how deeply involved they should become with the subjects of their films. For example, the director and producer of *Born into Brothels*, Zana Briski, as part of her film, recounts her personal efforts to get the children of Indian sex workers into school so they could escape the poverty and work choices the Calcutta slums seem to provide. Michael Moore does not hide his personal opinions in films such as *Roger and Me*, where his anger at General Motors CEO Roger Smith's decision to close a Flint, Michigan, factory is palpable throughout. Moore, a Flint resident, honed his reporting chops with the alternative newsweekly *The Flint Voice*, and his radical roots are forefront in his films. Documentarians often invest their own funds and months of their unpaid time to capture images, scenes, and dialogue that make a narrative work. This commitment to a single source and point of view is rare for journalists and can blur the line between essential source and friend. On the one hand, documentarians are concerned about exploiting those whom they become close to; on the other, they worry about becoming the prisoner of a single point of view or a source who likes to be on camera to the point where the director loses control over the content of the film itself.

Editing also raises a host of issues for documentarians, everything from the often in-your-face shots of people in joy or pain to the construction of a narrative that requires significant omissions and emphases for aesthetic purposes that edge the resulting film away from the initial truth, or just well-rounded examination, that both the filmmaker and the sources sought. Adding music, archival footage, and building a narrative structure all require hours in the editing room and, as documentaries have become more profitable, significant investment in production values and post-production efforts. Raising the money to make these sorts of films is not easy, and documentarians also worry about becoming the intellectual and artistic prisoners of those who fund their work. For example, documentarian Craig Atkinson accused Netflix of blacklisting his film *Do Not Resist*, about the militarization of police and the protests in Ferguson, Missouri, after he turned down their offer to buy his film and brand it as a Netflix Original because the streaming service required full creative control.

And, there is the role of emotion in documentary film. These are films that are designed to provoke audience response. Strategic communication professionals would recognize the call to action embedded in many documentaries. Documentarians seek to overtly link emotion, fact, logic, and action in a way that journalism, perhaps with the exception of investigative reporting, seldom does. Along the way, there are real ethical questions that are not readily answered by the too common response, "but, I am an artist." In the documentary *Inside Job*, which won an Academy Award in 2010, the filmmakers accepted the Oscar by noting that no one had yet been jailed in the financial scandal that precipitated the recession of 2008. The film was an artistic success; however, its political impact was less so. If Plato were alive today, there is little doubt that documentary film, through its artistry as well as investigations, would be on the list of highly suspect professions in the modern-day democratic republic.

AESTHETICS IS AN ATTITUDE

Artists see the world differently. While most people perceive only what is needful, the artist works with what some have called an "enriched perceptual experience." This aesthetic attitude is one that values close and complete concentration of all the senses. An aesthetic attitude is a frankly sensual one, and one that summons both emotion and logic to its particular ends.

For example, the theatre audience knows that Eugene O'Neill's plays are "merely" drama. But they also provide us with an intense examination of the role of family in human society—an experience that is both real and personal to every audience member. Such intense examination is what gives the plays their power to move.

The makers of mediated messages, whether they are the executive producers of a television sitcom or the designers of a newspaper page, share this aesthetic impetus. These mass communicators are much like architects. An architect can design a perfectly serviceable cube-like building, one that withstands the elements and may be used for good ends. But great buildings— St. Paul's Cathedral in London or Jefferson's home at Monticello—do more. They are tributes to the human intellect's capacity to harmoniously harness form and function.

In fact, philosophers have argued that what separates the commonplace from the excellent is the addition of an aesthetic quality to what would other- wise be a routine, serviceable work. These qualities of excellence have been described as:

- an appreciation of the function realized in the product;
- an appreciation of the resulting quality or form; and
- an appreciation of the technique or skill in the performance.

These three characteristics of aesthetic excellence characterize excellence in mass communication as well.

Take the newspaper weather page. *USA Today* literally recalibrated the standard from tiny black and white agate type to a colorful full page. They understood what the late political columnist Molly Ivins knew: when people aren't talking about football, they talk about the weather. They devoted more space to it and printed it in color. They added more information in a more legible style and form. In short, they gave newspaper weather information an aesthetic quality. While much about *USA Today* has been criticized, its excel- lent weather page has been copied.

Although mass-communication professionals are infrequently accused of being artists, we believe they intuitively accept an aesthetic standard as a component of professional excellence. As philosopher G. E. Moore (1903, 83) noted in *Principia Ethica*:

> Let us imagine one world exceedingly beautiful. Image it as beautiful as you can; put into it whatever on this earth you most admire: mountains, rivers, the sea, suns and sunsets, stars and moon. Imagine these all combined in the most exquisite proportion so that no one thing jars against another, but each contributes to increase the beauty of the whole. And then imagine the ugliest world you can possibly conceive. Imagine it just one heap of filth, containing everything that is most disgusting to you for whatever reason, and the whole, as far as may be, without one redeeming factor. . . . Supposing (all) that quite apart from the contemplation of human beings; still it is irrational to hold that it is better that the ugly world exists than the one which is beautiful.

Substitute film, record, poem, news story, photograph, or advertising copy for Moore's word "world" and we believe that you will continue to intuitively agree with the statement. While we may disagree on what specifically constitutes beauty in form and content, the aesthetic standard of excellence still applies.

Philosopher John Dewey (2005) noted, "Aesthetic experience is a manifestation, a record and celebration of the life of a civilization, a means of promoting its development, and is also the ultimate judgment upon the quality of a civilization." In an interview on the PBS series *The Promise of Television*, commentator Bill Moyers (1988) said,

> The root word of television is vision from afar, and that's its chief value. It has brought me in my stationary moments visions of ideas and dreams and imaginations and geography that I would never personally experience. So, it has put me in touch with the larger world. Television can be a force for dignifying life, not debasing it.

Though Moyers' comments were made specifically about television, the same argument can be made for a good book, a favorite magazine, music, or a film. And whether the media are a force for dignifying humanity or debasing it is largely in the hands of those who own and work in them.

SUGGESTED READINGS

Bunton, K., & Wendy, W. (2012). *Reality television: A philosophical examination.* New York: Continuum International.

Calvert, C. (2000). *Voyeur nation: Media, privacy and peering in modern culture.* Boulder, CO: Westview Press.

Jensen, J. (2002). *Is art good for us?* Lanham, MD: Rowman & Littlefield.

Medved, M. (1992). *Hollywood vs. America.* New York: HarperCollins.

Montgomery, K. C. (1989). *Target: Prime time. Advocacy groups and the struggle over entertainment television.* New York: Oxford University Press.

Postman, N. (1986). *Amusing ourselves to death: Public discourse in the age of television.* New York: Penguin Books.

CASES

CASE 10-A

GET OUT: WHEN THE HORROR IS RACE

MICHAEL FUHLHAGE
Wayne State University

LEE WILKINS
Wayne State University
University of Missouri

The 2017 horror film *Get Out*, made by first-time director/writer Jordan Peele for $4.5 million—a very modest budget by current standards—grossed more than $254 million worldwide. While profitability is one mark of success in Hollywood, the film also received critical acclaim. After its Sundance Film Festival preview in January 2017, it received the Oscar for Best Original Screenplay and three other Oscar nominations, two Golden Globe nominations, and more than 20 other nominations from a variety of groups for acting, directing, the music, and the screenwriting.

But, more than that, it was a film that made people think—an uncomfortable essay on the actual bodies of black people being colonized by white minds.

Most critics interpreted the film as a commentary on how Caucasian liberals can make life unintentionally difficult for African-Americans. A *Guardian* reviewer noted, "It exposes a liberal ignorance and hubris that has been allowed to fester. It's an attitude, an arrogance which in the film leads to a horrific final solution, but in reality, leads to a complacency that is just as dangerous." In an interview with CBS News, Peele explained that the film reflected "my truth as a black man. My perspective that I haven't seen in film before."

The film plays on references to other films that make political and or social points, among them the original *Invasion of the Body Snatchers*, *The Stepford Wives*, and *Guess Who's Coming to Dinner*.

Much of the film's commentary about race is tucked into the film's visuals. The movie opens with a young, African-American man walking down a street in a tidy suburban neighborhood. He's followed by a white sports car, and eventually kidnapped off the street by a man wearing a medieval helmet suggestive of a knight.

The next scene shows a young couple in an urban environment. She's bringing him breakfast in preparation for a weekend of meeting her family—upscale liberals, by her description of it. "Do they know I'm black," asks Chris Washington, played by Daniel Kaluuya. He doesn't really receive an answer from his girlfriend Rose Armitage (Allison Williams)—although that answer becomes clear by the end of the film.

On the drive to the weekend of introductions, their car runs into a deer—a foreshadowing of the plot to come. The police officer who stops at the scene of the accident plays on all of tropes of the current "arrested for driving while black" incidents common in the United States, while Rose keeps the cop from getting ID from Chris by arguing that he wasn't even driving so he shouldn't have to show proof of anything. Of course, it would turn out that Rose played the white-privilege card for the selfish reason of preventing a paper trail in the event that Chris' absence was missed once her real reason for taking him home was revealed. The stone planters on the porch of her family's country home are adorned with the Omega symbol, the last letter of the Greek alphabet, foreshadowing that the Armitage house is "the end."

Dean and Missy Armitage, Rose's dad and mom, say the kinds of inadvertently embarrassing things to Chris that parents typically say when their child brings home a significant other. But their comments devolve into ambiguously racist asides. Then Missy offers to hypnotize Chris, supposedly for the well-meaning purpose of helping him quit smoking, eventually doing it without his consent. All the while, she drinks tea in bone china—sugar and tea having been the colonial products that formed the commercial chains of the slave trade in the Western Hemisphere. It would turn out that the Armitages saw black bodies as commodities, just like tea, for consumption and profit.

When Chris is hypnotized, his mind "falls" into the sunken place, a mental state that leaves his body paralyzed and consciousness only capable of witnessing what is happening around him but incapable of controlling his body. This context and visuals are a callback to the captivity of Africans who, similarly, lacked control over their own bodies as they were transported in the holds of slave ships.

And the help—both African-American—are simply odd. The caretaker, Walter, uses an archaic vocabulary to describe Rose—"one of a kind, top of the line, a dog-gone keeper!" The housekeeper, Georgina, obeys orders to the letter, prompting Chris to muse that she "missed the (civil rights) movement."

From this point on in the film, the real intent of the family weekend emerges. A "family reunion" turns out to be a viewing period for bidders to assess Chris, the main attraction in a silent auction reminiscent of ones during the slave trade. Again, the cultural stereotype of African-Americans as "strong physically" becomes part of the plot. The goal, immortality—or at least greatly extended life—through a very immoral means is revealed. Walter and Georgina are actually the bodies of black victims used to extend the lives of Rose's grandparents. That fate awaited Chris unless he could avoid it in the only way possible: Get out!

Peele initially wrote two endings for the film but settled on the happier one because he was concerned about how the film would be received by Caucasian moviegoers. Regardless of which ending you prefer, the movie stands as a disturbing satire of American horror movies with the message that African-Americans can rely only on themselves to overcome exploitation by the very people who claim to want to help them.

Micro Issues

1. If you have seen the film, how many of the visual cues did you recognize as symbols of racial oppression or white privilege?
2. W. E. B. Du Bois wrote about what he called double consciousness—the idea that African-Americans simultaneously lived with the identity of an American and a black person, an individual feeling of being divided into multiple parts so it was impossible to have a single unified identity. How is that concept woven into the film? Do you find it meaningful today?
3. Evaluate Jordan Peele's decision to use a happier ending for the film in order to make it more palatable for Caucasian audiences.

Midrange Issues

1. Peele has said that he wrote the film to illustrate a system that is dominated by white power. Do you think a horror film is an effective vehicle for such a social critique?
2. Some reviewers have noted that the film also illustrates an additional social problem: the fact that African-Americans constitute about 14 percent of the US population but more than 24 percent of Americans "missing" due to some form of criminal activity. Contrast this film with *Wind River*, a drama that makes the same point with regard to Native Americans. Which do you believe is more effective?
3. Compare and contrast the social and political message of *Get Out* to similar films such as *Invasion of the Body Snatchers*, *The Stepford Wives*, and *Guess Who's Coming to Dinner*.

Macro Issues

1. Audience response to *Get Out* varied. One of the authors of this case saw the film in Detroit, where the largely African-American audience cheered at the ending. The other saw the film in a Midwestern college town where the audience did not applaud at the ending. What might be the reasons for such divergent responses?
2. *Get Out* takes a historic injustice and gives it a modern expression. How are the various theories of justice outlined in the text reflected in the film?
3. If you were unaware of racial exploitation before seeing the movie, what is your responsibility given your awareness of Peele's interpretation of America?

CASE 10-B

TO DIE FOR: MAKING TERRORISTS OF GAMERS IN *MODERN WARFARE 2*

PHILIP PATTERSON
Oklahoma Christian University

The scene on the screen is brutal. Bullets fly indiscriminately. Bodies fall to the floor. An airport terminal becomes a killing field for Russian terrorists who want the massacre to incite a US-Soviet war. Fortunately, it's only a game—*Call of Duty: Modern Warfare 2*—but one with very real decisions that have to be made by the viewer/gamer.

At the beginning of the mission, entitled "No Russian," the player is only a bystander as Russian terrorists fire randomly and ruthlessly into crowds at a fictitious Russian airport terminal. But the player quickly discovers that he or she can fire as well—only not at the perpetrators, but at the civilians. In one of the most controversial "first-person shooter" gaming decisions of all time, *Modern Warfare 2* (*MW2*) allows players to decide whether to join in the carnage.

First-person shooter (FPS) games had been a staple of video gaming since the earliest days of the industry beginning with *Maze War*, released in 1974. Today, FPS games are the most commercially viable of all video games, accounting for 27 percent of all video game sales in 2016, according to statista.com. But prior to *MW2*, the target of the shooting had been enemy combatants, fleeing criminals, zombies, and the like. Few FPS games and no bestsellers had featured the gamer firing at innocent bystanders.

MW2 challenged that convention. Here is a description of the gamer's option according to a reviewer for the gaming website kotaku.com (Klepek 2015):

> Bullets unload on an unsuspecting crowd, and the body count quickly begins to rise. Most players, thinking they needed to play along, probably decided to start shooting—at the time, I did. But the game never forces you do *anything*, and it's entirely up to the player whether a single shot is fired from their gun. Dozens of people will die, regardless of what you decide to do, but active participation is left to the player.

In some locations, becoming an active shooter was *not* left up to the player. In Japan and Germany, if a player attempted to join the shooting, he or she was met with a "mission failed" screen, the game having been altered at the insistence of the government. The entire segment was removed from versions released in Russia.

One of the game's designers, Mohammad Alavi, said in an interview that he took pride in forcing players to make an uncomfortable decision, telling interviewer Matthew Burns (2012) in an interview three years after the release of the game:

> In the sea of endless bullets you fire off at countless enemies without a moment's hesitation or afterthought, the fact that I got the player to hesitate even for a split second and actually consider his actions before he pulled that trigger—that makes me feel very accomplished.

Despite the controversies surrounding the game—or perhaps because of them—sales were brisk. The game grossed $310 million on Nov. 10, 2009, the first day of its release and has since earned more than $1 billion. It was well reviewed including winning "Game of the Year" honors from several retail and fan sites online. Eight years after its release, *Call of Duty: Modern Warfare 2* ranked as the 24th bestselling game of all time, selling nearly 23 million units. Industry estimates placed the cost of developing *MW2* at $40–$50 million along with a marketing budget of $200 million to launch the game.

Knowing that some players would choose not to shoot at the civilians in the terminal, the designers of *MW2* allowed players to bypass the "No Russian" segment and still move on in the game. Before starting the game, players were shown a screen that read:

> Disturbing Content Notice
> Some players may find one of the missions
> disturbing or offensive. Would you like to have
> the option to skip this mission?

[You will not be penalized in terms of Achievement or game completion]

The options given the player were these:

Yes, ask me later
No, I will not be offended

All "unlockables" were removed from the segment and a player could reach the highest levels of the game and earn the highest rewards even if they chose to either skip "No Russian" or not participate as a shooter in the segment.

One of the detractors of the civilian violence in *Call of Duty: Modern Warfare 2* is Walt Williams, lead writer for the 2012 game *Spec Ops: The Line*. Williams, who would write the killing of civilians into his war game (crossing "the line" in the game's title), criticized the "No Russian" sequence of *MW2* for its "clumsiness" (Hamilton 2012). In commenting on the civilian violence in that earlier game, he told a reviewer for kotaku.com:

> The thing that got me the most was that you could opt out of playing it. And that struck me as saying, "We wanted to do something that would cause controversy, but it's actually not necessary to the game, which is why you don't have to play it."

FPS games are often debated in the aftermath of mass shootings such as one in Las Vegas, Nevada, in the fall of 2017. In that event, a lone gunman shot into a crowd of 22,000 outdoor concertgoers from a high floor of a nearby hotel, killing 58 of them and injuring 546. While no direct evidence links FPS games to events such as Las Vegas, researchers note the similarities of such random shootings to FPS games and claim that hours of playing such games can desensitize the player to real-world violence.

But in the case of *MW2*, the controversy is not merely a hypothetical debate. On July 22, 2011, Anders Behring Breivik, a far-right Norwegian terrorist killed eight persons in a car bomb in Oslo and then killed 69 participants of a Worker's Youth League summer camp at an outing on an island 24 miles away. He would later claim to have been motivated in the attack by the game, but no evidence has been produced that supports the claim. Though he is still alive in prison today, he has been diagnosed as a paranoid schizophrenic and has never been questioned further about the relationship of the game to his actions.

Micro Issues

1. Should FPS games be regulated? If so, in what way?
2. Should the killing of innocent bystanders be banned in FPS games?
3. The game was modified in Japan and Germany and banned in Russia. Critique the actions of these countries in their actions toward this game.

Midrange Issues

1. What does the decision by the developers to make the segment optional say to you?
2. Critique the claim of Breivik above. Is it credible to you? Does it have any bearing on whether FPS games should be regulated?
3. Critique the remarks of Williams above. He allowed the killing of civilians in his game while criticizing the violence of *MW2*. Do you see a difference in the two games?

Macro Issues

1. Violence has long been a part of art and entertainment. What standards, if any, should we place on the artist in terms of how much violence we wish to see in our art?
2. Do you place any credibility in the research that indicates that violence in games, on the television and movie screens, etc., desensitize the audience and make us more tolerate of violence in real life?

CASE 10-C

DAILY DOSE OF CIVIC DISCOURSE

CHAD PAINTER
University of Dayton

One aspect that *The Daily Show* is known for is the civil, substantive, and thoughtful discussions and debate between host Trevor Noah—and Jon Stewart before him—and his guest. The interview segment is a model of civil discourse, where guests are provided time to discuss their ideas in a rational and critical back-and-forth discussion, even when the host disagrees (Barbur and Goodnow 2011; Williams and Delli Carpini 2011; Young and Esralew 2011).

Stewart, during his 16-year run as host, often interviewed conservatives such as Grover Norquist, John McCain, and Bill O'Reilly, who appeared on the show 11 times.

Noah, Stewart's hand-picked successor, similarly hosts guests who hold opposing political views, such as conservative talk show host Tomi Lahren, who appeared on the Nov. 30, 2016, episode. During the 26-minute talk, Noah and Lahren discussed Donald Trump's election victory, the Affordable Care Act, and Black Lives Matter, among other topics. Noah "expressed his opinions and challenged her on views he found confusing at best and offensive at worst. But he also just kept asking for clarity, for more information on why, exactly, Lahren thinks the way she does" (Framke 2016).

Lahren, at the time, was a host and commentator at *The Blaze*, a conservative news and entertainment network founded by Glenn Beck. She regularly criticized political and cultural figures such as Barack Obama and Colin Kaepernick on the "Final Thoughts" segment on her show, which routinely garnered millions of YouTube and social media views. Lahren was suspended from, and then left, *The Blaze* in March 2017 for saying that women should have legal access to abortion. She now works for the conservative Great America Alliance PAC and is a commentator on Fox News.

The key moment of the discussion occurred when Lahren said Kaepernick was not protesting "the right way." That comment led to the following exchange:

Noah: When people say that, I'm always fascinated. What is the right way? So here is a black man in America who says I don't know how to get a message across. If I march in the streets, people say I'm a thug. If I go out and I protest, people say that it's a riot. If I bend down on one knee, then it's not [the right way]. What is the right way? That is something that I've always wanted to know. What is the right way for a black person to get attention in America?

Lahren: Why would you take out your perceived oppression of black people on our national anthem and our flag? A country that you live in. A country that you benefit from. A country that people of all races have died for, have died to protect, have died for the vote. How do you then go and disrespect the flag and the anthem of that country? Why is that the outlet?

Noah: Well, maybe you're a person who's lived and read through history and you realize that a lot of those people of every color who died for this country, some of them didn't have the rights that their fellow servicemen had when they came back to the country after fighting for it. Maybe you're one of those people who realizes that the penal system in America was designed to oppress black people. It was designed to enslave people. It's a relic of slavery. Maybe you're one of those people. So what I don't understand is, a guy is kneeling in the corner. I don't understand why that offends you so much. It's not even like he's trying to sing over you. He's not doing anything that affects you. I don't understand why that gets to you. I genuinely don't.

Deborah Tannen, in her book *The Argument Culture*, describes modern communication more like warfare than discourse. Most issues, Tannen argues, are framed as having two sides, which limits the scope of public discussion and causes polarity instead of thoughtful discussion aimed at resolving issues (Tannen 1999).

Stewart famously argued against "the argument culture" during an appearance on the CNN show *Crossfire* (2004). Hosts Tucker Carlson and Paul Begala, their bosses, and the audience believed they were booking a comedian. But Stewart was far from funny. Instead, he lambasted Carlson, *Crossfire*, and the television news media in general for doing bad political theater rather than their jobs. In a curious way, the media's reduction of the complexities of a presidential campaign to a "horserace" complete with each party and hundreds of journalists for both old and new media alike playing a daily game of "gotcha" with the candidates, had made a show like Stewart's and Noah's, which ridiculed the process, not only popular but quite possibly necessary.

Just before Jon Stewart and Stephen Colbert departed from Comedy Central in 2015, a poll from the Public Religion Research Institute, quoted in the *Washington Post*, had 11 percent of millennials saying that Comedy Central was their most trusted source of news, ranking it fourth behind CNN (24 percent), the three major networks (19 percent), and Fox (19 percent). This is a decade after a Pew Research Center poll found 21 percent of viewers under 30 got their election news from Comedy Central.

Micro Issues

1. Compare Trevor Noah's interview of Tomi Lahren with similar interviews on a cable news channel such as CNN, Fox News, or MSNBC.

Midrange Issues

1. Trevor Noah was criticized—even called a "sellout" and "devil"— for giving Tomi Lahren a platform to express her ultra-conservative views, for example, equating Black Lives Matter with the Ku Klux Klan. Is such criticism justified?

2. Compare Trevor Noah's decision to invite Tomi Lahren with Megyn Kelly's decision to interview *Infowars* Alex Jones on her NBC news program?

Macro Issues

1. Jon Stewart often would deflect criticism by saying that he was just a comedian trying to get laughs. What is the role of a political satirist in modern political debate and discussion?
2. Evaluate Deborah Tannen's claim that the argument culture distills every issue or debate into two polarized sides.
3. As polls have consistently shown that Comedy Central is used as a source for news by 10–20 percent of younger viewers, does this impose any kind of responsibility on the channel and its most prominent show to adhere to conventional journalistic standards?

CASE 10-D

THE ONION: FINDING HUMOR IN MASS SHOOTINGS

CHAD PAINTER
University of Dayton

A lone gunman opened fire Oct. 1, 2017, during the Route 91 Harvest Music Festival in Las Vegas, killing 58 and injuring 546. News coverage was nearly around the clock, mostly following a similar, well-rehearsed playbook, according to the *Washington Post*:

> Deploy reporters to the scene quickly. Interview eyewitnesses and families of the victims and the shooters. Check social media for clues to the attackers' identity. Bring on the law enforcement experts for comment (Farhi 2015).

Coverage was a bit different, however, for one "news" organization. In *The Onion*, readers were greeted with a familiar headline: "'No Way To Prevent This,' Says Only Nation Where This Regularly Happens." The full text of less than 200 words, reads:

> LAS VEGAS—In the hours following a violent rampage in Las Vegas in which a lone attacker killed more than 50 individuals and seriously injured 400 others, citizens living in the only country where this kind of mass killing routinely occurs reportedly concluded Monday that there was no way to prevent the massacre from taking place.

"This was a terrible tragedy, but sometimes these things just happen and there's nothing anyone can do to stop them," said Iowa resident Kyle Rimmels, echoing sentiments expressed by tens of millions of individuals who reside in a nation where over half of the world's deadliest mass shootings have occurred in the past 50 years and whose citizens are 20 times more likely to die of gun violence than those of other developed nations. "It's a shame, but what can we do? There really wasn't anything that was going to keep these individuals from snapping and killing a lot of people if that's what they really wanted." At press time, residents of the only economically advanced nation in the world where roughly two mass shootings have occurred every month for the past eight years were referring to themselves and their situation as "helpless."

The Onion had published versions of the same story five times changing only the date, location of violence, and number of people killed. The story was first published after a May 23, 2014, attack at the University of California where a gunman killed six people and injured 14 others. It later ran, almost verbatim, after the June 17, 2015, shooting at the Emanuel African Methodist Episcopal Church in Charleston, South Carolina; the Oct. 1, 2015, shooting at Umpqua Community College in Oregon; the Dec. 2, 2015, shooting at a Christmas party for the San Bernardino County Department of Public Health; and the Feb. 14, 2018, shooting at Parkland High School.

The *Onion* has not run the story after every mass shooting; notably, it didn't appear after the June 12, 2016, Orlando nightclub attack. The repetition, though, underscores the problem that mass shootings are a regular occurrence in US life. *Onion* managing editor Marnie Shure told *Vice* in a September 2017 interview that "by re-running the same commentary, it strengthens the original commentary tenfold each time. In the wake of these really terrible things, we have this comment that really holds up." The not-so-subtle commentary is an attempt by *Onion* writers to tap into a shared sense of frustration coupled with futility and hopelessness. The satire here is not just used for humor; instead, it has a larger purpose regarding social and political life (Feinberg 1967).

The Onion, which dubs itself as "America's Finest News Source," is a satirical web site that covers both real and fictional current events in the tone, format, and design of traditional news organizations such as the Associated Press. It came to national prominence for its acclaimed coverage of the 9/11 terrorist attacks; *Onion* writers were among the first humorists to address the attacks and their aftermath.

Micro Issues

1. Does *The Onion*'s mass shooting story gain or lose impact with each retelling?
2. The story is fictional, though it does include real information, including statistics. Does this blending of fiction and nonfiction aid or detract from the overall message? Compare this story to news coverage of these shootings that appeared in local newspapers.

Midrange Issues

1. *The Onion* publishes the story after only some mass shootings. Discuss this editorial strategy.
2. Does *The Onion's* approach trivialize these events? What might be the impact of this story on the victims' families should they see it?
3. Is *The Onion's* story fake news?

Macro Issues

1. What are the ethical implications of using humor to discuss mass shootings or other tragic events?
2. Compare *The Onion's* coverage of mass shooting to that provided by columnists such as Nicholas Kristof of the *New York Times*. Evaluate their effectiveness as a form of political communication as outlined in chapter 6.
3. Satire typically has a larger social or political purpose. Discuss that purpose in relation to mass shootings.

CASE 10-E

HATE RADIO: THE OUTER LIMITS OF TASTEFUL BROADCASTING

BRIAN SIMMONS
Portland State University

Trevor Van Lansing has what some would call the greatest job in the world. He is employed by KRFP-AM, an all-talk-format radio station in a large city in the West. His program airs weekdays from 3–7 p.m., and he is currently rated No. 1 in his afternoon drive-time slot. Van Lansing is, quite simply, the most popular radio personality in the market. He is also the most controversial.

Each afternoon Van Lansing introduces a general topic for discussion and then fields calls from listeners about the topic. However, Lansing's topics (and the calls from his listeners) revolve around a recurring theme: the world as viewed by a Caucasian, Anglo-Saxon Protestant who also happens to be vocal, uncompromising, and close-minded.

A sampling of his recent programs typifies his show. On Monday, Van Lansing discusses a woman in a small Indiana town who quits her job in a convenience store to go on welfare because there is more money to be made on the federal dole than in the private sector. Says Van Lansing, "All these irresponsible whores are the same. They get knocked up by some construction worker, then expect the taxpayers to pay for them to sit around the house all day and watch Oprah Winfrey."

Callers flood the airwaves with equally combative remarks in support of and opposition to Van Lansing's comments. On Tuesday, the topic of racial discrimination (always a Van Lansing favorite) comes up. According to Van Lansing, "Those Africans expect us Americans to make up for two hundred years of past mistakes. Forget it. It can't be done. If they are so keen on America, let them compete against Caucasians on an equal basis without the 'civil rights crutch.'"

When one African-American caller challenges Van Lansing's thinking, the host responds, "Why don't you tell your buddies to work for what they get like us Caucasians? All you do anyway is steal from the guys you don't like and then take their women."

Wednesday finds Van Lansing lashing out against education: "The problem with today's schools is that our kids are exposed to weird thinking. I mean, we tell our kids that homosexuality is okay, that we evolved from a chimp, and that the Ruskies are our friends. It all started when we elected women to school boards and started letting fags into the classroom. It's disgusting."

Thursday features an exchange between Van Lansing and an abortion-rights activist. At one point they are both shouting at the same time, and the airwaves are peppered with obscenities and personal attacks. By comparison, Friday is calm, as only a few irate Jews, women, and Mormons bother to call in.

Critics have called Van Lansing's program offensive, tasteless, rude, racist, obscene, and insensitive. Supporters refer to the program as enlightening, refreshing, educational, and provocative. The only thing everyone can agree on is that the show is a bona fide moneymaker. Van Lansing's general manager notes that the station's ratings jumped radically when he was hired and that advertising revenues have tripled.

In fact, Van Lansing's popularity has spawned promotional appearances, T-shirts, bumper stickers, and other paraphernalia, all designed to hawk the station. "Sure, Trevor is controversial, but in this business that's good," says KRFP's general manager.

"Van Lansing is so good that he will make more money this year than the president of the United States. Besides, it's just a gimmick."

Does Van Lansing see a problem with the content and style of his program? "Look," he says, "radio is a business. You have to give the audience what they want. All I do is give them what they want. If they wanted a kinder, gentler attitude, I would give it to them." He continues, "Don't get mad at me. Thank God we live in a country where guys like me can express an opinion. The people who listen to me like to hear it straight sometimes, and that's what the First Amendment is about, right?"

Finally, Van Lansing points out that if people are really offended by him, they can always turn the dial. "I don't force these people to listen," he pleads. "If they don't like it, let them go somewhere else."

Others disagree. The National Coalition for the Understanding of Alternative Lifestyles, a gay- and lesbian-rights group, calls Van Lansing's show "reprehensible." "Trevor Van Lansing is hiding behind the First Amendment. What he says on the air isn't speech; it's hate, pure and simple," says the group's director. "His program goes well beyond what our founders intended."

Adds a representative of the National Organization for Women: "Van Lansing is perpetuating several dangerous stereotypes that are destructive, sick and offensive. Entertainment must have some boundaries."

Micro Issues

1. Would you be offended by Van Lansing's program? If so, why?
2. Would Van Lansing's program be less offensive if the station aired another talk show immediately after his that featured a host holding opposite views?
3. How are the lyrics of rapper Eminem like or unlike Van Lansing's rants? Is an artist subject to different restrictions?

Midrange Issues

1. Who should accept responsibility for monitoring this type of program? Van Lansing? The radio station KRFP? The FCC? The courts? The audience?
2. What, if any, are the differences between Van Lansing's *legal* right to do what he does and the *ethical* implications of what he does?
3. Legal scholar Mari Matsuda (1989) has called for a narrow legal restriction of racist speech. She notes, "The places where the law

does not go to redress harm have tended to be the places where women, children, people of color, and poor people live" (Matsuda 1989, 2322). She argues that a content-based restriction of racist speech is more protective of civil liberties than other tests that have been traditionally applied. Could such an argument be applied to entertainment programming?

4. In the current American media landscape, talk radio is supposedly the stronghold of the right while the majority of major daily newspapers are supposedly controlled by the left. Does the evidence validate this widely held assumption? Is democracy well-served by this arrangement of entire media systems leaning to one side of the political spectrum?

Macro Issues

1. Are entertainers relieved of ethical responsibilities if they are "just giving the audience what they want"? Do Van Lansing's high ratings validate his behavior, since many people are obviously in agreement with him?

2. How does Van Lansing's narrow view of the world differ from a television situation comedy that stereotypes blondes as dumb, blue-collar workers as bigoted, etc.?

3. Van Lansing says that it's great that a guy like him can have a radio show. Is tolerance one of the measures of a democracy? If so, are there limits to tolerance, and who draws those lines?

4. Supreme Court Justice William O. Douglas has said, "If we are to have freedom of mind in America, we must produce a generation of men and women who will make tolerance for all ideas a symbol of virtue." How should democratic societies cope with unpopular points of view, particularly as expressed through the mass media?

CASE 10-F

SEARCHING FOR SUGAR MAN: REDISCOVERED ART

LEE WILKINS
Wayne State University
University of Missouri

What makes a hit record has never been reduced to a formula. During the decades of the 1960s and early 1970s, hundreds of talented artists were never heard beyond a small group of fans because their records didn't sell. That was the case with a young Detroit musician, Sixto Rodriguez, who produced one album—*Cold Fact*—in 1970 and a second in 1971. With a voice reminiscent of James Taylor and lyrics with the edge and poetry of Bob Dylan, Rodriguez's career never made it out of Detroit. Years later, his Motown-based producer, then living in California, told Danish documentary filmmaker Malik Benbdielloul that Rodriguez had sold exactly six records in the States.

Which was true—sort of. What his producer may have known—but Rodriguez unquestionably did not—was that the *Cold Fact* album and its title song had become the anthem of young people half a world away. In South Africa, in the early 1970s, Rodriguez was better known than Elvis, sold more records than the Rolling Stones, and had become the voice of a generation that wanted to challenge the apartheid political system in that country. His two records were considered so inflammatory that government censors deliberately scratched vinyl copies housed at radio stations so they could not be broadcast over the air. In the days before the internet, Rodriguez was an underground pied piper—everyone knew his songs just as everyone in a certain generation in the United States knew that "the answer was blowin' in the wind."

His South African fans also knew something else: Rodriguez was dead. No one was quite sure how he died, but there were conflicting newspaper reports that he had committed suicide—everything from setting himself alight on stage to protest apartheid to shooting himself. In an era of untimely rock musician deaths—Janis Joplin, Jimi Hendrix, Jim Morrison—it seemed only too reasonable. The mystery and the assumption of Rodriguez's demise persisted in South Africa for more than two decades. However, as the country changed, his largely Africanse fans did not forget, including two now-middle-aged fans-turned-music journalists who set out on an unlikely quest to find out how Rodriguez actually had died.

Solving that mystery became the focus of the documentary film *Searching for Sugar Man* that Benbdielloul reported, shot, and produced in the early 21st century. The film chronicles the efforts of the South Africans, one of whom is nicknamed Sugarman, to track down Rodriguez, with the most profoundly startling result.

In response to an internet posting about the circumstances of the musician's death, Rodriguez's adult daughter emailed back that her father is alive, he's living as he has for decades in Detroit supporting himself through heavy construction work, and he has literally no idea about his impact on the nation and the people of South Africa. When the South Africans find and then telephone Rodriguez, he hangs up the phone, thinking that the call is a prank. But, thanks to this initial connection, in the late 1990s, Rodriguez ultimately travels to South Africa where his concert performances are sold out and he plays to audiences in the thousands who can sing every word of every song. Benbdielloul reports it all, including lengthy interviews with Rodriguez, his daughter, his South African fans, and a sound track shot through with music that still seems timely even in the next century.

But, to report this different sort of magical mystery (Rodriguez had stopped playing professionally many years before), Benbdielloul makes what he admits are some uneasy compromises (personal communication 2012). In order to track down information about Rodriguez himself, Benbdielloul needs to interview his former producer—who had received some royalty checks for South African sales. The film can't go forward without his cooperation, so Benbdielloul makes the decision not to confront the producer about potential financial chicanery in order to learn more about Rodriguez's early recording and artistic career. Benbdielloul, himself, is working on a shoestring budget—while he's shooting the film, he spends some nights on Rodriguez's couch to defray expenses. And, Rodriguez himself is vague about some things. The finished documentary, for example, never mentions a marriage or a lover—although he has three children who appear in the film—nor does it delve deeply into why a person with such enormous talent—having learned he is a phenomenon—fails literally and artistically to capitalize on it during the late 1900s and early 2000s.

The documentary debuted formally in the United States in July 2012. Rodriguez and Benbdielloul were both interviewed in the *New York Times* and NPR, where audiences learn that Rodriguez had been politically active in Detroit, running unsuccessfully for mayor more than once. Rodriguez's US artistic career also begins to take off; he plays gigs such as South by Southwest and his music is covered at the Newport Jazz Festival.

Micro Issues

1. In crafting the narrative, Benbdielloul behaves more like a feature writer than he does an investigative journalist, even though it is clear that there are things worthy of investigation about Rodriguez's royalty payments. Analyze this choice, from the point of role. Is this a case of leaving out important facts to tell a better story?
2. Should the filmmaker have literally lived with his subject to produce this film? Justify your answer using ethical theory. How would you respond if a journalist had done the same thing with an important source?
3. Is the filmmaker using Rodriguez as a means to his ends?

Midrange Issues

1. How hard should the filmmaker have "pushed" to get information about the potentially less seemly parts of Rodriguez's life?
2. Rodriguez says on camera that he is a shy person. Indeed, in his early Detroit career, he often played at a bar called the Sewer with his back to the audience. Does a film such as *Searching for Sugar Man* invade his obviously valued privacy?

Macro Issues

1. Based on the above facts and what you can find on the internet, analyze how Rodriguez's lack of success in the United States might be explained by the concept of popular culture.
2. In today's environment, where musicians often make it on the web before making it on the road, do you think Rodriguez and his music would find a US audience? Does it matter?
3. Is the documentary film responsible for changing Rodriguez's life? Should the director have been concerned about this potential as he made the film?

11

Becoming a Moral Adult

By the end of this chapter, you should be able to

- know the stages of moral development as described by Piaget and Kohlberg
- understand the ethics of care
- understand the stages of adult moral development
- understand how these theories have been applied to journalists' ethical thinking

Graduation is not the end of the educational process; it is merely a milestone marking the beginning of a new era of learning. College studies should not only equip you for entry into or promotion within the workforce but also equip you to be a lifelong learner.

The same is true about moral development. There is no "moral graduation," marking you as an upright person capable of making right choices in life's personal and professional dilemmas. It's a lifelong process of steps—some of which you've taken; others lie ahead. Where you are now is a function of both age and experience, but the person you are now is not the person you will be 10 years from now. In a decade, you'll have added insight. Growth may, and probably will, change your decisions. This process is not only inevitable but also desirable. Contemporary scholarship suggests moral development begins within the mind-enhanced brain (Gazzaniga 2011).

This chapter is designed to provide you with an overview of some psychological theories of moral development. It attempts to allow you to plot your own development not only in terms of where you are but also in terms of where you would like to be.

BASIC ASSUMPTIONS ABOUT MORAL DEVELOPMENT: THE RIGHTS-BASED TRADITION

People can develop morally just as they can learn to think critically (Clouse 1985). Scholars base this assertion on the following premises.

First, *moral development occurs within the individual*. Real moral development cannot be produced by outside factors or merely engaging in moral acts. People develop morally when they become aware of their reasons for acting a certain way.

Second, *moral development parallels intellectual development*. Although the two may proceed at a slightly different pace, there can be little moral development until a person has attained a certain intellectual capacity. For this reason, we exempt children and people of limited mental ability from some laws and societal expectations. While you can be intelligent without being moral, the opposite is not likely.

Third, *moral development occurs in a series of universal, unvarying, and hierarchical stages*. Each level builds on the lower levels, and there is no skipping of intermediate stages. Just as a baby crawls before walking and babbles before speaking, a person must pass through the earlier stages of moral development before advancing to the later stages.

Figure 11.1. *Calvin and Hobbes* © Watterson. Distributed by Universal Uclick. Reprinted with permission. All rights reserved.

Fourth, *moral development comes through conflict*. As moral development theorist Lawrence Kohlberg notes, "A fundamental reason why an individual moves from one stage to the next is because the latter stages solve problems and inconsistencies unsolvable at the present developmental stage" (1973, 13). Just as a baby learns strategies other than crying to get its needs met, the developing moral being learns more complex behaviors when older, more elementary strategies no longer work.

The two most cited experts in the field of moral development did their work decades and continents apart yet came to remarkably similar conclusions. Jean Piaget conducted his research in Switzerland in the 1930s by watching little boys play marbles, and Lawrence Kohlberg studied Harvard students in the 1960s. They are often called "stage theorists" for their work in identifying and describing the stages of moral development.

THE WORK OF PIAGET

Piaget watched as boys between the ages of 3 and 12 played marbles, and he later tested his assumptions about their playground behavior in interviews. The box on the next page presents the basics of Piaget's theory.

The children under ages 5 to 7 didn't really play a game at all. They made up their own rules, varied them by playmate and game, and delighted in exploring the marbles as tactile objects. Their view of the game was centered exclusively on what each child wanted.

The younger boys (ages 7 and 8) did follow the rules and played as if violations of the rules would result in punishment. The boys believed the rules were timeless, handed down from some "other," and that "goodness" came from respecting the rules. Boys in this stage of moral development believed "Right is to obey the will of the adult. Wrong is to have a will of one's own" (Piaget 1965, 193).

Children progressed to the next stage of moral development at about age 11 when the boys began to develop notions of autonomy. They began to understand the reasoning behind the rules (i.e., fair play and reciprocity) that were the foundation of the rules themselves. Children in this stage of moral development understood that the rules received their power from their internal logic, not some outside authority.

These children had internalized the rules and the reasons behind them. Understanding the rules allowed the boys to rationally justify violating them. For example, children in this stage of moral development allowed much younger children to place their thumbs inside the marble circles, a clear violation of the rules. But the younger boys' hands were smaller and weaker,

Table 11.1. Piaget's Stages of Moral Development

Early Development (before age 2)

Interest in marbles is purely motor (e.g., put the marbles in your mouth).

First Stage: Egocentrism (years 3–7)

Children engage in "parallel play"; there is no coherent set of rules accepted by all.

The moral reasoning is "I do it because it feels right."

Second Stage: Heteronomy (years 7–8)

Children recognize only individual responsibility; obedience is enforced through punishment.

Each player tries to win.

Rules are regarded as inviolate, unbreakable, and handed down from outside authority figures, usually older children.

The children do not understand the reason behind the rules.

Third Stage: Autonomy (begins about age 11)

Children internalize the rules; they understand the reasons behind them.

They develop an ideal of justice and are able to distinguish between individual and collective responsibility.

They ensure fair play among children.

Children can change the rules in response to a larger set of obligations.

Authority is internal.

Children understand universal ethical principles that transcend specific times and situation

Children internalize the rules; they understand the reasons behind them.

and by allowing them a positional advantage, the older ones had—in contemporary language—leveled the playing field. They had ensured fairness when following the rules literally would have made it impossible.

Although Piaget worked with children, it is possible to see that adults often demonstrate these stages of moral development.

Take the videographer whose primary motivation is to obtain a great shot, regardless of the views of those he works with or his story subjects. This journalist operates within an egocentric moral framework that places the primary emphasis on what "I" think, "my" judgment, and what's good for "me."

Beginning journalists, the ones who find themselves concerned with the literal following of codes of ethics, may be equated with the heteronomy stage of development. This journalist knows the rules and follows them. She would never accept a freebie or consider running the name of a rape victim. It's against organizational policy, and heteronymous individuals are motivated largely by such outside influences.

Just as the boys at the third stage of moral development were more willing to alter the rules to ensure a fair game for all, journalists at the final stage of moral development are more willing to violate professional norms if it results in better journalism. The journalist at this stage of moral development has so internalized and universalized the rules of ethical professional behavior that he or she can violate some of them for sound ethical reasons.

However, people seldom remain exclusively in a single stage of moral development. New situations often cause people to regress temporarily to a previous stage of moral development until enough learning can take place so that the new situation is well understood. Perhaps the immediacy of the internet or the power of social networking sites caused such a regression for some at first. But in any case, such regression would not include behaviors that would be considered morally culpable under most circumstances, for example, lying or killing, even despite the new context.

THE WORK OF KOHLBERG

Harvard psychologist Lawrence Kohlberg mapped six stages of moral development in his college-student subjects. The accompanying box outlines Kohlberg's stages of moral development, divided into three levels.

Kohlberg developed a lengthy set of interview questions to allow him to establish which stage of moral development individual students had achieved. He asserted that only a handful of people—for example, Socrates, Gandhi, Martin Luther King, or Mother Teresa—ever achieved the sixth stage of moral development. Most adults, he believed, spend the greater portion of their lives in the two conventional stages where they are motivated by society's expectations.

Doing right, fulfilling one's duties, and abiding by the social contract are the pillars upon which the stages of Kohlberg's work rest. Under Kohlberg's arrangement, justice—and therefore morality—is a function of perception; as you develop, more activities fall under the realm of duty than before. For instance, reciprocity is not even a concept for individuals in the earliest stage, yet it is an essential characteristic of people in the upper stages of moral development. Conversely, acting to avoid punishment is laudable for a novice, yet might not be praiseworthy for a news director functioning at a more advanced stage. The further up Kohlberg's stages students progressed, the more they asserted that moral principles are subject to interpretation by individuals and subject to contextual factors yet able to be universalized.

Kohlberg's stages are descriptive and not predictive. They do not anticipate how any one individual will develop but suggest how most will develop. Kohlberg's formulation has much to recommend it to journalists, concerned

Table 11.2. The Six Moral Stages of Kohlberg

LEVEL 1: PRECONVENTIONAL

Stage 1: Heteronymous morality is the display of simple obedience.

Stage 2: Individualism is the emergence of self-interest. Rules are followed only when they are deemed to be in one's self-interest and others are allowed the same freedom. Reciprocity and fairness begin to emerge, but only in a pragmatic way.

LEVEL 2: CONVENTIONAL

Stage 3: Interpersonal conformity is living up to what others expect, given one's role (e.g., "brother," "daughter," "neighbor," etc.). "Being good" is important and treating others as you would have them treat you becomes the norm.

Stage 4: Social systems is the recognition that one must fulfill the duties to which one has agreed. Doing one's duty, respect for authority, and maintaining the social order are all goals in this level. Laws are to be upheld unilaterally except in extreme cases where they conflict with other fixed social duties.

LEVEL 3: POSTCONVENTIONAL

Stage 5: Social contract and individual rights is becoming aware that one is obligated by whatever laws are agreed to by due process. The social contract demands that we uphold the laws even if they are contrary to our best interests because they exist to provide the greatest good for the greatest number. However, some values such as life and liberty stand above any majority opinion.

Stage 6: Universal ethical principles self-selected by each individual guide this person. These principles are to be followed even if laws violate those principles. The principles that guide this individual include the equality of human rights and respect for the dignity of humans as individual beings regardless of race, age, socioeconomic status, or even contribution to society.

as they are with concepts such as free speech, the professional duty to tell the truth, and their obligations to the public and the public trust. However, Kohlberg's work was not without its problems. At least two aspects of his research troubled other moral development theorists.

Many scholars have argued that any general theory of moral development should allow people who are not saints or religious leaders to attain the highest stages of moral development. While perhaps only saints can be expected to act saintly most of the time, history is replete with examples of ordinary people taking extraordinary personal or professional risk for some larger ethical principles. Some felt that Kohlberg's conception—unlike Piaget's—was too restrictive.

Still more troubling was that in repeated studies, men consistently scored higher than women on stages of moral development. This gender bias in Kohlberg's work prompted discussion about a different concept of moral development founded on notions of community rather than in the rights-based tradition. It is called the ethics of care.

PARALLEL ASSUMPTIONS ABOUT MORAL DEVELOPMENT: THE ETHICS OF CARE

The psychologists who developed the ethics of care disagree with at least two of the fundamental assumptions underlying Piaget and Kohlberg. First, they say, moral development does not always occur in a series of universal, unvarying, and hierarchical stages. Second, moral growth emerges through understanding the concept of community, not merely through conflict. The rights-based scholars believe that moral development emerges from a proper understanding of the concept "I." Proponents of the ethics of care say that moral development arises from understanding the concept of "we."

Carol Gilligan (1982) provides the clearest explanation of the ethics of care. Gilligan studied women deciding whether to abort. As she listened, she learned that they based their ethical choices on relationships. The first thing these women considered was how to maintain a connection. Gilligan argued that the moral adult is the person who sees a connection between the "I" and the "other." The women spoke in a "different voice" about their ethical decision-making. Like many feminist ethicists, Gilligan reasoned that the ethical thinking emerged from a lived experience, not through the imposition of the top-down moral structure or set of rules.

For example, Gilligan presented the women with Kohlberg's classic ethical dilemma: the case of the desperate man and the greedy pharmacist. In this scenario, a man with a terminally ill spouse doesn't have enough money to purchase an expensive and lifesaving drug. When he explains the situation to the pharmacist, the pharmacist refuses to give him the medication.

Under Kohlberg's system, it would be ethically allowable for a man at the highest stages of moral development to develop a rationale for stealing the drug, an act of civil disobedience for a greater good. However, women made this particular choice less often. Instead, they reasoned that the most ethical thing to do was to build a relationship with the pharmacist, to form a community in which the pharmacist viewed himself or herself as an active part. In that situation, the women reasoned, the pharmacist ultimately would give the man the drug in order to maintain the connection.

Gilligan proposed that the women's rationale was no more or less ethically sophisticated than that expected under Kohlberg's outline. However, it was different, for it weighed different ethical values. Whether those values emerged as the result of how women are socialized in Western culture (an assertion that has often been made about Gilligan's work) or whether they merely reflected a different kind of thinking still remains open to debate. For our purposes, the origin of the distinction—and whether it is truly gender-linked—is not as important as the content.

Gilligan's notion of moral development is not neatly tied into stages. Her closest theoretical counterpart is probably the theory of communitarianism (see chapter 1 for a description) with its emphasis on connection to community and its mandate for social justice.

If you were to carve stages from Gilligan's work, they would resemble

- **first**—an ethic of care where the moral responsibility is for care of others before self;
- **second**—an acknowledgment of the ethic of rights, including the rights of self to be considered in ethical decision-making; and
- **third**—a movement from concerns about goodness (women are taught to believe that care for others is "good" while men are taught that "taking care of oneself" is good) to concerns about truth.

A complete sense of moral development, Gilligan observed, requires the ability "to [use] two different moral languages, the language of rights that protects separations and the language of responsibilities that sustains connection" (Gilligan 1982, 210).

Contemporary journalists have struggled with the issues of connection. Since much of our profession is based on an understanding of rights as outlined in various legal documents, ethical reasoning for journalists almost always assumes a rights-based approach. (You probably took this ethics course along with or immediately after a media law course, for example.) This historical rights-based bias, however, has led journalists into some of their more profound errors, including arrogance toward sources and readers and an unwillingness to be genuinely accountable to anyone.

If journalism as a profession is to mature ethically (or even survive economically), it must see itself as the vehicle to help people become the citizens they can be and to help reconnect and sustain communities that have become increasingly fragmented.

With the election of President Barak Obama, followed by the near-Depression of 2008–2009 and economic slump for the decade thereafter, and continuing with the election of President Donald J. Trump, the United States has found itself in an intense conversation about values, rights, community and class. The "Black Lives Matter" movement has shared a mediated stage with Nazis, white supremacists, and anarchists who have problematized the first amendment and our human connection to one another in ways that have challenged journalists and citizens. A *Newsweek* essay from 1992 anticipated these developments and the media's role in them.

Television brought the nation together in the '50s; there were evenings when all of America seemed glued to the same show—Milton Berle, "I Love Lucy" and yes, "Ozzie and Harriet." But cable television has quite the opposite effect, dividing the audience into demographic slivers. . . . Indeed, if you are a member of any identifiable subgroup—black, Korean, fundamentalist, sports fan, political junkie—it's now possible to be messaged by your very own television and radio stations and to read your own magazines without having to venture out into the American mainstream. The choices are exhilarating, but also alienating. The basic principle is centrifugal: market segmentation targets those qualities that distinguish people from each other rather than emphasizing the things we have in common. It is the developed world's equivalent of the retribalization taking place in Eastern Europe, Africa and Asia (Klein 1992, 21–22).

In the late 1990s, a movement called "civic journalism" mushroomed as an attempt to return journalism to what touched the everyday lives of people. Today, the buzzword is engagement, a broad professional heuristic that aims to foster a community of readers/viewers and listeners concerned with their networked civic life and employing the media as a way to share common thoughts and propose change. Neither engagement nor civic journalism allowed journalists—regardless of outlet and platform—to anticipate the national furor over these issues as they emerged in 2015 and 2016.

DEVELOPING AS AN ETHICAL PROFESSIONAL

In the 1970s, James Rest, a psychology professor at the University of Minnesota, took Kohlberg's schema of moral development and used it to create a paper-and-pencil test to measure moral development among various professions. In the ensuing years, the test, called the Defining Issues Test (DIT), has been administered to more than 40,000 professionals, among them doctors, nurses, dentists, accountants, philosophers and theologians, members of the US Coast Guard, surgeons, veterinarians, graduate students, junior high students, and prison inmates. Those taking the test read four to six scenarios and are then asked to make a decision about what the protagonist should do, and then to rate the factors that influenced that decision. Because the test is based on Kohlberg's work, test takers who rely on universal principles and who consider issues of justice score well. Most people who take the DIT score in the range of what Kohlberg would have called conventional moral reasoning—stages 3 and 4 of his scale.

Wilkins and Coleman (2005) asked journalists to take the DIT and compared journalists' scores to those of other professionals. Journalists do well on the DIT, scoring below only three other professions: philosophers/ theologians, medical students, and practicing physicians. Because the single biggest predictor of a good score on the DIT is education, and journalists as a group have less formal education than the three professions with scores "above" them, the findings are significant. Other professions, for example, orthopedic surgeons, scored lower than journalists on the test. In a follow-up study (Coleman and Wilkins 2006), public relations professionals also did well on the DIT.

The scenarios on the DIT are not directed at any particular profession but rather determine how people think about "average" moral questions. When journalists are presented with scenarios that deal directly with journalism, for example, problems involving the use of hidden cameras or whether to run troubling photographs of children, they score even better. In these tests, journalists often score in the fourth and fifth stage of Kohlberg's moral development schema. In an interesting side note, scholars found that having a visual image, such as a photograph, of some of the stakeholders in an ethical dilemma elevates ethical reasoning. However, research also has found that moving images can degrade ethical thinking just as still images can promote it (Meader, Knight, Coleman, and Wilkins 2015). Other scholars have studied journalists' ethical decision-making. Investigative reporters make moral judgments about the subjects of their stories, even though when they talk about their work they are reluctant to drop their professional objectivity (Ettema and Glasser 1998). Another study found that journalists who have been sued for invasion of privacy don't often think about the ethical issues their reporting creates (Voakes 1998). This leads to an indirect but plausible conclusion that solid ethical thinking may keep journalists out of court.

Finally, research shows that journalists do agree on what constitutes "good work" in their profession—an emphasis on truth-telling, taking a role as government watchdog, investigative reporting, and treating the subjects with dignity. However, journalists believe that the single biggest threat to continuing professional excellence is the increasing pressure to make a profit. Journalists are out of joint with a mission that includes the competing interests of public service and profit-making (Gardner, Csikszenthmihalyi, and Damon 2001). How that tension is resolved is the essential question facing news operations today. Taking inspiration from the feminist assertion that theory emerges from lived experience, Patrick Plaisance has studied professional moral exemplars. He found it is a combination of internal abilities (e.g., the ability to remain resilient in the face of challenges), a supportive work environment, and a sense of journalism as a "mission" rather than a job that has allowed individual professionals to make solid ethical choices throughout their careers as well as at particularly contentious decision points (Plaisance 2015). Such efforts also contribute to the larger project of feminist philosopher Martha Nussbaum, whose work on the impact of emotions on ethical decisions and whose theory focusing on human capabilities suggests that consistent and strong ethical thinking empowers both people and political society to "do" and "allow" choices that support human flourishing (Nussbaum 2001).

WHERE DO YOU GO FROM HERE?

William Perry (1970) postulates that one of the major accomplishments of college students is to progress from a simple, dualistic (right versus wrong) view of life to a more complex, mature, and relativistic view. Perry states that students must not only acknowledge that diversity and uncertainty exist in a world of relativism but also make a commitment to their choices (i.e., career, values, beliefs, etc.) out of the multiplicity of "right" choices available.

Unlike physical development, moral development is not subject to the quirks of heredity. Each individual is free to develop as keen a sense of equity as any other individual, yet not all reach their full potential. Kohlberg (1973) claims we understand messages one stage higher than our own. Through "aspirational listening"—picking a role model on a higher level—you can progress to a higher stage of moral development. This observation is not new. In fact, Aristotle suggested that virtues could be learned by observing those who possess them.

This book uses the case study method. Often in case studies, it is the reasoning behind the answer rather than the answer itself that is the best determiner of moral growth (Clouse 1985). *An important part of moral development is the recognition that motive, not consequence, is a critical factor in deciding whether an act is ethical.*

Elliott (1991) illustrates the difference in the following scenario. Imagine a situation where you are able to interview and choose your next-door neighbor. When you ask Jones how she feels about murder, she replies she doesn't kill because if she got caught she would go to jail. When you interview Smith, he says he doesn't kill because he believes in the sanctity of life. It takes little reflection to decide which neighbor you would prefer. Elliott concludes, "Ethics involves the judging of actions as right or wrong, but motivations count as well. Some reasons for actions seem better or worse than others" (1991, 19).

To the above quote we might add, "and some justifications are more deeply rooted in centuries of ethical thought than others." The goal of this book— and probably one of the goals your professor had for this class—is to ensure that your choices are not merely "right," as that's a debate for the ages, but to ensure that your choices are grounded in the ethical theories that have stood the test of time and are not subject to the vagaries of current popular thought. The work of Kohlberg and Piaget suggests that your journey is not finished, but that you *have* started. And with the set of tools you have now acquired, you have an excellent chance of reaching your destination.

SUGGESTED READINGS

Belenky, M. F., Clinchy, B. M., Goldberger, N. R., & Tarule, J. M. (1988). *Women's ways of knowing: The development of self, voice and mind*. New York: Basic Books.

Coles, R. (1995). The disparity between intellect and character. *The Chronicle of Higher Education*. 42.4. September 22.

Ettema, J., & Glasser, T. (1998). *Custodians of conscience: Investigative journalists and public virtue*. New York: Columbia University Press.

Gardner, H., Csikszentmihalyi, M., & Damon, W. (2001). *Good work: When excellence and ethics meet*. New York: Basic Books.

Gazzaniga, M. S. (2011). *Who's in charge? Free will and the science of the brain*. New York: HarperCollins.

Gilligan, C. (1982). *In a different voice: Psychological theory and women's development*. Cambridge, MA: Harvard University Press.

Wilkins, L., & Coleman, R. (2005). *The moral media*. Mahwah, NJ: Lawrence Erlbaum Associates.

References

Adler, S. (2017). *Radiolab: Breaking News*. National Public Radio, July 27, 2017. Retrieved from https://www.wnycstudios.org/story/breaking-news/.

Allcott, H., & Gentzhow, M. (2017). Social media and fake news in the 2016 election. *Journal of Economics Perspective, 31*(2), 211–236.

Allen, B. (2014). Report: Jenny Dell removed from NESN Red Sox broadcast. Retrieved from https://bostonsportsmedia.com/2014/01/30/report-jenny-dell-removed-from-nesn-red-sox-broadcast/.

Anderson, C. (2006). *The long tail: How the future of business is selling less of more*. New York: Hyperion.

Andrews, T. A. (2017). Why a TV station flew a drone over Kentucky governor's home. *Washington Post*, August 2, 2017. Retrieved from https://www.washingtonpost.com/news/morning-mix/wp/2017/08/02/why-a-tv-station-flew-a-drone-over-kentucky-governors-home/?utmterm=.66f9db179c40.

Ansen, D. (2006). Inside the hero factory. *Newsweek*, October 23, 2006, 70–71.

Arendt, H. (1970). *The human condition*. Chicago, IL: University of Chicago Press.

Aristotle. (1973). *Nicomachean ethics. Book II 4–5*. Translated by H. Rackham. Edited by H. Jeffrey. Cambridge, MA: Harvard University Press.

Associated Press. (2016). Chipotle says criminal probe into E. coli outbreak widens. February 2, 2016. Retrieved from http://www.nydailynews.com/news/national/chipotle-criminal-probe-e-coli-outbreak-widens-article-1.2518207.

Aufderheide, P. (2005). *Reclaiming fair use*. Oxford: Oxford University Press.

Axelrod, R. (1984). *The evolution of cooperation*. New York: Basic Books.

Baker, S., & Martinson, D. (2001). The TARES test: Five principles of ethical persuasion. *Journal of Mass Media Ethics, 16*(2 & 3), 148–175.

Baldasty, G. J. (1992). *The commercialization of news in the nineteenth century*. Madison: University of Wisconsin Press.

Barbur, J. E., & Goodnow, T. (2011). The arête of amusement: An Aristotelian perspective on the ethos of *The Daily Show*. In T. Goodnow (ed.), The Daily

Show *and rhetoric: Arguments, issues, and strategies* (pp. 3–18). Lanham, MD: Lexington Books.

Barnouw, E. (1997). *Conglomerates and the media.* New York: New Press.

Baym, G. (2005). The Daily Show: Discursive integration and the reinvention of political journalism. *Political Communication, 22*(3), 259–276.

Bell, M. (2011). Hillary Clinton, Audrey Tomason go missing in Situation Room photo in Di Tzeitung newspaper. *Washington Post*, May 9, 2011. Retrieved from https://www.washingtonpost.com/blogs/blogpost/post/hillary-clinton-audrey-tomason-go-missing-in-situation-room-photo-in-der-tzitung-newspaper/2011/05/09/AFfJbVYG_blog.html?utm_term=.e909bfbb8569.

Benoit, W. (1999). *Seeing spots: A functional analysis of presidential television advertisements.* Westport, CT: Praeger.

Berger, A. (1989). *Seeing is believing.* Mountain View, CA: Mayfield.

Berger, J. (1980). *About looking.* New York: Pantheon Books.

Bok, S. (1978). *Lying: Moral choice in public and private life.* New York: Random House.

———. (1983). *Secrets: On the ethics of concealment and revelation.* New York: Vintage.

Booth, C. (1999). Worst of times. *Time*, November 15, 1999, 79–80.

Borden, S. L. (2009). *Journalism as practice: MacIntyre, virtue ethics and the press.* Burlington, VT: Ashgate.

Bovée, W. (1991). The end can justify the means—but rarely. *Journal of Mass Media Ethics, 6*(3), 135–145.

Brooks, D. E. (1992). In their own words: Advertisers and the origins of the African-American consumer market. A paper submitted to the Association for Education in Journalism and Mass Communications, August 5–8, Montreal, Canada.

Bryant, G. (1987). Ten-fifty P.I.: Emotion and the photographer's role. *Journal of Mass Media Ethics, 2*(2), 32–39.

Bunton, K., & Wyatt, W. (2012). *Reality television: A philosophical examination.* New York: Continuum International.

Burns, M. (2012). A sea of endless bullets: Spec Ops, No Russian and interactive atrocity. Retrieved from https://www.magicalwasteland.com/notes/2012/8/2/a-sea-of-endless-bullets-spec-ops-no-russian-and-interactive.html.

Cain, B. (2017). He's the Raleigh man behind the Twitter account outing racists—and "I'm not going away." *Raleigh News Observer*, August 14, 2017. Retrieved from http://www.newsobserver.com/news/local/article167142317.html.

Calfee, J. E. (2002). Public policy issues in direct-to-consumer advertising of prescription drugs. *Journal of Public Policy & Marketing, 21*(2), 174–193.

Carey, J. W. (1989). Review of Charles J. Sykes' Profscam. *Journalism Educator, 44*, (3), 48.

Caron, C. (2017). Heather Heyer, Charlottesville victim, is recalled as "a strong woman." *New York Times*, August 13, 2017. Retrieved from https://www.nytimes.com/2017/08/13/us/heather-heyer-charlottesville-victim.html.

Carr, D. (2008). Jim Cramer retreats along with the Dow. *New York Times*, October 20, 2008.

Cassier, E. (1944). *An essay on man*, New Haven, CT: Yale University Press.

Caufield, R. P. (2008). The influence of "infoenterpropagainment": Exploring the power of political satire as a distinct form of political humor. In J. C. Baumgartner & J. S. Morris (eds.), *Laughing matters: Humor and American politics in the media age* (pp. 3–20). New York: Routledge.

CBS. (2017). Sinclair to buy Tribune Media, expanding its local TV reach. *CBS News*, May 8, 2017. Retrieved from https://www.cbsnews.com/news/sinclair-to-buy-tribune-media-expanding-its-local-tv-reach/.

Census.gov. (2017). Retrieved from https://www.census.gov/topics/income-poverty/poverty.html.

Centers for Disease Control and Prevention. (2017). Retrieved from https://www.cdc.gov/drugoverdose/data/heroin.html.

Chester, G. (1949). The press-radio war: 1933–1935. *Public Opinion Quarterly*, *13*(2), 252–264.

Christians, C. G. (1986). Reporting and the oppressed. In D. Elliott (ed.), *Responsible journalism* (pp. 109–130). Newbury Park, CA: Sage.

Christians, C. G. (2010). The ethics of privacy. In Christopher Meyers (ed.), *Journalism ethics: A philosophical approach* (pp. 203–214). Oxford: Oxford University Press.

Christians, C. G., Ferré, J. P., & Fackler, M. (1993). *Good news: Social ethics and the press.* New York: Oxford University Press.

Christians, C. G., Glasser, T., McQuail, D., Nordenstreng, K., & White, R. A. (2009). *Normative theories of the media: Journalism in democratic societies.* Champaign: University of Illinois Press.

Clouse, B. (1985). *Moral development.* Grand Rapids, MI: Baker Book House.

Coleman, A. D. (1987). Private lives, public places: Street photography ethics. *Journal of Mass Media Ethics*, *2*(2), 60–66.

Coleman, R., & Wilkins, L. (2006). *The moral development of public relations practitioners.* Presented to the Association for Education in Journalism and Mass Communication, August 2006, San Francisco, CA.

Collins, S. (2008). CNBC banking on Jim Cramer. *Los Angeles Times*, October 8, 2008.

The Commission on Freedom of the Press. (1947). *A free and responsible press.* Chicago, IL: University of Chicago Press.

Compton, J. (2011). Introduction: Surveying the scholarship on *The Daily Show* and *The Colbert Report*. In A. Amarasingam (ed.), *The Stewart/Colbert effect: Essays on the real impacts of fake news* (pp. 9–23). Jefferson, NC: McFarland.

Craft, S. (2017). Distinguishing features: Reconsidering the link between journalism's professions status and ethics. *Journalism and Communication Monographs*, *19*(4), 260–301.

Crouse, T. (1974). *The boys on the bus: Riding with the campaign press corps.* New York: Ballantine.

Cubarrubia, R. J. (2012). Adam Yauch's will prohibits use of his music in ads. *Rolling Stone*, August 9, 2012. Retrieved from https://www.rollingstone.com/music/news/adam-yauchs-will-prohibits-use-of-his-music-in-ads-20120809.

Culver, K. B., & Duncan, M. (2017). *Newsrooms should build trust with audiences in drone journalism.* Retrieved from https://ethics.journalism.wisc.edu/dronejournalism/.

Cunningham, B. (2003). Re-thinking objectivity. *Columbia Journalism Review*, July/August, 24–32.

D'Angelo, C. (2017). Journalist who exposed the racist creator of Trump's CNN tweet gets death threats. *Huffington Post*, July 4, 2017. Retrieved from https://www.huffingtonpost.com/entry/jared-sexton-trump-cnn-tweetus595a6656e4b0da2c7324d3d6.

Davies, J. C. (1963). *Human nature in politics*. New York: John Wiley.

Deitsch, R. (2017). ESPN suspends Jemele Hill two weeks for violating social media policy. *Sports Illustrated*, October 9, 2017. Retrieved from https://www.si.com/tech-media/2017/10/09/jemele-hill-suspend-espn.

Delk, J. (2017). Antitrust calls for hearing on Disney deal to buy Fox assets. *The Hill*, December 16, 2017. Retrieved from http://thehill.com/blogs/blog-briefing-room/365227-antitrust-senator-wants-investigation-of-disney-deal-to-buy-fox.

de Tocqueville, A. (1985). *Democracy in America*. New York: George Dearborn.

Deuze, M. (2008). The changing nature of news work: Liquid journalism and monitorial citizenship. *International Journal of Communication, 2,* 848–865.

Dewey, J. (2005/1932). *Art as experience*. New York: Penguin Putnam.

Dillion, S. (2007). Troubles grow for a university built on profits. *New York Times*, February 11, 2007. Retrieved from https://www.nytimes.com/2007/02/11/education/11phoenix.html.

Dionne, E. J. (1991). *Why Americans hate politics*. New York: Simon & Schuster.

———. (1996). *They only look dead*. New York: Simon & Schuster.

Dixon, T., & Linz, D. (2000). Overrepresentation and underrepresentation of Blacks and Latinos as lawbreakers on television news. *Journal of Communication*, *50*(2), 131–154.

Donohue, J. (2006). A history of drug advertising: The evolving roles of consumers and consumer protection. *Milbank Quarterly*, *84*(4), 659–699.

Douglas, D. M. (2016). Doxing: a conceptual analysis. *Ethics and Information Technology*, *18*(3), 199–210.

Duncan, E. (1970). Has anyone committed the naturalistic fallacy? *Southern Journal of Philosophy*, *1*(1/2), 49–61.

Dyck, A. (1977). *On human care*. Nashville, TN: Abingdon.

Eaton, M. L. (2004). *Ethics and the business of bioscience*. Stanford, CA: Stanford University Press.

Elliott, D. (1986). Foundations for news media responsibility. In D. Elliott (ed.), *Responsible journalism* (pp. 32–34). Newbury Park, CA: Sage.

———. (1991). Moral development theories and the teaching of ethics. *Journalism Educator*, *46*(3), 19–24.

Ellis, E. G. (2017). Whatever your side, doxing is a perilous form of justice. *Wired*, August 17, 2017. Retrieved from https://www.wired.com/story/doxing-charlottesville/.

Ellul, J. (1965). *Propaganda*. Trans by K. Kellen & J. Lerner. New York: Alfred A. Knopf.

Emerson, J. (2006). *The Bridge*. Retrieved from http://www.rogerebert.com/reviews/the-bridge-2006.

Entman, R., & Rojecki, A. (2000). *The black image in the white mind*. Chicago, IL: University of Chicago Press.

ESPN (2017). ESPN's social media guidelines. Retrieved from https://www.espnfrontrow.com/2017/11/espns-social-media-guidelines/.

Ettema, J., & Glasser, T. (1998). *Custodians of conscience: Investigative journalists and public virtue.* New York: Columbia University Press.

Fallows, J. (1996). *Breaking the news: How the media undermine American democracy.* New York: Pantheon.

Farhi, P. (2015). Media falls into pattern with coverage of mass shootings. *Washington Post*, December 3, 2015. Retrieved from https://www.washingtonpost.com/lifestyle/style/media-fall-into-pattern-with-coverage-of-mass-shootings/2015/12/03/ab5001e6-9a09-11e5-94f0-9eeaff906ef3_story.html?noredirect=on&utm_term=.8205f74aa3b8.

———. (2017). ESPN likes opinionated personalities. Until it doesn't. Just ask Jemele Hill. *Washington Post*, September 20, 2017. Retrieved from https://www.washingtonpost.com/lifestyle/style/espn-likes-opinionated-personalities-until-it-doesnt-just-ask-jemele-hill/2017/09/20/906ca3d8-9ce7-11e7-8ea1-ed975285475e_story.html?noredirect=on&utm_term=.59b282b227a1.

Farzad, R. (2005). The mad man of Wall Street. *BusinessWeek*, October 31, 2005.

Feinberg, L. (1967). *Introduction to Satire.* Ames: The Iowa State University Press.

Festinger, L. (1957). *A theory of cognitive dissonance.* Stanford, CA: Stanford University Press.

Fiegerman, S., & Byers, D. (2017). Facebook, Twitter, Google defend their role in election. *CNN*, October 31, 2017. Retrieved from http://money.cnn.com/2017/10/31/media/facebook-twitter-google-congress/index.html.

Finn, C. (2014). Jenny Dell's departure from NESN is official. *Boston Globe*, May 30, 2014. Retrieved from https://www.bostonglobe.com/sports/2014/05/29/jenny-dell-departure-from-nesn-official/svvOo0MvqNc4M4PyxMVvuJ/story.html.

Fischer, C. T. (1980). Privacy and human development. In W. C. Bier (ed.), *Privacy: A vanishing value?* (pp. 37–46). New York: Fordham University Press.

Fitzpatrick, K., & Bronstein, C. (eds.). (2006). *Ethics in public relations: Responsible advocacy.* Thousand Oaks, CA: Sage.

Fletcher, G. P. (1993). *Loyalty: An essay on the morality of relationships.* New York: Oxford University Press.

Folkenflik, D. (2017). Sinclair Broadcast Group has deal to buy Tribune Media's TV stations. *NPR*, May 8, 2017. Retrieved from https://www.npr.org/sections/thetwo-way/2017/05/08/527462015/sinclair-broadcast-group-has-deal-to-buy-tribune-medias-tv-stations.

Food and Drug Administration, Department of Health and Human Services (FDA/DHHS). (1969). Regulations for the Enforcement of the Federal Food, Drug, and Cosmetic Act and the Fair Packaging and Labeling Act. Federal Register 34:7802.

Framke, C. (2016). Trevor Noah didn't "destroy" Tomi Lahren on The Daily Show. What he did was much better. *Vox*, December 4, 2016. Retrieved from https://www.vox.com/culture/2016/12/4/13807584/daily-show-tomi-lahren-interview.

Gans, H. (1979). *Deciding what's news: A study of CBS Evening News, NBC Nightly News, Newsweek and Time.* New York: Vintage.

Gardner, H., Csikszenthmihalyi, M., & Damon, W. (2001). *Good work: When excellence and ethics meet*. New York: Basic Books.

Gazzinga, M. S. (2011). *Who's in charge? Free will and the science of the brain*. New York: HarperCollins.

Gert, B. (1988). *Morality, a new justification of the moral rules*. New York: Oxford University Press.

Gilen, M. (1999). *Why Americans hate welfare: Race, media and the politics of anti-poverty policy*. Chicago, IL: University of Chicago Press.

Gilligan, C. (1982). *In a different voice: Psychological theory and women's development*. Cambridge, MA: Harvard University Press.

Gillin, J. (2017). If you're fooled by fake news, this man probably wrote it. *Politifact*, May 31, 2017. Retrieved from http://www.politifact.com/punditfact/article/2017/may/31/If-youre-fooled-by-fake-news-this-man-probably-wro/.

Glionna, J. (2006). Uproar over film of Golden Gate suicides. *Los Angeles Times*, April 28, 2006. Retrieved from http://articles.latimes.com/2006/apr/28/local/me-bridge28.

Goffman, E. (1959). *The presentation of self in everyday life*. New York: Anchor.

Gold, H. (2017). Sinclair increases "must-run" Boris Epshteyn segments. *Politico*, July 10, 2017. Retrieved from https://www.politico.com/blogs/on-media/2017/07/10/boris-epshteyn-sinclair-broadcasting-240359.

GoldieBlox. (2017). About GoldieBlox. Retrieved from https://www.goldieblox.com/pages/about.

Gormley, D. W. (1984). *Compassion is a tough word. Drawing the line* (pp. 58–59). Washington, DC: American Society of Newspaper Editors.

Gough, P. (2006). "Mad" man adds insight to CNBC money news. *The Hollywood Reporter*, March 28, 2006.

Gramm, S. (2012). Apollo Group rolling higher again after long slide. *Forbes*, July 3, 2012. Retrieved from https://www.forbes.com/sites/scottgamm/2012/07/03/apollo-group-rolling-higher-again-after-long-slide/#525ec526257d.

Grcic, J. M. (1986). The right to privacy: Behavior as property. *Journal of Values Inquiry*, *20*(2), 137–144.

Green, S. (1999). Media's role in changing the face of poverty. *Neiman Reports*, September 15, 1999. Retrieved from http://niemanreports.org/articles/medias-role-in-changing-the-face-of-poverty/.

Greenwood, M. (2017). Kid Rock denies press credentials to Detroit paper. *The Hill*, September 12, 2017. Retrieved from http://thehill.com/blogs/in-the-know/in-the-know/350326-kid-rock-denies-press-credentials-to-detroit-paper.

Gross, A. (2017). Kid Rock denies Detroit Free Press credentials for Little Caesars Arena concert. *Detroit Free Press*, September 12, 2017. Retrieved from http://www.freep.com/story/news/local/michigan/detroit/2017/09/12/kid-rock-detroit-free- press-credentials-lca-concert/657462001/.

Gross, K., & Aday, S. (2003). The scary world in your living room and neighborhood: Using local broadcast news, neighborhood crime rates, and personal experience to test agenda setting and cultivation. *Journal of Communication*, *53*(3), 411–426.

Grow, J. M., Park, J. S., & Han, X. (2006). Your life is waiting! *Journal of Communication Inquiry*, *30*(2), 163–188.

Grunig, L., Toth, E., & Hon, L. (2000). Feminist values in public relations. *Journal of Public Relations Research*, *12*(1), 49–68.

Gulati, G. J., Just, M. R., & Crigler, A. N. (2004). News coverage of political campaigns. In L. L. Kaid (ed.), *Handbook of political communication research* (pp. 237–256). Mahwah, NJ: Lawrence Erlbaum Associates.

Gurevitch, M., Levy, M., & Roeh, I. (1991). The global newsroom: Convergences and diversities in the globalization of television news. In P. Dalhgren & C. Sparks (eds.), *Communication and citizenship*. London: Routledge.

Gutwirth, S. (2002). *Privacy and the information age*. Lanham, MD: Rowman & Littlefield.

Hadland, A., Campbell, D., & Lambert, P. (2015). The state of news photography: The lives and livelihoods of photojournalists in the digital age. Retrieved from https://reutersinstitute.politics.ox.ac.uk/our-research/state-news-photography-lives-and-livelihoods-photojournalists-digital-age.

Haiman, F. (1958). Democratic ethics and the hidden persuaders. *Quarterly Journal of Speech*, *44*(4), 385–392.

Halberstam, D. (2001). *War in a time of peace*. New York: Scribner.

Hamilton, K. (2012). How to kill civilians in a war game. *Kotaku*, July 24, 2012. Retrieved from https://kotaku.com/5928765/how-to-kill-civilians-in-a-war-game.

Hammargren, R. (1936). The origin of the press-radio conflict. *Journalism Quarterly*, *13*, 91–93.

Harp, D., Bachmann, I., & Loke, J. (2014). Where are the women? The presence of female columnists in U.S. opinion pages. *Journalism & Mass Communication Quarterly*, *91*(2), 289–307.

Hart, A. (2003). Delusions of accuracy. *Columbia Journalism Review*, July/August, 20.

Herman, E. S., & Chomsky, N. (2002). *Manufacturing consent: The political economy of the mass media*. New York: Pantheon.

Herreria, C. (2017). Kid Rock bans newspaper from his concert after critical column. *Huffington Post*, September 13, 2017. Retrieved from https://www.huffingtonpost.com/entry/kid-rock-bans-detroit-free pressus59b8b6b3e4b086432b027dcc.

Hess, A. (2011). Breaking news: A postmodern rhetorical analysis of *The Daily Show*. In T. Goodnow (ed.), The Daily Show *and rhetoric: Arguments, issues, and strategies* (pp. 153–170). Lanham, MD: Lexington Books.

Hess, S. (1981). *The Washington reporters*. Washington, DC: The Brookings Institution.

Hickey, N. (2001). The cost of not publishing. *Columbia Journalism Review*, November–December.

———. (2003). FCC: Ready, set, consolidate. *Columbia Journalism Review*, July/August, 5.

Hodges, L. W. (1983). The journalist and privacy. *Social responsibility: Journalism, Law, Medicine*, *9*, 5–19.

———. (1986). Defining press responsibility: A functional approach. In D. Elliott (ed.), *Responsible journalism*, (pp. 13–31). Newbury Park, CA: Sage.

————. (1997). Taste in photojournalism: A question of ethics or aesthetics? In *Media ethics: Issues and cases* (3rd ed., pp. 37–40). New York: McGraw-Hill.

Hoek, J. (2008). Ethical and practical implications of pharmaceutical direct-to-consumer advertising. *International Journal of Nonprofit and Voluntary Sector Marketing, 13*(February), 73–87.

Hoek, J., & Gendall, P. (2002). To have or not to have? Ethics and regulation of direct to consumer advertising of prescription medicines. *Journal of Marketing Communications, 8*(2), 71–85.

Holden, S. (2006). That beautiful but deadly San Francisco span. *New York Times*, October 27, 2006. Retrieved from http://www.nytimes.com/2006/10/27/movies/27brid.html.

Hollenbach, D. (2010). The Catholic intellectual tradition, social justice, and the university. *Conversations on Jesuit Higher Education, 36*(10), 20–22.

Huh, J., Delorme, D., & Reid, L. (2004). The information utility of DTC prescription drug advertising. *Journalism and Mass Communication Quarterly, 81*(4), 788.

Irby, K. (2003). L.A. Times photographer fired over altered image. *Poynter*, April 2, 2003. Retrieved from https://www.poynter.org/news/la-times-photographer-fired-over-altered-image.

Iyengar, S. (1991). *Is anyone responsible?* Chicago, IL: University of Chicago Press.

Itzkoff, D. (2014). Beastie Boys and toy company settle lawsuit over ad's use of "Girls." *New York Times*, March 18, 2014. Retrieved from https://artsbeat.blogs.nytimes.com/2014/03/18/beastie-boys-and-toy-company-settle-lawsuit-over-ads-use-of-girls/.

Jamieson, K. H. (1992). *Dirty politics*. New York: Oxford University Press.

————. (2000). *Everything you think you know about politics . . . and why you're wrong*. New York: Basic Books.

Jennings, L. (2016). Chipotle settles nearly 100 foodborne illness complaints. *Nation's Restaurant News*, September 9, 2016. Retrieved from http://www.nrn.com/fast-casual/chipotle-settles-nearly-100-foodborne-illness-complaints.

Johar, K. (2012). An insider's perspective: Defense of the pharmaceutical industry's marketing practices. *Albany Law Review, 76*(1), 299–334.

Johnson, T. (2017a). Four state attorneys general oppose Sinclair-Tribune merger. *Variety*, November 3, 2017. Retrieved from http://variety.com/2017/politics/news/sinclair-tribune-merger-opposiion-attorneys-general-1202606391/.

————. (2017b). FCC relaxes media ownership rules in contentious vote. *Variety*, November 16, 2017. Retrieved from http://variety.com/2017/politics/news/fcc-media-ownership-rules-sinclair-broadcasting-1202616424/.

Kaid, L. L. (1992). Ethical dimensions of political advertising. In R. E. Denton (ed.), *Ethical dimensions of political communication* (pp. 145–169). New York: Praeger.

Kaiser Family Foundation. (2014). *Opioid overdose deaths by type of opioid*. Retrieved from http://kff.org/other/state-indicator/opioid-overdose-deaths-by-type-of-opioid/?currentTimeframe=0.

Kang, C., & de la Merced, M. J. (2017). Justice Department sues to block AT&T-Time Warner merger. *New York Times*, November 20, 2017. Retrieved from https://www.nytimes.com/2017/11/20/business/dealbook/att-time-warner-merger.html.

Klein, J. (1992). Whose values? *Newsweek*, June 8, 1992, 19–22.

Keohane, J. (2017). What news-writing bots mean for the future of journalism. *Wired*, February 16, 2017. Retrieved from https://www.wired.com/2017/02/robots-wrote-this-story/.

Klepek, P. (2015). That time *Call of Duty* let you shoot up an airport. *Kotaku*, October 23, 2015. Retrieved from https://kotaku.com/that-time-call-of-duty-let-you-shoot-up-an-airport-1738376241.

Koehn, D. (1998). *Rethinking feminist ethics*. New York: Routledge.

Kohlberg, L. (1973). The contribution of developmental psychology to education. *Educational Psychologist, 10,* 2–14.

Kovach, B., & Rosenstiel, T. (2007). *The elements of journalism: What news people should know and the public should expect*. New York: Three Rivers Press.

Lacy, S. (1989). A model of demand for news: Impact of competition on newspaper content. *Journalism Quarterly, 66*(1), 40–48.

Landler, M. (2017). Trump resurrects his claim that both sides share blame in Charlottesville violence. *New York Times*, September 14, 2017. Retrieved from https://www.nytimes.com/2017/09/14/us/politics/trump-charlottesville-tim-scott.html.

Lazer, D., Baum, M. A., Benkler, Y., Berinsky, A. J., Greenhill, K. M., Menczer, F., et al. (2018). The science of fake news. *Science, 359*(380), 1094–1096, DOI: 1126/science.aao2998.

Lebacqz, K. (1985). *Professional ethics: Power and paradox*. Nashville, TN: Abingdon Press.

Lee, S. T. (2005). Predicting tolerance of journalistic deception. *Journal of Mass Media Ethics, 20*(1), 22–42.

Lee, D., & Begley, C. E. (2010). Racial and ethnic disparities in response to direct-to-consumer advertising. *American Journal of Health-System Pharmacy, 67*(14), 1185–1190.

Lee, D., Im, S., & Taylor, C. (2008). Voluntary self-disclosure of information on the internet: A multimethod study of the motivations and consequences of disclosing information on blogs. *Psychology & Marketing, 25*(7), 692–710.

Legum, J. (2017). ESPN struggles to explain how Jemele Hill violated its social media policy. *Think Progress*, October 10, 2017. Retrieved from https://thinkprogress.org/espn-jemele-hill-social-media-policy-3412c0e2a1d4/.

Leigh, D., & Harding, L. (2011). *WikiLeaks: Inside Julian Assange's war on secrecy*. London, UK: Guardian Books.

Len-Ríos, M., Hinnant, A., & Jeong, J. Y. (2012). Reporters' gender affects views on health reporting. *Newspaper Research Journal, 33*(3): 76–88.

Leshner, G. (2006). The effects of dehumanizing depictions of race in TV news stories. In A. Reynolds & B. Burnett (eds.), *Communication and law: Multidisciplinary approaches in research* (pp. 233–252). New York: Routledge.

Lester, P. (1992). *Photojournalism: An ethical approach*. Hillsdale, NJ: Lawrence Erlbaum Associates.

———. (1996). *Images that injure*. Westport, CT: Greenwood Press.

Li, S. (2014). Toy makers learn that construction sets aren't just for boys. *Los Angeles Times*, December 14, 2014. Retrieved from http://www.latimes.com/business/la-fi-girls-toys-20141214-story.html.

Linsky, M. (1986). *Impact: How the press affects federal policymaking*. New York: W.W. Norton.

Lippmann, W. (1922). *Public opinion*. New York: Free Press.

———. (1982). *The essential Lippmann*. Cambridge, MA: Harvard University Press.

Loftus, T. (2017a). Courier-Journal files complaint after public blocked from board visit to Matt Bevin's home. *Louisville Courier-Journal*, August 2, 2017. Retrieved from https://www.courier-journal.com/story/news/politics/2017/08/02/courier-journal-appeals-exclusion-inspection-matt-bevins-home/534585001/.

———. (2017b). A restored mansion or house in disrepair? Board to hear arguments Wednesday on value of Bevin's Anchorage home. *Louisville Courier-Journal*, July 19, 2017. Retrieved from https://www.courier-journal.com/story/news/2017/07/19/gov-matt-bevin-anchorage-home-hearing-decide-value-set-wednesday/491123001/.

Manly, L. (2005). U.S. network TV shows turn props into dollars. *International Herald Tribune,* October 3, 2005.

Marcus, R. (2017). Hillary Clinton, smash your rearview mirror. *Washington Post*, June 2, 2017. Retrieved from https://www.washingtonpost.com/opinions/hillary-clinton-smash-your-rearview-mirror.

Martens, T. (2013). Toy maker pulls Beastie Boys ad, says "we don't want to fight." *Los Angeles Times*, November 27, 2013. Retrieved from http://www.latimes.com/entertainment/music/posts/la-et-ms-beastie-boys-goldieblox-girls-ad-20131127-story.html.

Martin, E. (1991). On photographic manipulation. *Journal of Mass Media Ethics*, *6*(3), 156–163.

Marx, G. T. (1999). What's in a name. *The Information Society*, *15*(2), 99–112.

Matsuda, M. (1989). Public response to racist speech: Considering the victim's story. *Michigan Law Review*, *87,* 2321–2381.

Mattin, D. (2007). The Bridge. *BBC*, February 10, 2017. Retrieved from http://www.bbc.co.uk/films/2007/02/12/thebridge2007review.shtml.

May, W. F. (2001). *Beleaguered rulers: The public obligation of the professional*. Louisville, KY: Westminster John Knox Press.

McBeth, M. K., & Clemons, R. S. (2011). Is fake news the real news? The significance of Stewart and Colbert for democratic discourse, politics, and policy. In A. Amarasingam (ed.), *The Stewart/Colbert effect: Essays on the real impacts of fake news* (pp. 79–98). Jefferson, NC: McFarland & Company.

McCaffrey, K. (2015). Kim stands corrected: The limits of corrective promotion. *MM&M*, September 15, 2015. http://www.mmm-online.com/campaigns/kardashian-diclegis-duchesnay-corrective-advertising/article/438723/.

McChesney, R. (1997). *Corporate media and the threat to democracy*. New York: Seven Stories Press.

McCluskey, C. (2009). At best plagiarism, at worst outright theft: Courant covers towns with other papers' reporting. *Journal Inquirer*, September 2, 2009.

McGeough, R. (2011). The voice of the people: Jon Stewart, public argument, and political satire. In T. Goodnow (ed.), The Daily Show *and rhetoric: Arguments, issues, and strategies* (pp. 113–127). Lanham, MD: Lexington Books.

McLuhan, M. (1964). *Understanding media: The extensions of man.* New York: Signet Books.

McManus, J. (1994). *Market-driven journalism: Let the citizen beware?* Thousand Oaks, CA: Sage.

Meader, A., Knight, L., Coleman, R., & Wilkins, L. (2015). Ethics in the digital age: A comparison of the effects of moving images and photographs on moral judgment. *Journal of Media Ethics, 30*(4), 234–251.

Merrill, J. C. (1974). *The imperative of freedom: A philosophy of journalistic autonomy.* New York: Hastings House.

Metzl, J. M. (2002). Selling sanity through gender: The psychodynamics of psychotropic advertising. *Journal of Medical Humanities, 24*(1), 79–103.

Meyers, C. (2003). Appreciating W.D. Ross: On duties and consequences. *Journal of Mass Media Ethics, 18*(2), 81–97.

Michaels, S. (2013). Beastie Boys countersue GoldieBlox for toy video royalties. *The Guardian*, December 12, 2013.

Miller, C. (2013). Ad takes off online: Less doll, more awl. *New York Times*, November 20, 2013. Retrieved from https://bits.blogs.nytimes.com/2013/11/20/a-viral-video-encourages-girls-to-become-engineers/.

Mills, C. W. (1956). *The power elite.* New York: Oxford University Press.

Mills, K. (1989). When women talk to women. *Media and Values* (Winter), p. 12.

Molotch, H., & Lester, M. (1974). News as purposive behavior: On the strategic use of routine events, accidents and scandals. *American Sociological Review, 39,* 101–112.

Montgomery, K. C. (1989). *Target: Prime time. Advocacy groups and the struggle over entertainment television.* New York: Oxford University Press.

Mooney, M. J. (2012). The man in the middle of Bountygate. *GQ*, September 19, 2012. Retrieved from https://www.gq.com/story/nfl-bountygate-saints-sean-pamphilon.

Moore, G. E. (1903). *Principia ethica.*

Moses, L. (2017). The Washington Post's robot reporter has published 850 articles in the past year. Retrieved from https://digiday.com/media/washington-posts-robot-reporter-published-500-articles-last-year/.

Moyers, B. (1988). Quoted in *The promise of television*, episode 10. Produced by PBS.

National Association of Broadcasters. (1985). *Radio: In search of excellence.* Washington, DC: NAB.

Nelkin, D. (1987). *Selling science: How the press covers science and technology.* New York: W.H. Freeman.

Nerone, J. C. (1995). *Last rights: Revisiting four theories of the press.* Urbana: University of Illinois Press.

Neville, R. C. (1980). Various meanings of privacy: A philosophical analysis. In W. C. Bier (ed.), *Privacy: A vanishing value?* (pp. 26–36). New York: Fordham University Press.

Newsom, D., Turk, J. V., & Kruckeberg, D. (1996). *This is PR: The realities of public relations.* Delmont, CA: Wadsworth.

New York Times. (2015). Staging, manipulation and truth in photography. *New York Times*, October 16, 2015. Retrieved from https://lens.blogs.nytimes.com/2015/10/16/staging-manipulation-ethics-photos/?r=0.

Niles, R. (2009). What are the ethics of online journalism? *Online Journalism Review*. Retrieved from http://www.ojr.org.

Nissenbaum, H. (2010). *Privacy on context: Technology, policy and the integrity of social life*. Stanford, CA: Stanford Law Books.

Nuccitelli, D. (2014). John Oliver's viral video: The best climate debate ever. *The Guardian*, May 23, 2014. Retrieved from https://www.theguardian.com/environment/climate-consensus-97-per-cent/2014/may/23/john-oliver-best-climate-debate-ever.

Nussbaum, M. (2001). *Upheavals of thought: The intelligence of emotions*. Cambridge: Cambridge University Press.

———. (2006). *Frontiers of justice: Disability, nationality and species membership*. Cambridge, MA: Harvard University Press.

———. (2016). *Anger and forgiveness: Resentment, generosity, justice*. Oxford: Oxford University Press.

Ohio State Bar Association. (2017). *Fighting Ohio's heroin epidemic*. Retrieved from https://www.ohiobar.org/NewsAndPublications/OhioLawyer/Pages/Fighting-Ohios-heroin-epidemic.aspx.

Oz, M. (2014). Red Sox reporter Jenny Dell reassigned after Will Middlebrooks relationship goes public. *Yahoo Sports*, January 31, 2014. Retrieved from https://ca.sports.yahoo.com/blogs/mlb-big-league-stew/red-sox-reporter-jenny-dell-reassigned-nesn-because-012818455--mlb.html.

Park, S., Holody, K., & Zhang, X. (2012). Race in media coverage of school shootings: A parallel application of framing theory and attribute agenda setting. *Journalism & Mass Communication Quarterly*, *89*(3), 475–494.

Patterson, P. (1989). Reporting Chernobyl: Cutting the government fog to cover the nuclear cloud. In L. M. Walters, L. Wilkins, & T. Walters (eds.), *Bad tidings: Communication and catastrophe*. Mahwah, NJ: Lawrence Erlbaum Associates.

Patterson, T. (1980). *The mass media election*. New York: Prager.

Payton, A. R., & P. A. Thoits. (2011). Medicalization, direct-to-consumer advertising, and mental illness stigma. *Society and Mental Health*, *1*(1), 55–70.

Petty, R., & D'Rozario, D. (2009). The use of dead celebrities in advertising and marketing: Balancing interests in the right of publicity. *Journal of Advertising*, *38*(4), 37–49.

Pfanner, E. (2005). Product placements cause a stir in Europe. *International Herald Tribune*, October 3, 2005. Retrieved from https://archive.nytimes.com/www.nytimes.com/iht/2005/10/03/business/IHT-03products03.html?pagewanted=all.

Piaget, J. (1965). *The moral judgment of the child*. Trans. by M. Gabain. New York: Free Press.

Picard, R. (1988). *The ravens of Odin: The press in the Nordic nations*. Ames: Iowa State University Press.

Plaisance, P. (2015). *Virtue in media*. New York,: Routledge.

Pojman, L. (1998). *Ethical theory: Classical and contemporary readings*. Belmont, CA: Wadsworth.

Priest, S., & Hall, A. (2007). Soldiers face neglect, frustration at Army's top medical facility. *Washington Post*, February 18, 2007. Retrieved from http://www.washingtonpost.com/wp-dyn/content/article/2007/02/17/AR2007021701172.html.

Raab, C., & Mason, D. (2004). Privacy, surveillance, trust and regulation. *Information, Communication & Society*, *7*(1), 89–91.

Radin, M. J. (1982). Property and personhood. *Stanford Law Review*, *34*(5), 957–1015.

———. (1993). *Reinterpreting property*. Chicago, IL: University of Chicago Press.

———. (1996). *Contested commodities*. Cambridge, MA: Harvard University Press.

Rainville, R., & McCormick, E. (1977). Extent of racial prejudice in pro football announcers' speech. *Journalism Quarterly*, *54*(1), 20–26.

Rawls, J. (1971). *A theory of justice*. Cambridge, MA: Harvard University Press.

Reaves, S. (1987). Digital retouching: Is there a place for it in newspaper photography? *Journal of Mass Media Ethics*, *2*(2), 40–48.

———. (1991). Personal correspondence to the author quoted in digital alteration of photographs in consumer magazines. *Journal of Mass Media Ethics*, *6*, 175–181.

Reuters Institute for the Study of Journalism. (2015). How mobile phones are changing journalism practice in the 21st Century. Retrieved from www.reutersinstitute.politics.ox.ac.uk.

Ricchiardi, S. (2009). Share and share alike; once considered unthinkable, content-sharing arrangements are proliferating rapidly, often uniting newspapers long seen as bitter rivals. *American Journalism Review*, *28*(8), February–March.

Rieder, R. (1999). A costly rookie mistake. *American Journalism Review*, November/December, 6.

Robinson, M., & Sheehan, G. (1984). *Over the wire and on TV*. New York: Basic Books.

R0B0F1SH. *Read a Book (Dirty Version)*. Comment posted.

Ronson, J. (2015). How one stupid tweet blew up Justine Sacco's life. *New York Times*, February 12, 2015. Retrieved from https://www.nytimes.com/2015/02/15/magazine/how-one-stupid-tweet-ruined-justine-saccos-life.html.

Rose, M., & Baumgartner, F. (2013). Framing the poor: Media coverage and US poverty policy 1960–2008. *Policy Studies Journal*, *41*(1), 22–53.

Rosen, J. (2000). *The unwanted gaze: The destruction of privacy in America*. New York: Random House.

Rosenthal, A. M. (1989). Trash TV's latest news show continues credibility erosion. Syndicated column by *New York Times News Service*, October, 10, 1989.

Ross, W. D. (1930). *The right and the good*. Oxford: Clarendon Press.

———. (1988). *The right and the good*. Indianapolis, IN: Hackett.

Royce, J. (1908). *The philosophy of loyalty*. New York: Macmillan.

Ruiz, M. (2017). No, Hillary Clinton, the first woman to win a major-party presidential nomination, does not need to shut up about it. *Vogue*, September 11, 2017. Retrieved from https://www.vogue.com/article/hillary-clinton-what-happened-doesnt-have-to-shut-up.

Russell, B. (ed.). (1967). *History of Western philosophy*. New York: Touchstone Books.

Sabato, L. J. (1992). *Feeding frenzy: How attack journalism has transformed American politics*. New York: Free Press.

———. (2000). Open season: How the news media cover presidential campaigns in the age of attack journalism. In D. A. Graber (ed.), *Media power and politics* (4th ed., pp. 161–171). Washington, DC: CQ Press.

Sandel, M. J. (1982). *Liberalism and the limits of justice*. Cambridge, MA: Harvard University Press.

———. (2012). *What money can't buy: The moral limits of markets*. New York: Farrar, Straus and Giroux.

Schoeman, F. D. (ed.). (1984). *Philosophical dimensions of privacy: An anthology*. New York: Cambridge University Press.

Schudson, M. (1978). *Discovering the news*. New York: Basic Books.

Schwartz, T. (1973). *The responsive chord*. Garden City, NY: Anchor Press.

Scott, C. (2017). Report: Robot journalism will continue to grow in newsrooms despite its limitations. Retrieved from https://www.journalism.co.uk/news/report-robot-journalism-s-limitations-not-halting-its-onward-march/s2/a700429/.

Seabrook, J. (2003). The money note. *New Yorker*, July 7, 2003, 46.

Sen, A. (2009). *The idea of justice*. Cambridge, MA: The Belknap Press.

Shaw, D. (1999). Journalism is a very different business—Here's why. *Los Angeles Times*, December 20, 1999, V3.

Shepard, S. (2017). Politico Poll: 46 percent think media make up stories about Trump. *Politico*, October 18, 2017. Retrieved from https://www.politico.com/story/2017/10/18/trump-media-fake-news-poll-243884.

Shepardson, D. (2017). Sinclair Broadcast Group praises FCC media ownership, TV rule changes. *Reuters*, November 1, 2017. Retrieved from https://www.reuters.com/article/us-tribune-media-m-a-sinclair-ma/sinclair-broadcast-group-praises-fcc-media-ownership-tv-rule-changes-idUSKBN1D1645.

Shihipar, A. (2017). Antifa history and politics: A historian weighs in. *Teen Vogue*, October 25, 2017. Retrieved from https://www.teenvogue.com/story/antifa-history-and-politics-explained.

Shoemaker, P. J., & Reese, S. J. (1996). *Mediating the message: Theories of influences on mass media content*. White Plains, NY: Longman.

Smith, C. (1992). *Media and apocalypse*. Westport, CT: Greenwood Press.

Smith, A., & Banic, V. (2016). Fake news: How a partying Macedonian teen earns thousands publishing lies. *NBC News*, December 9, 2016. Retrieved from https://www.nbcnews.com/news/world/fake-news-how-partying-macedonian-teen-earns-thousands-publishing-lies-n692451.

Snider, M. (2017a). Two big reasons Sinclair-Tribune TV merger should be nixed, opponents say. *USA Today*, August 7, 2017. Retrieved from https://www.usatoday.com/story/money/business/2017/08/07/two-big-reasons-sinclair-tribune-tv-merger-should-nixed-opponents-say/546158001/.

———. (2017b). $4 billion TV deal creates nation's largest broadcaster. *USA Today*, May 7, 2017. Retrieved from https://www.usatoday.com/story/money/business/2017/05/07/sinclair-broadcasting-buy-tribune-media-4-billion-deal-reports-say/101409222/.

Sorkin, A. R. (2008). What goes before a fall? On Wall Street, reassurance. *New York Times*, September 30, 2008. Retrieved from https://www.nytimes.com/2008/09/30/business/30sorkin.html.

Spencer, J. (2001). Decoding bin Laden. *Newsweek*, October 11, 2001. Retrieved from http://www.nbcnews.com/id/3067564/t/decoding-bin-laden/#.WznMMtIzY2w.

Spangler, T. (2017). Cord-cutting explodes: 22 million U.S. adults will have canceled cable, satellite TV by end of 2017. *Variety*. Retrieved from http://variety.com/2017/biz/news/cord-cutting-2017-estimates-cancel-cable-satellite-tv-1202556594/.

Spicer, R. N. (2011). Before and after *The Daily Show*: Freedom and consequences in political satire. In T. Goodnow (ed.), The Daily Show *and rhetoric: Arguments, issues, and strategies* (pp. 19–41). Lanham, MD: Lexington Books.

Sterling, D. (2013). *TED Talk: Inspiring the next generation of female engineers*. Retrieved from https://www.youtube.com/watch?v=FEeTLopLkEo.

Stock, K. (2016). Chipotle's sales have dropped by 10.3 million burritos. *Bloomberg*, February 2, 2016. Retrieved from https://www.bloomberg.com/news/articles/2016-02-02/chipotle-s-sales-have-dropped-by-10-3-million-burritos.

Stone, I. F. (1988). *The trial of Socrates*, Boston, MA: Little, Brown.

Stoycheff, E. (2016). Under surveillance: Examining Facebook's spiral of silence effects in the wake of NSA internet monitoring. *Journalism & Mass Communication Quarterly*, *93*(2), 296–311.

Stray, J. (2016). The age of the cyborg. *Columbia Journalism Review*. Retrieved from https://www.cjr.org/analysis/cyborgvirtualrealityreuterstracer.php.

Strupp, J. (2009). AP to track online content usage. *Adweek*. Retrieved from https://www.adweek.com/digital/ap-track-online-content-usage-112972/.

Swanberg, W. A. (1972). *Luce and his Empire*. New York: Charles Scribner's Sons.

Szarkowski, J. (1978). *Mirrors and windows*. New York: Museum of Modern Art.

Tannen, D. (1999). *The argument culture: Stopping America's war of words*. New York: Ballantine Books.

Taylor, K. (2016). Chipotle gave away tons of free food to fix its battered image. It didn't work. *Slate*, September 23, 2016. Retrieved from http://www.slate.com/blogs/businessinsider/2016/09/23/chipotlesrewardscampaigndidntfixitsbatteredimage.html.

Thorson, E., Duffy, M., & Schumann, D. W. (2007). The internet waits for no one. In D. W. Schumann & E. Thorson (eds.), *Internet advertising: Theory and research* (pp. 3–14). New York: Routledge.

Tolstoy, L. N. (1960). *What is art?* Translated By A. Maude. New York: MacMillan.

Tomlinson, D. (1987). One technological step forward and two legal steps back: Digitalization and television news pictures as evidence in libel. *Loyola Entertainment Law Journal*, *9*, 237–257.

Toulmin, S. (1988). The recovery of practical philosophy. *The American Scholar*, Summer, 338.

Tur, K. (2017). *Unbelievable: My front row seat to the craziest campaign in American history*. New York: HarperCollins.

van de Garde-Perik, E., Markopoulos, P., de Ruyter, B., Eggen, B., & IJsselsteijn, W. (2008). Investigating privacy attitudes and behavior in relation to personalization. *Social Science Computer Review*, *26*(1), 20–43.

van den Hoven, J. (2008). Moral methodology and information technology. In K. E. Himma & H. T. Tavani (eds.), *The handbook of information and computer ethics* (pp. 49–68). Hoboken, NJ: John Wiley.

Voakes, P. S. (1998). What were you thinking? A survey of journalists who were sued for invasion of privacy. *Journalism & Mass Communications Quarterly, 75*(2), 378–393.

Wahba, P. (2016). Lawsuit accuses Chipotle of misleading investors. *Fortune*, January 8, 2016. Retrieved from http://fortune.com/2016/01/08/chipotle-lawsuit-ecoli/.

Ward, S. J. (2004). *The invention of journalism ethics*. Montreal, Canada: McGill-Queens University Press.

Weaver, D. H., Beam, R. A., Brownlee, B. J., Voakes, P. S., & Wilhoit, G. C. (2007). *The American journalist in the 21st century: U.S. news people at the dawn of a new millennium (LEA's Communication Series)*. Mahwah, NJ: Lawrence Erlbaum Associates.

Weaver, D. H., & Wilhoit, G. C. (1996). *The American journalist in the 1990s: US news people at the end of an era*. Mahwah, NJ: Lawrence Erlbaum Associates.

Weisman, R. (2014). Are baby boomers ready to give marijuana a second chance? *Boston Globe*, April 13, 2014. Retrieved from https://www.bostonglobe.com/business/2014/04/12/baby-boomers-who-moved-may-ready-give-marijuana-second-chance/8UcflcGP1dKkanaLuX6wOM/story.html.

Werhane, P. (2006). Stockholder ethics in health care. Presented to the Association of Applied and Professional Ethics, February 2006, San Antonio, TX.

The White House. (2017). President's commission on combating drug addiction and the opioid crisis. Retrieved from https://www.whitehouse.gov/ondcp/presidents-commission.

Wilkins, L. (1987). *Shared vulnerability: The mass media and American perception of the Bhopal disaster*. Westport, CT: Greenwood Press.

Wilkins, L., & Christians, C. G. (2001). Philosophy meets the social sciences: The nature of humanity in the public arena. *Journal of Mass Media Ethics*, *16*(2,3), 99–120.

Wilkins, L., & Coleman, R. (2005). *The moral media*. Mahwah, NJ: Lawrence Erlbaum Associates.

Williams, B. A. (2009). The ethics of political communication. In L. Wilkins & C. G. Christians (eds.), *Handbook of Mass Media Ethics*. New York: Taylor & Francis.

Williams, B. A., & Delli Carpini, M. X. (2011). Real ethical concerns and fake news: *The Daily Show* and the challenge of the new media environment. In A. Amarasignam (ed.), *The Stewart/Colbert effect: Essays on the real impacts of fake news* (pp. 181–192). Jefferson, NC: McFarland.

Winslow, D. (2004). Peter Turnley's photo-essays to debut in Harper's Magazine. Retrieved from http://digitaljournalist.org/issue0407/winslow.html.

Women's Media Center. (2017). The status of women in the U.S. media 2017. Retrieved from http://www.womensmediacenter.com/reports/status-of-women-in-us-media.

Woodward, K. (1994). What is virtue? *Newsweek*, June 13, 1994, 38–39.

Wooley, S., & Howard, P. (2017). Executive summary: Oxford Computational Propaganda Project. Retrieved from http://comprop.oii.ox.ac.uk/wp-content/uploads/sites/89/2017/06/Casestudies-ExecutiveSummary.pdf.

Young, D. G., & Esralew, S. E. (2011). Jon Stewart a heretic? Surely you jest: Political participation and discussion among viewers of late-night comedy programming. In A. Amarasignam (ed.), *The Stewart/Colbert effect: Essays on the real impacts of fake news* (pp. 99–116). Jefferson, NC: McFarland.

Zhou, L. (2017). Sinclair's assist from the FCC. *Politico*, August 4, 2017. Retrieved from https://www.politico.com/tipsheets/morning-tech/2017/08/04/sinclairs-assist-from-the-fcc-221710.

Zillman, D. (1999). Exemplification theory: Judging the whole by some of its parts. *Media Psychology*, *1*(1), 69–94.

Index